ROUTLEDGE LIBRARY EDITIONS:
TIBET

I0130929

Volume 2

BRITISH INDIA AND TIBET:
1766–1910

BRITISH INDIA AND TIBET:
1766–1910

ALASTAIR LAMB

Routledge
Taylor & Francis Group

LONDON AND NEW YORK

First published in 1960 by Routledge & Kegan Paul Ltd
Second, revised, edition first published in 1986

This edition first published in 2019
by Routledge
2 Park Square, Milton Park, Abingdon, Oxon OX14 4RN

and by Routledge
711 Third Avenue, New York, NY 10017

Routledge is an imprint of the Taylor & Francis Group, an informa business

British Library Cataloguing in Publication Data
A catalogue record for this book is available from the British Library

ISBN: 978-1-138-32747-4 (Set)
ISBN: 978-0-429-44145-5 (Set) (ebk)
ISBN: 978-1-138-33437-3 (Volume 2) (hbk)
ISBN: 978-1-138-33442-7 (Volume 2) (pbk)
ISBN: 978-0-429-44537-8 (Volume 2) (ebk)

Publisher's Note
The publisher has gone to great lengths to ensure the quality of this reprint but points out that some imperfections in the original copies may be apparent.

Disclaimer
The publisher has made every effort to trace copyright holders and would welcome correspondence from those they have been unable to trace.

British India
and
Tibet

·

1766 – 1910

Alastair Lamb

Routledge & Kegan Paul
London and New York

FOR SIMON AND SARAH

First published in 1960
Second, revised, edition first published in 1986 by
Routledge & Kegan Paul Ltd
11 New Fetter Lane, London EC4P 4EE

Published in the USA by
Routledge & Kegan Paul Inc.
in association with Methuen Inc.
29 West 35th Street, New York, NY 10001

Set in 10 on 11 pt Bembo
by Columns of Reading
and printed in Great Britain
by St Edmundsbury Press
Bury St Edmunds, Suffolk

Library of Congress Cataloging in Publication Data

Lamb, Alastair, 1930-
British India and Tibet, 1766-1910.
Includes bibliographies and index.
1. India—Foreign relations—China—Tibet.
2. Tibet (China)—Foreign relations—India.
3. India—Foreign relations—China. 4. China—
Foreign relations—India. I. Title.
DS450.T5L36 1986   327.54051   86-3232

British Library CIP Data also available

ISBN 0-7102-0872-3

CONTENTS

Preface   vii
I   First Contacts: 1766 – 1792   1
II   Nepal: 1792 – 1816   26
III   Western Tibet: 1816 – 1861   43
IV   The Opening of Sikkim: 1817 – 1861   68
V   The Sikkim Route: 1861 – 1874   88
VI   The Chefoo Convention and the Macaulay
Mission: 1876 – 1886   114
VII   The Sikkim-Tibet Convention and the Trade
Regulations: 1886 – 1893   139
VIII   Yatung: 1894 to 1898   165
IX   Curzon's Tibetan Policy: 1899 – 1902   193
X   The Younghusband Mission: 1903 – 1905   222
XI   The Aftermath: 1905 – 1910   256
Notes   286
Bibliography   323
Index   339

Maps

Sketch map of Tibet   *facing page* 1
Sketch map showing trade routes between Bengal
and Central Tibet in the latter part of the
eighteenth century   24
Sketch map of Western Tibet and the adjacent regions   45
Sketch map of Sikkim   77
Sketch map of Giaogong and the disputed portions
of the Sikkim-Tibet frontier   180

PREFACE

THE Northern frontier of the British Indian Empire along the Himalayas, in contrast to the North West Frontier which separated British territory from Afghanistan, enjoyed a surprisingly tranquil history during the course of the late eighteenth and nineteenth centuries. Early in the nineteenth century there was a major conflict between the East India Company and the largest of the Himalayan states, Nepal, which might have produced prolonged instability on the Afghan pattern. In the event it brought about by the middle of the century the emergence of a Nepal which was really the model of what a buffer state should be. Other British encounters with Himalayan states, with Bhutan and Sikkim, were on a far smaller scale and, in both cases, resulted ultimately either in total British domination (Sikkim) or effective neutralization (Bhutan). Where there were actual conflicts originating in the Himalayan range itself, as with a number of crises in Tibeto-Nepalese relations between 1788 and 1856 and with the war between Tibet and the State of Jummu and Kashmir (not yet under British influence) in 1841-2, the impact on British India was extremely indirect and produced at most a minor measure of British diplomatic activity.

This tranquillity, relative to the North West Frontier, meant that until fairly recently the history of British relations across the Himalayas was a subject both neglected and obscure. It gave rise, perhaps, to but one episode which might have come to the notice of the proverbial schoolboy, that of the Younghusband Mission to Lhasa in 1904. This dramatic event was the prelude to a fairly turbulent era culminating in the Chinese military occupation of Central Tibet from 1910-12. Chinese power in Lhasa, however, collapsed in 1912. Calm, it could be argued, thereupon returned. There were British Indian officials in the 1930s who detected threats to imperial security to the north of the Himalayas which required serious consideration; but their voices received scant publicity. At the moment of the transfer of power in 1947 most observers would have said that the Himalayan border of India was, to mix a metaphor, a political backwater.

This view, of course, was changed by the Chinese 'aggressions' of the 1950s and 1960s. Now for the first time the history of the Himalayan border began to be studied with an intensity generated by the vehemence of international polemic. The literature which has emerged since 1960 is of a truly formidable volume. The archives have been combed through by armies of research students, not to mention officials of foreign ministries, seeking evidence to support or challenge conflicting Chinese and Indian claims. Because national interests have become involved, the arguments between proponents of different views easily diverge from the strict path of scholarship.

When I first became interested in the origins of the Younghusband Mission the subject was indeed obscure. In 1951 I came across Landon's account of this strange British invasion of the Tibetan plateau. I was intrigued to find how little information was available concerning the background to the affair. What was the history of this sector of the British Indian border between the age of Warren Hastings in the late eighteenth century and that of Lord Curzon in the early twentieth century? Francis Younghusband in his own account of the 1904 venture, *India and Tibet* (London 1910), argued that there was a continuity of policy linking Hastings' missions to the Panchen (or Tashi) Lama and his own endeavour to open a dialogue with the Dalai Lama. Was this so? I decided to make the answer to this question the subject of my research for a doctorate at Cambridge which I began in 1953.

The material in my dissertation, which was successfully presented in 1958, I rewrote as a book during the course of 1959 while I was living in Malaya. This was published in 1960 by Routledge & Kegan Paul as *Britain and Chinese Central Asia. The Road to Lhasa 1767 to 1905*. The book was written at a period when I was actively engaged in archaeological research in the north of Malaya in an environment which did not include good libraries among its delights. It was impossible to check my notes against the original sources in London in the PRO and the India Office Library; and I lacked even the more common standard works of reference. A number of errors, most of them fortunately rather minor, resulted; but I am still surprised that the final work came through as well as it did.

One serious consequence of being in Malaya at this particular time was that I was not able to carry the story on to its logical conclusion in 1910. When I was writing my dissertation the fifty-year rule was still in force; and this effectively limited me to sources up to 1904. Even this last year, crucial in the story of the Younghusband Mission, did not become open until I was actually writing up my dissertation. It is not surprising, therefore, that the final chapter of *Britain and Chinese Central Asia* is far from satisfactory. My assessment of the consequences of the Younghusband Mission, as I discovered in 1962 when I was in fact able to go through the material in the PRO and the India Office Library, was defective in a number of important respects.

My original plan when I started research for my doctorate was that the work on the Himalayan border would be a preparation for further studies of other aspects of British Indian border history where Britain marched with the Chinese Empire and Republic. I had in mind a study of the history of British contacts with and policy concerning Chinese Turkestan (which in the 1880s became the Province of Sinkiang). I also contemplated a detailed examination of the evolution of the border between Burma and China. While *Britain and Chinese Central Asia* contains references to these projects, neither ever materialized. The Sinkiang book I abandoned because much of the subject was so well covered by G.J. Alder in his *British India's Northern Frontier 1865-1895* which was published in 1963; and Burma, in isolation, did not attract me very strongly. This does not mean, of course, that I entirely gave up the subject. I devoted two further volumes to the story of British relations with Tibet from 1904 to 1914: these, which were written while I was living in Australia (again removed by great distances from the original documents), were published as *The McMahon Line* in 1966. The theoretical nature of the Sino-Indian and Sino-Burmese border was examined in *Asian Frontiers* which came out in 1968. A great deal of material which might have gone into the Sinkiang volume was used in *The China-India Border* (1964) and *The Sino-Indian Border in Ladakh* (1973).

Everything that I wrote after the publication of *Britain and Chinese Central Asia* was produced in an atmosphere dominated by the Sino-Indian border question which, in 1962, resulted in a major armed conflict in the Himalayas. It is an unfortunate feature of the Sino-Indian dispute that it has been couched very much in the language of history. The issues are indeed complex; but in essence they derive from the nature of the Indo-Tibetan border in the British period which was inherited by independent India in 1947. How much of that border had been defined before 1947? What alignments, even if not formally accepted, had been the *de facto* limits separating British and Tibetan administration? What agreements had the Tibetans made with the British during that period after 1912 when the Chinese had been effectively expelled from Central Tibet; and, if they had come to any understanding with British India, had they the right to do so without Chinese approval? What was the status of Tibet? Since 1960 it has been very difficult to write about the relations between India and Tibet without concentrating on such questions to the exclusion of many other matters of great interest. Obscure points relating to the minutiae of the whereabouts of the Indo-Tibetan border at any particular moment tend to attract attention at the expense of general issues of British imperial policy.

When I was working on *Britain and Chinese Central Asia* I was not particularly concerned with the problems of boundary alignment confronting the Republic of India and the Chinese People's Republic. Indeed, until I actually visited the Tibetan border in the Spiti Valley in 1955, by which time the bulk of my research in the British archives had already been carried out, I was not really aware that there was a Sino-Indian boundary dispute. By 1959, when I wrote the final version of *Britain and Chinese Central Asia*, it was of course impossible to ignore the deterioration in Sino-Indian relations; but by then I was living in Malaya with no access to the primary sources. *Britain and Chinese Central Asia*, therefore, is virtually untouched by polemical considerations arising from the Sino-Indian question, though it is, of course, not free from potential controversies over the nature of British imperial policy. I was, for example, inclined to doubt the widely held view that in the latter part of the nineteenth century imperial policy was determined primarily by economic considerations; and I could detect no evidence of significant capitalist influence (in the Hobsonian sense) behind the Younghusband Mission of 1904 which I interpreted purely in terms of the application of a policy of frontier defence (even if a mistaken one).

The lack of contamination from Sino-Indian conflict is apparent throughout *Britain and Chinese Central Asia*. The treatment of the British annexation of Kumaon and Garwhal after the Gurkha War, for example, almost completely ignores the problems of defining the border that was now created between directly administered British territory and that under Tibetan jurisdiction, and which in the 1950s was to become the Middle Sector of the Sino-Indian boundary dispute. Again, there are implications for the western Sector of that dispute in the situation following the Dogra occupation of Ladakh in the 1830s which I but touch upon superficially. The whole question of the whereabouts of the British border in the Assam Himalayas after 1826, and of the relations between the British administration in Assam and the hill tribes, is likewise mentioned only in passing: after the extent of the theoretical Chinese claims to NEFA had become public in the late 1950s it would have been difficult to have been so casual, for example, about the history of the Tawang tract. Even in my consideration of the Anglo-Chinese demarcation of the Sikkim-Tibet border in the 1890s, a process which was of enormous importance in the genesis of the Younghusband Mission, I did not explore the Tibetan attitude *after* Younghusband towards the boundary markers which the British and Chinese had jointly set up on that border. Had I been writing after 1960 I would surely have commented on the fact that in the 1930s the Tibetans were still refusing to accept this border alignment and that, in 1935, Tibetan officials once more knocked down the very boundary markers that they had been removing or defacing in the 1890s. The Sikkim-Tibet border, in other words, which by virtue of the Convention of 1890 looked like one of the stretches of the Sino-Indian boundary which had been settled beyond doubt, was still in the 1930s under active Tibetan challenge, a fact not without relevance to the Sino-Indian arguments of the late 1950s and the 1960s, but of no great importance in the context of British imperial policy as described in *Britain and Chinese Central Asia*.

The story in the present volume begins with the British acquisition of the *diwani*, the revenue rights, to Bengal, Bihar and Orissa from the Moghul Emperor in 1765, an event which was to involve the East India Company in the direct administration of vast areas of Indian hinterland; and from this in time emerged the mighty edifice of the British Indian Empire with one border along the Himalayan range. The rise of British India was paralleled, as will be noted in Chapter 1, by an increase in Chinese influence to the north of the Himalayas with the effect that the first stages of British contact with Tibet took place in an atmosphere already dominated by those same concepts of exclusion which were such a feature of European relations with China proper.

In earlier times Tibet had not been quite so difficult to penetrate. The Jesuits entered Tibet from India in the early seventeenth century and established themselves in Lhasa where

they remained until 1721. The last of the Jesuit mission, Ipplito
.Desideri of Pistoia, compiled *An Account of Tibet* which was not
published in full until 1904; but a great deal of information
derived from Desideri and his predecessors was available in the
eighteenth century, some of it in the final volume of Du Halde's
*Description géographique, historique, politique et physique de l'empire de
la Chine et de la Tartarie chinoise* which was published in Paris in
1735. This work, moreover, contained D'Anville's map of Tibet
based on the data assembled by Jesuits in China on behalf of the
Manchu Emperor K'ang Hsi. After 1721 the Christian missionary
presence was maintained in Lhasa for a while by the Capuchins
who reported c.1730 the visit to Lhasa of a lay traveller, the
Dutchman Van der Putte (whose own narrative has not survived).
In the 1740s, in the face of a growing crisis in the internal affairs
of Tibet, the Capuchins withdrew to the Vale of Nepal. Here they
were able to preserve a foothold in the Himalayas until, ironically,
the first British attempts to establish contact with Nepal in the late
1760s (described below in Chapter 1) precipitated their departure
in the face of Gurkha conquest.

By the time that Warren Hastings embarked upon a policy of
establishing diplomatic contacts across the Himalayas, therefore,
there no longer existed either in Tibet or in the Himalayan states
any European presence. Neither the Jesuits nor the Capuchins
made any direct contribution to the evolution of the Tibetan
policy of the East India Company. Their work did, however,
make available to the agents of that policy a great deal of
information about Tibet. George Bogle, for example, carried with
him on his Tibetan mission of 1774-5 a copy of D'Anville's map
which at least identified some of the major features of Tibetan
topography including the correct position of part of the course of
the great Tsangpo river (as Bogle noted when he crossed it on the
way to the Panchen Lama's residence).

The story of these pre-British explorers, which is not touched
upon in the pages that follow, has been told in a number of places.
John MacGregor's *Tibet. A Chronicle of Exploration* (London 1970)
is excellent; and it contains an adequate bibliography.

The present book is a revised version of *Britain and Chinese
Central Asia*. A final chapter extends the story until 1910 when a
Chinese expeditionary force occupied Lhasa. The first chapter has
been considerably modified. Elsewhere a number of errors have
been corrected and minor alterations in the text made. The maps
have been redrawn. The bibliography has been expanded to
include some of the more important works which since 1959 have
either been published or have come to my notice. The index has

been altered to accommodate these various changes and additions. A large number of appendices in *Britain and Chinese Central Asia* dealing with Indo-Tibetan trade have been omitted. The present title has been adopted in the belief that it reflects more accurately the subject matter of the book.

In the process of revision a number of changes have *not* been made. Romanized Chinese words have not been transformed into the *pinyin* system which is currently in vogue.

In deciding to undertake this revision I was much influenced by kind opinions as to the merits of the original *Britain and Chinese Central Asia* expressed by Peter Hopkirk and Jeffrey Somers. I am also indebted to Jeffrey Somers for some ideas about the Russian Buriat visitors to Lhasa who were so important in the initiation of the Younghusband Mission. Crown copyright material quoted in this book appears by permission.

Alastair Lamb
Hertford 1985

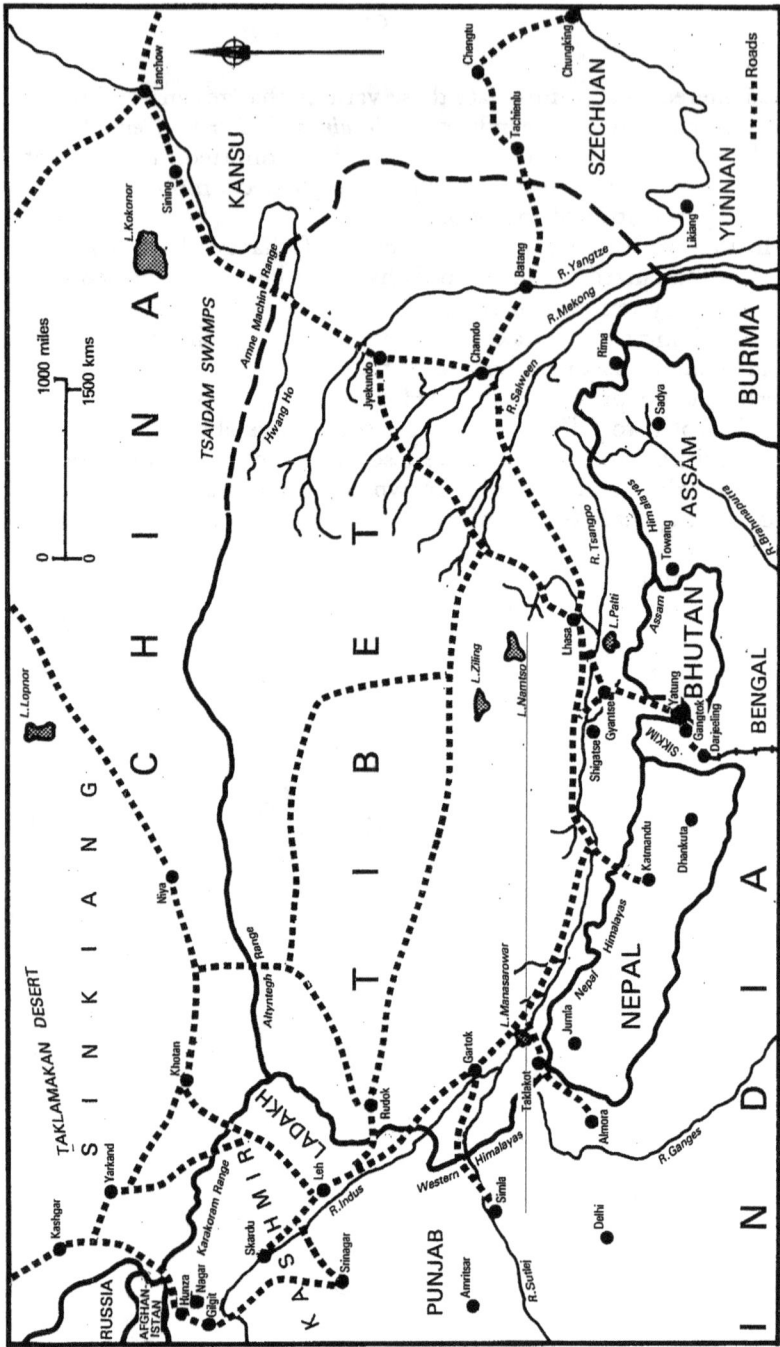

Sketch map of Tibet

FIRST CONTACTS

·

1766 – 1792

BY THE second half of the eighteenth century, Tibet was already well on the way to becoming that closed country which was to confront the British throughout the nineteenth century. This development was due to the consolidation of Chinese control over the land of the Dalai Lama. In the seventh century Tibet became a state of considerable importance in the political history of the Far East. The great Tibetan leader Song-tsan Gam-po, who unified Tibet and established its capital at Lhasa, made his influence felt both in India and in China. He forced the rulers of T'ang China to enter into an alliance with him, and created the precedent for the close relations between Lhasa and Peking which were to be such a feature of subsequent Tibetan history. But it was probably not until the Yuan period that the Chinese could claim to have established any suzerainty over Tibet, and not until the arrival of the Ch'ing Dynasty that they were able to give much practical effect to such suzerainty. Sino-Tibetan relations were closely connected with the place that Tibet occupied in the world of Buddhism, a faith whose hold over the Tibetans was consolidated by Song-tsan Gam-po, but which did not approach its present form until much later. Towards the end of the fourteenth century the Tibetan religious reformer Tsong Ka-pa founded the Yellow (or *Gelupka*) Sect and laid the foundations for that system of incarnate Lamas which has characterized Tibetan government ever since. As the Dalai Lamas, who owe their origin to Tsong Ka-pa, increased in power and influence, they became involved in Central Asian politics. The Yellow Sect spread rapidly among the tribes of Mongolia, and it was a Mongol chieftain, Altan Khan, who at the end of the sixteenth century conferred on the Lama at Lhasa the title of Dalai ('the all embracing'). The Manchus were not slow to appreciate the importance of the influence of the Dalai Lama in any policy which aimed to control events in Mongolia. In the eighteenth century, first under K'ang Hsi and then under Ch'ien Lung, the Chinese established a protectorate over Tibet which culminated in the constitutional revolution of 1750, when the last of the Tibetan lay rulers was removed. From that date the Dalai Lama became the Tibetan ruler in temporal as well as religious matters. A Chinese Resident, or Amban, and an Assistant Amban, were stationed in Lhasa to make sure that the Tibetans kept in line with Chinese policy.

The Dalai Lama carried out his government through a Chief Minister and a cabinet of four subordinate ministers, the Khalons or Shapes, who were referred to collectively as the Kashak. The Dalai Lama was by no means an unrestrained autocrat. The Amban and the Assistant Amban watched his actions; he was obliged to conciliate the great monastic establishments of Tibet and the great aristocratic families; and since the seventeenth century his power was somewhat limited, in practice if not in theory, by the existence of the potentially rival influence of the Tashi, or Panchen Lama at Tashilhunpo near Shigatse. The significance of the Incarnation at Tashilhunpo became apparent in the latter part of the eighteenth century. In 1751 the Chinese had recognized the Dalai Lama as the temporal head of the Tibetan state, and they do not seem to have given a constitutional position to the Tashi Lama - the term Panchen is more correct, but Tashi will, in the main, be used here as it was the name by which until the end of the nineteenth century, the British were accustomed to refer to this dignitary. During a minority of a Dalai Lama, however, the Regent at Lhasa inevitably found it difficult to ignore the great prestige of the Tashi Lama, whose real influence extended much further than the environs of Shigatse, to which his temporal powers were in theory confined. When, in about 1758, the Dalai Lama died, the 6th Tashi Lama began to acquire for himself a position which threatened to rival that of the Incarnation at Lhasa. The 6th Tashi Lama was respected in Mongolia and in China. His influence extended to the Court of the Chinese Emperor. His intelligence and his ability well qualified him to make the most of the opportunity provided by the temporary weakness of Lhasa during a minority of a Dalai Lama. It was this

2

Lama who made possible the first British missions to Tibet.[1]

That the British should have some sort of contact with Tibet was inevitable. The influence of Tibet extended, and still extends, far beyond its political frontiers. All along the Himalayas, in Ladakh, Lahul, Spiti, Garwhal, Kumaon, Nepal, Sikkim, Bhutan and Assam, as well as in Burma and Western China from Yunnan to Kansu, were to be found people with close ties of race and religion ,to Tibet. Many states outside the normally accepted political frontiers of Tibet owed political allegiance to Lhasa, as in the case of Ladakh, Sikkim and Bhutan. The political relations of these states with Lhasa, as we shall see in the case of Ladakh (in Chapter III), were intimately involved with commercial relations. Trade across the Himalayas and trade between China and Tibet was an expression of politics as well as of economics. Trade was also connected with religion, in that many of the Tibetan monasteries were involved in trade, and many goods coming to and from the markets of Tibet were carried by pilgrims. Political changes, therefore, on either side of the Tibetan frontier had commercial consequences; and attempts to alter the traditional patterns of trade had political effects. This fact can be seen in the developments which followed, for example, the conquest of the Vale of Nepal by the Hindu Gurkhas under Prithvi Narayan in the 1760s, or the conquest of Ladakh by Gulab Singh, the Raja of Jammu, in the 1830s.

While Indo-Tibetan trade has never been 'a vital element in the commerce of the Indian subcontinent, it has always been of great importance to the economic life of the Himalayan states; and, in consequence, any change in its volume or direction has had an effect on the political stability of India's northern frontier. To the East India Company, when its territory first began to extend towards the Himalayas, this trade had an added importance in that in the eighteenth century, it would seem, Tibet bought more from India than it sold, and the balance was made up in gold and silver.

The English were aware of some of the commercial possibilities of Tibet from the moment when they first set foot on the Indian subcontinent, but they took no steps to develop trade across the Himalayas until, in the years following Plassey, they found themselves in control of territory stretching from the Bay of Bengal to the foothills of the mountain barrier to the north.[2] The establishment of English rule in Bengal coincided with the explosive expansion of the Gurkhas who in the 1760s engulfed the many small states in that part of the Himalayas which now forms Nepal, including the Newar states of Katmandu, Bhatgaon and

3

Patan through which ran the traditional trade routes between the Gangetic plain and Tibet, the most important of which having its Indian terminus at Patna. The conquest of the Newar states, which possessed close ties of race and religion with Lhasa, by the Hindu Gurkhas brought about a marked decline of that trade across the Himalayas which the East India Company was beginning to appreciate as a possible source of specie to redress the adverse balance of the China trade. It was 'an advantageous trade . . . by which a considerable quantity of gold and many other valuable commodities were imported' and the Company had no wish to see its territories 'deprived of the benefits arising from the former intercourse, at a period when a decline of trade and a scarcity of specie render it of the greatest importance that every spring of industry should flow freely and without interruption'.[3]

Thus the Company responded in 1767 to a plea from the Raja of Patan for aid against the Gurkhas. Captain Kinloch and a small force were despatched to the Vale of Nepal to help the Newars. Kinloch and his men suffered much from the unhealthy climate of the Nepalese Terai, that disease-ridden lowland through which they had to pass on their way to the hills, and, in fact, they never reached their destination though they seem to have created a diversion sufficient to delay the Gurkha conquest of Patan for over a year.[4] This abortive campaign, however, sufficed to convince the Court of Directors of the East India Company of the need for opening some kind of commercial and diplomatic relations with the hill states which lay on Bengal's northern frontier. The Court appreciated that to the north of its Indian possessions lay a means of access not only to the local trade of Tibet and the Himalayan hill states, but also to the fabulous markets of the Chinese Empire. A land route to China in the exclusive possession of the Company had obvious advantages both as a way round the restrictions of Canton and as a source of specie for remittance home from India. As the Court wrote to Bengal in February 1768: 'We desire you will obtain the best intelligence you can whether trade can be opened with Nepaul, and whether cloth and other European commodities may not find their way thence to Thibet, Lhassa and the western parts of China.'[5]

It was with this policy in mind that James Logan, a surgeon in the Company's service, proposed towards the end of 1769 that he be sent to Nepal 'to endeavour to establish a trade with Tibett and the Western Provinces of China by way of Neypall'. Logan had, he said, long been interested in those mountain lands beyond

4

Bengal and had come to the conclusion that 'a person of integrity, properly authorized by the Company, is wanted to go into the countries themselves and report on their commercial possibilities'. He spoke of the great value of the trade that had existed between Tibet and Patna before the Gurkha attacks, and he urged that every effort be made to support the Newar Rajas of the Vale of Nepal in their hour of need. Such a policy, he added, could hardly fail to please the Tashi Lama of Tibet, who had long enjoyed the closest of relations with the Newar Rajas. This was an interesting plan, with its anticipation of the policy which Hastings was soon to pursue in the suggestion that the friendship of the Tashi Lama was worth cultivating; and it was a policy which received the support of John Cartier, Governor of Bengal from 1769 to 1772. Logan evidently set out on his mission some time before June 1770 only to be frustrated by the victorious Gurkhas whose completion of the conquest of the Vale of Nepal put an end to British projects of this kind.[6]

The Gurkha conquest of Nepal seems to have resulted for a while in an almost complete stoppage of the trade between Bengal and Tibet. The Company was anxious that it should revive. It decided that, since there was little prospect of the Gurkhas being expelled from Nepal by the original rulers, whose pleas for British aid it now ignored, its best policy would be to find new routes to Tibet to replace the route through Nepal. Thus, in 1771, the Court of Directors suggested that the exploration of the Assam and Bhutan might disclose a fresh channel for the Tibet trade.[7]

When Warren Hastings began his administration of Bengal in April 1772, the opening of some kind of diplomatic and commercial relationship with Tibet by means of a channel of communication which did not run through Nepal had already become an object of Company policy which, even before the failure of the Kinloch expedition to Nepal of 1767, had been directed towards Sikkim, Bhutan and the adjacent tracts of Assam between the hills and the Brahmaputra valley.

In the years immediately after Plassey in 1757 the pattern of established authority in this zone, wedged between Bengal on the one hand and the Himalayan states of Sikkim and Bhutan on the other, had been much disturbed. Not only was there pressure on the western edge from the conquering Gurkhas but also the Bhutanese took the opportunity to consolidate or expand their influence into the Duars, the Bhutanese equivalent of the Terai, and even further south into states like Cooch Behar. In this the Bhutanese were helped by armed bands of *sanyasis* (a peculiar blend of bandit and holy man or fakir who flourished in these unsettled times). By 1765 the situation in Cooch Behar, where the Bhutanese and their *sanyasi* allies had involved themselves in a disputed succession, had attracted Company attention; and early in 1766 a Company force under Lieutenant Morrison, responding to an appeal for aid from the Nazir Deo, the hereditary commander in chief of the Cooch Behar army, clashed with a band of these invaders near the junction of the Dharla and Brahmaputra rivers a few miles north-east of Rangpur. Present on this occasion was James Rennell, the very youthful first Surveyor-General of Bengal who was working in this neighbourhood and who was seriously wounded in the fight. Rennell's involvement indicated a Company interested in this sector of the Bengal frontier and the territories beyond it which was leading to active investigation by officials with direct access to the highest levels of Company administration.

The 1766 clash convinced Lord Clive, then serving his second Governorship of Bengal, that the Surveyor-General should have on subsequent ventures here an adequate military escort of at least a company of sepoys. With such a force did Rennell in the cold season of 1767-8, having recovered fully from his wounds, set out again through Cooch Behar towards both the Brahmaputra valley and, it would seem, the Bhutanese hills. There is, indeed, some evidence that on this occasion Rennell was trying to make his way to Tibet, and that he was only checked by the Bhutanese after penetrating deep into the Himalayan foothills. In other words, in 1767-8 there was considerable British activity, including the movement of a fairly impressive military force (since a sepoy company with servants and camp followers would have involved a thousand or more people), across Cooch Behar and into Bhutan. This seems to have been repeated in 1771 when Rennell was given command of an expedition, clearly military rather than geographical, against an enemy which, although the records lack precision on this point, would seem to include Bhutanese and *sanyasi* elements.[8]

In 1772 yet another crisis developed between Bhutan and Cooch Behar, an event which hitherto has generally been taken as the starting point of Anglo-Bhutanese and Anglo-Tibetan relations, but which, if our interpretation of Rennell's work is correct (not to mention the implications of Company Nepalese policy since at least 1767), really but marked a stage in a process which had been going on for several years. The great importance of the 1772 crisis was not that it was the beginning of a policy but, rather, that it resulted in a wider diplomatic interest which made the implementation of policy possible. The outbreak of conflict between Bhutan

6

and Cooch Behar in 1772 arose, as had several earlier crises, from Bhutanese objections to a succession to the Cooch Behar throne over which they considered they had some kind of suzerain rights. The anti-Bhutanese faction in Cooch Behar appealed to the Company. In return for the acceptance by treaty of British Protection, Warren Hastings, who had just taken over the Governorship of Bengal, agreed to help, perhaps seeing this as the logical conclusion of the policy with which Rennell had been associated since 1766. He sent a company of troops under the command of one Captain Jones. In 1773 Jones inflicted a series of defeats on the Bhutanese, and in so doing alarmed the Gurkhas, who were reluctant to see the British established in an area which they probably wished to occupy themselves. The Gurkhas sent an embassy to Tibet to point out to the Tashi Lama the danger of a British occupation of Bhutan. The Tashi Lama, who did not relish the prospect of the British taking over a Tibetan dependency, wrote to Hastings on behalf of the Bhutanese. In this letter, which reached Calcutta in March 1774, Hastings saw the chance to implement the policy which the Court of Directors had been suggesting since 1768. He decided to treat the Bhutanese with leniency and to send a friendly mission to the Tashi Lama.[9]

The mission, which set out in May 1774, was entrusted to George Bogle, a young Scot who in three years of Company service had attracted the favourable notice of Hastings. Its objective was fourfold. Firstly, by a treaty of 'amity and commerce' with Tibet and by similar means Bogle was to 'open a mutual and equal communication of trade' between Tibet and Bengal. Secondly, Bogle was instructed to study the markets and resources of Tibet and acquire the data without which no plans for the increase of Indo-Tibetan trade could be devised. Thirdly, the young envoy was to investigate the relations between Tibet and China with an eye to the possibility of the influence of the former country being used to bring about an improvement in English trade and diplomacy with the latter country. Finally, Bogle was to find out all he could about the people, politics, manners and morals of Tibet for the satisfaction of the personal curiosity of Warren Hastings.[10]

Bogle reached Tashilhunpo, the seat of the Tashi Lama, in December 1774 and he remained in Tibet for five months. He was the first Englishman, though by no means the first European, to cross the Himalayas and to see the strange land which lay beyond. Bogle was able to meet the Tashi Lama on many occasions and established a firm friendship with him. The Lama was interested in all that Bogle had to tell of the outside world, of the story of the rise of British power in India, of the relations between England and Russia, of the technical developments of Europe. Bogle, in turn, was impressed by the sanctity and wisdom of the Lama. This strange friendship between Tibetan priest and British official was the greatest achievement of Bogle's mission. Without the co-operation of the Tashi Lama there was scant hope of any significant revival of the Indo-Tibetan trade which had been so severely damaged by the conquests of the Gurkhas. With his co-operation, however, there was some hope that the Bhutanese, who appeared to exist in a constant state of civil war, might be prevailed upon to permit some trade to pass through their territory.[11]

Bogle's mission, in fact, did very little to open up the alternative trade route through Bhutan. Despite a treaty which Bogle was able to negotiate with the ruler of Bhutan, the Deb Raja, on his return from Tashilhunpo in the spring of 1775, and despite Hastings' attempts to encourage Bhutanese merchants to visit an annual fair at Rangpur in Bengal, which lay convenient to the Bhutanese frontier, the Government of Bhutan continued to place obstacles in the way of merchants crossing its territory to and from Tibet and India.[12] Alexander Hamilton, who had gone with Bogle to Tibet, reported that when he returned to Bhutan in late 1775 he found that no merchants were coming through and that he was experiencing great difficulty in sending and receiving letters to and from Tashilhunpo.[13] A decade was to pass, in fact, before the Bhutan route began to show much promise. The lack of commercial success, however, was more than compensated for by the real political achievements of Bogle's Tibetan journey.

When Bogle returned to India in the early summer of 1775 he was able to give Hastings some shrewd advice on the future conduct of relations across the Himalayas. In the first place, it was clear that Bogle's success depended on his personal relationship with the Tashi Lama; he had been unable to visit Lhasa and the Regent there – the Dalai Lama was then a minor – had observed his mission with a suspicion which was probably shared by the Chinese Amban.[14] In the second place, Bogle emphasized that there must be no question of trying to rush the opening of Tibet by requesting the right for Europeans to travel freely in that country. Formerly, Bogle observed:

When Europeans were settled in Hindustan merely as merchants, there would have been no difficulty in establishing factories and freedom of trade; but the power and elevation to which the English have now risen, render them the objects of jealousy of all their neighbours. . . . The Government at Lhasa considered me sent to explore their country, which the ambition of the British might afterwards prompt them to invade, and their superiority of arms render them successful. I was at much pains during my stay among the inhabitants of Bhutan and Tibet to remove their prejudices; but I am convinced that they can be effectually conquered only by the opportunities which a greater intercourse and more intimate acquaintance with the English may afford them of observing their fidelity to engagements, and the moderation of their views, and by an interchange of those good offices which serve to beget confidence between nations as well as between individuals.[15]

It seemed to Bogle that at the conclusion of his mission British relations with Tibet rested somewhat insecurely upon two supports. Firstly, the existence of the 6th Tashi Lama, a man of ability and independent mind, during the minority of the Dalai Lama enabled Bogle to deal with a prominent Tibetan personality away from the centre of Chinese influence at Lhasa. Secondly, the Gurkha conquests had seriously alarmed Tibet and the Himalayan states with close ties to Tibet. The Tashi Lama saw, as Bogle put it, that nothing was more likely to make the Gurkha Raja 'confine himself to his own country than the knowledge of a connection between the government of this country [Tibet] and that of Bengal'.[16] The British could best allay Tibetan suspicions by standing as the protectors of the Tibetans against Gurkha encroachment. The Gurkha conquests, which had provided the initial stimulus for the establishment of Anglo-Tibetan relations, should be exploited to extract lasting diplomatic benefit from those relations. This fact, of course, the Gurkhas also appreciated, and they did their utmost, while Bogle was in Tashilhunpo, to prevent the Tashi Lama from having any dealings with the British envoy.[17]

From his experience in Tibet Bogle concluded that from a friendship with the Tashi Lama the Company could derive much more than the profits of a flourishing trade across the Himalayas. Tibet was the back door to China and might well prove to be the way round the obstructions imposed upon British trade and diplomacy at Canton. It seems likely that Hastings was aware of the possibility before he sent his envoy to Tibet; but it was Bogle, through the friendship he established with the Tashi Lama, who showed in detail how Tibet might be made to play a part in Anglo-Chinese relations. The incarnate Lamas of Tibet, Bogle discovered, possessed considerable influence with the Chinese Emperors of the Manchu Dynasty, who, 'being of Tartar extraction, profess the religion of the Lamas, and reverence them as the head of their faith'. In this respect the 6th Tashi Lama wielded exceptional influence; 'his character and abilities had secured him the favour of the Emperor' so that 'his representations carried great weight at the Court of Peking'. The Tashi Lama promised Bogle that he would write to an influential Lama in Peking in praise of the British and held out the hope that it might eventually be possible for an envoy of the Company to make his way through Tibet to the Chinese capital. While Bogle was 'not so sanguine' about the prospects of this plan, he did not quite despair of 'one day or other getting a sight of Peking'.[18]

Bogle's mission showed that there were three distinct but closely related objectives of British policy beyond the Himalayas. The friendship of the Tashi Lama could be of the greatest value in keeping in check the turbulent Bhutanese and thus in avoiding border incidents like that which had resulted in British intervention on behalf of Cooch Behar in 1773. The influence of the Lama could help in keeping open a trade route from Bengal to Tibet by way of Bhutan. The intercession of the Lama at Peking offered some hope of paving the way for the visit of an envoy of the Company to the capital of the Chinese Empire, and from such a visit, it was hoped, a marked improvement of the conditions of British trade at Canton might result. All these objectives were, in one sense, financial. Border incidents might result in expensive campaigns by the Company's troops. The revival of the former Indo-Tibetan trade might bring about an increased flow of specie into the Company's possessions. Improvements of the conditions of trade at Canton might well enable the Company to sell more British manufactured goods in China and thus reduce the quantity of bullion that had to be laid out to finance the tea trade. These aims, in fact, accorded well with the general policy of the Company at this period in India and towards the East Indies and China, a policy which was to lead to Hastings' deputation of Chapman to Cochin China in 1778 under instructions which strongly recall those of Bogle in 1774.[19] The same financial problems which made Tibet so attractive to Hastings as a source of specie were to be one of the factors behind the founding of Penang in 1786 by Hastings' successor Macpherson, who saw in a settlement in Malaysia a market where English and Indian goods could be exchanged for specie 'to be applied as funds on the Chinese market for the purchase of Tea, instead of the ruinous export of specie from this country'.[20] Tibet was but one of several directions in which some solution to the problems implicit in British relations, diplomatic and commercial, with the Chinese Empire might be sought; and these were problems which, as Holden Furber has shown for the period 1783–93, were of the greatest concern to many interests in Europe as well as India.[21] Thus it is not surprising that the Court of Directors considered Hastings' overtures towards the Tashi Lama with approval.[22] Even Philip Francis felt obliged to admit that there might be something in the Tibetan scheme, although 'my Expectations of Commercial Advantages to be derived from a Communication with Tibet are by no means so sanguine as those expressed by the Governor-General'.[23]

The achievement of the benefits which might arise from British relations with Tashilhunpo certainly required more than the sending of a single mission. This fact Hastings appreciated; and in the years immediately following Bogle's return a number of attempts were made to reinforce the successes of the first mission to the Tashi Lama. Letters continued to pass between Tashilhunpo and Calcutta. The Tashi Lama wished to establish a religious house in Bengal and in 1775 land was rented to him for this purpose which, in 1778, was made over to the Lama in perpetuity as a gift of the Company.[24] At the end of 1775 the Lama sent Hastings a gift of a small quantity of gold and silver which was promptly sent off to the Court for assay.[25] In all this correspondence the intermediary between Hastings' and the Lama was Purangir, a *gosein* or trading pilgrim, who had brought the first letter from the Lama of 1774 and who had accompanied Bogle to Tashilhunpo. An attempt to send another European, Hamilton, to visit the Lama in 1776 was not successful. Hamilton, another of Bogle's companions, went up to Bhutan towards the end of 1775 to investigate conditions of trade through that country and to try to keep in touch with Tibet; but, as he wrote to Hastings in May 1776, 'from the particular situation of affairs at Tashilhumpo and the unreasonable jealousy of the Lassa Government, the expectations which I had formed of visiting Thibet are now at an end'.[26] A further visit by Hamilton to Bhutan in 1777 was no more successful.[27]

The reasons why Hamilton could not repeat Bogle's journey are good enough instances of the basic insecurity of British relations with Tibet at that time. As both Bogle and Hastings were convinced, the Tashi Lama was genuinely well disposed towards the Company. He was struggling to build up for himself and his office a position of independence both from the Tibetan authorities at Lhasa and from the Chinese. No doubt he was also looking for some support in the event of an attack on his territory by the Gurkhas. He had established relations not only with the Company - it was the Lama who had taken the first step leading to the Bogle mission - but also with other rulers as far apart as Benares and Mongolia; but in all this he had acted with considerable caution. He had no wish to make an open challenge to the authority of the Chinese. The presence of a Chinese ambassador at Tashilhunpo, he said, made it impossible for Hamilton to come to see him. Lhasa, moreover, would certainly object strongly to another Englishman following so closely in Bogle's footsteps. Finally, an assembly of Mongol chiefs was shortly to take place at Tashilhunpo and they would surely resent the presence of a European.[28] In a letter which reached Calcutta in July 1775 he explained to Hastings the difficulties of his position:

> As this country [he wrote] is under the absolute Sovereignty of the Emperor of China, who maintains an active and unrelaxed control over its all affairs, and as the forming of any connexion or friendship with Foreign Powers is contrary to his pleasure, it will frequently be out of my power to dispatch any messengers to you - however, it will be impossible to efface the remembrance of you out of my mind, and I shall pray always for the increase of your happiness and prosperity - and in return - I hope you will frequently favour us with accounts of your health.[29]

In 1779 it seemed to Hastings that the time was ripe for a second Bogle mission to Tashilhunpo. The death of the Regent at Lhasa, who was thought to have been hostile to the Company, and the coming of age of the Dalai Lama, who had just been invested with the insignia of full authority by the Tashi Lama, seemed to favour this plan. The purpose of the second Bogle mission was less to improve the conditions of Indo-Tibetan trade than to try to exploit the relationship existing between the Tashi Lama and the Chinese Emperor to bring about a British mission to Peking. As Hastings put it:

> by means of the Teshoo Lama . . . I am inclined to hope that a communication may be opened with the court of Peking, either through his mediation or by an Agent from the Government; it is impossible to point out the precise advantages which either the opening of new Channels of Trade, or in obtaining redress of Grievances, or extending the privileges of the Company, may result from such an

Intercourse; like the navigation of unknown seas, which are explored not for the attainment of any certain and prescribed object, but for the discovery of what they may contain. In so new and remote a search we can only propose to adventure for possibilities, the attempt may be crowned with the most splendid and substantial success, or it may terminate in the mere gratification of useless curiosity, but the hazard is small, the design is worthy of the pursuit of a rising state, the Company have both approved and recommended it, and the means are too promising to be neglected, while the influence of the Teshoo Lama joined to the favourable disposition which he has hitherto manifested to our nation, affords so fair a prospect, and that the only one which may ever be presented us of accomplishing it.

Thus, Bogle was instructed to 'endeavour by means of the Lamas of Tibbet to open a communication with the Court of Peking, and, if possible, to procure leave to proceed thither'.[30] As Bogle remarked, there was a crying need for some means of direct communication between Company and the Chinese Court, if only to enable the English at Canton to collect the vast sums, between £1,500,000 and £2,000,000 Bogle estimated, which were owed to them by Chinese merchants. The Company's business at Canton was 'often harassed and oppressed, and its conductors are entirely without any channel of communication or representation to the Court of Pekin'.[31]

News that the Tashi Lama was about to set out for China to pay his respects to the Emperor necessitated a postponement of Bogle's mission and thus left unanswered the question whether Bogle would, in fact, have been able to repeat his exploit of 1774-75. But there was still, in these altered circumstances, some hope of an improvement in Anglo-Chinese relations since the Tashi Lama had promised that while in Peking he would do his best to obtain the passports which Bogle required to visit the Chinese capital. Once the passports were ready, word would be sent to India and Bogle would set out to join his old friend in Peking, probably travelling by way of Canton.

But the Tashi Lama died of smallpox in Peking in 1780, before he had made any progress in the matter of the passports – there was much rumour that he had been murdered by the Chinese because of the friendship he had shown towards the Company, but this is now generally discounted.[32] In the following year Bogle also died, and Hastings was deprived of the services of the Englishman with the most experience of Tibet. One may well speculate what would have been the outcome had Bogle been able to visit Peking. He would have done so as the envoy of the East India Company and not of the King of England, and he would not have been so concerned with matters of 'face' as were Macartney and Amherst. There might not have been the question of 'kow-tow'. Bogle possessed the skill and tact required for the tortuous conduct of oriental diplomacy, as his success with the Tashi Lama stands witness. He had the patience and the intelligence for the kind of negotiation which would produce results only by the establishment of a mutual good-will over a long period of time. Acting under the command of Hastings, he would have been allowed a freedom of action that was denied to later envoys, and his discretion was such that he would certainly have made the best use of any opportunity that came to hand.

Hastings did not abandon his Tibetan schemes on the deaths of Bogle and the Tashi Lama. The installation of the new Lama, an infant into whose body the soul of the 6th Incarnation was thought to have migrated, provided him with the opportunity for sending a second mission to Tashilhunpo to bring the good wishes of the Company on this auspicious occasion. This task was entrusted to Samuel Turner, a kinsman of Hastings, who set out for Tashilhunpo in 1783. There was no prospect of Turner repeating Bogle's triumphs, since the Tashi Lama was an infant. As Hastings told Macpherson in April or May 1783: 'I expect no great things from Turner's Embassy, but it will at least satisfy curiosity',[33] and the Governor-General's chief satisfaction at this time was in having found in Turner a person who was 'not inferior' to Bogle in some of the latter's great qualities of 'Temper, Patience and Understanding'.[34] It seemed unlikely from the outset, therefore, that the second mission to Tashilhunpo could do much more than reinforce the good will established in 1774-75 by George Bogle. Turner was convinced that with patience the project which had been thwarted by the death of the 6th Tashi Lama might yet come about. It was essential that every effort be made to continue the friendly contacts which Bogle had established, and the best way to achieve this would be through the establishment of trade between India and Tibet. As Turner said, on his return from Tibet in 1784,

> Whenever a regular intercourse takes place between the agents of the government of Bengal and the Chiefs of Tibet, I shall consider it to be the sure basis of an intercourse with China: and it will probably be, by the medium of the former, that we shall be enabled to arrive at Peking.[35]

Turner urged the Company to do all it could to bring about a profitable trade across the Himalayas; and, immediately following Turner's return from Tibet, Hastings acted on this advice. In April 1784 he instructed that an advertisement be circulated inviting native Indian merchants to join an 'adventure' in trade with Tibet through Bhutan, where Turner's diplomacy seems to have at last secured a promise of reasonable conditions of passage. The party of merchants was to assemble in February of the following year. A detailed list of goods likely to find a ready market in Tibet was posted along with the advertisement, suggesting such items as second-quality cloth, coating, cheap watches, clocks, trinkets, snuff-boxes, smelling-bottles, pocket-knives, scissors, conch shells, indigo, coral, large imperfect pearls, amber, gloves and coarse cottons. In return the merchants might bring back gold dust, silver, musk from the musk deer, yak tails (used as fly whisks) and wool. This first venture, so that it should have every chance of success, was to be exempted from all duties.[36] In 1785 the 'adventure' took place according to plan, and a reasonably flourishing and profitable trade seems to have resulted. But by the time that Purangir, who had accompanied the merchants to Tashilhumpo, returned to India to report this success, Hastings had already set out for England and the many trials that faced him there.[37]

The departure of Hastings resulted in a decrease in the tempo of Anglo-Tibetan relations but not in its oblivion. In January 1786, for example, Macpherson, who was acting as Governor-General since Hastings' departure, remarked that the increasing trade with Tibet and the steady flow of friendly letters from the Tashi Lama's advisers gave good grounds for hope that a direct correspondence with the Emperor of China might soon be arranged through Tibet.[38] In the following year the Court observed that Bhutan still seemed to be friendly to the Company and was placing no obstacles in the way of trade across the mountains to Tibet. It expressed its hope that 'a most beneficial trade will soon be established with that distant country, to the great advantage of the Bengal Provinces, by a regular importation of Bullion'. It urged that Bhutan should not be alarmed by any action 'affording the least cause for suspicion that we have any schemes of ambition to accomplish, which, in truth, we have not'; and it added that it might be as well to continue to woo Tashilhunpo, perhaps by the offer of another temple site in Bengal. It was sure that the Regent at Tashilhunpo, who was then ruling during the minority of the 7th Tashi Lama and with whom Turner had made friends on his visit to Tibet, would welcome such a gift.[39]

15

It has been seen that one of the most attractive features to the Company of the trade between Bengal and Tibet lay in its potential balance of payments in favour of India. Mercantilist theory objected to the export of bullion; yet it had proved impossible to finance the purchase of China tea at Canton by the export of British manufactures. One solution to this problem was to increase the flow of specie into the Company's territories by the encouragement of local Indian trade; another was to search for some commodity like opium which would command a ready sale in China; yet a third was to try to become independent of Chinese tea through the cultivation of this plant in India. The latter part of the eighteenth century saw the beginning of the history of Indian tea planting with the quest by the Company for samples of the Chinese tea plant. Here again Tibet was thought to be of importance as the back door not only to the Chinese capital but also to the tea-growing districts of Western China. Towards the end of 1789 there was a proposal to send a certain Mr. Foster to China by this route; and when it was shown that no European then stood much chance of travelling through the length of Tibet, it was inevitable that Purangir should be named for this task, with instructions for 'obtaining either the seed or plant of the Tea with promise of a suitable reward in case of success in procuring the proper kind and delivering it in a state of vegetation to the Chief at Rungpoor, and if possible with a native practised in the cultivation'. This scheme, as one might have suspected, came to nothing, and the difficulty of obtaining skilled cultivators of the tea plant from China effectively held up the development of the Indian tea industry until after the Treaty of Nanking in 1842. But Sir Joseph Banks, President of the Royal Society, was vocal in support of Indian tea plantation, as was Lord Macartney on his return from his Embassy to China in 1794.[40]

Shortly after Hastings' return to England, the difficulties of the Company's position at Canton convinced the Court of Directors and the Board of Control that a British mission must go to Peking. It may well be that the lessons of the missions to Tashilhunpo of Bogle and Turner, resulting in such cordial relations with important officials within the Chinese Empire, had a part to play in the genesis of this idea. In 1787 Lt.-Col. Cathcart was deputed to travel to Peking. A hint that this mission was not wholly unconnected with the earlier Tibetan ventures is provided by the suggestion that Cathcart might proceed to China via Tibet. When this was vetoed by the Board of Control on the grounds that such a journey would be 'too long and hazardous to be entered upon, as well as very doubtful in the result',[41] Cathcart then proposed that after reaching Peking by way of Canton he should send his secretary, Agnew, home through Tibet.[42]

The establishment of relations between the British and the centre of Chinese power by means of a channel of communication through Tibet had obvious advantages for the East India Company. Any improvements in the condition of trade with China by sea which an ambassador from the King of England might secure would have to be open to all the King's subjects. As Dundas told the Court of Directors in 1787, it was unthinkable that 'in negotiating with the Emperor of China, the King of Great Britain is obliged to accept a settlement with such a restriction in it, as of necessity obliges him to carry on the trade of China by an exclusive Company'.[43] But improvement in a trade of which one terminus lay within the Company's territory was clearly another matter. Improvement in the trade across the Himalayas carried no threat to the Company's monopoly.

The Cathcart Mission failed owing to the death of its leader while at sea on the way to China. The project was revived with the sending of Lord Macartney on a similar mission in 1792. Here again, while the immediate object was to improve conditions of trade at Canton, there are still hints that some thought had been given to the Tibetan route. In Macartney's instructions, as in those of Cathcart, Dundas at the Board of Control was at pains to state categorically that the British Ambassador should not travel to China by way of Tibet.[44] And, as in the case of the Cathcart Mission, Macartney gave serious thought to the possibility of exploring the Tibetan route as a means of communication between Peking and the East India Company. He was musing on this idea on the voyage out to China; while off the coast of Sumatra he wrote to Dundas that he had just suggested to Cornwallis, then Governor-General of India, that Cornwallis should 'communicate with me not only by way of Canton but also by Tibet, and I propose to try that way also from Peking in order to let you know, if possible, the sooner of my arrival at that Capital, and what may be the likelihood of my success there'.[45]

When Macartney wrote to this effect he was not aware of a radical alteration in the situation in the Himalayas that had ruled out completely the Tibetan route. He knew of the policy of Hastings towards Tibet - he was Governor of Madras at the time of Turner's return from Tashilhunpo - but the slowness of communications had kept him in ignorance of the chain of events that not only upset the work of Hastings but also endangered the success of his own mission to China.

In 1788 the Gurkhas invaded the territory of the Tashi Lama

and occupied several points across the Tibetan border. The immediate causes of this development are by no means clear; but the chief factor was undoubtedly the expansionist nature of the Gurkha state. Checked to some extent in their designs on Sikkim and Bhutan by the establishment of British relations with Tashilhunpo, the Gurkhas began to look northwards to Tibet, where they could acquire plunder, counter the British and keep their own soldiers occupied. It is not surprising that the Gurkhas should listen to one of the brothers of the late Tashi Lama who had found himself obliged to flee to Nepal, and who referred to the great wealth of Tibet as an incentive to bring the Gurkhas on to his side against his enemies in Tashilhunpo. Once they had decided on an attack on the Tibetans, the Gurkhas had no difficulty in finding a *casus belli* in long-standing disputes over the Nepalese claim to rights of minting coinage for circulation in Tibet, and over the duties which the Tibetans charged on salt which they exported to Nepal. The Tibetans had no force with which to oppose the Gurkhas, and only persuaded the invaders to withdraw after the promise of the payment of a substantial indemnity.[46] But before this arrangement had been negotiated, the authorities at Tashilhunpo remembered the promises of friendship which had been made to them by the two envoys of Hastings and appealed to the British for help against the Gurkha invaders. Lord Cornwallis, the Governor-General, replied in a somewhat ambiguous manner. It was clear that he did not want to be involved in a Himalayan war or take any action which might be construed as hostile by the Gurkhas; yet he wished to derive some benefit from this development in the Himalayan situation. He promised, in his reply to Tashilhunpo, that he would give no assistance to the Gurkhas; but he added that neither could he give any active help to the Tibetans. The Company could not afford the expense of a hill war; it had received no provocation from the Gurkhas; it did not want to intervene in a matter which concerned a dependant of the Chinese Emperor without first being asked to do so by that ruler. Perhaps, Cornwallis concluded rather disingenuously, his answer would have been different if the Company had possessed a representative in Peking and had been in a closer relationship with the Chinese Government. It was not too late, Cornwallis implied, for Tashilhunpo to use its influence to bring this about; it was very much in its interest to do so.[47]

It is clear from this correspondence that Cornwallis was less interested in the value of the local trans-Himalayan trade, of which he was well aware,[48] and which was bound to suffer from any increase in the power and extent of Nepal, than in the

18

opportunity which the Tibetan hour of need promised to give for the establishment of a British representative in Peking through Tibetan mediation.

But the reply of Cornwallis to the Tibetan appeal was sent too late to have any effect on Tibetan policy. By the time it reached Tashilhunpo the Tibetans had already come to terms with the Gurkhas. The only result of this response to the Tibetan call for assistance was, in all probability, to suggest to the authorities in Tashilhunpo that the friendship of the Company towards Tibet was not as disinterested as the professions of Bogle and Turner might have suggested.

In 1791 the Gurkhas once more invaded Tibet. Only part of the indemnity promised in 1789 had been paid and Lhasa, which was the financial centre of Tibet, refused to provide the balance. Lhasa had watched with great suspicion the rise in influence and independence of Tashilhunpo. It must have appreciated that failure to pay the Gurkhas in full would result inevitably in a fresh invasion, which in turn would provide an excuse for requesting Chinese intervention and the consequent squashing, once and for all, of the pretentions of Tashilhunpo. If this was the policy of Lhasa, it succeeded beyond all reasonable expectations. The Gurkhas renewed their attack, and this time they advanced far into Tibet, capturing Shigatse and plundering the great monastery of the Tashi Lamas at Tashilhunpo. In early 1792, while the Gurkhas were withdrawing slowly to their own territory, loaded with their booty, a powerful Chinese force arrived in Tibet. The invading Gurkhas were decisively defeated and obliged to come to terms with the Chinese. They surrendered their loot and they agreed to send a tribute mission to Peking once every five years. The Chinese took the opportunity afforded by their intervention to strengthen their control over Tibet, and in so doing they devised a new method of selection of the Dalai Lama. A sort of lottery was instituted whereby the names of several likely candidates were placed in a golden urn and the final selection was made by the Amban, the Chinese Resident in Lhasa, who drew out one name. This system gave the Chinese a considerable say in the selection of a new Lama, since it is not to be supposed that the draw was as random as it might at first sight seem.[49] After 1792 the Chinese had more power in Tibet than they had ever possessed before.

British diplomacy during the second Tibeto-Nepalese crisis was no more successful than it had been during the first outbreak of hostilities in 1788-89. The Company received letters from both the Gurkhas and the authorities in Lhasa, Tibetan and Chinese.

The former sought Company assistance, and the latter, in an admonishing tone, requested British neutrality. The Company's policy was to try to play one side against the other. The mediation of the Company was offered to both parties, while in secret the Company, through Jonathan Duncan, Resident at Benares, seems to have hinted that it might supply armed help to the Gurkhas in return for a commercial treaty opening up Nepal to British trade. The commercial treaty was duly signed in March 1792, stipulating no more than a 2½ per cent. duty on the goods of Indian merchants trading in and through Nepal; but the Gurkhas, when they found that no help beyond Company mediation would be forthcoming, felt, naturally enough, that they had been tricked. In Tibet, on the other hand, there seems to have been a definite impression that the British had sent troops to help the Gurkhas against the Chinese and Tibetans. The Company gained the good-will of neither side.[50]

Cornwallis, in fact, was serious in his offer of the Company's mediation. In September 1792 Colonel Kirkpatrick was sent up to Nepal for this purpose, but by the time he got there the war had long been over and the Gurkhas had come to terms with the Chinese. Kirkpatrick saw clearly that a change had taken place in the Himalayas which was adverse to British interests. In the first place, the trade between Bengal and Tibet was now dead, and the only hope for its revival lay through Nepal: British goods could perhaps be carried to Katmandu for onward transmission to Tibet in the hands of Nepalese traders.[51] In the second place, the Chinese intervention seemed to have changed Tibet from a possible help towards the improvement of Anglo-Chinese relations to a positive danger to the position of the British traders at Canton. As Kirkpatrick perceived in 1792, when the extent of the new Chinese control over Tibet was not yet clear, if 'the Chinese were to establish themselves permanently in our neighbourhood, the border incidents always incident to such a situation, would be but too liable to disturb, more or less, the commercial relations subsisting between them and the East India Company in another part of Asia'.[52] Kirkpatrick argued that this was a matter of sufficient gravity to be included in the agenda of subjects which Lord Macartney, in his impending embassy to Peking, should discuss with the Chinese Emperor.[53]

Macartney's Embassy coincided with these events in Tibet, but no information about them from a British source reached the Ambassador until he arrived at Canton in December 1793, on his way home, his mission completed. Thus Macartney was most surprised to hear from the Chinese, when he was on his way to

meet the Emperor at Jehol, that they were very angry at the way
in which the British had fought against them in the recent war in
Nepal. As he noted in his diary, on 16th August 1793, 'I was very
much startled with this intelligence, but instantly told them that
the thing was impossible and that I could take it upon me to
contradict it in the most decisive manner.' He then thought that
the story that the British had helped the Nepalese might have been
'a mere feint or artifice to sift me, and to try to discover our force,
or our vicinity to their frontiers', and he was reinforced in this
conclusion a few days later, when the Chinese asked him whether
'the English at Bengal would assist the Emperor against the rebels
in those parts'. Since Macartney had denied the first charge on the
grounds, quite untrue, that the distance between British territory
and the scene of the recent war in the Himalayas made British
intervention on either side quite impossible, he could only
consider this second question as a trick to test his sincerity, and he
was forced to say that the British could give no assistance to the
Chinese.[54] Macartney, however, was soon obliged to admit that
the Chinese at Peking genuinely believed that the British had
opposed China in the recent war, perhaps because of the deliberate
misrepresentations of Fu-k'ang-an, the Chinese commander in
Tibet, who, Macartney suggested, might have been insulted by
some Englishman during his recent tenure of office as Viceroy at
Canton, and was now getting his revenge. He had met the
Chinese commander, just back from the wars, and found him to
be most unfriendly despite every exertion of the Ambassador's
charm.[55]

Macartney was convinced that this misunderstanding on the
part of the Chinese as to the nature of the British role in the recent
Himalayan crisis was a major factor behind the failure of his
mission. Staunton, who accompanied Macartney and later wrote
the standard account of the Embassy, thought it was a tragedy
that the Cathcart Mission had not reached its destination, for then
there would have been a British representative in Peking at the
time of the opening of the Gurkha attack on Tibet. The Emperor,
he argued, would in such a case have surely asked for British
assistance in defending his Tibetan dependants, rather than have
relied on his own forces who had not been too successful on the
field of battle in recent years. From the giving of such help the
British would have reaped valuable diplomatic benefits.[56] The
misunderstanding, moreover, in conjunction with the great
increase in Chinese power so close to the borders of British India
might have serious consequences for the future unless it was
explained away. As Staunton put it:

21

Should an interference take place in future, on the part of His Imperial Majesty (of China), in the dissentions which frequently arise between the princes possessing the countries lying along the eastern limits of Hindostan . . . there may be occasion for much mutual discussion between the British and Chinese Governments; and no slight precaution may be necessary on their parts to avoid being involved in the quarrels of their respective dependents or allies.

Macartney felt that the need to clear up this misunderstanding. justified another mission to Peking, not only because no improvement of Anglo-Chinese relations could result until the Chinese had been disabused of their suspicions of the nature of British policy in the Himalayas, but also because the existence of such suspicions created a dangerous situation on the very borders of the Company's possessions in India. Once Chinese doubts had been removed, moreover, the British might begin to derive some positive benefit from the recent chain of events in the Himalayas. The Chinese had learnt, Macartney was clearly implying in his letter to Sir John Shore of 3rd February 1794, that the British possessed great strength in an area which lay virtually on the Chinese frontier. 'Our political situation in Bengal,' he wrote, 'may even contribute, with other motives, to procure for us the full extension, we desire, of our commerce throughout the Empire of China.'

While a second Embassy was not immediately sent, as Macartney advised, the misunderstanding about the Tibeto-Nepalese War was considered of sufficient importance in London to lead in 1795 to a correspondence with Peking in which the British case was stated. In the following year, in a letter to King George III, the Emperor Ch'ien Lung indicated in a most patronizing manner that perhaps the British had not helped the Gurkhas after all. British mediation had been offered, but it came too late to have any effect on the course of the war, and no debt of gratitude was owed to the British on this account.[58]

The Macartney embassy failed to bring about a significant improvement in Anglo-Chinese relations; the correspondence of 1795-96 was equally fruitless.[59] The reasons for this failure lay rather in the nature of the Chinese conception of foreign relations than in any misunderstandings about the British role in the Himalayan crisis of 1788-92. The Chinese Emperor could have no relations with foreign powers on terms of equality; to the Chinese foreign ambassadors were bearers of tribute coming to Peking to recognize the supremacy of the Son of Heaven. On such terms no properly accredited embassy from the King of England to the Emperor of China could have had any result other than that achieved by Macartney. Only a mission of the type envisaged by Bogle and Hastings, opportunist and flexible, ready to sacrifice dignity to commercial advantage, stood any chance of success. Tibet and the Himalayas played little part in the failure of the first British Ambassador to China. But the reason why this should be so was not fully understood by the British at that time. The memory of a causal connection between the crisis of the Tibeto-Nepalese War and Lord Macartney's failure remained, and it was to affect subsequent British policy.

The two Tibeto-Nepalese crises resulted in a great augmentation of Chinese power in Tibet, and this was a decisive blow to any policy of the type which Hastings and his immediate successors had tried to pursue. The demonstration of Chinese military efficiency was a lesson which would deter for many years any Tibetan who might otherwise have given thought to following in the footsteps of the 6th Tashi Lama. It was not until after the Chinese defeat at Japanese hands in 1895 that Tibet, under the leadership of the young 13th Dalai Lama, was to feel itself strong enough to try to carry out at all openly an independent foreign policy. The Company, of course, knew well enough that a decisive change had taken place in the political alignments of the Himalayas since, so Turner wrote to Hastings, his former chief, in November 1792, the recent events in Tibet 'will give the Chinese a much greater hold of those countries than they ever had, and rivet that authority which had before the respect only of a superior power'.[60] But the Company was not certain as to how exactly its interests had been affected. After 1792 it became very difficult to obtain accurate intelligence on what went on in Tibet and the Himalayan States; for one thing, Purangir and trading pilgrims like him, who were firmly identified in Tibetan and Chinese minds as agents of the Company, were now banned from Tibetan territory. Lack of information, however, did not prevent the Company from taking an interest in Tibet: the projects of Hastings' day, indeed, were revived periodically right up to the end of the Gurkha War of 1814–16. As will be seen in the next chapter, the Company still hoped to set the gold and silver of Tibet flowing into its territories, and it made a number of attempts to open up Nepal for this purpose. It still appreciated that its relations with Tibet and the Himalayan States might be connected closely with its position in Canton; but in exactly what way no longer seemed so clear as it had when Hastings thought about sending George Bogle on a second mission to Tashilhunpo.

Would British activity and diplomacy in the Himalayas, by convincing the Chinese at Canton of Company strength, help the Company merchants in China; or would it only irritate the Emperor and confirm him in his distrust of the barbarous Europeans? The problem was a difficult one in the absence of reliable information. Company opinion, especially during the Gurkha War, wavered from one alternative to the other. British policy towards Tibet was for this reason rather ineffective; but, as we shall see shortly, continued interest in the land beyond India's northern mountain border was to play a part in the advance of British influence in the Himalayas, into Kumaon, Garwhal, the

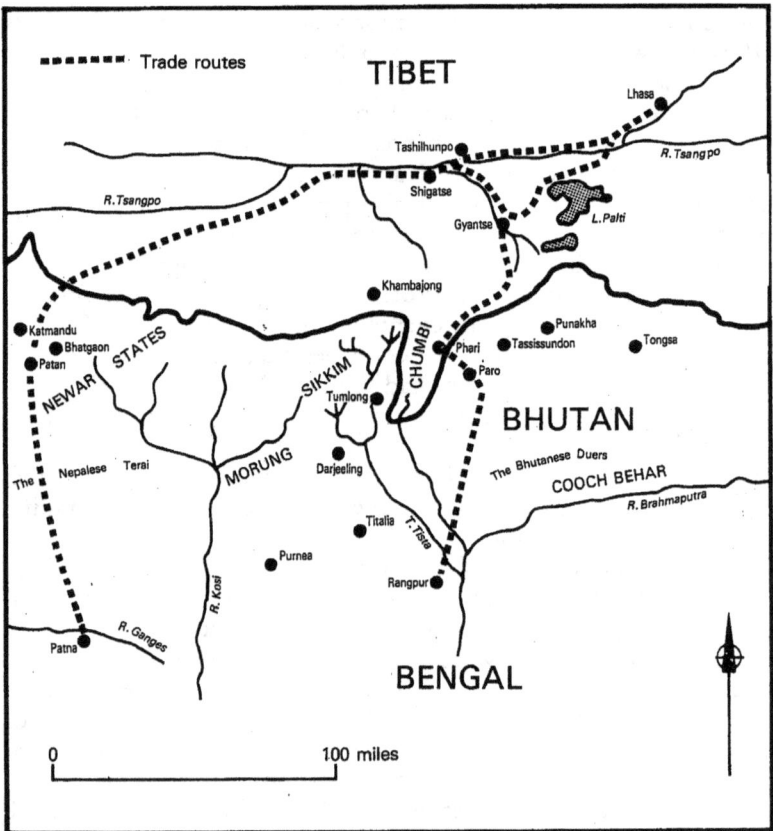

Sketch map showing trade routes between Bengal and Central Tibet in the latter part of the eighteenth century

Sutlej Valley, Spiti, Lahul and, to some extent Kashmir on the west, and into Sikkim, Bhutan and the Assam Himalaya in the east. Even the continued independence of Nepal after the Gurkha War was to be a consequence of the Company's interpretation of the significance of the Chinese position in Tibet. It is clear enough that British interest in Tibet did not disappear with the departure of Warren Hastings, or, even, with the disasters of 1792. It would be true to say, however, that under Warren Hastings British influence had penetrated further into the heart of Tibet than it was to again until the opening years of the twentieth century saw the energetic frontier policy of Lord Curzon.

II

NEPAL

·

1792 – 1816

AFTER THE Chinese intervention in the Himalayas in 1792 there remained but one route linking Bengal and Tibet which offered any promise for a revival of Indo-Tibetan trade. Bhutan, a Tibetan dependency, was now closed to Indian merchants. The potentialities of Sikkim, later to be traversed by the main road between Calcutta and Lhasa, had not yet been discovered by the Company. Nepal alone, bound somewhat tenuously to the Company by the commercial treaty of 1792, offered any chance of access for Indian merchants and British goods to the Tibetan plateau. It is an indication of the importance with which Tibetan trade was regarded that serious thought was given to the exploitation of this sole remaining route, and that the company did not despair following the upsets to its Tibetan diplomacy during the two Tibeto-Nepalese wars.

Kirkpatrick had suggested that the Nepalese route might be developed as an alternative to that through Bhutan; and under the Governor-Generalship of Sir John Shore an attempt was made to follow this advice. Relations between the Company and Katmandu, such as they were, were managed from Benares. It was Duncan, the Resident at Benares, who had negotiated the commercial treaty of 1792; and it was to be Duncan, and his successor Lumsden, who were to try to develop the Nepalese route. Benares seems to have remained in some sort of contact with Tibet after the Nepalese debacle in 1792. We hear, for instance, of letters and presents from the Dalai Lama reaching the Benares Residency in 1794 and 1795.[1] To Benares came Gurkha officials – often men who had fallen from grace in Katmandu – and Indian merchants who still, in small numbers, could trade in Nepal even if Tibet was closed to them. One such merchant, the Moslem holy man Abdul Kadir Khan, had been in close touch with Duncan – during the second Tibeto-Nepalese crisis he had acted as Duncan's agent in Katmandu[2] – and he seemed an obvious choice for the execution of the policy now proposed. In early 1795 Abdul Kadir Khan was provided by the Company with a stock of Indian and English manufactures and sent up to Nepal with instructions to see if he could find a means of getting these goods into Tibet, and to report generally on the prices and prospects of this route. 'The attempt', Shore wrote to Dundas in February 1795, 'is made upon so moderate a scale, that the loss will be trifling even if it should entirely fail; but I have better hopes.'[3] Abdul Kadir Khan's mission was also watched with interest in London. David Scott, then Deputy Chairman of the East India Company, observed that English woollens had 'lately sold to a loss at China',[4] and the Court hoped that 'a vend may be found for cloth of British manufacture in Thibet and Tartary to a considerable amount', as a result of Abdul Kadir Khan's mission.[5]

Abdul Kadir Khan returned from Nepal at the very end of 1795 and at once submitted a most interesting report. His broadcloths, of all colours except yellow, and much of his Indian produce had found a ready sale in Nepal at very satisfactory prices. Many of his wares, moreover, were purchased for re-export to Tibet. The bulk of Nepalese commerce, in fact, was concerned with goods in transit to the north. Profits were so high that the ruling Gurkha families had tried their best to make Nepalese international trade into their monopoly. They had succeeded sufficiently in this to make it very hard for any outsider to make much profit. The circumstances of Abdul Kadir Khan's mission had been exceptional, and it seemed that in regular trade the Company could only hope to gain if it could find a way of eliminating the Nepalese middlemen and dealing directly with Tibetan merchants. Could this be done, there awaited much profit. Abdul Kadir Khan estimated that English broadcloth on sale at Lhasa would make ten annas in the rupee, and that such articles as conch shells, mirrors and knives would bring in a profit of one rupee for each rupee of capital outlay. The avaricious Gurkhas alone stood between the Company and this wealth. Tibetan merchants were eager for trade, but could make no money in the face of Gurkha greed. Moreover, relations between the Gurkhas and the Chinese in Tibet were still strained. Large numbers of Chinese troops still guarded the Tibeto-Nepalese border and political conditions hardly favoured merchant enterprise. Abdul Kadir Khan suggested a number of steps which the Company might take to improve matters. A mart could be established on the Indo-Nepalese frontier which might attract Tibetan merchants, and friendly letters could be written to 'the Subadar of Lhassa and to the Delai Lama'.[6] It seemed, however, that a good trade was likely to develop by this route only, so Lumsden noted to Sir John Shore, 'if it should be found practicable hereafter to carry on direct trade with the natives of Thibet or of China . . . without the agency or intervention of the inhabitants of Napaul'.[7]

From his reading of Abdul Kadir Khan's report Shore was inclined to wonder whether the Company would have been better off had the Chinese in 1792 occupied the whole of Nepal and driven out the Gurkhas as the Gurkhas had previously expelled the Newar Rajas.[8] It seemed, in any case, that it might be necessary to induce the rulers of Nepal to accept a British Resident at their capital, providing, of course, that the Chinese did not oppose such a plan; and if this were done, Shore did not 'despair of extending the sales of the manufactures of Great Britain into Thibet and Tartary; at all events it is an object worthy of our attention'.[9] Thus the company took advantage of a crisis in the politics of Nepal in 1800 to place a Resident at Katmandu. In that year Ranbahadur, the Raja of Nepal, was forced to flee to India, where he established himself in exile at Benares. Vanderheyden, the Resident at Benares, was instructed to make the most of this situation in order to persuade the Gurkhas to accept a new commercial treaty with the Company. The Nepalese Government, apparently fearing lest the Company should begin to intrigue with the exiled Ranbahadur, agreed to discuss such a treaty with the British envoy who should go up to Katmandu for this purpose and who should remain there as British Resident. Captain Knox was deputed to this task, and he reached Katmandu in 1801.[10]

Knox's instructions show how much interest the Company still had in the trade of Tibet. He was told that

you will direct your attention to the means of opening a beneficial trade with the countries of Bootan and Tibet either directly with the Company's Provinces, or through the medium of the merchants of Nepal. The importation into the Company's Provinces of Gold and Silver bullion is an object of considerable importance. The territories of Bootan and Tibet are said to abound with Gold and Silver mines - the produce of which may perhaps, by proper encouragement, be rendered an article of trade, and by the exchange of commodities, the produce of Europe or of the provinces of India, may find its way into the Company's Territories.[11]

But, in carrying out these instructions Knox was to act with great caution. One lesson drawn from the outcome of the Macartney embassy had been that a Chinese misunderstanding of British diplomacy in the Himalayas could, perhaps, have adverse affects on the Company's trading position in China. It was only decided to allow Knox to go to Katmandu after the Governor-General, Lord Wellesley, had made up his mind with considerable optimism that 'the Kingdom of Nepaul is not in any degree dependent on the Chinese Empire'. All the same, 'considerations . . . connected with the security of the interests of the Hon'ble Company in China rendered it necessary to observe a considerable degree of caution in contracting political engagements' with the Gurkhas.

Captain Knox secured a treaty with the Gurkhas, carefully framed so that it would not strain British relations with China, in October 1801; and, as provided for in the treaty, he became the first British resident in Katmandu. Anglo-Nepalese relations, however, soon became strained owing to a palace revolution at the Gurkha court. In 1803 Knox was withdrawn. In the following year Lord Wellesley dissolved the 1801 treaty in the evident hope that Anglo-Gurkha relations would be happier without any formal framework. In this Lord Wellesley was to be disappointed. Shortly after Knox's departure Ranbahadur returned to Katmandu from his Benares exile to assume power as Regent for his young son who had been Raja since Ranbahadur's flight in 1800. Ranbahadur, however, did not long survive his return, being murdered by one of his queens. The outcome was the assumption of effective power over the Gurkhas by Bhim Sen Thapa who was, until 1836, to dominate the policy both internal and external of Nepal.[12]

Bhim Sen Thapa adopted an expansionist outlook which inevitably brought Nepal into conflict with the British. The central issue was to be found in the Terai, the low lying tract along the Himalayan foothills, much of it swampy and disease ridden, but of considerable economic value not least for its hardwood forests. The Terai was the Nepalese equivalent of the Duar tracts along the southern Bhutanese border into which the Company had been penetrating since at least 1766, and which, indeed, were a factor in the initiation of the Bhutan–Cooch Behar war in 1772 as they were to be in other Anglo-Bhutanese crises in the nineteenth century. In the Nepalese Terai, as well as in the comparable tract of Morung, adjacent to both Nepal and Sikkim, there existed complex conflicts of sovereignty between states in the Gangetic plain and those in the Himalayan range. When these claims were acquired, directly or indirectly, by the Company on the one hand and the Gurkhas on the other, a major confrontation could only have been avoided by a degree of conciliatory statesmanship to which Bhim Sen Thapa certainly did not aspire.

The potential as a source of Anglo-Nepalese conflict of the Terai was apparent as early as 1768 when the Company had begun to be interested in the value of Morung, the Terai adjacent to east Nepal and Sikkim, as a source of ship timber. From this date they watched with concern the gradual encroachment of the Gurkhas into this valuable source of raw materials. Sikkim, which derived most of its revenue from these fertile lowlands, was even more concerned. Hastings gave serious consideration to the possibility of driving the Gurkhas out of Morung by force of arms; he was probably deterred from such a project by the extreme difficulty of the country in which such a campaign would have to take place. Not only in Morung did the Gurkhas threaten British interests; after the completion of their conquest of Nepal they gradually encroached on a number of small states under British protection which bordered the hills, and they provided, moreover, a refuge for dacoits and escaped criminals from British territory. Frequent incidents along the border between Nepal and British-controlled territory were accompanied by the steady advance of the Gurkhas, excluded from northward expansion in 1792, along the Himalayan range: westwards until, where the Sutlej cuts through the mountains they encountered the fringes of the Sikh empire of Ranjit Singh which blocked them; eastwards far into Sikkim, whose ruler they drove to a fugitive existence in the hills. By 1813, when Lord Moira, later Marquess of Hastings, became Governor-General, it looked as if 'there could never be real peace' between the Gurkhas and the British 'until we should yield to the Gorkhas our provinces north of the Ganges, making that river the boundary between us'.[13] In the following year, all attempts at negotiation having proved fruitless, Lord Moira went to war with Nepal.[14]

In 1814 Nepal was no longer an independent state; since 1792 it had been a Chinese tributary. How this fact would affect the course of the war was not known with any certainty in India since the events of 1792 had made it hard to obtain information on Tibet, whence the Chinese might come to Nepal's aid; and the

Company had not been very alert to opportunities for obtaining such information when they presented themselves. There was, for example, no attempt to make use of that pleasantly eccentric English scholar, traveller and friend of Charles Lamb, Thomas Manning. Manning came to Canton in 1807, armed with a letter from the Court of Directors to the Select Committee, with the intention of learning the Chinese language and then setting out to explore the Chinese interior. Having failed to enter China from Canton or Macao, and then from Cochin China, Manning made his way to Calcutta in 1810 with the aim of approaching the Chinese Empire by way of the Himalayas and Tibet. While he did not get through to China, Manning, in the somewhat ineffective guise of a Chinese gentleman, did manage to reach Lhasa in 1811, where he met the Dalai Lama. Manning made it plain that he thought that great advantage could be derived from relations between the Company and Tibet; of those Company officials who refused to give him any diplomatic commission or status when he was preparing for his journey in Calcutta, he wrote: 'Fools, fools, fools, to neglect an opportunity they may never have again!'[15]

William Moorcroft was another enterprising Englishman who, in the years just before the outbreak of the Gurkha War, was given no official encouragement in his ambitions to explore Tibet. Moorcroft was a veterinary surgeon who received an appointment with the Bengal Government in 1808 and was soon made super-intendent of the Company's stud farm near Patna. In 1812, accompanied by Hearsey, he made his way in a not very effective disguise to Gartok in Western Tibet to seek out new breeds of horse and to investigate the possibilities of the trade in shawl wool of Western Tibet, of which Gartok was the centre. To Government at this date Moorcroft's journey seemed to be 'replete with danger . . . and not likely to be productive of advantage to the public service'.[16] Moorcroft continued his travels in the years that followed, exploring in the Hindu Kush, the Pamirs and the Karakoram. In 1825 he died at Andkhui in northern Afghanistan and was buried at Balkh: though a legend has persisted, for which the two French missionaries Huc and Gabet seem to have been responsible, that after 1825 he in fact made his way to Lhasa in disguise, and remained in Tibet until his death in 1835.[17]

With the outbreak of the Gurkha War Lord Moira came to appreciate the value of Moorcroft's experience of Chinese Central Asia and of the contacts he had made with native merchants trading in those regions. A crucial question in 1814 was what would be the attitude of the Chinese to a war between the Company and Nepal. How, for instance, would the Chinese react to a British annexation of their Nepalese tributary, an event which the exigencies of the war might well make necessary? Dr. Buchanan, who had accompanied Captain Knox to Katmandu in 1801, and who was now the most experienced adviser on Gurkha affairs at the disposal of the Company, thought that a British annexation of this state might have unpleasant consequences: 'a frontier', he said, 'of seven or eight hundred miles between two powerful nations holding each other in mutual contempt seems to point at anything but peace'.[18] Moorcroft was able to provide factual information in support of this opinion. One of his informants, Mir Izzut Ullah, who was a member of a Kashmiri merchant house with its headquarters at Patna and with widespread branches in Kashmir, Nepal, Western China, Tibet and Bengal, had told Moorcroft this story which he passed on to Government. The Raja of Nepal, fearing a British attack, had appealed to the Chinese at Lhasa for help should this come to pass. The Chinese in reply had expressed their willingness to bring assistance if needed, and had asked how much money and how many men would be required. Moorcroft suggested that the truth of this information could be checked by sending native agents to Ladakh and Kashgar, where news would surely be available of any unusually large purchase of grain for Tibet of the type that would be required to supply a large body of troops coming into a country with such meagre resources. Such native agents could then go on to Lhasa without arousing any suspicion, coming in this way from outside the British dominions; from the Tibetan capital they could send reports to the British troops advancing into Nepal.[19] There is no record to suggest that this scheme was ever put into effect, but there can be no doubt that Lord Moira looked on the Chinese as a source of real danger.

His fears received further confirmation as the war developed. In March 1815, for example, the British captured the draft of an appeal from the Nepalese Raja to the Chinese Emperor, which made unpleasant reading in British eyes. After acknowledging the 'supremacy of the Emperor of China above all other potentates on earth', the appeal went on to point out that the Gurkhas could not hold out indefinitely against the British without Chinese help. It begged the Chinese to attack Bengal from Tibet, thus creating a diversion which would take the pressure off Nepal and spreading 'alarm and consternation among the Europeans as far as Calcutta'. It was in the Chinese interest to do this. The English had 'subjugated all the Rajahs of the plains, and usurped the throne of the King of Delhi; and, therefore, it is to be expected that they would all unite in expelling Europeans from Hindostan'; otherwise 'the English, after obtaining possession of Nepal, will advance . . . for the purpose of conquering Lassa. . . . I beseech you . . . to lose no time in sending assistance, whether in men or in money, that I may drive forth the enemy, and maintain possession of the mountains, otherwise, in a few years, he will be master of Lassa.'[20] There was sufficient truth behind this sort of argument to make it seem plausible to a Chinese official, as Macartney's experience so clearly indicated. It was necessary to try to allay Chinese suspicions, and two methods suggested themselves.

Firstly, since the British wished only to punish the Gurkhas and to maintain their rights, they ought not alarm the Chinese by annexing Nepal. This was the advice of Dr. Buchanan; but he added that the Chinese were hardly likely to object if Nepal was restored to those Newar chiefs who had been dispossessed by the Gurkhas. The Chinese, he noted, were 'fully as tired of the insolence of the Goorka as the British Government appears to be'.[21] It was decided not to annex Nepal; but since no descendants of the original rulers could be found, there was no alternative to leaving the Gurkhas in possession. Thus Nepal was able to survive to the twentieth century as a sovereign state. There seemed to be no objection, however, to the Company taking over those territories in the western Himalayas, Kumaon and Garwhal, which the Gurkhas had acquired since 1792 and which were not held, in consequence, to form part of Nepal as understood in the Sino-Nepalese treaty of that year.[22]

Secondly, it was felt that the Company should present to the Chinese, to prevent them from misunderstanding British aims and intentions, a clear statement of the Company's case against the Gurkhas. The opening of relations with Sikkim, a small hill state with the closest of ties with Tibet, might, in the opinion of J. Adam, the Secretary to the Indian Government, provide a channel whereby this could be achieved, since 'the Princes of Sikkim are closely connected with the Lamas of Lassa and Bootan, and their restoration of their former possessions would, no doubt, be highly acceptable to the authorities in those countries, and induce them to regard our proceedings with satisfaction'.[23] The war with Nepal provided an excellent excuse to establish contact with Sikkim, which had been under Gurkha attack since 1775; and rumours that Nepal and Bhutan, only separated by this tiny state, were about to conclude an alliance made such a step all the more necessary. British assistance to Sikkim had military as well as political objectives; not only did it prevent the Gurkhas and the Bhutanese from intriguing together, but also it constituted an attack on the Gurkha flank. For these reasons David Scott, who held Bogle's old post of Collector at Rangpur, was instructed in

December 1814 to try to establish contact with Lhasa, either through Sikkim or through Bhutan; and Captain Latter of the Bengal Army was ordered to take a force into Sikkim and in every way to encourage its Raja to go on fighting the Gurkhas.[24] At the same time, a letter was sent to the Bhutanese rulers to warn them in polite terms not to try to oppose the British on that section of the frontier.[25]

In the spring of 1815 Latter entered Morung with a force of over 2,000 men and immediately established contact with the Sikkim authorities. In return for some ammunition and a promise of restoration of territory lost to the Gurkhas, the Sikkimese were easily persuaded to co-operate with the British and to act as a link between Calcutta and Lhasa.[26] Letters were sent by this route to the Chinese Ambans to explain the reasons which obliged the Company to wage war on Nepal. At least 'one reply was received, which, as Lord Moira observed, although expressed in a tone of loftiness, there is nothing offensive, still less hostile, in its tenor, and we are disposed to believe that the disposition of the Chinese Umpahs [Ambans] is as expressed in that letter, that our affairs with the Nepalese should be settled without their intervention'.[27] He thought that here at last might be the beginning of a promising approach for British diplomacy to Peking and the realization of the hopes of Bogle, Turner and Hastings.[28] David Scott's attempt to get in touch with Lhasa through Bhutan did not succeed, however. In January 1815 he sought from the Bhutanese authorities permission to send an agent to their capital and thence to Lhasa. The Bhutanese seemed willing enough to receive this mission, but the envoy sent, Kishen Kant Bose, failed to get into Tibet.[29] 'I am sorry to observe', Scott wrote, that Kishen Kant Bose 'seems not to possess all the discretion requisite for such an employment.'[30]

Lord Moira's Government had feared genuinely enough that the Chinese might come to the aid of their Gurkha dependents. It had gone so far as to issue orders in 1815 to British commanders in Nepal not to fire on Chinese troops unless it was absolutely certain that they were hostile.[31] It had also had to consider what its policy would be were defeated Gurkha armies to take refuge in Tibet in preference to surrender to the British.[32] At the end of the war a fresh danger emerged. While there no longer seemed much likelihood of the Chinese reacting to the war, there appeared to be a definite chance that they might take objection to the circumstances of the peace that followed with the Treaty of Segauli of March 1816. Had the Nepalese, as far as China was concerned, the right to make any binding agreement with a foreign power? In what light would the Chinese consider the British annexation of Kumaon and Garwhal and the placing of the former Gurkha conquests in Sikkim, a state dependent on Tibet, under British protection? Would the Chinese agree to the appointment of a British Resident at Katmandu?

In the summer of 1816 these questions began to cause Lord Moira some anxiety. During the course of the war, it will be remembered, the Gurkhas appealed to the Emperor for assistance. In July or August, when peace had already been signed, news reached Katmandu that a Chinese force was at last on its way to the Himalayas. It was clear to Gardner, the new Resident at the Nepalese capital, that the Gurkhas did not welcome this development: indeed, they seemed convinced that the Chinese had come to punish them, firstly for going to war with the Company, and secondly for making peace with it.[33] 'The Chinese business', Gardner wrote at the end of August, 'is really I think getting very serious', and the Gurkhas were now looking for British support.[34]

Lord Moira's Government very much hoped that this crisis, whatever might be the truth behind it, would blow over without a decision having to be made whether the British would help the Gurkhas or not. There could be no question, of course, of any armed assistance to Nepal since British policy must be based on 'the avoidance of any engagement with the Nepalese which might embroil us with or give umbrage to the Chinese'. The Company might offer its mediation in the dispute which appeared to be about to break out between China and Nepal; but only as the friend of both sides, and 'even this degree of interference however it appears to His Lordship in Council to be extremely desirable to avoid'. The true Company interests in this situation were clear enough:

The maintenance of Peace and Amity with the Emperor of China is an object of such vast consequence to the Commercial Interests of the Company, and indeed of the United Kingdom, that no effort ought to be spared on the part of this Government to prevent the present state of things from taking a turn which might occasion even any suspension of relations.

It was evident that a better means of communication with the Chinese than that through Sikkim must be established as soon as possible, and Lord Moira suggested the deputation to Lhasa of a European agent, perhaps 'one of the Gentlemen of the Residency' at Katmandu, so that the Chinese could see for themselves 'the open and candid dealings of an English Officer'.

This agent, should he be able to meet with senior Chinese

officials in Tibet, was to deliver a concise history of the recent war with Nepal. He was to argue that the Treaty of Segauli in no way affected existing Nepalese relations with China, and he was to point out the harmless nature of the Katmandu Residency. In order to avoid any ambiguity he was to have with him a document in Chinese with these points clearly made. Another topic on which Lord Moira felt some anxiety was the extension of Company rule into Kumaon and Sikkim. The agent was to justify this if he could and was on no account to commit his Government to withdrawal from these regions. He could, however, if it seemed essential, promise the Chinese that the Katmandu Residency would be withdrawn; but this bargaining card was only to be used as a last resort. If it should come about that the Chinese began to invade Nepal, the worst possible eventuality in this crisis since it would create a long Anglo-Chinese frontier and a breeding ground for border disputes, the Katmandu Residency was to be withdrawn in any case. But Lord Moira had little fear that this would happen.[35]

Lord Moira took care to warn Lord Amherst, then about to set out on an embassy to Peking, that he might be questioned on the situation in the Himalayas.[36] He also arranged for explanations to be sent to the Chinese in Lhasa by the Sikkim route;[37] and this, as it turned out, was the only way that the Chinese heard from the Company, since Gardner decided against the deputation of a European to Tibet at that time and showed that such a mission was too delicate to be entrusted to a native agent.[38] A reasonably amicable correspondence between Calcutta and Lhasa continued until 1818. The Chinese seem to have admitted that they had no grounds for intervention in the relations between the Company and Nepal, though they did request politely, and in vain, for the withdrawal of the Katmandu Residency 'out of kindness towards us, and in consideration of the ties of friendship'.[39]

No one in India knew quite what lay behind this crisis. A Chinese force, which Kishen Kant Bose put at some 2,000 men, did arrive in Lhasa, and the Bhutanese were warned to be ready to help the Chinese if the need arose.[40] It may be that the Chinese force was sent by the Viceroy of Szechuan Province, under whom lay the administration of Chinese interests in Tibet, to investigate the Himalayan situation. It seems unlikely that Peking knew much about it. The matter of the Gurkha War does not appear to have been mentioned to Lord Amherst by any Chinese official during his embassy.[41] The effect of the crisis on Lord Moira was to confirm him in his belief in the dangers to the Company's position at Canton inherent in any British action in the Himalayas.

The English at Canton did not entirely share this belief.

In June 1814 Lord Moira had been very careful to explain to the Select Committee of the Supercargoes at Canton, that governing body of the Company's officials in China, the reasons for the war against Nepal; he told them, moreover, that the war might well increase the difficulties of their position. The Supercargoes, however, were far more optimistic: they did not think that news of the war would ever reach Peking; and it would do no harm if it did, for the knowledge in the Chinese capital that the Company had at its disposal a means of retaliation on Chinese territory was 'the best if not only security for the preservation of their trade with this country'.[42] But Lord Moira continued to be uneasy. In June 1816 he sent to Canton, to be included in the despatches to await the arrival of the forthcoming Amherst Mission, a detailed account of the British case for war with Nepal which was suitable for presentation to the Chinese Emperor.[43] But the Supercargoes adhered so firmly to their original optimism that in August 1816, when Lord Moira was justifying his conduct of the Gurkha War to the Court of Directors, he was able to refute the charge that he had endangered the Canton trade by remarking that

> the Committee at Canton were of so different an opinion that they regarded our having secured a communication with Tartary, through Kumaon, as an important protection for the tea trade; because the Viceroy at Canton, comprehending the facility with which we could transmit representations to Peking overland, would fear to indulge himself again in these vexatious practices with which he had of late harassed the Supercargoes.[44]

In the next few years the English at Canton continued to have hopes of the recently secured 'communication with Tartary'. The Select Committee at Canton felt that the *Topaz* affair of 1822 provided just the sort of occasion which demanded a better means of communication with Peking.[45] A crisis had arisen at Canton as a result of an affray between members of the crew of H.M.S. *Topaz* and some Chinese at Lintin Island. Several Chinese were killed and the local authorities demanded that those responsible be handed over to the tender mercies of Chinese justice. This particular situation had arisen several times in the past and the English had sometimes sacrificed one of their subjects for the sake of peace; on this occasion, however, they stood firm and refused to hand over any Englishman for trial in a Chinese court. The Supercargoes found themselves, as a result of their determination, obliged to leave Canton and trade was closed there for several months. They sent off a long despatch to India, outlining the causes of the present dispute and showing the difficulties which faced them in getting for their point of view a fair hearing by the Chinese. They described how at one time they had been obliged to submit any petition they wished to make to Peking to the local authorities, and in the English language; and how they were convinced that distortion took place in the process of translation into Chinese. At present they were permitted to petition in Chinese, but they had still to rely on the agency of the Canton officials for the forwarding of such petitions to Peking; and they had no guarantee that they reached their destination unaltered, or, indeed, ever reached it at all. They requested Bengal, therefore, to look into 'the practicability and expediency of transmitting their representations overland to the Chinese frontier opposite Thibet, or by way of Sylhet and the province of Yunan whenever a crisis should occur of importance sufficient to require a reference to the Court of Peking'.[46] Nepal and Sikkim were investigated by the Indian Government as possible routes for this kind of communication; and it seemed likely that one letter might reach Peking by either of these routes but that the development of a regular channel of communication depended entirely on the wishes of the government of the Chinese Emperor at Peking.[47] The matter seems to have been dropped at this stage.

The Gurkha War, as it turned out, had no appreciable effect on the course of British relations with China; it did not, for instance, trouble the Amherst Embassy which made its futile journey to Peking in 1817. The fear that British Himalayan policy might produce such an effect, however, lingered on in India; it will be expressed, for example, during the crisis in the western Himalayas of 1841-42; but the idea that Tibet might provide the back door to Peking ceased, soon after 1816, to be a significant theme in the history of Anglo-Tibetan relations during the nineteenth century. British attempts to open relations with Tibet were made primarily to improve local trans-frontier trade and to find a solution to local problems of Himalayan policy. This change had become quite clear by 1842; soon the British were seeking to use their newly established relations with China, at first through Hong Kong, and, after 1861, through Peking, to solve local problems of Indian administration.

Many of these problems arose from the political settlement following the Gurkha War. The relations with Sikkim, for example, first developed out of war-time necessity, were further extended immediately after the war when it was decided that to prevent further Gurkha expansion in the British sphere Nepal should be surrounded on three sides by territory under British control or protection. In this policy Sikkim played a crucial part. It was necessary, to preclude further Gurkha advance in this direction, to 'conclude an engagement with the Raja of Siccim, for defining and recording the conditions of our future connexion with that State'. To ensure that the Raja would make such an agreement, the Nepalese conquests in Sikkim were to be surrendered to the British, who would then hand them over to their rightful owner if and when they saw fit.[48] With this bargaining card Captain Latter, in February 1817, was able to negotiate at Titalia a treaty with Sikkim which met all British requirements. The Company guaranteed Sikkim against Gurkha aggression. The Sikkimese agreed to place their foreign relations under a measure of Company control, promised to return fugitives from British justice who might seek shelter in the Sikkim hills, and assured to British Indian merchants protection and freedom from exorbitant taxation while carrying out their business in and through Sikkim. The Company thus acquired what it had lacked in Hastings' day, namely, the clearly defined right to trade up to the Tibetan frontier through the territory of a state under its protection.[49] Sikkim, indeed, seemed to afford 'a more ready communication with Lhasa and China' than the way through Bhutan which Bogle and Turner followed;[50] and Lord Moira rightly considered the establishment of relations with this small state to have been something of a diplomatic triumph 'which we never could have imposed by force of arms, from the extreme difficulty of the country'.[51] But the Sikkim route was not exploited at that time, and the Treaty of Titalia was allowed to lapse through desuetude – a fact which was to cause the Government of India some inconvenience in the future. The Company gains from Nepal in the Western Himalayas, Kumaon and Garwhal, seemed, in the years immediately following the Gurkha War, to offer better prospects than Sikkim as channels for Anglo-Chinese diplomacy and as means of access for British trade to the markets of Tibet.

During the course of the war Lord Moira had shown some interest in the trade of Tibet, mainly because of the enthusiasm with which Moorcroft had advocated the extension of British commerce into Central Asia. In 1815, on Moorcroft's proposal, Lord Moira had agreed to an 'attempt to ascertain the practicability of establishing a commercial intercourse with Lassa' which in some ways recalled the mission of Abdul Kadir Khan. A Kashmiri merchant, one Ahmad Ali, was to go up to Tibet with a stock of trade goods and to bring back a report on the 'quality of our manufactures which are likely to suit that market'. The plan, however, was marred by too much caution. Where Abdul Kadir Khan had been given his stock by the Company, Ahmad Ali was only lent the capital sum needed to equip himself at 6 per cent. interest. It is not surprising that Ahmad Ali decided in the end that he could not afford to co-operate with the Company on these terms, and the project was abandoned.[52]

The commercial value of Kumaon and Garwhal was also brought to Lord Moira's notice in the course of the Gurkha War,[53] and in his survey of the results of the war he drew special attention to the possibilities of these districts as a means of bringing to British territory the famed shawl wool of Western Tibet, the raw material of the profitable Kashmir shawl industry, and as a route 'into the inmost districts of Tartary'. This was 'a circumstance which opens views of great advantage to the commercial and manufacturing interest not only of this country but of Great Britain'.[54] The conclusion of the war, moreover, removed the objection to the development of this trade route, which had been voiced earlier by Government, that it might alarm the Chinese (who might consider such activity as but a cover for schemes of British expansion) and precipitate their intervention on the side of Nepal.[55] This route, Lord Moira thought, would also enable the British to compete with Asiatic Russian merchants who, he had heard, had found a good market in Tibet and other parts of Central Asia for cloth of French manufacture.[56]

Four factors contributed to make the western Himalayas rather than Sikkim the area in which the Indian Government expended the most effort to develop Anglo-Tibetan relations in the years immediately following the Gurkha War. Firstly, as has already been noted, this area gave access to the centre of production of Tibetan shawl wool, a commodity the value of which had been appreciated by the Company long before the war with Nepal. Secondly, in this area there was now a common Anglo-Tibetan frontier, a fact which it was hoped would bring about frequent and profitable contracts between British and Tibetan officials.[57] Thirdly, there was the possibility that in this region, so far from the centre of Chinese control at Lhasa, Tibetan isolation might not be so strictly observed as it was elsewhere; Moorcroft's visit to Gartok in 1812 gave some substance to this hope,[58] as did also Captain Webb's dealings with Tibetan frontier officials on the Kumaon border in May 1816.[59] Finally, during the war or just after it, British officers noted the advantages which the small village of Simla seemed to possess as a site for a hill station. Simla developed rapidly. In 1827 it was visited by Lord Amherst, the

Governor-General, 'who resided there with his family for several months and brought back to Calcutta a rosy complexion and some beautiful drawings by Lady Sarah Amherst to attest the healthful and picturesque properties of the spot'.[60] Simla became fashionable. By bringing British officials into contact with the Himalayas and with Tibet it was destined to play a part in the history of Anglo-Tibetan relations comparable to that played later by another hill station, Darjeeling.

As will be seen in the next chapter, however, the possibilities of trade with Western Tibet were not exploited by the Company with much energy, and that a trade did spring up in this region was very much due to developments in Himalayan politics outside British control. It has already been noted that Lord Moira saw in any British action along the Tibetan border a threat to the security of the Company's position at Canton. Even when the danger of Chinese intervention on behalf of Nepal no longer existed this fear remained, and no amount of argument to the contrary by the Supercargoes could quite remove it. Thus, while the Indian Government, in theory, thoroughly approved of the development of trade, especially in shawl wool, between Western Tibet and its territories, it was unprepared to take any very decisive step to bring this about. It preferred to leave the Chinese in Tibet to their own devices, and it hoped to avoid the risk, however slight, of the expense of another hill war. The Gurkha War had cost more than the combined cost of the campaigns against the Marathas and the Pindaris for which Lord Moira's administration is renowned: Sicca Rs. 51,56,961 as against Sicca Rs. 37,53,789.[61] This was the kind of fact which influenced greatly the policy of a Company government.

If it were necessary to put a date to the end of the Tibetan policy of the time of Warren Hastings, then 1816 or 1817 would be as good as any. Company relations with Nepal had been inextricably involved with Company attempts to open up a trade route with Tibet. When Bhutan became closed in 1792, Nepal became the obvious alternative, and, to a great extent, the crisis of the Gurkha War was influenced by British efforts to open this unco-operative country to their traders. In 1816 and 1817, by the Treaties of Segauli and Titalia, the Company acquired new routes to the Tibetan border. In the west, British territory now marched with that of Tibet. In the east, Sikkim provided a corridor of nominally British-protected territory to the Tibetan frontier which, in time, was to be seen as the ideal bypass to the old road through Bhutan. In another respect, also, the end of the Gurkha War marks a change in the pattern of Anglo-Tibetan relations.

Hastings had hoped that through Tibet British diplomacy might find its way to Peking. The same idea is expressed in the Supercargoes letter to the Indian Government of 1822 following the *Topaz* affair. This letter was a direct result of the correspondence between India and Canton during the course of the war, and it was to be the last reference to this possibility. Throughout the nineteenth century there were to be occasions when some branch of the British Government feared that British policy on the Tibetan border might upset the smooth running of Anglo-Chinese relations, but there were to be very few British officials indeed who would argue that the attempt to extend British influence into Tibet would ameliorate those relations. After the Treaty of Nanking in 1842 the Indian Government, when it thought of China in relation to Tibet, tended to think in terms of applying through the British representative in China, first at Hong Kong and then in Peking, pressure on the Chinese to make them co-operate in attempts to open Tibet to British influence and commerce.

III

WESTERN TIBET

·

1816 – 1861

THE GURKHA War, resulting in the acquisition of Kumaon and Garwhal, brought for the first time, British territory into direct contact with that under the sovereignty of the Chinese Emperor. As was the case in that portion of Tibet made familiar by the journeys of Bogle and Turner, Western Tibet extended its influence beyond its boundaries. Thus the Western Himalayan hill states possessed old and complex ties with Lhasa. Of the new territories under British control, Kumaon and part of Garwhal were annexed outright, while Tehri-Garwhal and the states around Simla and along the Sutlej valley, later classified as the Simla Hill States, remained under their local chiefs as protected states, of which the most important was Bashahr on the Sutlej, with its capital at Rampur. Beyond the Sutlej and outside British control, though now adjacent to British territory, lay the kingdom of Ladakh with its dependencies of Lahul and Spiti, which bounded the Tibetan border from the Himalayas to the Karakoram and formed a buffer between Lhasa and the Moslem, Sikh and Hindu states of Kashmir and the Punjab. In people, religion and culture Ladakh, with Lahul and Spiti, was Tibetan and its government showed many of those peculiar theocratic features associated with the government of Tibet. To some extent this was also a feature of those areas now under British control, though the states to the east of the Sutlej showed a considerable admixture of Hindu influences. On both sides of the Sutlej the influence of Tibet was considerable, taking expression in a complex of commercial, political and religious relationships. Ladakh exchanged periodic diplomatic and commercial missions with Lhasa, and Lahul and Spiti paid dues to Tibet of a politico-religious nature. Bashahr had close diplomatic contacts with Gartok, the political centre of Western Tibet, and in Kumaon, which was now under direct British rule, the Tibetans, as of old, continued to collect taxes from merchants engaged in the trans-frontier trade, sending collectors on to British soil for this purpose.[1]

In Western Tibet, moreover, are Mount Kailas and Lake Manasarowar, places sacred to Buddhists, Hindus and Muslims alike. For centuries pilgrims have thronged there from the plains to walk round the sacred mountain and bathe in the icy lake whence, according to one tradition, spring the great Indian rivers, the Ganges, Indus, Sutlej and Brahmaputra.[2]

The western provinces of Tibet were firmly under the control of Lhasa. The authorities in Gartok, despite their great distance from the capital, were as powerless to receive diplomatic overtures, and as opposed to the entry of Europeans as Tibetan officials elsewhere. There was, however, a significant distinction between Western Tibet and the provinces of Lhasa and Shigatse: while it is doubtful whether the trade with Bengal was ever of great economic importance to Lhasa, the life of Western Tibet depended very greatly upon commerce with its neighbours. Its chief place, Gartok, was nothing more than a trade mart, a sparse collection of mud huts to which, during the summer months, thousands of traders from the surrounding countries, from Chinese Turkestan and the Central Asian Khanates, even from as far afield as the Russian dominions, came to exchange their goods for the native products of Tibet, borax, salt, gold, shawl wool and ponies, and for goods carried overland from China, tea, porcelain and silks.[3]

In 1816 the main foreign trade of Gartok was with or through Ladakh, and trade between Gartok and the hill states now under British control did little more than supply local needs.[4] Trade between Ladakh and Gartok was closely connected with the political relations existing between Ladakh and Tibet. This continued to be the case throughout the nineteenth century, and when Ladakh, as part of Kashmir, had come under British protection, it was to cause the Indian Government some anxiety. In 1889, and again in 1899 and 1900, the foreign relations of Ladakh were made the subject of a detailed examination by British officials, and the following pattern was disclosed.[5] Two missions

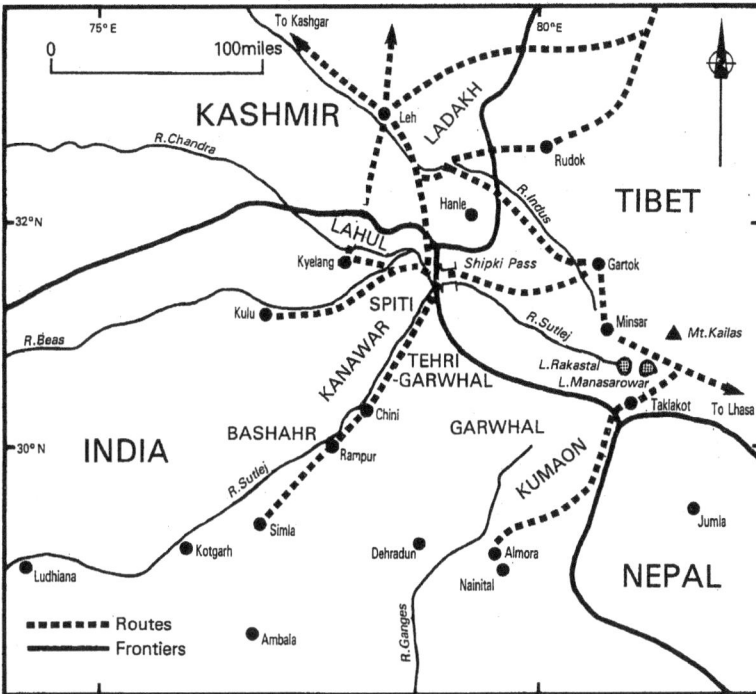

Sketch map of Western Tibet and the adjacent regions

of especial importance linked Leh, the Ladakhi capital, to Lhasa. The *Lapchak* mission went from Leh to Lhasa once every three years. Its object was in part trade and in part diplomacy. It was headed by a prominent Ladakhi or Tibetan resident in Ladakh, in either case a monk or abbot, and it was accompanied by a leading Ladakhi Moslem (*Arghun*) merchant of that class which had by long tradition been permitted to trade in Tibet. The mission carried letters and presents from the King, or *Gyalpo*, of Ladakh to the Dalai Lama. The *Lapchak* always passed through Gartok òn its way to Lhasa. The Tibetans looked on it as a tribute-bearing mission and they did not admit that the incorporation of Ladakh into Kashmir in 1834 altered its nature; they referred to the Kashmiri Governor of Ladakh as the 'man in usufructory possession of Ladak'. The Tibetans sent, in return for the *Lapchak*, an annual mission to Leh known as the *Chapba*, or 'tea man',

45

mission. Its head, the *Chapba* or *Zungtson*, was the Dalai Lama's personal trader to Ladakh, and was always a Tibetan official, either lay or monastic, of some importance. He held this office for a three-year term, during which he would visit Leh once. The *Chapba* mission left Lhasa each June, bringing with it Chinese brick tea for sale in Ladakh, and it arrived at Leh in December. It remained in Leh until the following April, when it set out once more for the Tibetan capital, taking with it Indian and European fabrics and other manufactured goods.

The *Lapchak* and the *Chapba* were the most important manifestations of the close relationship existing between Ladakh and Tibet which also gave rise to a number of lesser missions. Feudatories of the King of Ladakh like the Rajas of Stok and Matho were accustomed to send an annual trading mission to Gartok. Certain Moslem traders possessed special privileges in the trade in Chinese brick tea between Gartok and Leh. The Governors of Gartok, the Garpons, as well as the Tibetan commander of the fort at Rudok, came to Leh annually to trade. Several of the larger Buddhist monasteries in Ladakh sent periodically combined religious and trading missions to Lhasa. At about ten-year intervals a similar mission came to Leh from the great Tibetan monastic centre of Tashilhunpo. All these missions enjoyed the right of *begar*, that is to say of obtaining labour and baggage animals from the local inhabitants through whose districts they passed, a right which the British were later to find somewhat objectionable. The effects of the symbols of the traditional relationships between Ladakh and Tibet were felt in nearly every Ladakh village, and any alteration in those relationships could not fail to have profound economic consequences in both Ladakh and Western Tibet.

The trade of Ladakh, as one would expect from its situation and its sparse population, was primarily a carrying trade. A certain amount of Chinese brick tea was imported for local consumption, but by far the most important commodity in the commerce of this region was shawl wool, or *pashm*, the fine undercoat of that sheep or goat which seems to develop best in the dry climate of the Tibetan plateau. In 1853 this product made up a quarter of the trade of Ladakh; the proportion in 1816 was probably nearer half of the total trade.[6] By custom, usage and also by treaty, the Ladakhis had acquired a monopoly of this product, which they obtained in the neighbourhood of Gartok, and which they sold to the weavers of Kashmir as the raw material for the Kashmir shawl so prized as an article of clothing in Europe. It was a jealously guarded monopoly,[7] and only a very small quantity of shawl

46

reached the plains by any other route.[8]

This commodity, with its obvious value in Europe, was bound to attract the notice of the British. In 1799 the Board of Agriculture asked the Court of Directors whether they could secure samples of the shawl-bearing sheep of Tibet with a view to breeding it in England. Bengal was accordingly instructed to procure specimens, with precise directions as to the care of the animals during their long voyage back to England.[9] In 1810 a British merchant, Mr. Gillman of Bareilly, sent an agent to Gartok to obtain a small sample of shawl. When the Ladakh Government came to hear of this attempt, so it must have seemed, to break their monopoly, they protested to the Governor, or Garpon, of Gartok, who then issued an edict forbidding the sale of shawl to any but Ladakhis on pain of death.[10] Two years later the great traveller William Moorcroft made a journey to Gartok 'undertaken from motives of public zeal, to open to Great Britain means of obtaining the materials of the finest woollen fabric', though in no way under official auspices. Moorcroft succeeded in buying some of the wool, the first time, he was told, that a non-Ladakhi had done so; in his account of this journey, published in *Asiatic Researches* in 1816, he strongly advocated the possibilities of this trade. He argued that the Company might well coax it away from Ladakh by paying, to begin with, a little more than the market price.[11] During the Gurkha War the value of this and other aspects of the Tibet trade had aroused considerable comment and had been an influential factor in the decision to annex the hill territory freed from the Gurkhas.

In 1815, when Bashahr became a British protected state, the Company retained possession of the Bashahri village of Kotgarh, which gave them a vantage point on the Sutlej from which to tap the Tibet trade. After the Sikh conquest of Kashmir in 1819 and the consequent famine had driven many Kashmir weavers to seek shelter in the plains, in Amritsar, Ludhiana, Nurpur and the surrounding villages and thus created a new demand for the raw material of their craft,[12] the Company established, in 1820 or 1821, a factory here to purchase shawl from Tibetan traders. This venture 'was merely experimental, being intended to turn the trade in this article from Cashmere to our own territories'[13] and did not prove to be a success, as Kotgarh was situated further down the Sutlej than the Tibetans were prepared to travel.[14]

It was in Rampur, the capital of Bashahr, that the shawl trade was to develop, encouraged by the new demand in the plains, and unaided by the Company. This trade was soon destined to become the most important element in the economy of the hill states along the Sutlej. The figures collected by J.D. Cunningham, who spent a year in Kanawar on the upper Sutlej in 1841-42, show a rapid rise in the value of this trade in the late 1830s. In 1837 the value of Tibetan shawl sold at Rampur was Rs. 35,630; in 1839 this figure had increased to Rs. 73,080; and in 1840 it reached Rs. 94,807.[15] This increase took place in a period when the Government were less concerned with the commercial possibilities of the hill states than with the advantages they offered as sites for hill stations like Simla and Naini-Tal.

Nor, in the years immediately following the Gurkha War, was much official interest shown in the possibilities and dangers latent in the complex relationships between the hill states and Tibet, possibilities which would assuredly have aroused the enthusiasm of a Warren Hastings. When Moorcroft visited Ladakh in 1822 the *Gyalpo*, alarmed by the rapid expansion of the Sikhs, who had just completed the subjugation of Kashmir, offered him a treaty placing Ladakh under British protection and opening its trade to British subjects. Government not only rejected this proposal, but took pains to ensure that Ranjit Singh was informed that such an offer had been made and refused.[16] In 1834, just before the Dogra invasion of Ladakh, this offer was renewed, this time to one Dr. Henderson, botanist in the Company's service who was absent without leave from his post in Calcutta and, quite naturally, did not wish to advertise this fact by relaying the proposal to Fort William. In the event, it was the Lahore Durbar which first informed Government of this offer, in a protest, and Dr. Henderson was promptly disowned.[17] He was severely reprimanded by Government for having crossed into the territory of a Tibetan dependency without any permission.[18] Another traveller, Dr. Gerard, was also approached by the Ladakhis, who asked him to visit Leh to mediate, it is to be presumed, with the Sikhs on behalf of Ladakh; but Government resolved to ignore this overture.[19]

Government was inclined to oppose any action in this area which might be interpreted as an attempt to compete with the Sikhs, a fact, in the opinion of Alexander Cunningham, most unfortunate 'for the prosperity of Ladak and the commerce of British India'.[20] The advice of men like Moorcroft fell on deaf ears. Moorcroft argued, before such ideas had become as fashionable as they were to be later on in the century, that the outcome of the rivalry between Britain and Russia was to be the decisive factor in the future history of Central Asia, and he made the most of his travels to prove this point. To Moorcroft, Ladakh and Western Tibet were not only the means of tapping the profitable trade in shawl wool, but also routes to the commerce of the whole of Central Asia, of which Tibet was but one small part. The Russians, Moorcroft was convinced, had grasped the potentialities of this great market, and the British would have to act quickly if they wished to compete. Russian merchants were visiting the annual fair at Gartok.[21] Russian agents, armed with official credentials and suitable gifts, were intriguing at Leh and Lahore.[22] The choice that faced the British was a momentous one. The British, Moorcroft wrote, had to decide whether the inhabitants of Central Asia and Tibet

shall be clothed with the broadcloth of Russia or of England – whether they shall be provided with domestic utensils of copper, iron, or of pewter, with implements of iron and steel, with hardware of every description, from St. Petersburg or Birmingham – it is entirely in the decision of the government of British India. At present there is little doubt to which the prize will be awarded, for enterprise and vigour mark the measures of Russia towards the nations of Central Asia, whilst ours are characterised by misplaced squeamishness and unnecessary timidity.[23]

Though the British may well be blamed for missing opportunities in Ladakh, they can hardly be rebuked for failing to establish any relations with the authorities in Western Tibet. Since 1792 the Chinese seem to have been firmly in control at Gartok, and they appear to have been fully aware of the growing British power south of the Himalayas, which they watched with considerable suspicion. They knew of Moorcroft's travels in Ladakh, against which they protested,[24] and it is evident that they were alarmed by the many attempts by British travellers to enter Tibet by way of the Sutlej Valley or the passes of Kumaon. From 1818 this increasingly had become the favoured sport of British officials on leave or duty in the hills; the Sutlej route was particularly convenient to the new hill station at Simla. But, as one such traveller noted, 'the Chinese Tartars, on this remote frontier of their vast empire, are just as vigilant respecting the non-admission of strangers as their countrymen at Pekin: no sum of money, however great, will bribe them to infringe the orders of their superiors'.[25] In 1821 Captain Alexander Gerard wrote to the Garpons at Gartok requesting permission to visit Lake Manasarowara, and journeyed up the Sutlej in great hopes for a favourable reply. He was stopped at the Tibetan frontier, however, and informed by the Chinese frontier guards that 'orders had been received from Lhasa, some months ago, to make no friends with Europeans, and to furnish them neither with food nor firewood'. He was then handed the reply from the Garpon to the effect that reports of the movements of Moorcroft, then travelling in Ladakh, had alarmed the authorities in Lhasa, who had issued strict orders to stop all Europeans from crossing the frontier, and in future 'he could neither receive nor answer letters from Europeans; and he must return them unopened'. Despite this setback Gerard was 'greatly pleased with the frank and open manner of the Chinese'. As soon as he agreed to turn back he was given every assistance in the provision of food and fuel. He concluded that 'the Tartars are of a very mild and peaceable disposition, and this character develops progressively on acquaintance'.[26] The Chinese policy was to ensure that early warning of the impending advance of European would-be-frontier crossers was received from the local inhabitants on the British side of the frontier; to meet the traveller at the frontier and with every courtesy to request him to turn back; and if he refused, to prevent his further progress by withholding supplies. This was, for example, the experience of the French traveller, Victor Jacquemont, in 1830.[27] In no case did there result an unfortunate incident that could lead to international complications.

Avoidance of such complications was just as much the wish of the Indian Government as of the Chinese. In 1827 the Gartok authorities ventured to remonstrate with the Raja of Bashahr for allowing British travellers to enter Tibet through his territory. They pointed out the increasing frequency of this practice, which had aroused the displeasure of Lhasa. If the British wished to make an alliance with China, they should go by sea to Peking, and not to Tibet. They concluded by warning the Raja not to rely excessively upon the strength of British arms, for the Emperor was infinitely more powerful, and a war with China would result in overwhelming Chinese victory. The Raja passed this on to Government, in the hope that he no longer be placed in a position in which he must displease one or another of his powerful neighbours, and Government, though mildly pained at the somewhat arrogant tone of this communication, decided, 'in order to restrain this spirit of curiosity and research which might lead to unpleasant and embarrassing discussions', to instruct British officers in future not to cross the Tibetan frontier, a prohibition which does not seem to have been applied to private individuals.[28]

After 1816, in contrast to the considerable degree of imagination shown during the Gurkha War, it can be said that Government ceased to have any policy towards Tibet other than an expressed wish to avoid all entanglements with the authorities, Tibetan and Chinese, in that country. It did not ignore Tibet entirely, of course, as it would be hard to ignore a land with so many miles of common border. Thus it encouraged the Tibetan researches of the Hungarian scholar Csoma de Körös; and from the 1820s until his death at Darjeeling in 1841 while about to set out on an attempt to visit Lhasa, it paid this gentle eccentric a small pension.[29] It approved the proposal of B. H. Hodgson, Resident at Katmandu, to try to get in touch with the Tashi Lama with the intention of obtaining from him copies of Tibetan religious texts. The 327 quarto volumes which Hodgson secured from the Lama in exchange for a few yards of red broadcloth were despatched to the Court of Directors in November 1835.[30] But it was not until 1837, with the Pemberton mission to Bhutan to which reference will be made in the next chapter, that any serious attempt was made to establish political contact with Tibet along the lines of the projects of the Gurkha War period.

The needs of the Company were changing. The problems of British trade and diplomacy with China were rapidly approaching a solution in China itself. The initiative in Anglo-Tibetan relations came increasingly to be provided by events in the Himalayas for which the British were not responsible and over which they had little control. Thus the Company found itself obliged to take a more active interest in the border between its possessions in Kumaon and Garwhal and the territories of Western Tibet, less because it wished to establish contact with the Chinese for those reasons and in those ways which Lord Moira had suggested, than because it discovered that it could not ignore political developments along its frontiers. In the 1830s the balance of power on the north-western frontier of India was being altered. The Raja of Jammu, Gulab Singh, the Dogra ruler who was a feudatory of the Sikh kingdom of Lahore, was busy creating an empire of his own out of the small states of the Upper Indus. In 1834, through his general Zorawar Singh, he undertook the successful invasion of Ladakh, thus bringing the Sikh Empire into contact with that of China.[31] Though this expedition was undertaken with the tacit approval of the British,[32] it was none the less destined to threaten British interests. There can be little doubt that it was the attraction of the Ladakh carrying trade, particularly in shawl wool, which brought Dogras into this barren and mountainous region, and there can be equally little doubt that the Dogra conquest and the consequent exactions imposed upon this trade upset the long-established commercial framework of this area. The trade between Ladakh and Tibet was largely based on a system of traditional relationships which could hardly fail to be disturbed by the conquests of a power alien in culture and religion. One result was a large increase in the trade of Gartok with the states to the south of the Himalayas, to the detriment of that with Ladakh. Before 1834 the shawl exports to Rampur seem to have been very small; the rapid rise after 1837, the first year for which any figures are available, of nearly two hundred per cent. in four years has already been noted. Such a spectacular change in the direction of trade could not fail to have widespread effects. A rise in the production of finished shawls by the weavers of Amritsar and Ludhiana could only be at the expense of those of Kashmir, and a loss to Gulab Singh. An economic revolution took place in the hill states through which the new trade was carried; new capital was needed, and the indebtedness of the hill men to money lenders in the plains increased greatly.[33]

The reaction of Gulab Singh to this change can cause no surprise. In the spring of 1841 his general Zorawar Singh was sent to invade the shawl producing areas of Western Tibet, and was soon in possession of all that territory up to the sacred lakes of Rakas-tal and Manasarowara, so that Dogra dominions now included the Tibetan towns of Rudok and Gartok, and stretched to the frontier of Nepal. K. M. Panikkar, whose life of Gulab Singh is a standard work on this period, gives no explanation for this act of aggression; he is full of admiration for the daring conception of this Indian ruler who was prepared to undertake conquests beyond the natural mountain frontiers of Hindustan.[34] But British officials, in 1841, were not so favourably impressed. Clerk, Agent to the North-West Frontier, had no doubt in his mind that Gulab Singh, relying on the traditional relationships between Ladakh and Western Tibet which included the payment of complimentary dues by Rudok and Gartok to the Ladakh king, which he now claimed were due the Dogras by right of conquest, had laid claim to this part of Tibet with the express object of monopolizing the shawl trade.[35] Events soon justified this conclusion. One of the first acts of the conquerors was to stop trade between Tibet and British territory;[36] the shawl imports at Rampur dropped in 1841 to a value of Rs. 17,766.[37] Such a rapid decline - in 1840 the value of shawl passing through Rampur had been Rs. 94,807 - had political consequences. As Thomason observed:

If we submit to this injury, loss of influence and loss of

consideration must inevitably follow, and the arrogance and presumption of our neighbours will be proportionally increased. The value of the trade from a political point of view is of little moment, but the simple fact of it being stopped for any length of time must dispirit our own people and give confidence to those who have achieved this act, to attempt others.[38]

But this was not all. The year 1841 found the British involved in war in Afghanistan and in China. A British army was in Kabul with a line of communication stretching across the territory of the Sikhs, who, since the death of Ranjit Singh two years before, were of doubtful loyalty to their British allies. Action against Dogras in Tibet might not only involve troops needed elsewhere, but gravely endanger the position of the army in Afghanistan. The continued presence of Zorawar Singh on Chinese territory, however, could complicate, if not nullify, negotiations then in progress for a peace in China. Clerk thought that

the hostile position towards tributaries of the Chinese Government, in which the Sikhs are now exhibited, might prove embarrassing under such circumstances as an approaching pacification at Pekin; for that Government will, of course, in the present state of affairs there, impute the invasion of its territories by the Sikhs, to the instigation of the British Government.[39]

Gulab Singh also seems to have been aware of this problem; in October 1841 he proposed that he should 'co-operate in force with the British Government in an invasion of the Western Frontier of China', a proposal which aroused no British enthusiasm.[40]

A further danger lay in the attitude of Nepal. Since 1837 the Gurkhas had been in the throes of a political conflict in which the issue at stake was whether they should follow a policy of hostility or of neutrality towards the British. With the British at war with China, it seemed likely that the fact that the Gurkhas were Chinese feudatories might decide the issue against the British. It might prove highly embarrassing if the Gurkhas should choose to consider Gulab Singh's attack on Western Tibet as having been British inspired or British supported. Gulab Singh, after all, was a subject of Lahore, and Lahore was allied to the British. Thus Hodgson watched with some anxiety the arrival in Katmandu in June 1841 of envoys of the former king of Ladakh seeking aid

53

against the Dogras.[41] It would seem that the Gurkhas did, in fact, offer to help their Chinese suzerain by waging war against British India, but that their proposals were rejected by Peking despite arguments in favour of acceptance by such prominent Chinese officials as Lin Tse-hsu, who had dealt closely with Europeans at Canton, and the Amban at Lhasa.[42] When the Gurkhas were turned down by China, however, they did not abandon hope of extracting some advantage from the Himalayan situation. They began to consider coming to some sort of arrangement with Gulab Singh, whose territory now approached close to Nepal, and this development, of course, threatened to .break that political isolation of Nepal from other Indian states which had been an important object of British policy at the conclusion of the Gurkha War. As Clerk reported in September 1841:

> There would be a degree of insecurity to British interests in the connection of Nepal to any Hill State to the west of it, and that insecurity would, I conceive, be imminent in an union of the abundant resources of the Jummoo Rajas with the malevolence and bravery of the Gurkha Army.

He felt that such a connection could well have been a 'more remote object' of Gulab Singh's attack on Western Tibet.[43]

Yet another aspect of Dogra invasion distasteful to the British was that the activity of the Dogra in Tibet led to a Dogra military presence in Lahul, Kulu and Spiti, on the southern side of the Tibetan frontier between Ladakh and the Sutlej. In Spiti, through which passed the route from Bashahr to Ladakh, all trade had stopped, and in view of the extreme complexity of the relations of Spiti with its neighbours, it was by no means clear that the sovereignty of Bashahr, a British protected state, had not been violated.[44] There seemed little doubt that Gulab Singh was trying to spread his influence into the Hill States under British protection; it was reported that he was negotiating for the marriage of the daughter of the Raja of Bashahr to his son.[45] He was claiming, moreover, the customary presents that these states were wont to make to Ladakh. Government rapidly decided that open Dogra interference in British protected territory must be stopped; and by military action should this prove to be necessary.[46]

As Hodgson noted, the Dogra invasion was 'a most untoward event', which, in view of 'the political and military imbecility of the Chinese in this quarter', was very likely to endure.[47] It was difficult to see what action could be taken without the risk of more unpleasant consequences. In September 1841 two non-committal though not very promising steps were decided upon. The Lahore Durbar was requested to secure the withdrawal of Gulab Singh from Tibet; and this they agreed to do, though the question whether the Jammu Raja would have obeyed the orders of Lahore in this respect was never put to the test.[48] A British officer, Lieutenant J. D. Cunningham, the future historian of the Sikhs, was instructed to travel up to Sutlej to a point near the Tibetan frontier, where he could observe and report developments.[49]

In December 1841 the Tibetans reacted to the Dogra advance. Zorawar Singh was cut off by a superior force of Chinese and Tibetans after he had rashly decided to winter in Tibet with his lines of communication made impassable by snow; and he was decisively defeated, he and most of his officers being killed. The Chinese followed up by invading Ladakh and laying siege to Leh. This reversal of the situation made British neutrality no easier to maintain. The Dogras at once appealed to the British for help. What would be the attitude of the Chinese to this in view of the war then in progress in China? The danger of friction between the British and the Chinese was brought home when some Dogra soldiers escaping from the Tibetan debacle sought asylum on British soil in Kanawar. Would the Chinese, if they demanded the surrender of these men and were refused, look on the British as Dogra allies, as in fact they were, and would they use this excuse to stop the trans-frontier trade?[50] What would be the reaction of Nepal? Clerk refused to allow the fear of such developments to lead him from the path of strict neutrality. He wrote to Cunningham that British policy desired nothing more than the restoration of Gartok to the Chinese; Cunningham's role should be that of observer, or, if called upon, of mediator.[51] The nature of the country made the sending of military assistance to the Sikhs quite impracticable,[52] and the opposite course of forcibly restraining them, which had to be considered once more, when, in September 1842 Gulab Singh resumed the offensive, was thought to offer no advantages. The British were not likely to gain any credit, even if they did assist the Chinese, since the local Chinese commanders would never report such a fact to Peking.[53]

Thus it was without British participation that the Chinese and Dogras came to terms, signing a peace treaty at Leh on 17th October 1842. No text seems to have been officially communicated to the British, though a version was received from the Raja of Bashahr. This was a simple document of three articles restoring the *status quo ante*; to the second article only, which stated that 'in conformity with ancient usage, Tea and Pushm shall be transmitted by the Ladakh road', could exception be taken, as it was thought to confer on Gulab Singh a monopoly of the export trade in shawl wool, the main object of his campaign in Western Tibet.[54] The treaty was reinforced by a further document signed by the Chinese, Tibetans and the Lahore Durbar, confirming the engagements into which Gulab Singh had entered.[55] The British did not obtain an official text of Gulab Singh's treaty until 1889, when the situation on the frontier between Sikkim and Tibet led them to investigate closely the relations still existing between states under their protection and Tibet. Captain Ramsay, British Joint Commissioner at Leh, then produced the following document:

> Whereas we, the officers of the Lhassa country, viz., firstly, Kalon Sukanwala and, secondly, Bakhshi Sapju, Commander of the forces of the Emperor of China, on one hand, and Divan Hari Chand and Wazir Ratnu on the side of Gulab Singh, on the other, agree together and swear before God that the friendship etc. between Raja Gulab Singh and the Emperor of China and the Lama Guru-Sahib Lhassa-wallah will be kept and observed till eternity; no disregard will be shown to anything agreed upon in the presence of God; and we will have nothing to do with the countries bordering on Ladak. We will carry on the trade in Shawl, Pasham and Tea as before, by way of Ladak; and if one of the Sri Raja's enemies comes to our territories and says anything against the Raja, we will not listen to him, and will not allow him to remain in our country; and whatever traders come from Ladak shall experience no difficulty from our side. We will not act otherwise but in the same manner as it has been prescribed in this meeting regarding the fixing of the Ladak frontier and keeping open the road for the traffic in Shawl, Pasham and Tea.[56]

These terms agreed substantially with those communicated by the ruler of Bashahr, though they seemed to imply a greater extent of Tibetan influence over the affairs of Ladak than the Indian Government had suspected. By 1900 the Indian Government had still not made up its mind whether this treaty affected in any way its status of paramountcy over Kashmir.[57]

Gulab Singh's invasion of Western Tibet did not result in any of the unpleasant possibilities which so worried the Indian Government at the time. Trade between British territory and Western Tibet did not, it is true, increase to any great extent, but more trade existed than would have been the case had Gulab Singh managed to incorporate Western Tibet into his dominions. The danger of an alliance between the Jammu Raja and the Gurkhas passed away, thanks, in part, to the skilful diplomacy of B. H. Hodgson, whose tenure of the Katmandu Residency marked an important stage in the conversion of the Gurkhas from British enemies to British allies. Compared to events in Afghanistan, the Himalayan crisis of 1841 to 1842 seems insignificant enough, and it has earned scant mention in the histories of India. Yet this crisis was to have a significant effect on the subsequent course of British Himalayan policy. In the first place, it had become clear that some policy was needed on the complex relationships existing between the Himalayan hill states and Tibet. The British would have to try to prevent the existence among their protectorates of any form of dual allegiance. As J. D. Cunningham wrote:

> A multiplicity of relations and a diversion of allegiance naturally arise during the contests of barbarous people and short lived dynasties, and such a state of uncertainty is always agreeable to the wishes of aspiring and able rulers who occasionally appear. But of late the consolidated empires of China and England have met one another along the Himalaya Mountains, and it is time that doubt should be put at an end. It is not for us to share with others the allegiance of petty princes, nor should we desire that our dependents should have any claims on the territories of other states. Our feudatories should have no political connection with strangers, although we may allow them to interchange friendly letters, and even visits, with their neighbours under the rule of others.[58]

In the second place, it had been shown that trade on the British side of the Himalayan frontier was often dependent upon events in areas outside British control. The trade at Rampur, for instance, did not revive to the expected extent once Gulab Singh had left Tibet,[59] and was unlikely to do so unless the British could secure some form of political and commercial settlement with the Chinese and Gulab Singh. It was also evident that without such a settlement Gulab Singh might well be tempted once more to seize Gartok and Rudok and again threaten the peace of the frontier.

The Sikh War, which broke out in 1845, provided an opportunity for securing such a settlement. Gulab Singh, the Raja of Jammu, managed to dissociate himself from any act of overt hostility to the British with such skill that in 1846, when the army of the Khalsa had been defeated at Sobraon, he was rewarded with recognition by the British as sovereign ruler of Jammu and Kashmir. The way in which this was carried out was significant.

By the Treaty of Lahore of 9th March 1846 all the Sikh hill possessions between the Sutlej and the Indus, including Jammu, Kashmir and Ladakh, were annexed by the British. At Amritsar, a week later, Jammu, Kashmir and Ladakh were made over to Gulab Singh and his family in perpetuity with certain vital provisions. The new state was to be under British protection in that it was obliged to pay a small annual tribute, to refer boundary and other disputes to the arbitration of Government, to refrain from the employment of European or American subjects without permission, and to allow its boundaries with the Chinese Empire to be determined by a joint frontier commission.[60] The last provision was crucial. Now that Gulab Singh was freed from the control of Lahore, in the words of Alexander Cunningham, who was to play a leading part in the settlement of the Kashmir-Tibet border:

> It seemed not improbable that the hope of plunder and the desire of revenge might tempt him to repeat the expedition of 1841 in the Lhassan territory. Such an occurrence would have at once stopped the importation of shawl wool into our territory, and have closed the whole of the petty commerce of our hill states with Tibet. It was possible also that our peaceful relations with the Chinese Emperor might be considerably embarrassed by His Celestial Majesty's ignorance of any distinction between the rulers of India and the rulers of Kashmir. . . . The British Government decided to remove the most common cause of all disputes in the East - an unsettled boundary.[61]

Accordingly, in July 1846, Captain Alexander Cunningham and Mr. Vans Agnew were deputed to proceed to the new territories ceded by the treaty of Lahore.[62] From their instructions, however, it is clear that much more was intended than a mere demarcation of frontiers. The trade question was to be settled, and an enquiry conducted into the prospects of British commerce not only in Western Tibet but also in the whole of Central Asia. In so far as Tibetan trade was concerned, before a satisfactory settlement could be reached, the fact that Kashmir might be able, even now, to prevent the export of shawl wool to Rampur and other markets had to be faced. In this context the Spiti Valley with its approaches in Lahul and Kulu became significant. It joined Ladakh to the upper Sutlej, and whoever controlled it was in a position to exert considerable influence over the road from Gartok to Rampur; this was one lesson learnt in 1841. Accordingly, the Boundary Commissioners were instructed to secure this area, 'geographically part of Ladak . . . in order to prevent the interposition of a foreign state between Rampur and the shawl-wool districts of Chanthan', compensating Gulab Singh by concessions elsewhere.[63]

There were also signs that the Tibetan authorities might be willing to enter into some form of agreement. In 1845 the Raja of Bashahr was led to believe that if the British were to request the Garpons of Gartok to free the export of shawl from any restrictions that might have resulted from a treaty with Gulab Singh, they would be heard with favour. It would seem that the heavy taxes imposed on this trade by the Kashmir officials in Ladakh were as distasteful to the Tibetans as they were to the British.[64] With this possibility in mind, Hardinge, the Governor-General, prepared a letter to the 'Vizier of Lhassa-Gartope', to be transmitted by the Boundary Commissioners, which set out the ingenious thesis that whatever treaty engagements Gulab Singh may have made with Tibet in 1841-42 were now made over to the British Government, since any such engagements were in fact those of Lahore, and by the Lahore treaty of 1846 had been surrendered to the British along with the Sikh hill territory. It was thus arguable that British traders should enjoy the same rights of trade with Gartok as those of Ladakh or elsewhere. If this was accepted, then a formal agreement between Tibet and the British, though doubtless it would be welcomed, was not essential. Rather, it was felt that once a regular trade was authorized with British territory, the advantages of freedom from duty to which the Governor-General was at pains to refer in his letter would attract a traffic which 'will soon find its way where best protected and least taxed'.[65] As Hardinge wrote to the Court of Directors in August 1846:

> I am in hopes that the measures now in progress for opening a line of communication with the Chinese frontier and Lhassa, running entirely through our territories, or those under our control, and unmolested thro' its whole length by transit duties, will have a very beneficial effect on the trade between our provinces and those of Chinese Tartary.[66]

A problem to be solved in any attempt to open relations with Tibetan officials was how to ensure that letters from the British Government should reach their destination. Hitherto the authorities in Gartok had shown a most unwelcoming attitude to British overtures and had explicitly stated on more than one occasion their inability to entertain any communication with Europeans. But without some means by which British views and intentions could be conveyed to the Tibetans there were grave risks of misunderstanding. For instance, in what light would the British annexation of Spiti, which had long been accustomed to pay a tribute to Gartok which had now been stopped in accordance with the policy suggested by J. D. Cunningham in 1841, be regarded? An alternative method of sending letters to Lhasa was needed. Consequently a copy of Hardinge's letter was sent to Hong Kong with a request that Sir John Davis should arrange for its transmission to the Tibetan capital by way of Peking.[67]

This was the first occasion on which the Indian Government had attempted to carry out a Tibetan policy through China – previously it had been the other way about, to establish relations with China through Tibet. It was now possible as a result of the Treaty of Nanking. Moreover, the surprisingly powerful Chinese reaction to Gulab Singh's invasion had seemed to demonstrate beyond doubt that the Chinese were the real masters in Tibet. Thus the Chinese could perhaps play a larger part than that of postman. Sir John Davis was asked to suggest to the Chinese authorities in Canton that the Emperor should depute Commissioners to proceed to the western frontiers of Tibet to carry out a demarcation jointly with the British and Kashmir Commissioners. Davis seems to have received a favourable reply to this suggestion, though with no prospect of any developments in 1846.[68]

Vans Agnew and Cunningham spent the summer of 1846 laying down the boundaries of the new British possessions of Lahul and Spiti. They were not so successful in establishing contact with Gartok. Their interpreter, one Anant Ram, an official of the Raja of Bashahr, was sent to deliver the Governor-General's letter. On his return Anant Ram reported that the Garpons had shown great reluctance in accepting the letter, and only agreed, after much argument, to send it on to Lhasa because it had been brought to them by an agent of Bashahr and not by a British official with whom the Garpons declared they could have no dealings whatsoever. They added that there was little chance of a reply being received for a year at least.[69] There is later evidence to suggest that Anant Ram was not quite truthful in his report; that the letter was not transmitted to Lhasa and that, in any case, it was written in such execrable Tibetan that the Garpons took it to be a demand, on the part of the British, for a strict adherence to the terms of the treaty with Gulab Singh.[70] This is not the only occasion in which the employment of native agents to carry out diplomatic missions was to prove to be unsatisfactory, since suitable agents for such work, particularly in the case of Tibet, were often personally interested in the maintenance of the existing state of affairs. Anant Ram, as an official of Bashahr, was almost certainly financially involved in the Tibet trade and could lose by its general extension to British subjects; in any case, he could hardly be pleased at a commission that would compromise him in the eyes of the Tibetan authorities as a British agent.

In the spring of 1847 news was received through Bashahr that two Chinese officials had arrived in Gartok, with the suggestion that they were the Chinese Boundary Commissioners whose deputation had been asked for through Hong Kong.[71] Although Hardinge suspected that they had come 'as much for the purpose of preventing our Commissioners from crossing the boundary, as for defining it', he decided, none the less, to send out a new Commission to continue the work of the previous year.[72] Alexander Cunningham was to be in command, assisted by Lieutenant Henry Strachey, who had just made an adventurous journey to Lake Manasarowara, and Dr. Thomson, a well-known naturalist. Its instructions were ampler than those of the year before. Not only was it to define the Kashmir–Tibet frontier, with, it was hoped, the assistance of Chinese Commissioners, but it was also to endeavour 'to place on a more satisfactory footing than at present the commercial relations between Tibet and the provinces of British India'.[73] Cunningham was to explore the prospects of Central Asian trade by travelling through Ladakh and Kashmir to Gilgit and Hunza, while Strachey was to visit Western Tibet and, if possible, to travel along the Upper Brahmaputra or Tsangpo River, visit Lhasa, and return to British territory by way of Bhutan or Sikkim, though in this attempt no force was to be employed.[74] If a meeting with Chinese or Tibetan officials should take place, the Commissioners were to secure, if possible, the abandonment of any clause in any treaty between Gulab Singh and Tibet respecting a Ladakh monopoly of the shawl trade. It is clear from Hardinge's report to the Court of Directors that behind these instructions lay an irritation, if not anxiety, at the presence of Russian traders and Russian goods in Tibet and other parts of Central Asia, and the hope that traders from British territory could now be placed in a favourable position to compete, as Moorcroft had urged two decades earlier.[75] The prospect of a British official visiting Lhasa was welcomed also by Major Jenkins, Agent for the North-East Frontier, who saw in a closer contact with the authorities of Tibet a means to control the turbulent tribes of Bhutan and the hill districts of Assam: his proposals on this occasion will be discussed in the next chapter.

Both Gulab Singh and the Tibetans looked on the Commission with the deepest suspicion. Gulab Singh had much to lose if a trade agreement was reached; the Tibetans remained convinced that the Commission was spying out the land in preparation for a future invasion.[76] And, as one would have expected, the negotiations through Hong Kong, which continued through 1847 and 1848, achieved nothing. Sir John Davis sent several notes to the Emperor, by way of the Chinese authorities in Canton, and through agents of his own. Although he was informed that Peking would send the Chinese Resident in Lhasa 'proper instructions',[77] the Chinese attitude was clearly 'that the borders of those territories have been sufficiently and distinctly fixed so that it will be best to adhere to this ancient arrangement, and it will prove far more convenient to abstain from any additional measures for fixing them'. This was all the less surprising when it is remembered that the Chinese Resident in Lhasa had previously been High Commissioner at Canton, the notorious Ch'i-shan. As Lord Dalhousie remarked in his review of the achievements of the Boundary Commission, 'it is not to be wondered at that he should take every possible means of abstaining from any intercourse with British officers on another remote frontier of the Empire'.[78] Ch'i-shan, after his failure to restrain the British at Canton from which had emerged the Opium War, was degraded, condemned to death and, at the last moment, had this harsh sentence commuted for what amounted to exile in Tibet. His tenure of office in Lhasa was made memorable by the two French Lazarist missionaries, Huc and Gabet, who managed to make their way to that forbidden city in 1846, and for whose expulsion from the Tibetan capital Ch'i-shan was responsible.[79]

Thus no Chinese Commissioners arrived; the earlier reports that they had were shown to be false. The British Commissioners were subjected to obstructions in Ladakh itself, Strachey being virtually imprisoned for several weeks at Hanle owing to the refusal of the abbot of that place to provide him with supplies; and this was doubtless at the instigation of Gartok, which showed nothing but hostility to the Commission. Further letters to the Garpons were ignored, and it was plain that the Commissioners would not be permitted to set foot on Tibetan soil, let alone carry out a joint demarcation.[80] The Commissioners of Gulab Singh were scarcely more co-operative; they put off joining their British colleagues for several months, and when finally they did arrive on the scene they gave the impression of but wishing to postpone any boundary settlement for as long as possible,[81] though this does not seem to have deterred Gulab Singh from requesting that the

British use their influence to secure the release of the many prisoners still remaining in Tibetan hands following his disastrous invasion of Western Tibet of 1841.[82] All Cunningham and Strachey could do was to define the frontier unaided, in which task they were greatly helped by the clear marking of much of the Tibet-Ladakh border by boundary pillars set up c. 1687, and to collect much information on these little-known regions which was to gain wide circulation in Cunningham's *Ladak* and Strachey's *Physical Geography of Western Tibet.*[83] With this Government had to be content; in May 1848 it decided to abandon further attempts to enter into discussions with the Tibetans or Chinese, though greatly regretting the loss of 'this favourable opportunity' for improving relations with the Chinese Empire.[84]

Thus the Boundary Commission resulted in no political settlement, and the story of its origins and its activities has been given scant mention in accounts of Anglo-Tibetan relations.[85] Although no settlement resulted from them, however, it is not true to say that these events, and those of the crisis of 1841-42, had no political significance. In the correspondence, instructions and reports of this time can be discerned the elements of a frontier policy, the development of which was to constitute the major part of the future history of the relationship of India to Tibet. For example, the appreciation of the complex relationships between the hill states and Tibet led J. D. Cunningham to suggest that such states under British protection should only be allowed to pay to a dependency of the Chinese Empire a tribute of a specifically religious nature, a doctrine that was first put into effect on the case of Spiti. This was a principle that was to govern the settlement of Burma in 1886 and of Sikkim in 1890, and was to lead the Indian Government to examine with interest and some anxiety the tributary status of Nepal to the Chinese Empire.

The Boundary commission marked the first occasion on which the British attempted formal imperial boundary negotiations with representatives of the Chinese Empire, in this case along the western Himalayan range. Though a mountain chain is in many ways a natural barrier of great strength, it does present questions of policy; whether the limit of British control should be in the foothills, or in the centre, or on the glacis on the other side. On the whole, it was preferred, where possible, to maintain friendly independent states in physical possession of the mountain areas as in the case of Nepal, Bhutan, and at first, Sikkim. The creation of Kashmir can largely be interpreted in this light.[86] From a commercial point of view, however, this policy was not entirely satisfactory, since the friendly, independent states could never

63

resist extorting the utmost revenue from their transit trade. Hence in areas where the trans-Himalayan trade was of importance, as in Sikkim, for instance, there was a strong argument for annexation right up to the Tibetan frontier, and we can see this applied in the case of Lahul and Spiti. In such cases, where a frontier had to be laid down in mountainous territory, the Boundary Commission, 'to preclude any possibility of future dispute', adopted 'a boundary of such mountain ranges as form watershed-lines between the drainages of different rivers'.[87]

Another result was an appreciation of the futility of attempting direct contact with the Dalai Lama and the Government in Lhasa. Strachey reported in 1848 that nothing but obstruction was to be expected from a Tibetan Government which refused to recognize any political changes in its neighbouring states; in his view the question of the clauses in a treaty between Gulab Singh and Lhasa was an academic one, since Lhasa still officially considered Ladakh to be an independent kingdom, and did not even recognize the existence of the Jammu Raja. He felt that the best chance of success lay in the encouragement, despite the obvious dangers of such a course, of friendly contacts with local Tibetan officials through native agents. He also urged that if any letters should in future be written to Tibetans greater care should be taken in their translation – indeed the interest in Tibetan studies shown by Government is most probably an outcome of this period. Finally, Strachey emphasized that if it was found necessary to approach the Chinese Resident, or Amban, at Lhasa, it was better to do so through Peking than through any of the means of direct communication at the disposal of the Indian Government. This view was accepted by Government.[88]

In the years immediately following the Afghan War the Indian Government seems to have taken note of the fact that Russian commerce was penetrating the markets of Tibet, as it was extending into other regions of Central Asia. This fact, of course, had been remarked upon before. Bogle referred to Kalmuk merchants who carried on trade between Siberia and Tibet.[89] During the Gurkha War, as has been noted, Lord Moira commented on the sale that Russian (presumably Asiatic) merchants had found for French cloth in Tibet, and so did Moorcroft. In 1831, from his vantage point in Katmandu, B. H. Hodgson pointed out the strange fact that British goods were finding their way to Tibetan bazaars by way of St. Petersburg.[90] In 1838 Pemberton seems to have concluded that the Russians had political as well as commercial influence at Lhasa.[91] But none of this sort of information seems to have aroused much interest on the part of the Indian Government until Lord Dalhousie's day, when that energetic Governor-General thought that British trade should try to compete with that of Russia in a market so close to the borders of British India. Dalhousie admitted that the value of the foreign trade of Tibet was small, but he saw no reason why it should be allowed to become a Russian monopoly. He did not appear to have been worried lest Russian merchants in Tibet should turn out to be political agents as well.[92] How should the Indian Government act in order to improve the trade between British India and Tibet? The Boundary Commission had shown that political methods had little chance of success. If the British wished to improve their trading position on the Tibetan plateau, they would have to do so by measures confined to their own territories. They could remove duties on goods passing to and from Tibetan markets, and they could build roads up to the Tibetan border.

With this policy in mind, transit dues in Bashahr were abolished in 1847.[93] In 1850 Lord Dalhousie authorized that work be set in hand on the construction of a road from the plains to Simla, whence it would eventually be extended up the Sutlej to the Tibetan border, by way of Chini. The road, the Hindustan-Tibet road as it came to be called, was originally suggested in 1841 by J. D. Cunningham, who thought it would induce merchants from Amritsar and Delhi to undertake the journey to Gartok in search of shawl wool.[94] Dalhousie saw a number of additional arguments in favour of this project. It would improve access to the important hill station at Simla; it would facilitate troop movements; it would end the system of *begar*, or compulsory porterage, which was then essential to hill travel and which Government found to constitute an unjust imposition on the hill villages; but its chief service would be to improve the conditions of trade with Tibet, and Dalhousie looked 'with interest to the political and commercial advantage likely to result from the opening of a line of communication with Tibet by way of Chini'.[95] The project was not carried out with much vigour, however, and in 1858 it was practically abandoned in favour of a concentration of effort on the building of the Grand Trunk Road. At that time doubts were also expressed on military grounds as to the advisability of creating such an easy route through the Himalayan barrier.[96] The last stages, from Chini to the frontier, were not completed in the nineteenth century.[97] In 1861 Major Montgomerie of the Survey of India reported that the best route to Tibet was by Darjeeling or through Assam, and that it was here that roads should be built and not in the remote regions adjacent to Western Tibet.[98]

On the whole the trade policy towards Western Tibet, of which the Hindustan-Tibet Road was a manifestation, did not succeed. A report on this trade of 1862, which analysed progress to that date, suggested that while many prospects existed, little had been achieved. A market for the purchase of Tibetan shawl, attended by European buyers, could be established in the newly annexed territory of Spiti, but as yet this had not been done.[99] From Spiti a route might be developed to Yarkand, passing only through Chinese territory – this had been a suggestion of Vans Agnew – and thus avoiding the excessive duties of the Kashmir Government;[100] at present trade with Chinese Turkestan still had to pass through Leh or other towns controlled by Kashmir, where it was mulcted to an almost prohibitive extent: textiles paid 30 per cent. transit duty, sugar 126 per cent. tea 78 per cent. and tobacco 99 per cent.[101] Diplomacy had failed to break the Ladakhi hold on the shawl trade, which the Maharaja of Kashmir still considered to be a state monopoly.[102] There had been no improvement in the diplomatic relations with the Tibetan authorities since the time of the Boundary Commission. When, in 1863, P. H. Egerton, Deputy Commissioner for the Kangra District, addressed the Garpons of Gartok to request a meeting on the Spiti frontier with a view to discussing 'the establishment of a fair, which should promote the advantage of both countries', by encouraging Indian and Tibetan traders to meet in Spiti, his letter was returned unopened. 'Well,' Egerton exclaimed, 'Lord Russell himself never received a more decisive checkmate in his diplomatic efforts than I did.'[103] The Tibetans were most suspicious of British intentions. A wealthy Tibetan landowner asked one of Egerton's native assistants: 'When are the English coming to take this country? There has been constant talk of roads the last four or five years, and yet they don't come. I will engage to buy two hundred yaks and send on every Englishman to Lhasa at my own expense.'[104] Until there was a revolution in Lhasa, however, Egerton was most doubtful whether much trade of value could make its way 'against the pertinacious obstructiveness of the Thibet officials, without a mandate from the Government of China under the Imperial "Red Chop" – which should be conveyed, I think, to Gartok or Lhassa by an imposing Embassy.'[105]

If the supply of shawl wool to the Punjab weavers was to be maintained – and its quality, since there was an increasing tendency to use the inferior wool of Kerman and Seistan, which depreciated the finished product of the Punjab in relation to that of Kashmir – and at the same time there was to be no improvement in the relations with Tibet, it followed that some arrangement must be made with the ruler of Kashmir, resulting, perhaps, in the stationing of a British official in Ladakh.[106] This policy was now pursued by the Indian Government; a tariff agreement was made with the Maharaja of Kashmir in 1864, and in 1867 Dr. Cayley was appointed the first British Agent in Ladakh.[107] But with these developments the importance of the shawl trade declined in relation to the possibilities of Central Asian commerce by way of Yarkand and Kashgar, which could now be carried on through Kashmir territory, and which offered a natural field for British competition with Russian traders. The Forsyth Mission to Yarkand of 1870 marks the beginning of a new phase in British expansion,[108] compared to which 'the trade with Chinese Tibet is quite unimportant'.[109] In 1883 the trade with Tibet formed a mere one per cent. of the total export and import trade of the Punjab.[110]

The important point of contact with Tibet moved from the west to Bengal, as it was bound to do once British influence had been established in that section of the Himalayas across which ran the shortest route from the plains of India to the Tibetan capital. This development had been almost completed by 1861, and it was not until the very last years of the century that Western Tibet was to play once more a significant part in the relations between India and Tibet.[111]

Note: Were there any Chinese, as opposed to Tibetan, forces involved in the expulsion of the Dogras from Western Tibet in 1841-2? The British sources are not clear on this point: they do not always distinguish between 'Chinese' and 'Tibetan'. The probability is that the number of Chinese military involved was minimal if it existed; but it is equally probable that the situation was closely watched by the Chinese Ambans in Lhasa who may well have had representatives or observers with the Tibetan army in Western Tibet.

IV

THE OPENING

OF

SIKKIM

·

1817 – 1861

THE TREATY of Titalia of 1817 did not result in an immediate flourishing of friendly relations between the Company and the rulers of Sikkim, as the more optimistic British officials had hoped during the Gurkha War. Nor were the possibilities seen in the establishment of a treaty with Sikkim to lead to trade and communication with the Chinese and Tibetans in Lhasa without further British pressure, exerted over a period of many troubled years. The British were not able to exploit the potentialities of Sikkim, of which they were able to catch a glimpse during the war with Nepal, until they had secured a new treaty in 1861 following the successful outcome of a military expedition to that state. After 1861 Sikkim was to become the main channel through which the Indian Government was to endeavour to carry out a Tibetan policy; for this reason the often trivial history of British relations with this small hill state was to be of great future significance.

Despite the provisions of the Treaty of Titalia, disputes occasionally broke out between Sikkim and her neighbours. Sikkim, like Bhutan, was very prone to internal feuds. The ruling family was largely Tibetan in its connections and outlook, while the bulk of the population, the Lepchas and other tribes, were the remnants of older states that had been conquered by invaders from Tibet in the legendary past. Between the Tibetan and indigenous factions there was constant friction; thus in 1826, when the Raja had one of the leaders of the Lepcha party assassinated, many of his followers fled to Nepal, whence they started a series of raids on Sikkim, abetted by the Gurkhas. News of this caused Government to send Captain Lloyd and G. W. Grant to investigate and settle the dispute under the terms of Titalia. While in Sikkim Captain Lloyd noted that a small village known as Dorjé-ling offered an ideal situation for a hill resort where Bengal soldiers could go to recover their health away from the scorching heat of the Plains in summer. Lord William Bentinck, who had recently been interested in the development of such a resort at Simla, was favourable to the proposal. Accordingly, in 1829 Grant and Lloyd were instructed to visit Sikkim once more, accompanied by a surveyor, Captain Herbert, to examine fully the possibilities of this site. Their findings suggested that Darjeeling, as the village was to be called, would not only make an ideal health resort but that its possession would confer considerable political benefits on the British Government. The situation of Darjeeling in the midst of Lepcha Sikkim made it an ideal observation point from which to keep an eye on the relations between the Lepchas and the Gurkhas which promised to be a danger to the peace of the frontier. An island of well-governed British territory in the prevailing sea of Sikkim misrule might persuade the Lepcha refugees in East Nepal, estimated to number about 1,200, to take up residence in the Darjeeling district, where they would provide a labour force for the construction of the proposed sanatorium. So eager did Captain Lloyd think they would be to escape the tyranny of the Sikkim Raja that he doubted whether in a few years a 'single Lepcha' would remain under his rule. They might even, he felt, come soon to prefer 'the Christian to the Lama religion'. Grant observed that were a road built from British territory to Darjeeling, 'passable even for cattle', the people of Sikkim would take the opportunity 'to open a traffic, not only between themselves and the inhabitants of Doorjeeling, but between Bengal and Chinese Tartary'.[1]

It was appreciated that the Raja of Sikkim might well object to these developments in his country, 'and no doubt a handsome douceur or some permanent advantage offered would be the only means of obtaining it'. Captain Lloyd thought that a person well acquainted with the customs and politics of Sikkim would have no difficulty in obtaining its cession to the British, but that if this did not prove the case, then it was well worth the while of Government to resume that territory, in which lay Darjeeling, that had been returned to Sikkim at Titalia. Though Government would not contemplate quite so forward a policy as this, it instructed Lloyd to obtain the cession of Darjeeling 'on the first convenient occasion'. Another incursion by the Lepcha refugees in 1834 provided the opportunity for British mediation which was offered in return for the cession of the Darjeeling tract. The Sikkim Raja tried, without avail, to offer concessions elsewhere; in February 1835 he agreed to hand over the site to the British by deed of gift. The Sikkim official history gives two explanations for this unusual act. In the first place, the problem of the Lepcha refugees in Nepal was a serious one, all the more so as the Sikkim Raja had failed to secure the promise of armed assistance from Tibet in the event of a future outbreak, and thus he found the friendship of the British of great value. In the second place, it would appear that the Lepcha refugees had themselves offered Darjeeling to the British in return for support for their cause, and this had forced the Raja's hand.[2]

In Government circles there was some opposition to the acquisition of Darjeeling; Sir Charles Metcalf, for example, urged strongly against this move on the grounds that the advantages of a sanatorium did not outweigh the risk of open hostility from the Gurkhas, who might well consider British control to pave the way for a future attack on Nepal. Hodgson, however, did not accept this conclusion; possession of a route by which the Gurkhas could attack Sikkim could bring nothing but advantage to the British, and it was this argument that won the day.[3]

The cession of Darjeeling was an event of the greatest importance in the history of the northern frontier of India. Not only did it place the British in close contact with the hill states, their peoples and their politics, but also it provided a constant reminder of the possibilities of trade with Tibet. Many Englishmen - Bengal government officials, soldiers, and influential merchants - came to pass the hot season in Darjeeling and thereby became aware of Tibet and the Tibetans. From the outset the hill station became a centre for Tibetan studies, and has remained such to the present day. Moreover, Darjeeling seemed particularly vulnerable to attack by the hill peoples; though such attacks never materialized there were frequent alarms which must have brought home to the English visitors in a very personal way the problems of this section of the Indian frontier. Whatever the policy of the Indian Government might be, from the early days of this hill station there were always English residents who strongly advocated the establishment of closer relations with Tibet; some of them enjoyed a reputation far beyond the boundaries of Bengal, and it would be hard to overestimate the part played by the residents of this town in the opening of Tibet.

The growth of Darjeeling was very rapid. In 1835 the original village had scarce one hundred inhabitants, a figure which by 1849 had grown to over ten thousand, and continued to increase every year. In 1839 the first Darjeeling hotel was built; three years later the settlement was linked to the plains by a military road. In 1848 a Convalescent Depot for British troops was established there. In 1850 the town became a municipality. At about this date the cultivation of tea, which was to bring into existence a group of planters who saw a good market for their produce to the north, was started in the area. By 1860 Darjeeling had become a commercial and tourist centre of considerable importance, a spearhead of Western influence among the old cultures of the hill states.[4]

From its inception the relations between Darjeeling and the rulers of Sikkim had been uneasy. Captain Lloyd, who in 1836 was appointed Local Agent to supervise the development of the new hill station, noted in his journal in 1837 that 'I hear that it is the Raja's intention to throw every obstacle he can in our way; he might as well have refused to give us the place in the first instance'. Dr. Chapman, Lloyd's assistant, observed that the Sikkim Government was trying to prevent native labour from going to Darjeeling, and was in other ways trying to obstruct the development of the hill station. An open conflict was inevitable, sooner or later.[5] The official history of Sikkim produces strong reasons to justify the resentment by the Sikkim people of the presence of the British on their soil. It placed the country in an embarrassing position in relation to its more powerful neighbours Bhutan and Tibet, who had some cause to complain that Sikkim had sold itself to the British. Relations with these two states deteriorated; the Tibetans curtailed traditional grazing rights of the inhabitants along the frontier in Tibetan territory. In 1844 the Bhutanese attempted to assassinate the Raja while on his way on pilgrimage to Lhasa.[6]

The very presence of an enclave of British territory in the midst of Sikkim carried its own troubles. The Sikkim authorities resented the refusal of the British to surrender slaves who had escaped to the free territory of Darjeeling. The British were likewise annoyed at the ease with which criminals escaped from their possession found asylum in Sikkim.[7] On one issue the Sikkim Government found itself placed between two opposing fires. The British took the Treaty of Titalia to give their officials the right to travel throughout Sikkim and up to the Tibetan border. But Sikkim had been clearly warned by the Chinese and Tibetans that they would regard with displeasure the presence of Englishmen on their frontier, and instructed the Raja to see that this did not happen.[8] It was not surprising, in view of the very close contacts that had long been in existence between Sikkim and Tibet, not the least of which was due to the habit of the Rajas of spending the monsoon season in the Chumbi Valley in Tibet, where the rainfall averaged a few inches per year compared to the many hundreds of inches a few miles south, that the Sikkim rulers should listen to Tibet, the power they knew and understood, rather than the British, who were new and unknown.

Two factors precipitated the inevitable crisis. One was the appointment of the energetic Dr. Campbell as Superintendent of Darjeeling in 1839.[9] The second was the death, in 1847, of the Sikkim Chief Minister or Dewan, Ilam Singh, thus, in the words of Dr. Campbell, losing to 'the Raja's Counsels the only man of any honesty, or to be trusted in word or deed', and his succession by Tokhang Donyer Namgyal.[10] Namgyal was a Tibetan who had married the sister of one of the Raja's concubines. He had used this petticoat influence in his rise to power. He was a man of considerable strength of character and of real ability, qualities which helped him to play a significant part in the history of British relations with Sikkim and Tibet. Englishmen who met him, on the whole, did not take to him, though they usually acknowledged his undoubted qualities.[11] He was certainly the most able and forceful figure in Sikkim politics, and until his death in 1888, even though he was permanently exiled to Tibet after 1861, his influence in Sikkim remained strong. His chief failing seemed to have been his consistent underestimation of the power of the British; but, as the Sikkim History put it, the Sikkim people were not used to the behaviour of a powerful European government. At the time of his appointment to the office of Dewan, Namgyal's power was increased by the fact that the Raja of Sikkim had removed himself from the cares of government and retired to a life of religious contemplation. He did not, however, lack opposition. He was a Tibetan, and was, therefore, opposed by the Lepchas. His dominating position in the trade of Sikkim was much resented. As a lay ruler he faced opposition from the monasteries. The opposing faction was led by the Chebu Lama, the only Sikkim personality who could in any way match Namgyal. The Chebu Lama favoured friendship with the British, for the support of which policy he was to be well rewarded.

The issue on which the opposition focused its attention was the question of the succession to the present Raja, whose only surviving son was a celibate Lama. The only other candidate to the throne was an illegitimate son of the Raja by Namgyal's sister-in-law. The Chebu Lama persuaded the Raja to take a new, young, wife; but no issue resulted. He then, in 1848, persuaded the Dalai Lama to dispense with the vows of celibacy of the Raja's Lama son, and arranged his marriage in December of that year. This, of course, was a threat to the Dewan Namgyal: if an heir was born, then the Chebu Lama would be the Dewan of the next reign. [12]

In 1848 the British became involved in this conflict of Sikkim politics. In that year Dr. Joseph Hooker, the distinguished naturalist, came to Darjeeling to explore in the Himalayas, and to study its flora and its glaciers. On his behalf, and with the approval of Lord Dalhousie, the Governor-General, Campbell sought permission from the Sikkim Raja for Hooker to travel in his territories; but only after a prolonged wrangle, which sorely tried Campbell's temper, was Hooker allowed to enter Sikkim. These transactions were carried out through the Sikkim Vakil, or Agent, at Darjeeling, and Campbell had a shrewd suspicion that his letters had never reached the Raja of Sikkim, to whom they were addressed, but had been handed over to the Dewan. Campbell felt that he could never come to a satisfactory arrangement with Sikkim unless he could be sure of access to the Raja, and, accordingly, he obtained permission from Government to visit that ruler in Sikkim. In November 1848 he set out for Tumlong, then the Sikkim capital. On reaching the Tista River Campbell met Sikkim officials who objected to his crossing what was at that date the frontier between independent Sikkim and British territory. He was told that he could not see the Raja, who was completely absorbed in religious contemplation. On the next day he heard that the Raja was on his way to meet him, but Campbell was still prevented from crossing the Tista. A flood of reasons was then produced why he could not, in fact, meet the Raja. The Raja was once more engaged in religious exercises; he was too old to stand the strain of such a meeting; the bridge across the Tista was in too bad a state of repair to enable Campbell to travel over it; the Tibetans would object to the meeting, and so would the Bhutanese; and finally, the protocol of such meetings demanded that they should take at least two years to arrange.

Despite this formidable array of argument, Campbell eventually achieved his object and talked with the Raja face to face, having in the meantime been joined by Dr. Hooker. At the meeting with the Raja the Dewan was able to gain a small diplomatic victory by arranging that the presents which Campbell had brought for the Raja should be presented before the audience, thus giving to the visit the character of a tribute mission. No improvement of relations resulted from this encounter, but it did give Campbell information upon which he could form a more accurate interpretation of the politics of Sikkim. He realized that 'on the real nature of our power in India and England they are woefully ignorant and not a little misinformed', and that this was unlikely to be remedied until there was a Dewan who was sympathetic to the British, or a Vakil in Darjeeling who could be trusted to report faithfully to his Raja the views of the Indian Government.

When, in April 1849, a person who was clearly not desirable from the British point of view, the 'Lassoo Kajee', a staunch supporter from Namgyal, was made Sikkim Vakil at Darjeeling, Campbell realized that he must pay another visit to the Raja of Sikkim. Hooker was then making a second tour in Sikkim, and Campbell's plan was to join up with Hooker as before; but on this occasion they would travel together up to the Tibetan border.[13] Campbell was badly smitten by what amounted to an occupational disease among British officials along the Tibet frontier, a burning desire to see for himself that mysterious and forbidden land whose tantalizing proximity to British territory was a continual challenge to a man of Campbell's enterprise and determination. He hoped that his visit would provide him, at last, with the chance to satisfy this craving. As he wrote in his diary, on setting out for Sikkim: 'I can scarcely believe that I am really *en route* for Tibet. For 20 years it has been a primary object of my ambition to visit that land, of which so little is really known.' This aspect of the journey was clearly closer to his heart than any political settlement.[14]

In October Hooker and Campbell reached the Tibetan frontier, which they crossed by the Kangralama Pass, returning to Sikkim by the Donkya Pass. This they did despite protests from Sikkim officials and the tearful entreaties of the commander of a Tibetan frontier guard who begged, without avail, that they should turn back. No doubt this news was reported to Lhasa, where it could not have been favourably received. It was said, many years later, that the unfortunate Tibetan officer who had allowed this to happen paid for his negligence with his life. In November, Hooker and Campbell arrived at Tumlong, where, the Dewan then being in Tibet, they hoped for a more successful interview with the Raja; and they asked the Cehbu Lama to arrange an audience. But the Dewan's supporters prevented a meeting despite the Lama's efforts and the help of the family of the late Dewan, Ilam Singh. Campbell decided not to waste any time at Tumlong in fruitless intrigues. He set out with Hooker for the Chola Pass which led from Sikkim into the Chumbi Valley in Tibet and which he wanted to investigate as a possible route for Indian trade with Tibet. He hoped also that he might meet the Dewan, who was then said to be residing in the Raja of Sikkim's summer palace in Chumbi. Once over the pass and in Tibetan territory, the two travellers met a considerable body of Tibetan troops whose leader suggested, with all due courtesy, that they should retrace their steps. They were told, tactfully enough, that the other passes into Chumbi were at that time unusable. They had no choice but to turn back.

On the way back, while still on Tibetan soil, Hooker and Campbell came upon some Sikkim men commanded by a Sikkim official who had been, a few months before, exceptionally obstructive to Hooker. The Sikkim men addressed the two Englishmen with scant respect, ordering them rudely to get off Tibetan soil. They seemed bent on trying to provoke Hooker and Campbell into some ill-considered action which might oblige the Tibetans, who were still in sight, to lay hands on the two travellers. Campbell thought the Sikkim men were hoping that the Tibetans, once they had resorted to force against British officials, would find themselves committed to active support to the anti-British policy of the Dewan. No incident, however, developed. Instead, the commander of the Tibetans approached the Sikkim men and rebuked them for their incivility. He then escorted the two Englishmen to the frontier, where he said, his jurisdiction ended; and there he left them.

The Sikkimese, having failed to enlist the Tibetans on their side, resorted to more drastic action. Hooker and Campbell were set upon and arrested as soon as they were safely out of sight of the Tibetan troops. Campbell was subsequently tortured - bamboo cords were twisted rightly round his wrists - to try to force from him an agreement that the British would refrain in future from trying to exert their influence in Sikkim; but, with considerable courage, he refused to sign anything; if he did, he said, he would immediately be repudiated by his own Government. The Chebu Lama, who had accompanied Hooker and Campbell throughout this journey, was also arrested, and it was clear that the whole affair was a *coup d'état* by the Dewan Namgyal's faction. It is significant that Hooker was at this time left free and unmolested. The animosity of the Dewan's party was directed entirely against Campbell.

Hooker and Campbell were escorted back to Tumlong, Campbell being forced to march with his hands bound to the tail of a mule while Hooker was left free to go on collecting species of Himalayan rhododendron. On their arrival at the capital on 10th November, both travellers were locked up. Campbell was very much concerned at stories he had been told of a Sikkim army which was on its way to attack the settlement at Darjeeling. And, in fact, when news of these events reached that town there was considerable alarm. Wild rumours flew about that Sikkim had obtained Tibetan support and that a Tibetan army, some said over 50,000 men, was on the march to expel the British from Sikkim. There had been such alarms before, because, Hooker observed, the British residents at Darjeeling were 'ignorant of the pacific disposition of the Lepchas, and of the fact that there were not fifty muskets in the country, nor twenty men able to use them'.

On 20th November the Dewan returned from Chumbi, and the prisoners were then allowed to inform their Government of their plight. In reply the Sikkim authorities received a despatch worded in the strongest terms, such as they were 'accustomed to receive from Nepal, Bhutan or Lhassa, and such as alone commands attention from the half-civilized Indo-Chinese, who measure power by the firmness of tone adopted towards them', as Hooker put it. The Dewan began to see that his coup had failed, and at once his manner became more pleasant, whilst the families of the Chebu Lama and other members of his faction began to flock into Tumlong. The Dewan started to deny any responsibility for the outrage, pointing out that he was in Tibet when it took place. He offered to sell Hooker and Campbell ponies at a reduced price, tried to win their sympathy by feigning an injured leg, and 'altogether behaved in a most undignified manner'.

There continued to be delays in their release. It was alleged that the letter from the Governor-General did not bear the proper seals, and other unlikely excuses were brought forward. The next development was that the Raja sent presents to the captives, and the Rani sent Campbell a fan and other trifles to give to his wife. Finally, on 9th December, they set off under guard and accompanied by the Dewan, who was calmly going to visit Darjeeling to sell ponies, for the British frontier. On 24th December 1849 they reached Darjeeling.

The curious behaviour of the Dewan Namgyal in this episode was by no means atypical of the Tibetan attitude to international relations. Ashley Eden was to meet with similar treatment at the hands of the Bhutanese a few years later. Examples can be found of similar attempts to extract agreements by force in the relations of the Himalayan states to each other. In 1904 the Tibetans were to try to coerce the powerful Younghusband Mission with a show of force and a surprise attack with complete disregard for the manifest consequences of thus trifling with British might. Nor was Namgyal's behaviour without its subtlety. The British, as will be apparent shortly, had no wish to

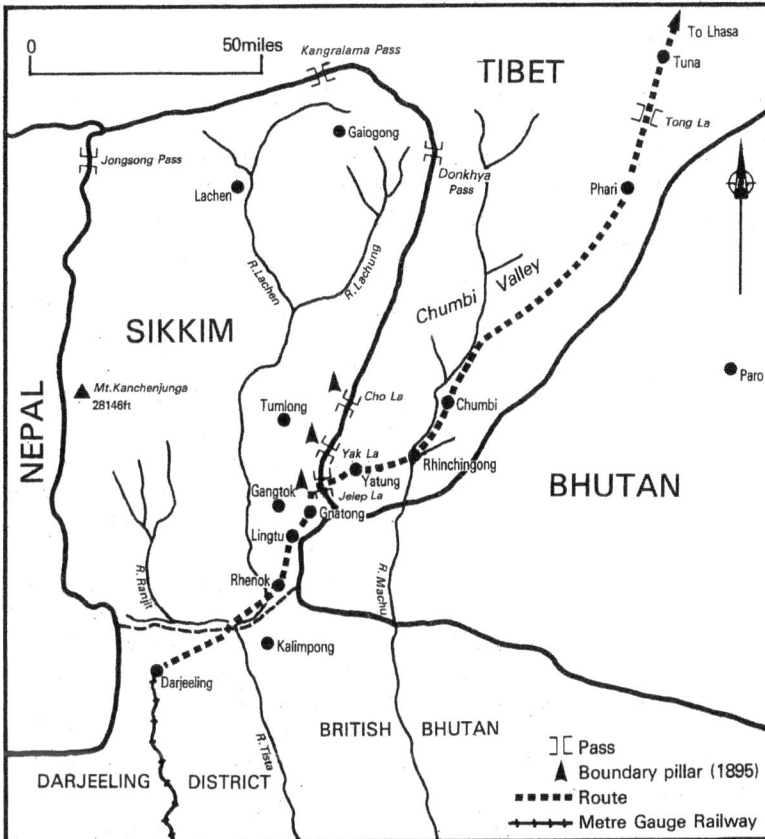

Sketch map of Sikkim

find themselves embroiled in a struggle with the Tibetans; had Namgyal managed to draw Tibet into his quarrel with Campbell, he might well have postponed the extension of British influence into Sikkim for many years. The imagined difficulties of hill warfare sufficed to make the British tolerate continual incidents along the Indo-Bhutanese frontier for nearly a century. As it was, the British reaction to the Hooker-Campbell incident was of surprising mildness.[15]

The allowance which the British had been paying since 1841 to Sikkim for the loss of Darjeeling - not as compensation, but as an act of grace - was stopped. The rest of Sikkim Morung (Terai) was annexed. A military expedition made a show of force along the Ranjit River, the new Indo-Sikkim frontier. The Chebu Lama became the Sikkim Vakil at Darjeeling. He was granted a large tract of land in the Darjeeling District, where he settled down to become for many years the unofficial adviser to the British on the affairs of Sikkim, Bhutan and Tibet. Throughout these proceedings Government was much influenced by the opinion of Sir Charles Napier that the hill country of Sikkim was quite unsuited to a campaign by European troops.[16]

In London the outrage on Hooker and Campbell was considered in quite a different light to that in which it had been regarded in India. There was no doubt that the cause of the affair lay in the two travellers' attempts to enter Tibet, which, in the eyes of the Political and Military Committee were, 'an infringement of Chinese regulations' and 'an act of grave indiscretion'. Far from being pitied, it was thought that Campbell should have been severely censured. One member went so far as to argue in favour of the action of Sikkim, noting that the crossing of the Tibetan frontier by Hooker and Campbell was 'an act certain to embroil the Sikkim Raja with the Chinese. A weak power between two great powers must doubly suffer - we seem to have punished the Sikkim Raja for his [Campbell's] offence.'[17] In fact, the affair might have had the most embarrassing consequences; if, for example, the rumours current in Darjeeling when news of the outrage was first received that Hooker and Campbell were about to be carried off to Lhasa had been well founded[18]: or if the Nepalese had persisted in their offers of military assistance in this crisis, thus creating the impression that the British were unable to manage their frontier without Gurkha help.[19] It is clear that there was no wish in London to exploit this affair as an excuse for the extension of British influence in the Himalayas.

As a result of the failure of his coup, Namgyal fell from power, but, according to Hooker, this was at the insistence of Tibet. He is said to have been rebuked by Lhasa in these terms:

> The Company is a great monarchy; you insulted it and it has taken its revenge. If you, or any other Tibetan, ever again cause a rupture with the English, you will be taken with a rope round your neck to Pekin, there to undergo the just punishment of your offence under the sentence of the mighty Emperor.[20]

But even Hooker did not take this report very seriously; the British had not seen the last of Namgyal, for considering his energy, a rare quality in these countries, I should not be surprised at his yet cutting a figure in Bhotan, if not in Sikkim itself; especially if, at the Rajah's death, the British Government should refuse to take the country under its protection.[21]

The Raja is also said to have retired in favour of his Lama son, and the faction of the Chebu Lama would seem to have been victorious. But within three or four years of the outrage the old Raja was again ruling through the Dewan Namgyal as if nothing had occurred. There was no improvement in the relations with the British and everything was as it had been before 1849, except that Sikkim had lost its low-lying possessions; though to a ruler who looked to Tibet in all things, it is doubtful whether the Terai held much importance. The one way in which this loss might have been felt, by resulting in a marked decrease in the revenues of the state, seems to have been offset by the Chinese and Tibetan authorities in Lhasa. Despite their rebuke to Namgyal, they appear to have come round to the view that the trouble with the British arose from the following of their instructions to exclude Europeans from Sikkim. Accordingly, they granted an annual subsidy to the Sikkim Government, to be paid in kind, in grain, salt and tea. They had cause to relent, for the action of Namgyal, in fact resulted in the keeping out of the British for a further ten years.[22]

The crisis of 1849 resulted in no great improvement in the relations between Darjeeling and independent Sikkim, and Dr. Campbell continued to look for an opportunity to avenge himself for those indignities to which he had been obliged to submit by the Dewan Namgyal. In March 1860 he decided to act, declaring that he could no longer tolerate the kidnappings by the followers of Namgyal of British subjects in the Darjeeling District. In November, with his usual impetuosity, he marched into Sikkim at the head of a company of native troops, intending to occupy a strip of Sikkim territory until the Raja made restitution for these fresh outrages, as Campbell described those incidents which had long been endemic on the Himalayan frontier. Campbell was suddenly attacked by Sikkim tribesmen and obliged to beat so rapid a retreat that all the baggage of his force had to be abandoned.[23]

However much Government might disapprove of Campbell's advance, for which it denied responsibility, it could hardly allow, for reasons of prestige, his discomfiture to go unavenged. It was decided to send an expedition into Sikkim, some 1,800 strong, commanded by Lt.-Col. Gawler, with Ashley Eden as Political Officer.[24] Namgyal was to be forced into exile. It was to be demonstrated to Sikkim that the British, if they wished, could make their influence felt in every corner of that State. But there was to be no question of annexing what remained of Sikkim, as Campbell had advocated in 1850 on the grounds that such an annexation would be the only way to give protection to those Sikkim subjects who might offer assistance to the British. Ashley Eden was instructed that the Governor-General 'does not wish that an independent state should cease to intervene between the British dominions and the vast regions and intractable people of Chinese Tartary'.[25] In other words, the Government were faced with the classic dilemma set out in 1864 in the famous memorandum of Prince Gorchakov; the frontier was disturbed by the peoples beyond, but an advance of the frontier merely brought an advance of the area of disturbance. In fact, when dealing with the primitive peoples of Central Asia, the problem often was not how to expand one's power but how to prevent its indefinite expansion. This very problem had arisen in connection with the Gurkha War. Now it was implicit in the Sikkim situation; if the British annexed Sikkim, who could say that a similar crisis would not arise in connection with Tibet, necessitating an even more arduous campaign?

The Sikkim expedition, both from a military and a political point of view, was reasonably successful. The Dewan was forced to flee into Tibet, though he was received here with some distinction. By a new treaty with the Raja all the British requirements were met. Namgyal was never again to set foot in Sikkim; free trade between Sikkim and British India was assured; Sikkim was to be opened to European travellers; the Sikkim Government was to assist the British in developing a trade through their country between India and Tibet, and for this purpose they were to help build roads to the Tibetan border. The Raja agreed not to reside in Tibet for more than three months in any one year and to devote himself more earnestly to the affairs of his state. The Chebu Lama was to remain the Sikkim Vakil in Darjeeling.[26] The British appeared to have lost nothing by not annexing outright this small state. In the long run, however, the continued theoretical independence of the Sikkim state was to have its own disadvantages. It was realized at the time that the Tibetans considered that they exercised some degree of suzerainty over Sikkim, but it was not known precisely what this amounted to. By failing to annex Sikkim, and by failing to define with precision what Sikkim's relations to her Tibetan neighbour were, or even where Sikkim stopped and Tibet began, the British, in effect, admitted that the Tibetans might have claims over this state. In years to come, when the British had come to assume that Sikkim formed part of the British Empire, they were embarrassed to find what a gulf still existed between Sikkim's *de jure* and *de facto* status.

But in 1861 there was no fault to be found with non-annexation. 'Had any other policy been pursued,' Eden wrote to Government, 'we should, I firmly believe, have been embroiled with the whole of the frontier and the Indo-Chinese States, and the result would have been a long, tedious, and most expensive war.' Sikkim, Bhutan, Nepal and Tibet had very close relations with each other. None of them showed that scrupulous concern over the observation of frontiers so characteristic of the British, and they tended to regard the British attempts to enforce treaty obligations as an example of their 'proverbial acquisitiveness'. It was this fear that resulted in the policy of excluding all Europeans; European travellers were looked on as spies, and surveying operations were considered the first step to invasion. But he felt that British moderation in Sikkim had aroused none of these fears. The Tibetans were convinced of British good faith. In a few years, Eden wrote:

> A very considerable trade will spring up between Lassa . . . and Darjeeling. The Thibetans will only be too glad to exchange gold dust, musk, borax, wool and salt for English cloth, tobacco, drill etc.; and the people of Sikkim will gain as carriers of this trade, and their government will raise a considerable revenue from the transit duties.

As a proof of Tibetan good will, Eden reported that a party of officers had recently been up to the Tibetan frontier at the Chola Pass, where they had been very courteously treated by the Tibetan frontier officials. All that was needed to produce this flourishing trade with Tibet was an annual fair at Darjeeling to which the Tibetans could bring their wares, and a good road to Tibet. A road from Darjeeling to the Tista had been built as a result of the expedition. The Sikkim Government had promised to help in its continuation to the Tibetan frontier at the Chumbi Valley, and they anticipated no difficulty in 'persuading the Thibetan authorities to repair the road between Phagri and the Chola pass, and beyond that there is an excellent road to Lhassa and Jigutishar [Shigatse]'.[27] Eden's optimism was quite unfounded.

The Sikkim campaign of 1861 was without doubt one of the

factors leading to the Bhutan War of 1865. By this time Bhutan had long ceased to be the important element in the attempts to develop trade and relations across the Himalayas that it had been in the time of Warren Hastings; but British officials who were directly responsible for the peace of the Indo–Bhutanese border continued to argue that the establishment of British relations with Lhasa might make their task easier. In 1792, presumably on orders from the north, Bhutan became closed to merchants from the Company's possessions who wished to pass through to Tibet. At that moment Bhutanese relations with the Company, never very satisfactory, began to deteriorate. The Indo–Bhutanese border became the scene of an interminable series of disputes and incidents which only increased in frequency when the British occupation of Assam in 1826 extended this troublesome frontier. The Bhutanese raided the foothills. They gave refuge to escaped criminals from British territory. They levied taxes on British dependants. The Company saw little prospect of a diplomatic solution to this continual friction, since it had come to appreciate the instability of the Bhutanese Government. Nominally under the control of the Deb Raja, an elected ruler, and of the Dharma Raja, an incarnation on the lines of the Dalai Lama of Tibet, Bhutan was in fact at the mercy of two of the more important chieftains, the Tongsa and Paro Penlops, who were almost continually at war either with one another or with their titular overlords.

There seemed but three solutions to the Bhutanese problem. A diplomatic settlement might be achieved by yet another mission to Bhutan in the footsteps of Bogle, Hamilton, Turner and Kishen Kant Bose. This was to be attempted twice more in the nineteenth century, in 1837 and in 1863; but in neither case, one suspects, with much hope of lasting success. A treaty could be imposed by force of arms and reinforced by the creation of a dependence among the Bhutanese chiefs on British subsidies: and this policy was followed with reasonable success in 1865. Finally, the Indian Government could try, as had Hastings, to exercise some measure of control over Bhutan through the mediation of the authorities in Tibet. This possibility had the advantage of cheapness. It seemed likely, moreover, that the Tibetans and Chinese were no more in favour of Bhutanese chaos than were the British. There was a chance, therefore, that Lhasa might welcome British offers of assistance in the controlling of this turbulent dependency and that, as in 1774, Bhutan would prove to be the instrument for closer relations between Tibet and British India. In this sense Bhutan might indeed become a means to the

82

improvement of Indo-Tibetan trade, even if the trade route did not lie through its territory. So thought Major Hopkinson, Commissioner and Governor-General's Agent for the North-East Frontier, when he wrote in 1861 that the establishment of a permanent British agent in Bhutan 'would be the best instrument for paving the way for friendly intercourse with Lhasa'.[28]

Jenkins, who occupied the North-East Frontier Agency during much of the 1830s and 1840s, was an ardent advocate of a policy of this sort. In 1837 relations between the Bhutanese and the British had so deteriorated that it seemed essential to make some attempt to reach a settlement. Captain R. B. Pemberton was deputed to Bhutan to do his best to secure a treaty from its rulers. In his account of this venture, which appeared in 1838, Pemberton described at length the series of trivial, but none the less intensely irritating, incidents which led up to the decision to try once more where Bogle, Hamilton, Turner and Kishen Kant Bose had failed to achieve lasting results. One issue in particular was directed to Pemberton's attention. The Bhutanese had for long been in the habit of levying tribute - Jenkins called it 'black mail' - from their neighbours in British territory. This practice seems to have owed its origins to traditional relationships extending back to a period long before the English first set foot in India, and it appeared to Jenkins that it might best be discussed in co-operation with Lhasa. As he wrote to Lord Auckland in April 1837:

> It appears to me that it would be a good opportunity if I were to address the Dalai Lama or the Governor of Lhassa to whom I believe they are all subject, inviting him to send a person to settle these disputes and to arrange for the collection of the black mail on a less objectionable footing than has hitherto prevailed.

At the same time, he added, it might be as well to remark on 'the wish of our government for the restoration of the friendly intercourse and traffic that formerly existed between Assam and Tibet'. He wondered whether Lord Auckland knew the correct forms of address for letters to the Dalai Lama and the Chinese Governor at Lhasa.[29]

Lord Auckland welcomed these proposals, which at once reminded his government of the mission of Turner. But he regretted that 'the records of this office do not furnish the means of supplying you with the proper titles of the Dalai Lama or the Chinese Governor of Lhassa', Jenkins had best 'have recourse to the best available authorities in your neighbourhood'.[30] A letter to

the Dalai Lama was drafted in English, reminding that theocrat of
the friendship that had subsisted between Tibet and the Company
in the time of Warren Hastings.[31] These references to the mission
of Bogle and Turner, of course, turned Jenkins' thoughts towards
further plans for the revival of Indo–Tibetan trade. 'There can be
little doubt', he observed, 'that if we could establish a perfectly
free intercourse with Tibet the commerce of that country would
become as valuable to us if not superior to that carried on with
any neighbouring state.' There was slight chance of this at
present, but Jenkins did not see why some arrangement should
not be made 'for the promotion and extension of the present petty
commerce by the establishment of periodical fairs along our
frontier at which the Tibetan caravans might be prevailed upon to
meet our merchants'.[32] With these ideas in mind, Pemberton was
told to try, once he arrived in Bhutan, to make his way 'to the
Dalai Lama and the Rajah of Thibet', though on this point 'much
caution must be exercised'.[33] As might have been guessed from
the experience gained on the frontier of Western Tibet, Pemberton
found that he had not the slightest hope of getting through to
Lhasa. His negotiations in Bhutan were hardly more successful,
since the treaty which he secured was ignored by the Bhutanese
from the moment that it was signed.

Jenkins, however, did not forget the project of 1837. Ten years
later, when there was some hope of a meeting between British,
Tibetan and Chinese commissioners in Western Tibet, and when
Strachey was proposing to set out for Lhasa by way of Gartok, he
returned to this theme. The immediate problem now was in East
Bhutan and the Assam hills, that area sometimes referred to as the
Tawang Tract, where Jenkins and other British officials in Assam
had for many years seen a possible trade route to Tibet. Here, as
in Kumaon, British territory, in theory at least, extended up to
the Tibetan border, and a route here would be unobstructed by
independent hill states. Were the petty chieftains of this hill
district, who mostly owed some sort of traditional allegiance to
Tibet, to realize that the British had established diplomatic
relations with Lhasa, they might well be more co-operative in the
matter of opening up trade routes. Jenkins hoped, therefore, that
one of the British officers from the Boundary Commission might
be authorized to make his way back to India through Tibet and
Assam. Should this be impracticable, he asked permission to send
an officer of his own to Lhasa through Tawang. Government felt
that any member of the Boundary Commission who might reach
Lhasa would only do so in a private capacity, and thus be
ineligible for work of the type proposed by Jenkins; but there was

no objection to Jenkins sending his own man to the Tibetan capital if he could.[34]

Once more, an imaginative proposal was proved to be unworkable in practice, and was abandoned. There was, however, sufficient political sense behind schemes of this sort to ensure their revival from time to time. Bhutan did owe some measure of allegiance to Tibet, as did many of the hill tribes of the Assam Himalaya.[35] With political contact with Tibet went traditional commercial associations. There had been a considerable trade between Assam and Tibet through the agency of some of the Assam hill tribes in the years before the British occupation of Assam in 1826. The change in the political status of Assam seems to have affected this trade in the same way that similar changes in Nepal affected the trade with Bengal and in Ladakh disrupted the shawl trade. After 1826 British officers in Assam tried from time to time to revive this trade. In 1833, for example, Lt. Rutherford opened a mart at Udalguri in the Darrang District in hopes of attracting merchants from Tibet and from the hills. The Mönpas and other Buddhist hill tribes of the Tawang tract held a particularly important position in the trade across the Assam Himalaya between Tibet and the plains. Since 1844 a subsidy had been paid by the British to certain chiefs in this tract which the Indian Government certainly considered at this time to be under Tibetan rule. A crisis on the Tawang-Assam border in the 1850s disturbed trade for a while; and there were further problems in 1864. In 1872-3 the Tawang-Assam border, running along the edge of the plains a few miles north of Udulguri, was demarcated by Major Graham, Deputy Commissioner for Darrang, and some Tibetan officials from either Tawang monastery or its mother house in Lhasa, Drebung. This unique act of Anglo-Tibetan border definition appears to have secured lasting peace along this sector of frontier.[36]

The Assam route to Tibet continued to be discussed from time to time throughout the nineteenth century. As will be seen shortly, T.T. Cooper tried to approach Tibet by this route in 1869. The possibilities of the Brahmaputra Valley as the great high road to Tibet were remarked on by several observers, and not only by those who had no more knowledge of the terrain than that provided by small-scale maps. Needham and Molesworth, with first-hand experience of the Assam hills, argued in this sense in 1886.[37] As will be seen, at the time of the Younghusband Mission there was some discussion of the possible opening of a trade mart on the Tibet side of the Assam frontier, perhaps at Zayul. And in 1908 Sir Thomas Holdich still thought that the best approach to Tibetan markets lay along the Brahmaputra.[38] It is true that the hill trade of Assam was by 1876, when the first figures were kept, an important element in the economic life of that region. But there seemed to be little reason for hope that it would ever develop into the great trans-Himalayan commerce of the more visionary writers. The Assam Himalaya is by no means easy to penetrate, and it is inhabited by a variety of extremely warlike tribes. There never was a route through it to compare with that through Nepal or Sikkim, and it possessed no hill station like Simla or Darjeeling to focus British attention on its possibilities.

One can, on the whole, look on the Assam-Tibet border in the nineteenth century as an interesting sideline in the story of Anglo-Tibetan relations. Not so, however, with Bhutan. While this state was not, in the nineteenth century, to provide a route to Lhasa, it was to retain some importance as a factor in the conduct of relations across the Sikkim-Tibet frontier. Its proximity to the point where the Sikkim route crossed into Tibet tended to keep it before British eyes; and its close historical association with Sikkim meant that Bhutanese reactions could never be overlooked for long in British dealings with that small hill state. And finally, as Major Hopkinson said, Bhutan might yet have a part to play in the establishment of British influence in Lhasa, if only a passive one. After the Sikkim campaign the Bhutanese gave asylum to many of the friends and followers of the now exiled Dewan Namgyal, and they refused to surrender them to British justice. This fact provided the immediate excuse for the deputation, in 1863, of Ashley Eden to a mission to Bhutan. Eden intended not only to make an attempt to settle those many border disputes which had by no means disappeared after Pemberton's visit of 1837, but also to try to use Bhutan as a jumping-off point for some attempt at closer contact with Lhasa. Lord Elgin, the Governor-General, who had a personal interest in the attempts to penetrate the Himalayan barrier, and who was shortly to lose his life while inspecting the trade routes of Lahul,[39] gave thought to accrediting Eden to the Dalai Lama and to securing for him some document from the Chinese Emperor; though this project was abandoned in the face of practical difficulties.[40] The results of Eden's mission, in any case, put off for a while any further plans for the exploitation of Bhutan in this sense, though British officials continued to look to Tibet as a possible aid in controlling Bhutan. Eden was maltreated by the Bhutanese in a manner very reminiscent of the way in which Campbell suffered at the hands of Namgyal's faction in 1849. But, unlike 1849, the Indian

Government, with the example of the Sikkim campaign of 1861 before it, no longer feared to embark on a military expedition into the Himalayas. War with Bhutan broke out in 1865, and it was destined to settle the shape of Anglo-Bhutanese relations for many years to come. In the first place, the Bhutanese gave a far better account of themselves than had the men of Sikkim. The British, indeed, suffered a surprising series of initial reverses. In the second place, the treaty produced by the final British victory gave reasonable promise of controlling the most turbulent of the Bhutanese chiefs, the Tongsa Penlop, through the payment of a substantial subsidy. After 1865 anxiety continued as to the stability of Bhutan, but the Indian Government preferred to rely on British gold to keep Bhutan in line, and showed no desire to test again the military prowess of those hardy hillmen by meddling with a political settlement that seemed to be working reasonably enough. It realized, moreover, that Lhasa had watched the war with Bhutan with a close interest recalling that of the Tashi Lama in 1774, and may have even given the Bhutanese more than moral support. It seemed clear that a fresh outbreak of war with Bhutan would find no favour in Tibet, and might even undo those results, however slight, of patient diplomacy on the Sikkim-Tibet frontier.[41]

V

THE SIKKIM ROUTE

.

1861 – 1874

THE SIKKIM Treaty of 1861 took place at a period when a number of events were working together to focus attention in India and in England on the Tibet trade and on routes by which it might be tapped. The Treaty coincided with the final stages of the opening of China, and this fact, of course, suggested that Chinese assistance might at last be forthcoming for the establishment of some sort of British representation at Lhasa. Already in 1857, when Lord Elgin was on his way to China, B. H. Hodgson urged that the British Ambassador should seek from the Chinese the right for a representative of the Indian Government to reside in Lhasa, or, failing that, Chinese help in the creation of a regular trade mart somewhere on the Indo-Tibetan border, where Indian and Tibetan traders could meet to exchange their wares.[1] In 1861, with British Legation established in Peking, suggestions of this kind were to become increasingly frequent.

In the years immediately preceding the Sikkim campaign of 1861 the advantages of Sikkim as a trade route between Bengal and Tibet had received considerable publicity. Hodgson, who had long advocated the extension of British trade to Tibet from his vantage point at Katmandu, now in his retirement in Darjeeling advised development of the road through Sikkim. Dr. Campbell, who looked on Darjeeling as his own creation, lost no opportunity to press for an improvement in the conditions of trade and travel in the Himalayas, 'which would greatly improve the resources of Darjeeling and add to its attractions as a Sanatorium'.[2] The hands of these two men can be detected behind the report of W. B. Jackson of the Bengal Civil Service on trade between Darjeeling and Tibet, which appeared in 1854 and enjoyed a wide circulation.

The report argued that the route to Tibet from Darjeeling could be of considerable commercial importance. In 1854, despite the many restrictions and duties imposed in Sikkim and Tibet, trade on this road had a value of Rs. 50,000 p.a.; once free of all obstacles, there was no telling to what value it might attain. British manufactures could be exchanged for Tibetan gold, salt and a wool which was said to equal the quality of the finest Australian merino, and to excel it in length of staple.[3] This report led the *Calcutta Review* to remark in 1857 that Darjeeling was 'cast in our way for a higher purpose than that of securing health and recreation for the sick and the weary from the scorching plains of India'; it was the gateway through which the commerce and civilization of the West could reach the barbarous expanses of Central Asia.[4] Its publication coincided with a growing awareness that the tea industry which was so rapidly developing in Kumaon, Darjeeling, British Bhutan and Assam might have a valuable outlet for its produce among the avid tea drinkers of Tibet in favourable competition with the brick tea of Szechuan, separated from its markets by such a long and arduous road.[5] It also came at a time when the English Chambers of Commerce were just beginning to appreciate the potentialities of the markets of the Chinese interior; an appreciation which, in the 1860s, was going to give rise to ambitious plans for developing communications between India and the Chinese Empire, and to subject the India and Foreign Offices to a bombardment of memorials. The most popular route was from Burma to Yunnan, often suggested as a line for a railway; but Tibet came into its share of attention.

The opening of China gave great encouragement to those missionaries who had for many years been knocking at the doors of Tibet. In 1838 the Protestant Gützlaff had urged the conversion of the Tibetans from their worship of Buddha under the leadership of the Dalai Lama, a 'Moloch in human shape - a worthless abject being'.[6] In the 1840s the Church of England Missionary Society began its labours on the Tibetan border with the founding of mission stations at Darjeeling in 1842 and at Kotgarh on the Sutlej in the following year.[7] The Moravians, who had been working with Mongol peoples since they founded a settlement on the Volga in 1765, and who had tried in the first decades of the nineteenth century to penetrate Tibet from China,

89

by Government invitation settled down in the 1850s among the Tibetan-speaking people of Lahul and Spiti to do good works and to study the Tibetan language. Here they remained until Indian Independence, and a number of local industries, the knitting of socks for one, survive to testify to their zeal.[8] The Catholics, of course, with their memories of their earlier achievements in Tibet and Nepal, made the most determined attempts to enter the forbidden land. In 1846 the two Lazarists, Huc and Gabet, made their astonishing journey to Lhasa, and in that year the Catholic Mission to Tibet was revived under French auspices. It was to remain very much a French preserve, and to become, so some cynical British Consuls in West China thought, an instrument of French imperialism. In the 1850s the French Fathers made a number of attempts to emulate the feat of Huc and Gabet. Desgodins tried to enter Tibet from Ladakh and from Sikkim and Nepal. Krick and Boury made a gallant attempt through Assam, in which they lost their lives at the hands of Mishmi tribals. In 1854 Fage and Renou established, albeit precariously, a mission settlement at Bonga, just on the border of Eastern Tibet. From their base in Szechuan Province the French Fathers gave much encouragement to would-be Tibetan explorers. Realizing that their best hope for entering Tibet was in the train of foreign merchants and diplomats, they were loud in support of the many schemes of the Indian Government to bring itself into closer contact with Lhasa. They studied the language, industry and politics of Tibet, and some of them, like Desgodins, became much-valued advisers to the British in India. They were strong protagonists of the argument that the Tibetans were eager to throw off not only the yoke of Chinese rule but also the oppressive burden of subservience to the Lamas and the Monasteries. And this was to be a thesis which was destined, as the nineteenth century drew to a close, to influence greatly the thinking of British officials concerned with the conduct of the Indo-Tibetan border.[9]

The improvement of the British diplomatic position in China, the commercial agitation in England and in India for the opening up to British trade of the Chinese interior, the British acquisition by the Sikkim Treaty of 1861 of access to the Tibetan border along one of the shortest routes to Lhasa, the loudly expressed wish to various missionary bodies to bring the Gospel to the benighted inhabitants of the roof of the world, all these factors in combination could but cause the Indian Government to give more serious thought to a mission to the Tibetan capital than it had since the days of the Gurkha War. It should, therefore, cause no surprise that in 1861 the Indian Government sanctioned the sending of a British mission to Lhasa, provided passports could be obtained for it from the Chinese Government at Peking.

The proposed mission to Tibet of 1861 emerged from a suggestion of Captain E. Smyth of the Bengal Army, who was then serving in the Kumaon Education Department. Smyth had proposed in May 1860 that he should be deputed to explore 'Chinese Tartary N.E. of Ladak', but it was not until he had interested the Royal Geographical Society in London, and not until the Sikkim campaign had been waged and won, that his plans received any official support.[10] When Smyth again approached the Indian Government in February 1861, he found them most receptive to his proposals. His plan was that he and several companions, two of whom at least having a scientific training, should be granted indefinite leave to undertake the exploration of Tibet and of Chinese Turkestan up to the Russian frontier. Government should supply him with a liberal quantity of suitable gifts, and should seek from the newly established British Minister in Peking the necessary passports for travel in Tibet. The Indian Government, while generally approving of the proposed expedition, could not say under exactly what conditions Smyth would be travelling until the matter had been referred to Peking. It observed that Lord Elgin had, not so long ago, asked the Governor-General 'that great caution should be used in allowing officers to enter Chinese Tartary'.[11]

Smyth's plan was, basically, of the same type as those put forward at the time of the Boundary Commission of Cunningham, Agnew and Strachey. But, unlike Strachey's projected journey to Lhasa, which was little more than an expression of optimism, the Smyth expedition developed into a serious project almost comparable to the later scheme of Colman Macaulay. Three officers, Lt. D'Aguilar Jackson of the Bengal Engineers, Dr. I. L. Stewart of the Bengal Medical Service and J. S. Medlicott of the Geological Survey, were deputed by Government to accompany Smyth in May 1861; and a month later the party was increased to seven with the addition of three more officers, Major T. Jerdon, Capt. P. Lumsden and Capt. J. P. Basevi. The plan was for Smyth and his original three companions to enter Tibet from Kumaon, while the other three would travel by way of Sikkim. Both parties, it was hoped, would meet up with each other in Lhasa. Bruce, the newly established British Minister in Peking, was asked to get Chinese passports for the two groups. The Indian Government, after the Treaty of Tientsin, anticipated no difficulty in this and it wondered whether, in the case of subsequent Tibetan ventures, it would suffice to write to the British Consul in Canton for the necessary travel documents.[12]

Smyth's plans coincided with those of Captain Blakiston, now on his way from Hankow with the intention of travelling up the Yangtze to Szechuan, and thence, if possible, to India via Tibet.[13] Bruce thought that Smyth should wait until the outcome of Blakiston's venture was known. In any case, Bruce neither thought the Tientsin Treaty applied to British travellers wishing to enter Tibet, nor did he consider it to be the right time to raise this matter with the Chinese authorities.[14] This reply, which was to be characteristic of the answer Bruce's successors were to make to similar queries, with the clear implication that the unknown benefits of trade with an obscure Chinese dependency did not justify the risk of straining Anglo-Chinese diplomatic relations, decided the Indian Government to postpone the Smyth Expedition for the moment.

The hopeful tone of Eden's report on the conclusion of the Sikkim Campaign suggested that a flourishing trade might spring up between Indian and Tibet through Sikkim without any reference to the Chinese at Peking. There were signs confirming this optimism; it was even said that the Ambans had announced publicly in Lhasa that 'the English are permitted to visit Lhasa', and that an Imperial Edict had been posted in a public place to this effect, requesting that 'if any English Gentlemen make their appearance there, they are to be treated with courtesy and kindness and are to receive assistance from the local authorities'. So, at least, a Kashmiri merchant engaged on a regular trade between Lhasa and Katmandu told Ramsay, the British Resident in Nepal.[15] The Indian Government seems to have taken this sort of information seriously enough. It saw fit, at any rate, to allow Smyth to set out into Western Tibet in 1863 without any Chinese passports.

Smyth, of course, was told to go cautiously. He was authorized only to cross over into those very remote regions opposite the Kumaon border, and only then on the understanding that he would return to India if the Tibetans asked him to; and this is just what happened. His experiences, however, were most instructive. The local Tibetan frontier officials said that they could only let Smyth pass with express authority from the local seat of government, Gartok; but they would not let Smyth go to that place. They said, however, that all Smyth's difficulties would have disappeared had he possessed a passport issued in Peking. Smyth concluded that he might have made some progress with bribes, but these he refused to give. He was certain that with the proper passports he could have gone where he liked in Tibet, even to Lhasa. He thought that a mission to Lhasa would be the sure way of improving Indo-Tibetan trade. Smyth, in fact, had put his finger on a vicious circle of diplomacy which was destined to vex the Indian Government until 1886, when certain fallacies were revealed. The only way to bring about a big improvement in Indo-Tibetan trade was by a mission to Lhasa. The Tibetans would welcome such a mission if it possessed Chinese passports. These could only be obtained through the British Minister in Peking, and he felt that it would greatly strain Anglo-Chinese relations if he were to press too hard for documents which the Chinese were clearly reluctant to issue.[16]

The Indian Government at this period and right up to the 1880s tended to overestimate the Chinese strength in Tibet, just as it later on was disposed to ignore unduly the influence in Tibetan politics of the Amban. It was certainly true that the Taiping Rebellion and the wars with the Powers had seriously weakened Chinese control over the outlying portions of the Empire. In the 1860s direct Chinese rule was steadily disappearing in Eastern Tibet, always a centre of revolt,[17] and there is evidence to suggest that in Lhasa the great monasteries were fostering anti-Chinese sentiment. In these circumstances the Chinese were most unlikely to do anything so obviously calculated to bring on a general revolt under the leadership of the Lama hierarchy as to agree to open Tibet to European travel. The Chinese, however, were not as politically incompetent as some Europeans observers thought, and diplomatic skill made up to some extent for military weakness. The Dalai Lama, on whose person would inevitably devolve the leadership of a general Tibetan rising, was never permitted to reach his majority; somehow, until the time of the 13th Incarnation, he seemed to die shortly before or after his eighteenth birthday. Chinese gold was skilfully expended to buy the friendship of some, at least, of the monasteries. The Tibetans were dependent to a great extent on trade with China on which they relied for the supply of that tea to which they were so addicted. The adjustable taxing of the Tibetan tea trade, and the toleration of its tendency to become a monopoly of the monks, were powerful political weapons. Finally, the prestige of Chinese military power, so high in the days of Ch'ien Lung, had not quite disappeared. In the next few years, with the suppression of revolts in Chinese Turkestan and in Yunnan, it was even to revive somewhat. Gabet was no doubt correct when in 1854 he told Sir John Bowring, Governor of Hong Kong, 'that the Chinese yoke was oppressive to the Tibetans, and that they would avail themselves of any favourable occasion to revolt against their masters'.[18] But such an occasion was still in the distant future; it was not to arise until the Chinese Revolution of 1911. It is certain that in the second half of the nineteenth century the Chinese would have done nothing, if they could possibly help it, to pave the way for a British mission to Lhasa; it is equally certain that they could have done little to stop such a mission if it were pushed forward with determination and suitably escorted.

This contradiction between the reality of Chinese military weakness and the survival of Chinese prestige doubtless goes far to explain the Nepalese attitude towards Tibet. Nepal probably possessed the military strength and skill to occupy Lhasa, though it did not, perhaps, have the financial resources to maintain such an occupation for an extended period. The Tibetans had a healthy respect for the Gurkha army, which had won from them in 1856 an annual tribute and the right to station a Nepalese resident at Lhasa. They were treated to periodic exhibitions of Nepalese strength in the shape of the Tribute Missions to Peking which the Gurkhas had been obliged to send once every five years by the treaty of 1792. Neither the Chinese nor the Tibetans held much affection for these tribute missions. The Chinese saw them as a threat to Tibetan independence (from everybody except China) and resented the frankly commercial nature they had taken in recent years. The Tibetans, with good cause, suspected Nepal of harbouring ambitions of Tibetan conquest. The passage of a Nepalese tribute mission through Tibet was frequently accompanied by strained Tibeto-Nepalese relations. The mission of 1852-54 had been so rudely treated in Tibet and China that no further mission was sent for twelve years, during which period the Gurkhas fought and won their third war with Tibet, a fact which did not gain them much favour in the eyes of Peking and Lhasa. In August 1866 Nepal decided to resume its traditional relations with China, but the Tribute Mission of that year, which did not return to Katmandu until 1869, was a failure in many respects. Originally, it will be remembered, the Tribute Mission had been imposed on Nepal as a symbol of Chinese supremacy in the Himalayas. By the middle of the nineteenth century, however, this aspect had been overshadowed by the Gurkha discovery that these missions could bring much profit. The mission of 1866, for example, carried with it over £45,000 worth of opium, with which the Nepalese ruling families hoped to do good trade in Peking. The Chinese refusal to buy caused much annoyance in Katmandu, and this fact, coupled with the many petty insults which the Nepalese envoys were obliged to suffer, resulted in considerable tension along the Tibeto-Nepalese border. The Tibetans, of course, were eager for an opportunity to bring

94

Chinese support to their side in an attempt to avenge their defeat in 1856. But it was only once, in 1854-56, that the Tibetans and the Gurkhas came to actual blows. It may well be that the lesson of 1792, that a major Himalayan crisis could have unforeseen consequences, tended towards peace.[19]

The French Fathers in Szechuan and Eastern Tibet seem to have been quick to see that Tibeto-Nepalese tensions could be exploited to their own advantage. They badly needed some means of putting pressure on the authorities in Tibet who had done all in their power to resist missionary enterprise. The Nepalese Tribute Mission, which was delayed for several months in 1867 in Eastern Tibet while awaiting permission to enter China, seemed a heaven-sent gift for this purpose. It could carry back messages to the British Residency in Katmandu and thus bring to the notice of the Indian Government the intolerable persecutions and obstructions to which the Fathers were subjected. It might also be exploited to further embroil the Gurkhas with Tibet, and it must have seemed that Tibet under Nepalese control could hardly be more hostile to the missionaries than it was at present under the Chinese. With this last possibility in mind the Fathers sent letters by messengers of the Nepalese Mission to Colonel Ramsay, Resident at Katmandu. One of these letters, containing a graphic account of the insults which had been hurled at the Nepalese Mission by the Tibetans, was intended for the eyes of Sir Jang Bahadur, the Prime Minister of Nepal. Ramsay, prudently, did not pass on this missive 'because some parts of the French document are of a rather bellicose tendency'. While the scheme of the Fathers failed to provoke a Tibeto-Nepalese crisis of any value to them, it did succeed in bringing the light of considerable publicity to shine on their sufferings. Their letters to Ramsay and Sir Jang Bahadur were published in Catholic journals in India and in France. Copies of them were sent to the Emperor Napoleon III and, perhaps more realistically, to the British Minister in Peking. The Royal Geographical Society in London took note of this correspondence. The Indian Government tried hard to establish regular contact with the Fathers, and attempts were made to get messages through to them from India by way of the Nepalese Resident in Lhasa and through the agency of certain tribal chiefs in the Assam Himalaya. Thus the French fathers stimulated discussion of the opening of Tibet in a number of widely separated places.[20]

The Fathers were skilled in advocacy. They produced arguments in favour of the advantages of opening Tibet, and they were optimistic about the ease with which this would be accomplished. Tibetan opposition to European travel, so they

said, was due to the machinations of the Lamas, those unen-
lightened oppressors of the poor who aimed at nothing but the
preservation of their hold over the minds of the superstitious
Tibetans. 'People of Thibet', the Fathers wrote to Ramsay in their
quaint English, 'is so slave of powerful men that his deeds are to
be counted as nothing, but we know his good feelings for religion
as well as for Europeans. We know very well that he would feel
very glad had he become freed from the heavy yoke of the
Lamas.'[21] It is an extraordinary fact that this line of reasoning was
to be accepted by the majority of Indian Government officers
concerned with the Tibetan border, and that Younghusband was
to write memoranda in this sense. The concept, of course, was
attractive, but its wide spread must to a great extent be attributed
to the persuasiveness of the French Fathers. Their doctrine greatly
influenced T. T. Cooper, for instance, and through his writings
gained considerable publicity.[22]

Cooper, who described himself as a 'pioneer of commerce', set
out from Shanghai in early 1868, with the knowledge and support
of the British merchant community there, to travel overland to
India by way of Burma or Tibet. He failed to complete this
journey by either route, but he did penetrate some way into
Eastern Tibet. He hoped, at one time, to travel to Lhasa in
company with the Nepalese Tribute Mission, and even persuaded
the Nepalese Ambassador who headed the Mission to seek,
unsuccessfully, permission for this from the Tibetan Government.
He found the French Fathers in Szechuan and Eastern Tibet most
helpful. They fed him with information. They gave him
introductions to Chinese officials, and they managed even to get
him a passport from the Viceroy of Szechuan which authorized
him to enter Tibet, though the Tibetans, needless to say, refused
to honour this document just as they were to ignore similar pieces
of paper in years to come. Indeed, it is most probable that here is
to be found the reason why the Chinese ever issued passports for
Tibet: the Chinese knew that they were quite valueless. So helpful
and encouraging were the French Missionaries that Cooper
shrewdly concluded that they were trying to push him on into
Tibet in the hope that he would be arrested, thus forcing the
British to exert themselves in this area.[23] Cooper's Tibetan
journey did, in fact, give rise to much diplomatic argument. It
became something of a trial to successive British Ministers at
Peking, Sir Rutherford Alcock and Sir Thomas Wade; but, to the
disappointment of the French Fathers, it resulted in no British
intervention in Tibet, though it did add to British awareness of
that region.[24] Cooper was not daunted by his failure to reach India

from China. In 1869 he tried again, but in reverse, setting out from Sadya in Assam with the intention of making his way across the Assam Himalaya into Eastern Tibet. He was again turned back by the Tibetans, but not before he had concluded that this route offered great possibilities for an expansion of Indian commerce.

Cooper's writings on the commerce of Tibet are of greatest importance. In a 'Memorandum on Trade between India and China', which he read to the Calcutta Chamber of Commerce in March 1869, he summarized his conclusions. He did not see much prospect in the trade routes between Burma and Western China, routes much discussed at this time. The Yangtze, he felt, was the natural artery of commerce in this region, and a route at right angles to the great river would never have much economic value. The Tibetan route, however, was another matter. Cooper described the road from Lhasa to Chengtu in Szechuan by way of Tachienlu as 'the great highway along which the Chinese send their brick-tea, beads and tobacco into Central Asia, getting in exchange sheep, rhubarb, deer, horn for hatshorn, skins, musk and a variety of medicines'. The opening up of a route from British India to Central or Eastern Tibet would tap this great trade road. Cooper, moreover, felt 'little diffidence' in pointing out the political significance of such an enterprise. The British would find themselves in contact with Tibet, Mongolia and Western China, and would thus have the opportunity to extend their influence into these regions. But even if the political side was a bit visionary, no one could deny the real commercial advantage of being able to cut in on the Chinese tea trade with Tibet. Tibet, Cooper estimated, consumed annually 6,000,000 lb. of Chinese brick-tea, mainly produced in Szechuan Province. Could this but be replaced by the tea of India, and here would be a market of great value. This idea, that Indian tea could find a ready sale beyond the Himalayas, was an attractive one.[25] It had been considered before. Campbell and others had given thought to this possibility from the moment when tea was first planted in the Darjeeling District. Cooper, however, was the first person to give wide publicity to this prospect in India and in England, and his advocacy of this point was to have a profound effect on the subsequent shape of Anglo-Tibetan relations, though not, perhaps, to the extent that has sometimes been suggested.

Cooper did not think that the tea trade of Tibet would fall into Indian hands without a struggle. The Tibetan Lamas held a virtual monopoly of the Chinese tea imported into Tibet, and they were not likely to welcome the loss of this great source of revenue. It provided considerable revenue from export duties imposed at Tachienlu, the effective frontier between Szechuan and Eastern Tibet; and it was useful to their position in Lhasa as a means of transmitting funds there, for the practice had long existed of remitting duties at Tachienlu against payment in Lhasa. Remission of duties was also a convenient method of bribing the Lhasa monasteries who all engaged to some extent in this trade. British commerce would not find its way into ·Tibet, Cooper was convinced, 'until a British Minister resides in Lhasa, and the Lamas have been taught their utter helplessness when actually brought into contact with a British force'. Cooper, perhaps on the advice of the French missionaries, did not see that the establishment of a British Mission in Lhasa in this way would be an act of unjustified aggression. Far from it. The Tibetan laity would welcome their liberation from Lama oppression and their gratitude would make the British, 'in all but name', the real masters of Tibet. No time was to be lost if such a policy were to succeed. The Tibetan authorities, already frightened of the British, and always eager to free themselves from Chinese control, would sooner or later seek aid from a foreign power, and 'Russia, who is close at hand, will not be behind when an opportunity offers in making herself master of Central Asia'.

The French missionary influence behind these arguments is clearly indicated in Appendix I to Cooper's book, *Travels of a Pioneer of Commerce*, where there is printed a memorandum on Tibet by 'an old resident in Western China', who was none other than Mgr. Cheauveau, Vicar Apostolic of Lhasa and head of the French missions in Western China and Eastern Tibet. The French prelate argued that China was on the verge of collapse. Who should then take her place in Central Asia? The United States had no influence on this part of the world; France was a European power with no colonial destiny; and the 'Russian yoke is the most oppressive and tyrannical in existence'. It must follow that 'England is the only power sufficiently strong and wealthy to unite China and Thibet with India'; she alone had the skill, perseverance and experience in 'colonial questions' required to carry out this work. Chungking with its river communication with the sea, commanded the access to Lhasa which was 'undoubtedly the most attractive point in all higher or Central Asia'. Control of Lhasa meant influence throughout Central Asia, for Lhasa was the Mecca of the Buddhist world. Chungking, moreover, also commanded the trade of Yunnan which, while not so valuable as that of Tibet, was still an attractive prize. The way to Central Asian domination, the 'old resident' concluded, lay through Chungking.[26]

Sir Rutherford Alcock, the British Minister in Peking, advised his superiors in London to ignore this sort of reasoning. He pointed to a Memorial which the Amban had just sent off to the Emperor reporting the anxiety of the Tibetans lest there should be any relaxation of the prohibition of foreigners from entering the holy land of Tibetan Buddhism, an anxiety inspired by the recent exploits of a number of European travellers. Not only, the Memorial continued, did the Tibetans fear for their faith, but they thought that the Nepalese might resent the opening of Tibet to foreign influences, and might take some drastic action to preserve their special position there. The Amban hoped that the Emperor would demand that the British give up all thoughts of establishing relations with Tibet, commercial or political. The people of Tibet, the Memorial concluded, would fight to the last man in an attempt to exclude the European. Matters should never be allowed to come to such a pass, not only because of the useless slaughter of Tibetans that would inevitably result, but also because Tibetan resistance to European travellers could only lead to retaliation by the foreign governments concerned. Alcock thought this Memorial contained more than a grain of truth. He considered, in any case, that the first step in the 'old resident's' plan, the establishment of a treaty port at Chungking, was at present quite out of the question. He noted, however, that the Shanghai Chamber of Commerce had taken the 'old resident's' plan quite seriously and was showing great interest in trade with Lhasa by way of Chungking.[27]

West China in the 1860s seemed to the English merchant like a trader's paradise. The markets were there and so were the goods; all that was lacking was a means of access. Before 1868 the Chambers of Commerce of Manchester, Huddersfield, Leeds, Halifax, Bradford, Liverpool, Bristol, Gloucester and Glasgow, the Liverpool Shipowners' Association, the Manchester Cotton Supply Association, and the United Salt Proprietors of Cheshire and Worcester, and probably many more such bodies, had petitioned the India Office to do something about opening up Western China to British trade. The pet scheme of this time was that of a railway between Rangoon and Yunnan, but other projects, including routes through Tibet, were considered. The India Office, which saw danger of trouble with frontier tribes in any project to open up the Sino-Burmese frontier, was much attracted to a Tibetan alternative.[28] Thus merchants and officials both watched the progress of Cooper's travels with close attention. The Indian Government gave him all the help it could. On his first journey it made an attempt to send messengers by way of Assam to meet up with him in Eastern Tibet. His second journey was carried out in close cooperation with the Assam Government. In return, Cooper provided Government with detailed reports after both his Tibetan ventures.[29]

Cooper's conclusions on the potentialities of Indo-Tibetan trade were welcomed by British officials concerned with the Himalayan frontiers of Bengal and Assam. The Bhutan War had emphasized Jenkins' point that the friendship of the authorities in Tibet could be of great value in restraining the war-like propensities of the Bhutanese hillmen, a thesis which could be traced back to the days of Bogle and Turner; and the trade question provided as good an excuse as any for the reopening of Indo-Tibetan relations.[30] Thus Colonel Haughton, Commissioner for Cooch Behar, who had charge of British relations with Bhutan, was so impressed by Bogle's analysis of Himalayan politics, which he had been able to study in a manuscript copy of Bogle's journals, that he proposed to Bengal in October 1869 that another attempt be made to establish relations with the rulers of Tibet. Haughton had concluded that Bhutan might shortly become the scene of yet another civil war, and there was a definite possibility that both Nepal and Tibet might take an unwelcome interest in such an event. It was, of course, extremely unlikely that any Bhutanese would be so rash as to do anything which might run them the risk of war with the British so soon after the Bhutan War of 1865, but there was no denying that Bhutanese affairs should be watched vigilantly, and in this the help of Lhasa would be valuable.[31]

Bengal, also with the Bhutan War in mind, felt that any attempt to approach Tibet 'might excite suspicion as to our motives, and do more harm than good'.[32] Ashley Eden, now Secretary to the Bengal Government, said that the best policy was to leave well enough alone. It was most inadvisable to bring the Tibetans – and the Chinese – into any future discussions about the British frontier; otherwise, were they obliged to conduct at some future date a campaign like those recently carried out in Sikkim and in Bhutan, they might find themselves in the invidious position of 'choosing either to let the offending states go unpunished, or of refusing a request of a friendly power' to mediate in the dispute. It was best to act on the assumption that the Himalayan States were completely independent sovereign states; Eden, indeed, felt that it was only by acting on this assumption that the Sikkim and Bhutan campaigns had been concluded without giving rise to international complications.[33]

The Indian Government, however, felt that the advantages of Haughton's policy outweighed the disadvantages, in which decision it was undoubtedly influenced by the prevailing interest in Tibet which had developed to a great extent from the much publicized travels of T. T. Cooper. It could afford to treat this matter in a more academic light since it was not concerned with the day to day running of the frontier. Thus Haughton was authorized to make an attempt to get in touch with the Tibetan authorities, though with the proviso that at present he did so only through non-committal friendly messages. He was not to entangle the Government in any way with politics across the mountains.[34] The Duke of Argyle, the Secretary of State for India, agreed that

> a renewal of the amicable intercourse with the Lamas of Tibet, which has, unfortunately, been so long in abeyance, need not necessarily, and, if properly managed, is not likely to lead to any such unfavourable consequences as appear to be anticipated by . . . the Lieutenant-Governor of Bengal.

It was, he noted, but a reversion to the policy of Warren Hastings.[35] The matter was referred to Lord Granville at the Foreign Office with the observation that the reopening of relations with Tibet would have many benefits, the greatest being the trade in tea from the Darjeeling District to Lhasa, could the Tibetans but be persuaded to remove the present restrictions on such a traffic. It was requested that the British Minister in Peking should raise the matter with the Chinese Government 'should any further Treaty Negotiations with China be at any time in contemplation'.[36]

Colonel Haughton, thus encouraged, examined carefully the whole question of relations, commercial and political, with Lhasa. For the Tibet trade he had become convinced that the best route lay through Sikkim, or, perhaps, West Bhutan - there were disadvantages to the other routes currently under discussion through Ladakh, Nepal, Assam and Burma. The Sikkim route joined the tea-growing districts of Darjeeling and the Bhutan Duars to the markets of Lhasa and Central Tibet where great profits might be made. At present, of course, the import of Indian tea to Tibet was prohibited, as Haughton had cause to know from the experience of a Chinese merchant from Szechuan, now living in Darjeeling, who had prepared in 1865 some Darjeeling tea in brick form which he had sold to a Tibetan trader. The Tibetan carried the bricks to the frontier, where Tibetan guards promptly confiscated them and fined him most heavily as well. Haughton thought the Chinese authorities in Lhasa were to blame for this as they naturally feared that the much shorter carrying distance between Darjeeling and Lhasa would enable Indian tea to sweep that of China off the Tibetan market. This obstruction could only be overcome by negotiations in Peking, though something might be gained by contact with Tibetan officials through the mediation of the Sikkim Raja. Thus, in August 1870, Bengal agreed to request the Raja to ask the Tibetan Government 'what restrictions, if any, are placed on the importation of goods from British India into Tibet' and 'to cause a letter to the same effect, written in Tibetan, to be sent to the officer commanding in the Chola Pass for transmission to his superiors'.[37]

The Indian Government placed greater faith in the outcome of negotiations in Peking. Wade was told of the present state of the new attempt to open relations with Tibet, and it was hoped that he would take some action on the basis of this information.[38] Wade's reply, however, was disappointing. He doubted whether he could persuade the Chinese to grant any concessions in Tibet, even if they were in a position to do so, which he thought was far from the true state of affairs. He did not believe a word of the theory that it was the Chinese who were opposing the opening of Tibet, and that the Tibetans would welcome it if they were allowed to do so. The refusal of the Tibetans to accept the perfectly valid passport of T. T. Cooper proved this point. The British, he added, had no treaty right to travel in Tibet. All that he could suggest was that the Indian Government should try to buy the Chinese and Tibetan officials in Lhasa with suitable bribes. The Amban seemed particularly suited to such treatment, Wade wrote, because

> he is always a Manchu or Mongol, never a Chinese, and is nowadays certainly a needy man to whom a sum of money in our eyes of no great amount would be an important consideration. All that he receives from his own government is the pay of his proper office, probably from £500 to £1,000 a year, which in these times he most probably does not draw![39]

It was advice of this sort which made the Government of India sometimes suspect that the British Minister in Peking was not really interested in the needs of British India.

Colonel Haughton had no spectacular success to show for his efforts. In October 1870 he sent his Tibetan interpreter, Gellong, up to Phari, the Tibetan frontier town at the head of the Chumbi Valley. Gellong was told to convey to any Tibetan officer whom he might chance to meet the good wishes of the Indian Government, but on no account to discuss political matters. But the indiscreet interpreter, when he met the Phari Jongpen, the chief official at Phari and the commander of the local fort, could not refrain from adopting a somewhat minatory tone, remarking that only British benevolence prevented the Gurkhas from attacking and plundering Tibet, and that that restraint might not be applied much longer if the Tibetans did not try to accommodate themselves to British wishes. 'I am afriad', wrote Haughton, 'that there exists not a Bhutea whose discretion might be trusted in any diplomatic business'; and this was a great pity because, so a Kashmiri resident of Lhasa had told him, the use of native agents was the most promising way of getting in touch with the Tibetans, who, afraid of the Chinese, were unwilling to compromise themselves by accepting official letters from the British. The Kashmiri, not surprisingly, suggested that he and his like would be admirable intermediaries between Bengal and Lhasa. Haughton, reluctant to send his interpreter on another mission and possessing little confidence in the reliability of Kashmiri merchants who were inspired by nothing but self-interest, did not see what more he could do about approaching the Tibetans at that time.

In July 1871, however, Haughton found that he could not allow the Tibetan question to drop. News had just reached him that the Phari Jongpen had refused to accept that letter which the Indian Government had instructed to be sent him by way of the Sikkim authorities. It was not, the Jongpen said, the policy of Tibet to hold any communication whatsoever with the rulers of British India. Haughton saw this reply as an insult to the British name, which could not be allowed to pass unanswered without damage to British prestige in Sikkim and the other hill states. He proposed that a strongly worded letter be at once sent off to the Jongpen to show him the dangers of ignoring the friendly overtures of the British; and he urged that British efforts to open the Tibet trade be intensified by the appointment of an officer whose sole concern would be this task. On no account, Haughton warned, must the Jongpen's rebuff be allowed to appear to have resulted in a British abandonment of the policy of closer relations with Tibet.[40]

The Indian Government, however, now agreed that Tibet should be left alone for a while. In late 1871 the Lieutenant-Governor of Bengal was confirmed in this opinion by what he learnt from talking with Kashmiri merchants in Darjeeling, who gave him to believe that the Sikkim route was not so promising as it might at first sight seem. He does not seem to have appreciated that these Kashmiris enjoyed a very privileged position in the economic life of Tibet - a result of the traditional relationship between Lhasa and Ladakh - and were hardly likely to do anything to open the Indo-Tibetan trade to outside competition. Bengal, at any rate, determined to take no further action on the Tibetan border until another attempt had been made to obtain Chinese co-operation through the representations of Wade at Peking, and the Indian Government could but agree.[41] Haughton, in the meantime, was instructed to keep an eye on the Tibetan border, 'his qualifications for observing this subject' being sufficient 'guarantee that the matter will not be lost sight of'.[42]

Wade saw no good reason to change his mind since 1870. He could detect no sign of a more helpful attitude at the Yamen. He had just completed a long discussion with the Chinese on the ill-treatment to which T. T. Cooper had been subjected in Tibet and in Yunnan, which had given him the opportunity to 'feel the pulse of the Ministers of the Yamen' on this subject. The Yamen were as determined to keep Tibet closed as they had ever been, and they said that any attempt to open Tibet to foreign trade or influence would be violently resisted by the Tibetans. In any case, they argued, the western frontiers of China were so disturbed at present that it was quite impossible for them to enforce their wishes on the Tibetan authorities, even if they had wanted to. Wade could only assure the Indian Government that if an unexpected opening should present itself he would waste no time in exploiting it.[43]

The Indian Government remained convinced that Wade had not its interests at heart, and Wade felt obliged, in August 1872, to clear himself of this charge. He assured Lord Northbrook that he was

> not indifferent to the consideration of any scheme by which the trade of Her Majesty's subjects or dependents in any part of the world may be extended, and that no opportunity is ever missed by this Legation of supporting any such scheme.

But, until the minority of the Emperor came to an end, which event 'may be nearer than we think', there was no prospect of any Chinese minister accepting the responsibility for major changes in policy. As evidence of his willingness to promote the extension of Indian trade, Wade suggested using the reported intention of the rebel Muslims at Tali to send a mission to England as a lever for the extraction from the Yamen of concessions on Tibet. He requested authority from the Foreign Office 'to tell the Chinese that if they will assist us in opening trade with or through Tibet, we shall not encourage the Mohammedans of Tali-fu in their proposed treaty relations.'[44] The Panthay Rebellion, to which Wade was referring, was finally put down in 1873 when the victorious Imperial troops perpetrated a series of particularly horrible massacres in the region of Tali. It coincided with a similar rising of Moslem tribes in Chinese Turkestan under Yakub Bey, which continued for a little longer until 1878. The surprising Chinese victories over these rebels ruled out any chance of the British extracting any diplomatic advantage from the unsettled state of Chinese Central Asia, and thus Wade's proposal to use the Panthay Rebellion as a lever to secure concessions in Tibet came to nothing.

Wade saw little prospect of the Chinese allowing the British to establish a foothold beyond the Himalayas unless they were forced to do so by pressure generated by some grave crisis in their policy. It will be seen shortly that Wade continued in this belief; his suggestions as to the Panthay crisis were ignored, but similar suggestions as to the crisis of the Margary affair, the murder of a British consular officer while travelling on duty in Yunnan, were to lead to Wade's securing of Chinese treaty recognition of the right of the British to send a mission to Tibet. The India Office, however, did not seem to appreciate the difficulties of the Tibetan question. 'Surely', minuted a member of the Political Committee in 1871, 'what was done directly from India in the time of Warren Hastings, should not be quite impossible now?'[45] And when, on 25th April 1873, a deputation from the Society of Arts called on the Duke of Argyle to press for measures for the opening of trade with Chinese Turkestan and Tibet, the Duke gave them a very favourable reception.[46]

The deputation, in the organization of which T. T. Cooper had been concerned, contained several 'old Tibet hands'; Dr. Campbell, Lt.-Col. Gawler, Dr. Joseph Hooker and B. H. Hodgson. They argued for a more active commercial policy in Central Asia on strategic as well as commercial grounds, for they remarked that it had been reported recently that in 1872 a Russian exploring party had left Peking with Chinese passports and with the declared intention of travelling through Tibet. The deputation's Tibetan proposals were contained in a Memorial to the Duke. Access to Tibet, the Memorial stated, should be improved not only by developing new routes through Nepal and Bhutan but also by improving existing communications in Sikkim by extending roads to the Tibetan frontier and by completing the railway connection between Darjeeling and Calcutta. Conditions of trade should be regularized in Sikkim by the establishment of a trade mart on the Tibetan frontier after the pattern pioneered by the Russians at

Kiachta on the Siberia-Chinese Turkestan border, and by establishing a British consul or agent at either Lhasa or Shigatse. Wade should again be asked to extract from the Yamen their co-operation in the removal of obstacles in the way of this trade. The Memorial stressed that the best commercial approach to Tibet lay through Sikkim. Here was the shortest and most direct road between British territory and the Tibetan capital, which had become open as a result of the Sikkim Treaty of 1861, and which led up to the Tibetan plateau by way of the Chumbi Valley, a region which offered an ideal site for a trade mart and which promised to be of great importance to the future of the Tibet trade.

The Memorial, in fact, was a summary of proposals to improve trade between India and Tibet which had been in circulation for some time. The trade mart was just another fair near the Tibetan border of a type which had been discussed by Warren Hastings. The policy of encouraging Indo-Tibetan commerce by building roads had already been tried along the Sutlej with the first stages of the Tibet-Hindustan Road. The British agent in Lhasa had been advocated vigorously by Cooper, but it was an idea which he shared with Bogle and Turner. The Memorial, however, marked a decisive step in the history of British attempts to open Tibet in that it concentrated attention in England and in India on the Sikkim route, almost to the exclusion of all other ways across the Himalayan barrier. Its provisions, which the Duke of Argyle approved, were destined to become in time the declared policy of the Indian Government. On one point only, that of the location of a British representative at Lhasa, was there to be much argument; and those who later opposed this suggestion did so not on the grounds that it would be ineffective but because they thought that it would raise greater international complications than could possibly be justified by the profits of the Tibet trade.

In India, despite indications from the British Legation in Peking that the Tibetans had no great affection of the British and had no wish to see them travelling in the holy land of Buddhism, the conviction persisted that the Chinese alone were responsible for the exclusion of Europeans from Tibet. By now much evidence seemed to exist to support this conclusion. When, for example, W. T. Blanford in 1870 visited the Jelep La leading into the Chumbi Valley and talked with the Tibetan frontier guards, he was told that definite orders from the Chinese Emperor were in force to exclude all foreigners from Tibetan soil. The Chinese, he concluded, had kept the Tibetans in ignorance of the comparative freedom of movement which was permitted to Europeans in

China proper since the recent treaties. The Tibetan people, Blanford was convinced, felt no ill-will against the British in India, though they may have been prejudiced a little by the ex-Dewan Namgyal, who enjoyed a measure of Tibetan offical favour and who held a minor government post in Chumbi. The purchase of Namgyal's friendship with suitable bribes would clear up these misunderstandings easily enough. The obstacles in the way of better relations between British India and Tibet were, it would seem, twofold. Firstly, the old question of Chinese obstruction, which would probably require solution in Peking; and secondly, the fact that what trade did exist across the Sikkim-Tibet frontier was most liable to stoppages, temporary but annoying none the less.[47]

The precise mechanism of trade stoppages on this border was not fully understood by British officials at this time. Haughton, for instance, was puzzled when he learnt in November 1870 that 200 merchants and their baggage had been held up for some weeks at Phari, waiting for Tibetan permission to continue their journey down to Darjeeling.[48] One thing seemed certain; interruptions in the Indo-Tibetan trade were in some measure a reflection of political tensions along the Indo-Tibetan frontier. The British watched these crises, which were fairly frequent, with much interest. The visits to the Sikkim-Tibet border of Edgar in 1873 and Colman Macaulay in 1884 were partly motivated by the wish to investigate more closely the mechanism of these frontier troubles.

In 1873 trade was once more stopped at Phari, an event which was certainly connected with a developing crisis in the relations, never too happy, between Nepal and Tibet. The history of this affair is fairly typical of the tensions of the latter part of the nineteenth century; there were very similar crises in the 1880s and 1890s. It has already been noted that the Nepalese Tribute Missions on their passage through Tibet to and from China were generally accompanied by strained Tibeto-Nepalese relations. The Tibetans were frightened of Nepalese military strength, but not so much so as to treat Gurkha diplomats with sycophancy. They harboured a deep resentment against the terms of the Tibeto-Nepalese treaty of 1856, by which they had been forced to accept a Nepalese Resident in Lhasa and to pay Nepal an annual tribute. They were frightened lest the Nepalese might, by some subtle diplomacy in Peking, take over a share of the Chinese interest in Tibet. They felt, in any case, that it was likely that the Gurkhas would make another raid on to Tibetan soil, perhaps, this time, with the intention of more permanent conquest. They could see nothing reassuring in the close friendship which, since the period of the Mutiny, Sir Jang Bahadur had established with British India; this fact, indeed, only resulted in a diversion of some Tibetan animosity towards the Government of India, and led Lhasa to interpret British road-building in Sikkim as the prelude to military invasion.

There was some justification behind many of these Tibetan fears. After the return of the Tribute Mission of 1866 Sir Jang Bahadur did give serious thoughts to a fresh invasion of Tibet and a repetition of the victories of 1854–56. The Chinese did see in this a need to make some gesture of friendship to Nepal, and Chinese ambassadors came to Katmandu in 1871 to confer decorations on Sir Jang Bahadur. In 1871, at any rate, the Tibetans seem to have convinced themselves that the Chinese, with Bhutanese and Gurkha aid, were about to make a bid to reinforce their hold on Lhasa. A result was the rise of strong anti-Nepalese sentiment in the Tibetan capital which took expression in attacks on Nepalese traders, against which Sir Jang Bahadur delivered a most strongly worded protest. An ultimatum from Katmandu placed the Chinese Amban at Lhasa in a delicate position. He knew well that the monasteries and the Regent, who ruled during the almost continuous minorities of the Dalai Lama, were always plotting to expel him, and that nothing was more calculated to further their plans than for the Chinese to appear to be in league with Nepal, the Tibetan foe. The Amban seems to have decided to rally Tibetan sentiment to his side by delivering an insult to the Gurkhas. In the spring of 1871 some Chinese soldiers in Lhasa selected the house of the Nepalese Resident as a target for musketry practice, and the Amban showed himself most reluctant to punish these men at the Nepalese Resident's request. In the following year the Amban helped the Regent prepare fortifications along the Nepalese border, and this martial preparation produced the inevitable reaction in Katmandu, where by March 1873 the arsenals were working day and night. By then the crisis had progressed almost to the point of war. The Dalai Lama kept the Nepalese Resident waiting for several hours when that official made a courtesy call on the titular head of the Tibetan state. Sir Jang Bahadur broke off relations with Tibet, withdrew the Resident and closed the Nepalese frontier to Tibetan traders. The Tibetans, in the belief that the Indian Government stood behind Sir Jang Bahadur, then stopped all trade on the Sikkim-Tibet border.

Why did this sort of crisis not result in war? The Nepalese, it has already been noted, had not forgotten the lesson of 1792.

They were frightened of the Chinese army which they felt might still possess that superiority in cannon which had once brought it almost to the gates of Katmandu. The Amban, of course, once he had made his gesture of support to Tibetan national sentiment, was eager to compromise with Nepal. He had no more than 2,300 Chinese troops in the whole of Tibet and his official establishment was even lower, at 1,500 men. He doubtless had little confidence in the abilities of the 60,000 or so Tibetan levies on whom the main burden of defence fell. Thus a peace was patched up by the end of 1874, but of little durability since a very similar Tibeto-Nepalese crisis was to erupt in 1883.

The reaction of the British to these crises is interesting. The Indian Government, of course, deprecated any turbulence along its borders. It retained, moreover, a distrust of the Gurkha Government from the days of the Gurkha War which the policy of Sir Jang Bahadur and the recruitment of Gurkha troops into the Indian Army had not entirely dispelled. It had, as will be discussed later on, a suspicion that the Gurkhas used these crises as an excuse to request permission to buy from British territory modern arms for their own army, and it was not quite certain that those arms were intended for use to the north. In London, the India Office was less anxious: it did not have the responsibility of the day-to-day conduct of a difficult frontier. It even felt that some advantage might be wrested from Tibeto-Nepalese tension. As Owen Burne observed in 1874, these disputes

cannot but be productive of advantage to ourselves, as, whatever the issue, it must tend to improve our relations with Nepal and Tibet which are now closed doors, and will ever remain so as long as we rely on Mr. Wade and Sir Jang Bahadur.

He concluded with a remark which may cause surprise to more recent generations of Gurkha admirers:

The Goorkha army is a cowardly host, as was practically experienced in the mutiny, and may possibly receive rough treatment from the Thibetans, but anything that can open to us Nepal and Tibet, which are closed doors to our influence and trade, must be better than the present state of things.[49]

Major, later Sir Owen, Burne seems to have forgotten what happened in 1792.

The Bengal Government saw in the Tibeto-Nepalese crisis and

the stoppage of trade on the Sikkim-Tibet frontier the need for the deputation of a British official to the Tibetan border to enquire into the causes and the significance of these events. In June 1873 the Lieutenant-Governor gave an audience at Darjeeling to the Raja of Sikkim. The main topic of discussion was the increasing of the subsidy which the Indian Government had been paying to the Raja since 1841. Originally Rs. 3,000 per annum, it had been raised to Rs. 6,000 in 1846, stopped in 1850, restored in 1863 and raised to Rs. 9,000 in 1868. It was now proposed to raise it yet further to Rs. 12,000 at the Raja's request; but only, the Lieutenant-Governor said, if the Raja made greater efforts to open trade with Tibet, and if he would facilitate a visit to the Tibetan frontier by J. W. Edgar, the Deputy Commissioner for Darjeeling. Edgar's mission was justified on the grounds that it was the policy of Bengal to 'seize every opportunity of opening up the developing trade with Central Asia, and to secure, by increased frequency of communication with Sikkim, more full and accurate knowledge of what goes on in the hills'. Added reason was provided by a recent statement by the Chief Minister of Sikkim that the Tibetans were anxious to open relations with the Indian Government and were only prevented from doing so by fear of the Chinese. It seemed that Edgar might achieve much from friendly talks with Tibetan officials on the frontier.[50]

Edgar was instructed to go up to Sikkim in the autumn of 1873. The Sikkim authorities were told to inform the Phari Jongpen, the chief official in that important Tibetan frontier town, that a British representative was about to visit the border and would welcome a meeting.[51] The Phari Jongpen replied that he did not take this news very seriously. He had been hearing for years of impending British visits, and they never came to anything; so he was not going to risk making a fool of himself by asking Lhasa for permission to hold the talks which the Indian Government said it wanted.[52] But it seemed to Bengal that this answer did not reflect the Jongpen's true feelings. Indeed, so seriously did the Tibetans take the news of the forthcoming visit by Edgar that they had started to fortify the passes leading from Sikkim into Chumbi. Edgar felt, however, that the rude reply and the defensive preparations were nothing more than a bluff on the part of the Jongpen, who was eager to talk with the British but anxious, at the same time, to protect himself against the suspicions of the Chinese in Lhasa. In proof of this Edgar pointed to a recent report of the Jongpen's intention to winter in Chumbi, an unprecedented change in his normal routine.[53]

Edgar entered Sikkim in October 1873. He visited the passes

into the Chumbi Valley and talked with Tibetan officials, including the Phari Jongpen and the ex-Dewan Namgyal.[54] The Jongpen was very friendly and polite, but would not allow Edgar to set one foot into Tibet; it was evident that the Tibetans would not consider the entry of Europeans on any terms. On the other hand, from remarks made by the Jongpen, Edgar concluded that a new spirit was abroad, and many influential Tibetans were beginning to doubt the wisdom of the policy of isolation. But this was as yet a very delicate growth and any abrupt move on the part of the Indian Government would probably retard its development if not kill it completely. The soundest policy at present seemed to be to refer the matter once more to Peking; for with the removal of Chinese obstruction the Tibetans might be encouraged to declare themselves openly.

Edgar made the following proposals on his return from Sikkim in December 1873. Wade should be asked once more to try to obtain from the Yamen a promise that the obstacles which continued to be placed in the way of Indian traders entering Tibet should be removed. If possible, this should take the form of an Edict from the Emperor containing 'a formal expression of the Emperor's disapproval of the interference of his representatives at Lassa' in this matter. Put in this way Chinese approval would not appear to the Tibetan anti-Chinese faction to be quite so like Anglo-Chinese collusion towards the opening of Tibet as would a treaty agreement. At the same time, Edgar continued, the cultivation of the friendship of Tibetan frontier officials should be carried on, though care should always be taken here not to give the impression that the Indian Government was trying to open Tibet to European travel. The question of European entry into Tibet, Edgar thought like Bogle before him, was a tricky one which should be avoided if possible. A trade mart,' Edgar went on, should be established on the Sikkim side of the Tibetan frontier, and he suggested Gnatong at the foot of the Jelep La as a suitable site for a mart to which Tibetan traders might come, and where Nepalese and Kashmiri merchants might be persuaded to settle for part of the year to act as middlemen between Darjeeling and Lhasa. Finally, Edgar advised that a good road to the Tibetan frontier be completed as quickly as possible, even though the Tibetans might for a while look on such activity with suspicion. As soon as profitable trade sprung up, Edgar was convinced, the Tibetans would cease to believe that the British had any wish to attack or to occupy their country. Edgar made it clear, however, that measures on the British side of the Sikkim-Tibet frontier, while essential for the improvement of the Indo-

Tibetan trade, were unlikely to succeed by themselves. The co-operation of the Chinese was still of the greatest importance.[55]

On the strength of Edgar's recommendations Wade was instructed that 'Her Majesty's Government, looking at this question from an Imperial point of view, attach great importance to the resumption of the active commercial intercourse formerly existing between Thibet and Hindostan'.[56] But Wade still saw no hope of success from negotiations with the Chinese Government. He remarked that he had spent the last four years trying to 'disabuse the Government of India of any idea that the Chinese Government would lend itself to any measures that promised an increase of foreign trade, or of foreign intercourse, across its frontier'. India seemed to hope too much from the recent coming of age of the Emperor, and Wade was very surprised to find that so experienced an observer of Chinese politics as Sir Rutherford Alcock had thought that the young Emperor T'ung-chih was likely to grant any concessions in Tibet. It was only under pressure from his superiors that Wade was prepared to take any action at all on the Tibetan question, and he certainly was not prepared to approach the Yamen directly on this matter. He had told his Chinese Secretary, Mayers, not so long ago, to mention Tibet to the Yamen in the hope that he might elicit a clear declaration of the real obstacles existing in the way of improved trade between India and Tibet. The Yamen had shown Mayers that they were opposed to foreigners entering Tibet since the Tibetans would regard this as a threat to their religion, a fear, Wade noted, which was to some extent justified by the activities of the French Missionaries in Szechuan. The Yamen thought that the Tibetans would attack any European who might try to travel in their land, and the Chinese Government were not prepared to take the responsibility for this sort of outrage. All this seemed reasonable enough, but Wade felt that there was more behind it than fear of unwelcome incidents. The Manchus relied greatly on the support of the Buddhist hierarchy, and they had no intention of surrendering their influence in Lhasa.[57]

There was, moreover, another good reason for Chinese interest in Tibetan isolation. Wade had learnt that the present Viceroy of Szechuan Province, Wu T'ang, was strongly opposed to any relaxation of the rules which kept Tibet closed to foreign influence as he feared lest concessions in Tibet should lead immediately to similar concessions in his own Province. The influence and prestige of Wu T'ang sufficed to decide the Yamen and would continue to do so unless the Emperor himself could be persuaded to declare for a change in policy; and Wade remarked that so far as a more pro-foreign policy is concerned, we have nothing to reckon upon, except it be some serious crisis in foreign relations, the result of which would not be unmixed good; or the caprice of the Emperor, and of the direction of this in our favour we have not . . . the faintest symptom.[58]

All that Wade could suggest to the Indian Government was that, 'if the trade were worth the effort', a mixed commercial and political mission should be 'pushed forward' into Tibet without any reference being made to the Chinese Government. Most of the opposition in Tibet to such a venture could be eliminated by the distribution of suitable bribes. He offered, if the Indian Government were interested in sending a mission to Tibet under these conditions, the services as Chinese Interpreter of Byron Brennan of the Chinese Consular Service.[59]

It seems most unlikely that Wade thought the Indian Government would act on this advice. Progress in the opening of Tibet would have to await a 'serious crisis' in British relations with China. Wade may well have suspected that this was already in the making with the preparations of the Indian Government to send an exploring mission into Yunnan, from which was to result the Margary Affair and the consequent Chefoo Convention.

VI

THE CHEFOO CONVENTION
AND THE
MACAULAY MISSION

·

1876 – 1886

THERE WERE four routes open to British merchants by which to approach the commerce of the Chinese interior. The simplest of these lay through the Treaty Ports in China proper, along the coast and up the great rivers. There were, however, three overland routes into the Chinese Empire from the British possessions in India, and these, while still in the 1860s and 1870s little more than theoretical possibilities derived from the study of small-scale maps, inspired many who were concerned with the spread of British trade to pinnacles of optimistic prophecy. Chinese territory approached or touched on British India at three points; Lower Burma had a common frontier with Yunnan; along the Himalayas Indian territory marched with that of Tibet; and through Kashmir and across the passes of the Karakoram lay the road to Kashgar, Khotan, Yarkand and other markets in Chinese Turkestan. Two quotations can probably suggest better than any analysis of economic factors the enthusiasm with which the prospects of these routes were being considered in the 1870s. In 1873 one J. M'Cosh memorialized the India Office on the scheme which was then much discussed, and which continued to be discussed throughout the nineteenth century, of the construction of a railway linking India with Yunnan by way of Burma. Such a line, said M'Cosh, would lead to a time

when the Chinese shall cease to think of themselves as

celestials, and hold out the hand of good fellowship to the outside barbarians; when the prodigious commerce of the Indus, the Ganges, the Brahmaputra the Ning-tee, the Irrawaddy and the Yang-tsi-Kiang shall be hoisted upon trucks, and rolled from East to West, from West to East, in one grand tide, ever ebbing, ever flowing, everlasting, and when London and Liverpool, Manchester and Bradford, Glasgow and Paisley, Dundee and Aberdeen, shall dip their pitchers into the sacred stream, and deal out its bounty to the peoples of the land.[1]

And in 1878 D. C. Boulger, who possessed a reputation as an authority on Central Asian questions, wrote in the sober pages of the Journal of the Royal Asiatic Society of the time when

the people of Szechuen wear Manchester goods and use Sheffield cutlery, when they are forced to acknowledge that honesty is the guiding principle of English merchants, and when, on the other hand, the caravans bearing the silk and tea of China, come pouring in half the time and at half the expense they do at present, through the passes of Sikkim and Bhutan, to enrich the markets of India, then we may well feel confident that the Chinese people, who are, even at this moment, progressing towards more enlightened ideas, and whose virtues we have hitherto to a great extent shut our eyes to, will be more eager to recognize our position with regard to themselves, for this perception will have been brought home to them by the most forcible of all arguments, benefit to themselves.[2]

It is not surprising that in this climate of opinion the Indian Government should have taken steps to investigate the possibilities of these three overland routes during the 1870s. The prospects of Kashgaria were being probed by, for example, the Forsyth Mission.[3] The Sikkim route to Tibet was being explored. Plans were in hand for the survey of the Burma-Yunnan road; and it was through this last project that Wade obtained the opportunity for a general revision of British treaty relations with China which he saw as the prerequisite for any Chinese co-operation in the matter of opening Tibet. In 1874 an exploring mission was instructed to proceed across the Burma-Yunnan border under the command of Colonel Browne. Wade, who had made the necessary arrangements with the Yamen for its passage through Chinese territory, deputed one of his subordinates, A. R. Margary, to act as Chinese interpreter for the mission. While travelling in Yunnan in 1875 Margary was murdered, and there was a strong suspicion that the local Yunnan Government had some complicity in his death. This unfortunate occurrence constituted one of those 'incidents' out of which so much of the history of the relations of the Powers with China in the nineteenth century developed. The outcome was the negotiations at Chefoo in the summer of 1876 from which Wade secured the provisions of the Chefoo Convention.[4]

Wade needed no prompting to place Tibet on the Chefoo agenda. The collection of correspondence on this subject between India and the British Legation at Peking was already quite bulky, as was also that collection dealing with Kashgaria. There seemed to be an element of poetic justice in using the Chinese hostility, so it seemed, to British exploitation of one of the land routes between India and China to obtain Chinese agreement to the better development of the other two such routes. Thus the Separate Article of the Chefoo Convention contained provisions for the sending of British missions both to Lhasa and to Chinese Turkestan. Only Tibet will be discussed here, but it must not be forgotten that at this period Tibet and Kashgaria seemed to many to be but alternative means of achieving the same end of the increase of British commerce with the Chinese interior.

Wade requested that the Chinese should agree, despite the great reluctance they had shown during the past years, to the granting of passports for a commercial, political and scientific mission from British India to Tibet; and on 8th September 1876 the chief Chinese negotiator at Chefoo, Li Hung-chang, agreed to this, remarking that 'there need be no fear of any harm being allowed to befall another expedition. That sort of thing costs too heavily.' But on 11th September Li heard from the Tsungli Yamen that they were not prepared to accept the Tibet clause unless the granting of passports was made in some measure conditional on the opinion of the Chinese Resident in Tibet as to the risks which a mission entering Tibet would run of attack by the local population; the Chinese were not going to take the chance of another Margary affair. On 12th September Wade accepted this safeguard in return for a provision that the proposed mission could enter Tibet from China as well as from India. Thus the final article, as signed on 13th September 1876, read:

> Her Majesty's Government having it in contemplation to send a mission of exploration next year by way of Peking through Kansu and Koko-Nor, or by way of Ssu-Ch'uan to

Tibet, and thence to India, the Tsungli Yamen, having due regard to the circumstances, will, when the time arrives, issue the necessary passports, and will address letters to the high provincial authorities and to the Resident in Tibet. If the Mission should not be sent by these routes, but should be proceeding across the Indian frontier to Tibet, the Tsungli Yamen, on receipt of a communication to the above effect from the British Minister, will write to the Chinese Resident in Tibet, and the Resident, with due regard to the circumstances, will send officers to take due care of the Mission; and the passports for the Mission will be issued by the Tsungli Yamen, that its passage be not obstructed.[5]

Wade appreciated that this article was hedged about with precautionary clauses, but he felt that the Chinese fears of their being made responsible for another Margary affair were quite justified. In any case, such precautionary clauses were placed in all passports granted to foreigners of other nations travelling in the outlying parts of China. Finally, the right to enter Tibet by Szechuan seemed to Wade to be ample compensation for any vagueness in the phrasing of the article which did, at least, give the British the clear treaty right to send one mission to Lhasa.[6]

The Separate Article, once won, was ignored by the Indian Government for several years. The Chefoo Convention was not ratified in its entirety until 1886, and till then the Indian Government may well have doubted the validity of an instrument which, in any case, it did not find completely to its taste. The opium clauses, particularly, were felt to involve a sacrifice of Indian interests, and the Indian Government from time to time considered pressing for a revision of the Convention; it may have been unwilling to take advantage of the Convention until it had been so modified. Its attention, moreover, was absorbed elsewhere, for the forward policy of Lord Lytton was leading to the second Afghan War and a period of general crisis on the North-West Frontier. But the Article was not forgotten. Sir Charles Dilke, for example, asked in the House of Commons in February 1879 whether any mission had been sent to Tibet as authorized in 1876.[7] Writers like D. C. Boulger continued to point out the advantages of trade with Tibet. Wade at intervals reminded the Yamen that the article existed and would be implemented sooner or later; they had better persuade the Tibetans to adopt a more reasonable attitude towards Europeans or they would some day 'have to pay the penalty which had over taken Burmah and Annam'.[8] Thus the Separate Article gave the British Legation in

Peking a new interest in the affairs of Tibet. Tibet was now involved in British treaty relations with China, and after 1876 references to Tibet are frequent in the despatches from Peking.

In many quarters the Separate Article was considered with distaste or with suspicion. In Russia it was looked upon in much the same way as British observers of Central Asian affairs were accustomed to look upon further Russian advances towards the borders of the British Empire in India. One Russian newspaper, *Goloss* of 22nd December/4th January 1877/1878, gave what the India Office considered to be a typical Russian interpretation of this instrument. It was yet another step towards that policy of Warren Hastings which hoped for 'the exercise by the British of an influence over the Dalai Lama, the spiritual head of the greater proportion of the population of Asia'; and it was clearly implied that this policy was aimed against Russia.[9]

The Tibetans, of course, were much alarmed by news of this provision of the Chefoo Convention of which they learnt soon enough from the Amban.[10] They assumed that the mission so authorized would set out immediately, and they had good reason for coming to such a conclusion since there were abundant signs for an increase in the tempo of British pressure on the gates of Tibet. In 1876, for example, a Russian exploring party was provided with Chinese passports authorizing it to enter Tibetan territory,[11] and the most elementary understanding of the mechanism of the diplomacy of the Powers in China would suggest that what the Russians got the British would soon demand for themselves. In 1877 a British Consular Officer, E. C. Baber, was stationed in Chungking; and British influence this far up the Yangtze may well have suggested that further moves towards Eastern Tibet were not far off. English missionaries were already trying to reach Lhasa from West China by that route which the French Catholics had tried in vain for so long to open up; and the Tibetans, always fearful for the security of their faith, may well have seen the danger of the flag following in the footsteps of the missionaries. So, at least, Baber reasoned when he protested against 'the proselytizing stream' directing its 'full current' against Tibet.[12] The French Fathers on the border of Eastern Tibet certainly concluded that by April 1877 the Tibetans had convinced themselves that their independence, such as it was, was in danger and that they had no wish to replace Chinese control, to which they had long grown accustomed, by the influence of a European Power. In Lhasa, so the Fathers told Baber, it had been decided to resist by force any attempt to implement the Separate Article.[13] If further evidence of Tibetan hostility to the prospect of a visit to their capital by a foreign mission were needed, it could be found in the Tibetan treatment of the Nepalese Tribute Mission on its passage through Tibet in 1877. The Nepalese, it will be remembered, were suspect as possible allies of the Indian Government, and this fact goes far to explain the hostility shown to the mission in Tibet and in China, for the Chinese had no wish to show respect for a people who were regarded as enemies in Lhasa.[14]

By 1878 the Tibetans had become so convinced that a British mission, and, perhaps, one from Russia, was about to make a bid to reach Lhasa that they were interpreting every event on their frontiers in this light. Perhaps some trivial occurrence on their Indian or Chinese border convinced them that a British mission had actually set out, for by November 1878 a number of reports to this effect were circulating in Tachienlu which described the progress of this non-existent venture in the most circumstantial detail. Baber, at first, believed in their authenticity, and Fraser, the Chargé d'Affaires in Peking, could find no explanation for this news. India had denied that any such mission was then in contemplation. Fraser thought that the French Fathers in Szechuan, 'with whom the wish may perhaps have been to some extent father of the thought', had something to do with the detail of these reports, for it was through them that Baber had learnt of them. But he felt that 'there must be some remote foundation of fact' behind such rumours, and he hoped that this should 'be made clear before very long'.[15]

It would not be difficult to suggest a number of reasons for the growth and propagation of this sort of rumour. Apart from the suspicions of the Tibetans, which could have been aroused easily enough by some episode in the history of British exploration and road construction on the Indian side of the Himalayas, there were motives which might induce the Chinese authorities in Szechuan to encourage such rumours which always arose whenever a European approached close to the Tibetan border. It was a subtle method of suggesting to the Powers that the exploration of Tibet might prove dangerous. After the Chefoo Convention the Chinese found it hard to refuse passports for travellers who wished to enter Tibet - such documents, for instance, were given to the Austrian traveller Count Szechenyi in 1878[16] - and they had to resort to some subterfuge to render these passports ineffective. One method was the age-old one of petty obstruction. Another might well have been to create so many rumours about Tibetan hostility to such ventures as to justify the Yamen in cancelling passports to Tibet on the ground, of admitted validity in the

Separate Article, that circumstances in Tibet made travel there dangerous to the life of any European explorer.

Arguments with the Yamen over the right of Europeans to enter Tibet were frequent after the Chefoo Convention, and Wade and his successors found themselves obliged to take more notice of this remote portion of the Chinese Empire. This was also a consequence of the steady opening of Western China to foreign trade and influence. The establishment of a consular official at Chungking in 1877 made the collection of information about Tibet much easier. Baber, for example, visited Tachienlu in 1878, and his successor, Alexander Hosie, did likewise in 1882. In 1885 Chungking was opened to foreign trade and a full British Consulate was established there. The regular consular reports from that place did not ignore the trade and politics of Tibet. The reports of Baber, Hosie, Litton and their like were laid before Parliament and were widely studied. The Indian Government was quick to see the value of this British observation post so close to the border of Eastern Tibet and to those regions in Szechuan where was made the brick tea for the Tibetan market. In February 1880, for example, the Indian Government asked Baber to obtain for it samples of this tea as prepared for sale in Lhasa. Reports from Chungking played an important part in the propagation of the impression that vast profits might be made from the sale of Indian tea across the Himalayas.

The idea of selling Indian tea to Tibet was an inevitable consequence of the development of a tea industry in the foothills of the Himalayas. In the 1850s this possibility was being discussed by such Darjeeling residents as Campbell and B. H. Hodgson. The journeys of T. T. Cooper emphasized the importance of the existing tea trade between China and Tibet. The first quantitative studies of this commerce, however, were made by Baber and by Hosie. In 1881 Hosie found that the Chinese imported from Tibet through Tachienlu about £250,000 worth of Tibetan produce, skins, Tibetan felt, musk, horn, gold dust and herbs for medicinal purposes; and they exported to the value of £150,000, of which £120,000 was brick tea and the remainder made up of such items as cottons, ceramics, silks and foreign manufactured goods. Baber, in 1879, put the value of tea a little higher, at £160,000, and he thought that the tea which was smuggled past the *likin* station at Tachienlu and that which found its way into Tibet by other routes might raise the total value to about £300,000. It was a tea of the poorest quality, grown mainly in Szechuan province expressly for the Tibetan market and prepared in a special way. The leaves and bits of stalk were mixed with clay and pressed to form a brick with dimensions of about 9 by 7 by 3 inches. It was carried from Tachienlu westwards by porters who could sometimes bear loads of 400 lb. or more. Baber was convinced that, as the Szechuan tea was of such execrable quality, the Tibetans would welcome the superior Indian produce once political conditions made possible an Indo-Tibetan trade of any freedom. 'The Tibetans', he wrote, 'with their fondness for tea and their dislike of Chinamen would be the first to welcome the best wares to the best market by the shortest road.'[17]

In Sikkim the British had been busy in the five years following the signing of the Chefoo Convention in smoothing the way for the hoped-for Tibet trade by improving communications. In 1879 a cart road to the Jelep La Pass into the Chumbi Valley had been completed, bringing Darjeeling into easy reach of the Tibetan border. In 1881 a branch of the East Bengal Railway, narrow gauge, had been brought through a series of impressively engineered loops and gradients up to Darjeeling from the main line at Siliguri. It now took less than a week to reach the Tibetan border from Calcutta.[18]

The increase of British influence in Sikkim, greatly accelerated since Edgar's visit in 1873, was regarded with anxiety by the rulers of that State. In 1874, on the death of Raja Sidkyong Namgyal, it became an issue in the disputed succession which followed. Thutob Namgyal, one of the half-brothers of the late Raja, secured the throne, while another half-brother, Tinle Namgyal, fled to Tibet, where, advised by the ex-Dewan Namgyal, he began to intrigue against the incumbent Raja, whom he depicted as a tool of the British. He argued that the building of roads in Sikkim was a sign of British domination. He made political capital out of the fact that under British protection Sikkim had been opened to the influx of settlers from Nepal, a land with which Sikkim had a long history of hostility. The Nepalese settlers, by their industry and their fecundity, soon began to displace the original inhabitants, and the Sikkim Durbar had good cause to protest on this score. In 1878, as a result of Sikkimese representations, the Lieutenant-Governor agreed to limit Nepalese settlement to the south of a line drawn across Sikkim just to the north of Gangtok. But disputes between the new immigrants and the Sikkim people continued; in 1880, for instance, there were riots at Rhenok between the two groups. The Sikkim opposition in Chumbi did not fail to note these developments, and to point out to Lhasa what might happen if the British were once allowed to obtain a foothold in Tibet.[19]

It was probably to counteract these intrigues in Chumbi that in

1881 the Lieutenant-Governor of Bengal, Sir Ashley Eden, obtained the sanction of Government for the employment of two native explorers, Lama Ugyen Gyatso and Sarat Chandra Das, who had visited Shigatse in 1879 on behalf of the Survey of India, on a mission to Tibet to establish contact with the Tashi (or Panchen) Lama, and, if possible, to visit Lhasa. Both objectives were achieved. The Tashi Lama was very friendly to Das. He was about to visit the Tibetan capital and offered to take the Indian explorer there in his suite. The Lama, unfortunately, died suddenly before he could introduce Das to Lhasa in such promising circumstances, but Das went on alone, and managed to spend some time in Lhasa, where he had to remain in hiding in the house of a friendly monastic official. The Lhasa visit produced no positive political results, though its later discovery by the Tibetans did serve to increase their suspicions of British intentions. The visit to Tashilhunpo, on the other hand, resulted in a most promising friendship between Das and the Regent or Chief Minister who had assumed authority on the demise of the Tashi Lama. The Chief Minister was very interested in the outside world. He wanted European things, a lithographic press, a telephone and a photographic camera, and he gave Das money with which to buy these on his return to India. Bengal took the opportunity so provided to return the money and to send the things desired by the Chief Minister as gifts. A correspondence between Calcutta and Tashilhunpo ensued, and it looked as if Tashilhunpo at least was ripe to break out of that isolation which had been the characteristic of Tibetan foreign policy for so many years.[20]

It was unfortunate that Das' Tibetan journey coincided with another period of crisis on the Tibeto-Nepalese frontier. A new spirit of Tibetan independence was abroad, the causes of which will be discussed a little later on, and its effects can be detected in rioting in Lhasa which broke out during the Great Prayer festival in the spring of 1883.[21] This was directed against the Nepalese merchant community in the Tibetan capital, and it nearly gave rise to another Tibeto-Nepalese war. The cause of this incident was trivial indeed. A Tibetan woman tried to pilfer a small piece of precious coral from the shop of a Nepalese jeweller in Lhasa. The woman was spotted by the jeweller, and the inevitable argument broke out. The woman denied her guilt, and soon a crowd gathered round, mainly composed of monks who were assembled in Lhasa from all over Tibet at this festival period. The crowd was, naturally enough, strong in support of the Tibetan woman. The crowd soon became a mob, and the argument between woman and jeweller developed into an anti-Nepalese riot in which the Nepalese quarter in Lhasa was sacked and the houses of 84 Nepalese subjects were destroyed. The Nepalese, of course, objected strongly to this affair and demanded a huge compensation. The Tibetans refused to pay and threatened in their turn to cut off the subsidy of Rs. 10,000 which they had been paying Nepal since the treaty of 1856. Nepal began to prepare for war. As in 1871-3, the Amban found this crisis highly embarrassing. He did his best to make peace without appearing to be hostile to Tibetan interests, and by the end of 1884 he seems to have done so by pointing out to the Tibetans that if they did allow this situation to develop into a war the British would only come to Nepal's support. In September 1884 the Tibetans came to terms and agreed to pay Nepal Rs. 300,000 compensation for the damage done to Nepalese property in Lhasa in 1883.[22]

The Amban was right to suppose that a Tibeto-Nepalese war might result in British intervention of sorts. As in the previous crisis in the 1870s, the British found themselves unable to ignore the danger of war so near their border. There were awkward questions of policy involved in war between Tibet and Nepal. Though a Nepalese victory might favour British interests – it might even be a way of solving the question of Tibetan trade, though the Nepalese attitude to British commerce did little to encourage such a view – it would also be accompanied by a dangerous increase in Nepalese power and prestige. It would be difficult, in any case, to refuse a Gurkha request for facilities to buy arms in British India without arousing resentment in Nepal. Yet any increase in Gurkha armed strength would not only tempt Nepal into an expansionist policy, thus endangering the peace of the whole frontier, but it would also mean that many Gurkhas who would normally be recruited into the Indian Army would now be retained for the army of Nepal. This appeared to be, in the eyes of the Indian Government and the Indian Office, the lesser of two evils, and it was decided to supply arms to Nepal should they be requested.[23] While the solution of the crisis by Tibeto-Nepalese negotiation saved the British from active intervention, it did not save them, in Tibetan eyes, from becoming potential invaders of Tibetan soil. The Nepalese were quite open about their close friendship to the Indian Government, to whom, in 1885, they offered their military assistance in the event of a war with Russia.[24]

The Tibeto-Nepalese crisis was accompanied by tension along the Tibeto-Bhutanese border. In 1880 the Tibetans seem to have made one of their periodic assertions of suzerainty over Bhutan, and this the Bhutanese chiefs, who had grown greatly in independence from the north during many years of enjoyment of British subsidies, chose to resent. In 1883, when Lhasa was still recovering from the anti-Nepalese riots, the Paro Penlop attacked and plundered Phari.[25] The effect of these tensions on either side of the Sikkim-Tibet border was to make the trade with Tibet more than usually subject to stoppages which were apparent in Darjeeling. As in 1873, interruptions in trade invited investigation by the Bengal Government. A repetition of the Edgar mission to the Tibetan frontier seemed to be needed; and, in 1884, when following Das' journey to Tibet some measure of contact existed with the authorities at Tashilhunpo, the occasion promised to bring about concrete improvements in the relations between India and Tibet. With these considerations in mind, the Bengal Government in October 1884 deputed Colman Macaulay, Bengal Financial Secretary, to visit Sikkim.[26]

The account of Macaulay's visit reads in many ways like that of Edgar eleven years earlier. Instead of the Phari Jongpen of 1873, Macaulay met the Jongpen of Kambajong, a small town not far to the north of the Sikkim border on the road to Shigatse. The Jongpen, with Das interpreting, gave another version of that familiar story that the Chinese were entirely responsible for the continued isolation of Tibet. He spoke of a lay faction in Lhasa who would, in fact, welcome closer relations with British India in defiance of the obstinate conservatism of the monks. Many Tibetans, he said, had come of late to appreciate the utility and quality of European manufactures, and they would welcome an increase in trade. The monks, however, feared for their spiritual influence and for their lucrative commercial monopolies, and they would never cease to fight against any change unless compelled to do so. The monks, the Jongpen continued, still retained a measure of respect for Chinese power. If the Indian Government could obtain an order from the Chinese Emperor, duly signed and sealed, expressing a wish for an improvement in the conditions of Indo-Tibetan trade, then he, the Jongpen, would do his best to co-operate with Macaulay. Until then, whatever his private sympathies might be, he was obliged as an official of the Tibetan Government to oppose all efforts to alter the structure of the trans-frontier trade in his district. With Chinese approval, however, he felt that that trade had good prospects. 'Nowadays', he said, 'whenever a man gets an article of English manufacture, a hundred people come to look at it.' The Jongpen concluded by hinting that the British cause was more warmly accepted in Tashilhunpo than in Lhasa. In the former place it was said that

Queen Victoria was regarded as the incarnation of a protecting deity, while in the latter she was seen as the Goddess of War. Further evidence of the friendship of Tashilhunpo was detected in the willingness of the Jongpen to transmit letters and presents from the Indian Government to the Chief Minister.[27]

Macaulay was very much inspired by the prospect of a revival of the Tibetan policy of Warren Hastings. Unlike Edgar, he had no difficulty in uncovering traces of the memory of Hastings' two envoys to Tashilhunpo. The publication in 1876 of Markham's edition of Bogle's journal, of course, gave a much better picture of what Hastings had hoped for from Tibet than had been previously general. Macaulay, moreover, did not fail to be struck by the similarity of the situation at Tashilhunpo to that obtaining when Turner visited it in 1783. In 1884, as in 1783, friendly letters were passing between Tashilhunpo and the British. On both occasions a Tashi Lama who had shown himself well disposed towards the British - for such was the interpretation of the kindness shown to Das - had just died and an infant ruled in his place under a Regent who had proved to be by no means adverse to a closer relationship to the great power to the south. Macaulay, in some respects, acted in conscious imitation of Warren Hastings. He advised the Bengal Government, for instance, to offer to the Tashilhunpo authorities a plot of land near Calcutta on which they might build a hostel for Tibetans visiting Bengal, just as Hastings had given land for a religious house to the 6th Tashi Lama.[28]

Macaulay's report on his visit to the Sikkim-Tibet frontier in 1884 contained some of the most optimistic statements about the benefits to be derived from closer relations with Tibet to have been written by an official in the service of the Indian Government since the time of Hastings. The commercial advantages would be stupendous. If the Chinese once removed the prohibition of the import of Indian tea into Tibet, the Chinese product would be swept off the market. There would be an ever-increasing demand for English broadcloth, piece goods, cutlery and Indian indigo. The Tibetans in return would supply gold: 'there appears to be little doubt that gold is really plentiful'; and wool: 'the quantity of wool available for export is known to be enormous'. If a route were developed through the Lachen Valley in northern Sikkim, as well as one to the Chumbi Valley, British goods would have as easy access to Shigatse as they would have to Lhasa. All that stood in the way of the realization of these blessings was Chinese and monastic opposition. The monks, however, could easily be brought round to acquiescence in British plans by a skilful distribution of gifts to the great monasteries of Sera, Drebung and Gaden which, Macaulay wrote, 'represent the national party in permanent opposition to the Chinese', and would in consequence be quite glad to see a development which could but result in the decline of Chinese influence.

The Chinese, Macaulay thought, could hardly refuse a British request for permission to send a mission into Tibet. They had just granted passports to the Russian explorer Prjevalski for travel in Tibet, and they would have to give such documents to the British. Macaulay, therefore, urged most strongly that the Chinese be approached for passports for a political and scientific mission of the type specified in the Separate Article of the Chefoo Convention to go up to Lhasa, and there to confer with Chinese and Tibetan commissioners on the removal of obstacles at present imposed on Indian trade with Tibet. These discussions were not to involve the difficult question of the general admission of Europeans into Tibet. Once the passports had been obtained, overtures should be made to the abbots of the great Lhasa monasteries, to try to secure their good-will towards the mission. The present contacts with Tashilhunpo should be maintained; and if by some chance the Chinese should refuse to allow a large mission to Lhasa, then a smaller one should be sent to Tashilhunpo in its place. The forthcoming installation of the new Tashi Lama provided an excuse for such a mission which was as good now as it had been for Turner in 1783.[29]

Sir Rivers Thompson, the Lieutenant-Governor of Bengal, agreed to Macaulay's plans with enthusiasm.[30] But not so Lord Dufferin, the Viceroy, who was anxious about complications with China which might well result from any Tibetan venture. He was even worried lest the Chinese should construe the present correspondence between Bengal and Tashilhunpo as an infringement on their sovereignty in Tibet.[31] Sir Harry Parkes, the British Minister in Peking, saw no danger of this, however, though he very much doubted whether fresh attempts to open Tibet would be rewarded by better results than had similar attempts in the past.[32]

But Bengal soon found fresh evidence to justify its optimism. In January 1885 they had written to the Chief Minister to offer him the grant of land near Calcutta. He had replied in a most amicable manner, and had hinted that he might come down to Calcutta himself in the next cold season, which was more than Hastings' Tashi Lama had ever suggested. He also asked for various articles to be sent to him; English readers, a Tibetan-English dictionary, a book on the English language self-taught, another camera and plates, and perfumes and oils 'to make the complexion soft and fair'.[33] All this suggested that Tibet was beginning to wake to the existence of the outside world at last.

O'Conor, the British Chargé d'Affaires at Peking, retained that dislike of Tibetan schemes which had become traditional to the British Legation since the time of Bruce. The Yamen, he said, had told him that Tibet was not a dependency of China, but 'an integral portion of the Chinese Empire', and that the Tibetan authorities at Tashilhunpo had no power to initiate a new policy.[34] It was clear that the Chinese would not welcome any attempt to implement the Separate Article, and O'Conor did not want to press them for such a trivial reason as the Tibet trade, 'at best a poor trade with no prospect of increase'.[35]

Macaulay's visit to the Tibetan frontier was widely reported in England. *The Times* published accounts of it[36] which caused alarm in some quarters. A question was asked in the Commons as to whether the Indian Government intended to 'throw' opium into Tibet, an allegation which was denied.[37] The Society for the Suppression of the Opium Trade was not convinced, and its Secretary, Storrs Turner, was in any case deeply shocked at the very idea of British relations with the Tibetan Lamas. No Englishman, he protested to *The Times*, should be proud of this attempt by Macaulay 'to curry favour with the Tibetan Buddhists by pretending that the British Queen and people do not heartily disbelieve and repudiate the imposture of the re-incarnate Lamas'.[38]

But British merchants did not have these scruples. In May 1885 the Dewsbury Chamber of Commerce petitioned the Foreign Secretary to expedite the opening of Tibetan markets to British commerce, which would help alleviate 'the depression in trade which has now so long existed' by securing in Tibet an outlet for British manufactures in return for Tibetan wool and gold. It pressed for immediate negotiations at Peking on this subject.[39] In July 1885 the Manchester[40] and Birmingham[41] Chambers echoed these sentiments.

In the summer of 1885 Colman Macaulay came home on leave, taking full advantage of this opportunity to explain to Lord Randolph Churchill, the Secretary of State, the advantages of a mission to Tibet. Not only, he said, was 'Darjeeling the natural outlet for the trade of Tibet and South Mongolia', not only did a mission to Lhasa provide an opportunity for studies of great scientific value, but also there were enormous political advantages to be won from friendship with 'the two great Pontiffs of the Buddhist Church, who exercise boundless influence over the tribes of Central Asia – an influence so great that the present dynasty of China has had to conciliate it in order to secure its own existence'. The time, Macaulay went on, had passed for waiting 'till the wall of Chinese obstruction should fall as fell the walls of Jericho'. A special commissioner should go at once to Peking and there get passports for a British mission to Lhasa. Macaulay, in conclusion, referred to the reported desire of China for an alliance with Britain as an added reason for trying to open Tibet now. 'Our political influence in Central Asia', he wrote, 'would receive an enormous accession if, all misunderstanding and jealousy being removed, a British Envoy and the Chinese Imperial Commissioner were to meet at the Court of the Dalai Lama on cordial terms as the representatives of the two great Empires of Asia in alliance.'[42]

Lord Randolph was attracted by these Imperial visions. He agreed to send Colman Macaulay, the obvious choice for the task, first to Peking for passports, and then as head of a mission to Lhasa. Lord Dufferin, the Viceroy, on the other hand, could only think of the vast expense involved were the proposed mission to find itself attacked by the Tibetans and then have to be rescued or avenged by a campaign across the Himalayas. He asked that the mission be postponed a while, at least until the Afghan frontier was 'in a more settled state'. But the India Office prevailed.[43] It thought that 'the Government of India are quite demented' in trying to put off the mission when conditions seemed so favourable. Macaulay was instructed to leave England in August 1885, pick up S. C. Das at Columbo, and arrive in Peking in October.[44]

O'Conor did not relish the prospect of an Indian official meddling so directly in Anglo–Chinese diplomacy. He felt, moreover, that Macaulay's arrival in Peking would only serve to advertise without need the Tibetan project. He felt sure that he could do much better without Macaulay, and he could without doubt ensure greater secrecy if he was left to do the job on his own. With this Sir Robert Hart, the Inspector-General of the Chinese Maritime Customs who played such an important part in the conduct of British relations with China in the latter part of the nineteenth century, was in full agreement.[45]

O'Conor was right in supposing that Macaulay's plans could be kept no secret in Peking. Before Macaulay had left England, *The Times* of 9th July 1885 printed a detailed account of British dealings with Tibet, concluding with Macaulay's visit to Sikkim of 1884 and with a summary of the proposals he then made, which could only have been based on official sources.[46] But Macaulay could not understand these finer points of diplomatic reticence, and thought that O'Conor opposed his visit to Peking because he was 'cool' towards the whole Tibet enterprise, and he felt that it was essential to convert O'Conor to its support. He was sure that once he reached the Chinese capital he could put O'Conor into a better humour.[47]

Throughout these discussions Macaulay was greatly assisted by the Chinese Legation in London. The Secretary to the Legation, Sir Halliday Macartney, father of that George Macartney who was to play such a part in Kashgaria from the 1890s onwards, was very interested in Tibet. As a young man he had been much impressed by the adventures of T. T. Cooper. In 1875 he had prepared a plan to try to emulate his hero in an attempt to penetrate to Lhasa from Western China in the disguise of a wealthy Chinese merchant. His appointment to the Kuo Mission to London following the Margary affair put stop to this project, but he never forgot his early enthusiasms. In 1875 Macartney had been promised help in his Tibetan project by the young Marquis Tseng Chi-tse, son of that Tseng Kuo-fan who had been so instrumental in saving the Manchu Dynasty at the time of the Taiping Rebellion. Tseng was now Chinese Minister in London, shortly to return to China, and Halliday Macartney had no difficulty in persuading his old friend to promise to do all he could to smooth Macaulay's path. The Chinese Legation, moreover, prepared letters of introduction for Macaulay to the Yamen and to the Tientsin Viceroy, Li Hung-chang.[48]

Macaulay's instructions were a summary of the proposals which he himself had made in his report. He was to try for a mission to Lhasa; if this failed, then to Tashilhunpo; if this failed too, then for a declaration on the part of the Emperor that he disapproved of the obstacles at present placed in the way of Indo-Tibetan trade. Macaulay was empowered to waive discussion of entry to Tibet by Europeans, and he was to assure the Chinese that British subjects would only enter Tibet for trading purposes. His instructions considered the possibility that the question of the Tibet trade might be settled in Peking, without the necessity for a mission to Lhasa. If this was the case, Macaulay was to request that Indo-Tibetan trade should be free, or, at most, not subject to a duty higher than that in force at the Treaty Ports in China; and, in any case, there should be no *likin* or other internal taxes on this trade within Tibet. He was also to insist that Indian traders should have free access to Tibet; that their lives and property while in Tibet should be protected adequately; and, finally, that the trading monopolies of the Lamas should be broken.[49]

Macaulay and Das arrived in Peking in October 1885. They

soon discovered that no trade settlement could be made there, and that the Yamen was not going to give them passports for Tibet without a long and tedious argument. As O'Conor had feared, the reason for Macaulay's presence in Peking was common knowledge. The day after his arrival a Shanghai paper reported that he had come about Tibet. It was soon discovered that the Yamen had been aware of a contemplated British mission to Lhasa for several months. O'Conor was anxious lest the opening of the Tibet question would upset the settlement, then pending, of regulations for British trade with Kashgar, and was clearly more hopeful of Kashgaria than of Tibet as a field for the extension of British commerce. Macaulay, however, thought that he had soon convinced O'Conor that 'the Tibet question was the larger of the two'.[50] Li Hung-chang, while not personally opposed to the Tibetan project, doubted whether any Chinese offical would take on the responsibility involved in this. Li had seen with his own eyes a huge pile of petitions from Tibet begging that no foreigners be allowed to enter. Moreover, Li said, the tutor to the Emperor, Sung Kuei, a former Amban at Lhasa, was very much opposed to any relaxation of the restrictions now in force, and his opinions carried great weight. From the outset it was apparent that Macaulay's task was not as easy as he had once supposed.[51]

From the start the Yamen offered two arguments against the proposed mission to Lhasa. The Tibetans would oppose it, probably by force of arms. The Chinese did not have the power to impose their wishes on to the Government of the Dalai Lama. O'Conor and Macaulay, of course, denied that these arguments had any validity. They said that the Tibetans would welcome an improved trade with British India. They claimed that the present difficulties in the way of that trade were due not to Tibetan hostility but to Chinese obstruction. Macaulay remarked that on his visit to the Sikkim-Tibet border in 1884 he had seen on one of the passes leading into Chumbi a placard, written in Chinese and adorned with the Imperial Seal, prohibiting all passage to foreigners. So much for the Yamen's arguments. They were, in any case, as O'Conor pointed out, quite superfluous since the Separate Article of the Chefoo Convention was quite explicit that the Yamen should grant passports for a British mission to Tibet. The Yamen, however, had an effective counter on this point. The Separate Article had left a loop-hole in the reference to 'special circumstances', and in that category the Yamen classed the Tibetan petitions against European entry. The Yamen did not feel that it could grant any passport until it had had time to refer the whole question to the Amban. To this O'Conor remarked that there would be plenty of time to consult the Amban after the passports had been granted in principle.[52]

O'Conor had no doubt that passports would eventually be granted. The real problem was to ensure that the passports were respected in Tibet. For this reason O'Conor suggested that along with the passports he should extract from the Yamen a copy of the letter of instructions which the Yamen would send to the Amban concerning the reception to be given to the mission; and that he should also secure a firm undertaking by the Yamen that the Amban would in fact obey his orders. Even with these safeguards O'Conor did not doubt that the Yamen would do their best to make the sending of the mission impossible. He advised the Indian Government, once the necessary documents had been obtained, to slip the mission into Tibet with as little fuss and delay as possible. Moreover, since this was probably the last chance they would ever have of sending Europeans to the forbidden land, they should keep several members of the mission there for as long as they could, if not in Lhasa then in Shigatse.[53]

As the negotiations developed, O'Conor had to make several concessions to the Yamen. He had to promise that the Indian Government would make no agreement with the Tibetans without reference to China - an important concession in view of the hopes of relations with Tashilhunpo - and he had to emphasize the absolutely secular nature of the proposed mission. In no way was it to pave the way for the extension of the influence of the French Catholics into Central Tibet.[54]

In November 1885 the pasports were granted and the text of the letter of instructions from the Yamen to the Amban was agreed upon. O'Conor was still convinced that the hardest part of the business was yet to come. All the way from the frontier to Lhasa there would be difficulties, and it was more than likely that the mission would have to be content with reaching Shigatse or, even, Gyantse. To lessen Tibetan suspicions, O'Conor advised India to organize the mission on a commercial rather than a political basis, by which he meant that it should on no account be accompanied by a large military escort, which would certainly give the Tibetans the impression that the mission was an invading army. Great secrecy should be preserved; the mission should be pushed on quickly; and once begun it should continue with determination. O'Conor now thought the time was favourable for this venture to the extent that the Chinese had been much impressed by the strength and decision which the British were then showing in Burma.[55] O'Conor warned that delays in the mission's departure would only give the Chinese time to find an excuse to delay it further, if not to stop it altogether. From what he had heard at the Yamen, he felt sure that the Amban would send a very unfavourable report, 'most probably fictitious', as to the reception likely to be given to the mission by the Tibetans. If Tibet was not opened at this time, O'Conor said, it would, in all probability, never be opened.[56]

Sarat Chandra Das had, meanwhile, concluded that the Tibetans were indeed hostile to the mission. While Macaulay had been arguing with the Yamen, Das went to live in the Yellow Temple, one of the chief places of Buddhist worship in Peking, where he dressed and lived as a Buddhist monk. Here he met a Tibetan envoy sent by Lhasa to keep an eye on the negotiations in Peking, and from this person Das learnt that all the concessions offered by the Yamen were no more than a sham. The Chinese had every intention of stopping the mission, whatever promises the Yamen might make, for they knew that if they did not prevent it from entering Tibet the Tibetans would oppose it by force and a crisis would develop far worse than the Margary affair. But no one seems to have paid much attention to Das.[57]

Early in 1886 the mission assembled in Darjeeling. Instead of the quiet, modest affair advised by O'Conor, it had developed into an expedition of formidable proportions. Macaulay was Chief Envoy; he was to be accompanied by A. W. Paul as Secretary, Colonel Tanner as Surveyor, Dr. Oldham as Geologist, Dr. Leakey as Medical Officer, Mr. Warry of the China Consular Service as Chinese Interpreter, S. C. Das as Tibetan Interpreter, and Captains Elwes and Gwatkin in command of an escort of some three hundred sepoys. The size of the escort was later reduced somewhat – in May 1886 it had shrunk to fifty-eight sepoys – but not enough to allay suspicion that it was the vanguard of an invading army.[58]

The mission showed a reluctance to start despite O'Conor's advice that it should set out as soon as possible.[59] Lord Dufferin was largely to blame for these delays, and for good reason. In the latter part of 1885, as a result of a long history of complaints from British merchants in Rangoon combined with fear of French intrigues, Lord Dufferin had undertaken the conquest of Upper Burma: and that territory was brought officially under British rule in January 1886. This action was much criticized at home, and, since the annexed territory was by no means pacified, was likely to arouse much more criticism in the future. Lord Dufferin, therefore, was hardly likely to welcome the prospect of becoming involved in another border war through the Tibetan resistance to Macaulay's advance. Thus in February 1886, on hearing that a change of Ambans was about to take place, he suggested that the mission should wait until the new Amban could reach his post.[60] To O'Conor this seemed to be playing into the hands of the Chinese by giving them time to think up a method of stopping the mission altogether;[61] but Dufferin was not swayed by this sort of argument since he too was seeking excuses for a postponement of the mission. Thus in March he suggested that its departure be delayed until an agreement was reached with China over Burma, a country with traditional ties to China.[62] And in April he proposed that concessions should be made to Chinese claims of possession of some sort of suzerainty over Burma in return for a Chinese guarantee of improved conditions for Indian trade with Tibet.[63] But at this point the India Office were still impressed enough by Macaulay's scheme to inform Lord Dufferin that the arrangements already made with regard to Tibet 'are sufficiently satisfactory to render it unnecessary and unexpedient to mix the two questions'.[64]

During these delays the Chinese Government was becoming more and more alarmed at the way things were going. It was frightened by the reports it had seen in the English press as to the size of the escort, and it was by no means convinced that the annexation of Burma would not shortly be followed by the annexation of Tibet.[65] This, certainly, was the impression of that important Chinese official the Viceroy of Szechuan Province, who in May was proposing to send Chinese troops to Lhasa for the defence of Tibet against British invasion.[66] O'Conor managed to convince Li Hung-chang that no such invasion was contemplated, and Li thought he could calm down the Szechuan Viceroy; but he needed time, which it was impossible to deny him. Meanwhile the long-awaited report from the Amban on the Tibetan reaction to the Macaulay Mission reached Peking. It did not mince words. 'If the English incontinently enter Tibet,' the Amban reported, 'trouble will certainly ensue.' On the strength of this the Yamen asked for a further postponement of the mission on the grounds that, in the words of the Separate Article, 'a circumstance' now existed to which 'due regard' should be paid;[67] and this caused no surprise to the Foreign Office in London, which felt that the Macaulay Mission had been mishandled in India from its inception.[68] At the end of May the Yamen played their last card. They offered O'Conor an immediate settlement in Burma in return for a permanent abandonment of the Macaulay Mission.[69] Lord Dufferin agreed at once. With relief he telegraphed Lord Kimberley that 'I would not hesitate a moment in sacrificing the Tibet mission for settlement'.[70]

The Yamen at once saw that they were in a position of strength, and they now pressed home their advantage in an attempt to secure the cancellation of the Separate Article of the Chefoo Convention. This the Foreign Office and the India Office refused to do,[71] but, as O'Conor argued, the Separate Article was now to all intents and purposes dead. It had but provided for the sending of one mission, and one only. It did not specify that that mission should be successful or should reach its destination. This was a point hardly worth the discussion, since there seemed no prospect of any British mission to Lhasa for many years to come. Meanwhile, a final settlement was urgently required to counteract the rapidly mounting Chinese bad feeling over Burma.[72]

Thus O'Conor pressed for a solution, while he managed to keep the Yamen at the conference table throughout June and most of July 1886 by the clever use of the threat to send forward the Macaulay Mission regardless of how the Tibetans might react.[73] He continued to tell the Foreign Office that the British objective was Tibetan trade, and that the mission was but a means to this end which had proved unworkable in practice.[74] Dufferin, who was worried about the expenses being run up by the mission which could not be withdrawn from Darjeeling until an agreement was reached in Peking, was by July 1886 in favour of any settlement which gave him the chance to be quit of the whole business.[75] Thus, after some more haggling over words, O'Conor was able on 24th July 1886 to sign the following agreement with the Yamen as Article IV of a Convention between Britain and China 'relative to Burmah and Thibet', which read:

Inasmuch as enquiry into the circumstances by the Chinese Government has shown the existence of many obstacles to the Mission to Thibet provided for in the Separate Article of the Chefoo Agreement, England consents to countermand the Mission forthwith.

With regard to the desire of the British Government to consider arrangements for further trade between India and Thibet, it will be the duty of the Chinese Government, after careful enquiry into circumstances, to adopt measures to exhort and encourage the people with a view to the promotion and development of trade. Should it be practicable, the Chinese Government shall then proceed carefully to consider Trade Regulations; but if insuperable obstacles should be found to exist, the British Government will not press the matter unduly.[76]

This amounted to a total abandonment of British hopes for the opening of Tibet. 'Insuperable obstacles' would always have been discovered by the Chinese, and the British would not then be in a position to press the matter 'unduly'. Even if the British should find the occasion to reopen the question of Tibet, as, indeed, they soon were, the Chinese would be in a stronger position than they had been in 1885. Hitherto some doubt had existed as to the status of Tibet in relation to China. The Separate Article had obliged the Chinese to assist the British in getting a mission through to Lhasa; but it had in no way bound the British to deal with Tibet exclusively through China; indeed, it had recognized the British right to establish direct diplomatic relations with the Tibetans. The Convention of 1886, however, removed all ambiguity on this question. In future all British negotiations about Tibet were to be carried on through China. Among the consequences of this was the end to any hope of political results from British contacts with Tashilhumpo.

The India Office, however, soon came to agree with Lord Dufferin that they had done well by the Convention. By the sacrifice of problematical gains in Tibet they had won 'the formal recognition of the Chinese Government to the establishment of British rule in Upper Burmah'; 'complete freedom of action in dealing with any territorial claims on the Burmese border which China may advance in the future'; and 'a guarantee for the settlement of the frontier trade between Burmah and China, and for the opening of S.W. China to our commerce'.[77]

The Chambers of Commerce, on the other hand, were not so happy at this outcome of the Macaulay Mission. The Foreign Office and the India Office received petitions on the opening of Tibetan trade from the Chambers of Halifax, Huddersfield, London and Manchester.[78] The Chambers took note of the publication by Warry, the Consular officer lately attached to the Macaulay Mission as Chinese Interpreter, of an indignant account of the obstacles now placed by the Tibetans in the way of what trade there still was between Tibet and Darjeeling. Warry very much deprecated the abandonment of Macaulay's project. 'Cannot the present Government', he wrote, 'be induced to retrace a step which would involve the closing of Tibet for another generation and the perpetuation of a state of things which is a scandal and an insult to the British name?'[79] On reading this account, which the Indian Government described as 'a serious error of judgment', the Chambers of Commerce of Dewsbury and Leeds, both towns much interested in Tibet as a source of high-quality wool, were moved to press for a revival of the mission.[80] It is of interest that

Warry, the Chinese specialist, saw in the Tibetans the cause of obstructions which Edgar and Macaulay had attributed to the Chinese. As Lt.-Col. Bailey has noticed, the conduct of British relations with Tibet has been greatly influenced by the fact that the officials concerned have had strong preferences for one or other of the two races.[81]

Why did the Macaulay Mission fail? There seems to be little doubt that had it pushed on into Tibet in January 1886 it would have reached Gyantse if not Lhasa, and its very presence on Tibetan soil must have forced some settlement of the question of Tibetan trade. There seems to be equally little doubt that Macaulay was not the man for oriental diplomacy. He had great energy and enthusiasm, but he had little understanding of diplomatic method. The way he sold his project to Randolph Churchill over Dufferin's head was hardly calculated to inspire the Indian Government with much liking for the project, even if they had been in sympathy with its aims. Macaulay was obsessed about opening Tibet to a degree that seriously affected his judgments. He was always wanting to share his hopes with the whole world. When prevented by Government from publishing an account of his confidential mission to Sikkim in 1884, he wrote it up in a long poem, the *Lay of Lachen*, in a style which owed much to his namesake's *Lays of Ancient Rome*.[82] Sir Philip Currie of the Foreign Office in London was convinced that the size of the escort was due to Macaulay's inability to resist an Imperial gesture.[83] That Macaulay saw no need to keep secret the objectives of his visit to Peking is shown by his request for permission to publish a full account of his intentions,[84] and it may well be that he himself was responsible, even if indirectly, for the publication in February 1886 and subsequently of details of the size of the escort.

If the Indian Government had been wholeheartedly in favour of the mission, the unwelcome publicity it received and the consequent reactions might not have prevented its advance. But, as Sir Alfred Lyall pointed out in his life of Lord Dufferin, the Viceroy was not at all enthusiastic. He felt that the whole project 'has been imposed upon' him by instructions from England. Lord Dufferin doubted greatly the wisdom of the Macaulay Mission, and the moment that it seemed likely that opposition would be offered to Macaulay by the Tibetans, he saw his doubts confirmed. He agreed with the Duke of Wellington that the outcome of a successful military expedition in Asia was often no less embarrassing than a defeat. Where should it stop? In 1886 Afghan relations were still critical, an army was still tied down in Burma, and the prospect of further military commitments across the Himalayas, which must result if the Tibetans were to attack the mission, was truly alarming. Dufferin was only too glad to give up the mission for a settlement in Burma, and he must have hoped to hear no more of Tibet during his administration. The only justification for a military expedition into Tibet would be the threatened presence there of some other European power: in Lyall's view it was the presence of such a threat which marked the difference between the Tibetan policy of 1886 and that policy of the first years of the twentieth century which resulted in the Younghusband Mission to Lhasa of 1904.[85]

Finally, it must be admitted that O'Conor was never as pleased with the idea of a mission to Tibet as he might have been. The years 1885-86, when the Macaulay Mission was born and died, marked a particularly difficult period in the history of British diplomacy in the East. The rivalry between Britain and Russia in Asia had reached a point where war seemed more than likely. The Russian advance to Merv and the Panjdeh crisis created a condition in which the friendship of China, which O'Conor and Sir Robert Hart both thought might soon mature into a formal alliance, was worth cherishing.[86] Tibet, moreover, was by no means the only matter for discussion in the relations between Britain and China at this time. While the Macaulay Mission was developing, O'Conor was wrestling with the Yamen over the difficult question of the imposition of *likin* on opium. He was preparing the way for yet another of a series of ventures by Ney Elias to Kashgaria and the Pamirs to keep an eye on the Russians and to promote British commerce. He was attempting to solve the many problems which arose from Lord Dufferin's annexation of Upper Burma, including the question of what exactly was Burma's traditional relationship to the Chinese Empire, and what was the precise significance of the tribute missions which the Burmese had been accustomed to send to Peking at regular intervals. The questions of opium, Kashgar, Burma and Tibet were all, to some extent, interconnected. They were all concerned with trade between India and the Chinese Empire, and it should cause no surprise that O'Conor was prepared to concede in one question in return for advantages in another. Apart from the final exchange of Chinese recognition of the British position in Burma for the abandonment of the Macaulay Mission, O'Conor had at an earlier stage considered concessions to China in the opium question in return for Chinese concessions in Burma and Tibet. Tibet had always been an element in the course of Anglo-Chinese relations, and as such was affected by the prevailing policy of Britain towards China. In 1886

China seemed a potential bulwark against Russian expansion in Asia, and neither O'Conor nor the Foreign Office wished to bear down too hard upon her.[87]

VII

THE SIKKIM-TIBET
CONVENTION
AND THE
TRADE REGULATIONS

.

1886 – 1893

IN THE Burma-Tibet Convention of July 1886 the Indian Government saw a means by which it could slip quietly out of any entanglements on the Tibetan border. The Macaulay Mission would be disbanded and the Tibetan question left in indefinite suspension. If, at some future date, the Tibetans should appear willing to accept British representatives, the subject could be raised again: if not, it did not matter very much. The settling of the Burmese frontier and the avoidance of military commitments at a period when the Russian advance in Central Asia seemed more threatening, and more likely to lead to war than ever before, were solid benefits. Friendly relations with China, which might be of crucial importance in the coming struggle, were well worth the sacrifice of unknown, and, in all probability, trifling, benefits of the Tibet trade. Lord Dufferin's Government had always felt that Macaulay was engaged on a wild goose chase and they were glad to see the last of his plan. The dogma of a valuable Tibetan trade had lost many of its adherents; even 'Macaulay himself was soon constrained to admit that the commercial advantages to be derived from the mission were comparatively insignificant', and was forced to talk about the immense political advantages to be gained from opening Tibet. But Government could only see political advantage in the abandonment of the mission, and hoped that its hands would 'not be forced a second time for the sake of a little momentary and altogether undeserved popularity among the classes suffering from the commercial depression'. So wrote Mackenzie Wallace, Dufferin's private secretary; and he concluded with the following remarks:

> At present we ought to aim at establishing cordial relations with China and allaying her suspicions. Any attempt to resuscitate the defunct mission or to bring pressure of any kind on the Tibetans would have a most prejudicial effect on the negotiations which must sooner or later be undertaken for the delimitation of the Burma-Chinese frontier. Good relations with China can only be obtained by convincing the Chinese that having taken Burma, we have no aggressive intentions, and we should never forget that, apart from the frontier question just referred to, China is every day becoming a more important factor in the great Eastern Question.[1]

In the first week of July 1886, however, a chain of events began which was to lead to further pressure on the Tibetans. While O'Conor was still arguing with the Yamen as to the terms on which the Macaulay Mission should be abandoned, news began to reach Darjeeling of considerable Tibetan troop concentrations in the Chumbi Valley, just beyond the Sikkim border. Macaulay took this to be a reception committee assembled by the Tibetans to welcome his mission; but by 27th July it had become apparent that the Tibetans had advanced thirteen miles into Sikkim territory across the Jelap La and had fortified a hill top at Lingtu on the Darjeeling road. The Maharaja of Sikkim, then living in Chumbi, told his Durbar that the Tibetans had always possessed rights over this portion of Sikkim. They had for many years allowed Sikkim to look on this region as its own, but they were now resuming control over it as punishment for the way in which the ruler of Sikkim had allowed the British to travel and build roads through his land, and for his failure to stop the development of the Macaulay Mission which the Tibetans considered the spearhead of an impending British invasion.[2]

The reported Tibetan claims over Sikkim were very embarrassing to the Indian Government; and it seemed difficult to counter them. The precise extent of the Tibetan claims was not known at this time and it was hard to see how the Sikkim Treaty of 1861 might apply to them. Two articles of this treaty might have been relevant. Article 19 forbade the Raja of Sikkim - who in 1886 came to be called Maharaja by British officials, and will be so referred to henceforth - to cede or lease any of his territory to another state without British permission. Article 20 forbade the passage of the armed forces of any other state through Sikkim territory without British consent. The Maharaja was promptly reminded of these two articles. But what was the exact extent of Sikkim territory? It was known that Sikkim had long enjoyed the closest of relations with Tibet – Campbell, Hooker, Eden, Edgar and Macaulay all testified to this – and it might well be that the Tibetan claims, whatever they were, had good historical foundation. And how could these claims be discussed? They could not be considered in talks with the Tibetans alone, for the Burma-Tibet Convention of July 1886 stated that the British were to have no dealings with Tibet except through the Chinese. Thus, the Indian Government could only query the Tibetan claims through Anglo-Chinese negotiation, and it had no desire whatsoever to embark on discussions with the Chinese over its status in territory which it had long been accustomed to think of as British. Macaulay's proposal, that he should go at once to the border and try to settle the trouble by holding a general conference with representatives from Sikkim, Tibet and Bhutan, was rejected. The Chinese might see here a revival of the Macaulay Mission, and this might result in 'an embarrassing collision or rebuff'; it would, in any case, lead to those Anglo-Chinese discussions which Lord Dufferin wished to avoid.[3]

Thus Dufferin refused to heed the cries of Bengal officials that the Tibetan advance was resulting in severe damage to British prestige in the Himalayas, that it was causing alarm among the inhabitants of Darjeeling, native and European, and that it should be treated as a local police action. He told Macaulay that 'your mission must be broken up completely and expeditiously'. He hoped that the Tibetans would then retire of their own accord from a position which must be difficult to keep supplied at any time, and even more so when winter came. The India Office thought that 'the decision of the Government of India not to act hurriedly in this matter is a wise one. . . . If Mr. Macaulay is sent away and kept quiet we will hear little more of this. The Tibetans are not aggressive.'[4] The supporters of Macaulay's plans, of course, could not accept reasoning of this sort. They saw the Tibetan advance to Lingtu as the inevitable reaction to Lord Dufferin's timidity in allowing the mission to be abandoned, and many later writers adhered to this version. But it was soon apparent that the Tibetan move into Sikkim was symptomatic of profound changes which were then beginning to take place in the shape of Tibetan foreign policy, and that while the Macaulay Mission no doubt provoked the crisis, it was not its fundamental cause.

141

Lhasa had always looked on Sikkim as a Tibetan dependency; and after 1861 it still continued to influence to a considerable extent the course of Sikkim politics, partly through the ex-Dewan Namgyal, who retained a following in Sikkim despite his banishment to Chumbi, and partly through the Maharaja, who liked to spend as much time as possible in the dry atmosphere of his Chumbi estates. When the Raja Sidkyong Namgyal died in 1874, his successor and younger brother Thutob Namgyal was crowned in Chumbi at a ceremony attended by representatives of the lay and monastic authorities in Lhasa.[5] In 1881 Thutob Namgyal came under the influence of his Tibetan bride, who became the chief advocate of the Tibetan viewpoint in the Sikkim Durbar. Doubtless she acted as the mouthpiece for the views of the former Dewan Namgyal, who from his place of exile in Chumbi continued to plot for his return and for revenge for his defeat in 1861 until his death in 1888. In early 1886 the Maharaja affirmed his loyalty to the Chinese and Tibetans, and promised to do his utmost to prevent the entry of Englishmen into his dominions.[6]

This step seems to have been taken only after several years of pressure from the north. Lhasa, alarmed at the extension of British influence in Sikkim, the journeys of European travellers, the building of roads, and the influx of Nepalese settlers, had become far more strict in the enforcement of its grazing rights along the Sikkim-Tibet borders, and in other ways had brought its displeasure to the Maharaja's notice. The Maharaja was finally convinced that he would be well advised to make some sign of subjection to Lhasa by the outcome of events in Bhutan. In late 1884 the two Penlops of Bhutan, the Paro Penlop and the Tongsa Penlop, revolted against the Deb Raja as they had so many times in the past. The Deb Raja, the nominal lay head of the Bhutanese state, appealed to the Amban at Lhasa, who promptly summoned a conference at Phari to investigate the causes of this trouble. The two Penlops refused to attend. A Sino-Tibetan force was then assembled on the Bhutanese border, and the Tongsa Penlop prudently decided to make his peace. The Paro Penlop, however, continued in his defiance until he found himself surrounded by Chinese troops, whereupon he committed suicide. The Chinese underwent some anxiety in the early stages of this crisis lest the Bhutanese chiefs should request British assistance. A Memorial to the Throne from the Amban noted that 'the State of Bhutan being contiguous on its outward edge with British territory and on its inner edge with Tibet, it forms a screen or hedge upon the frontier, to which, in effect, it stands in the position of the lips to the teeth'. By their intervention, however, Bhutan was restored 'under our bit and bridle', and 'the preying designs of grasping people [the British] were put a stop to, so that it became possible to restore tranquility and content upon the border lands and so strengthen our frontier line'. The Amban, moreover, managed to acquire through this crisis some measure of control over the appointment of the Deb Raja and the Penlops.[7]

In early 1886 another conference was ordered by the Amban and the Tibetans, to meet at Galing in the Chumbi Valley. The occasion was the conferring on various Bhutanese chiefs of Chinese insignia of rank, a symbol of Chinese supremacy. The Maharaja of Sikkim was summoned to attend – he was then living in Chumbi – and he was so impressed by the recent display of Chinese strength in Bhutan that he made at Galing the declarations which the Amban requested without any struggle. He is said to have addressed the Amban and the Lhasa Government in these words:

> From the time of . . . [the first ruler of Sikkim] . . . all our Rajahs and other subjects have obeyed the orders of China. . . . You have ordered us by strategy or force to stop the passage . . . between Sikkim and British territory; but we are small and . . . [the Government of India] . . . is great, and we may not succeed, and may then fall into the mouth of the tiger-lion. In such a crisis, if you, as our old friend, can make some arrangements, even then in good and evil we will not leave the shelter of the feet of China and Tibet. . . . We all, king and subjects, priests and laymen, honestly promise to prevent persons from crossing the boundary.[8]

This version, which Riseley prints in the Sikkim Gazetteer, is probably a good indication of what took place, even if the actual words are not accurately reproduced. Thus the Amban managed to benefit from Chinese intervention in Bhutan. It was to be the last occasion on which he was able to do so, since one of the results of this crisis was to be the eventual emergence as supreme ruler of Bhutan of the Tongsa Penlop, Ugyen Wangchuk, who was to become a close ally of the British and to be rewarded with the title of Maharaja of Bhutan and with the award of the G.C.I.E. and the K.C.S.I.[9]

The Tibetans looked upon the Macaulay Mission as the first step in a British invasion of Tibet; but they had been given to believe by the monks of the Yellow Temple in Peking, who had

143

been so friendly with S. C. Das, that the mission would not enter Tibet if opposed by sufficient strength on the frontier. That the mission should be opposed all parties in Lhasa seemed to agree; but, once the Emperor had granted the passports and the mission appeared to be all set to move, there was a certain amount of division as to the best method of opposition. The monasteries, supported by the Nyechung or State Oracle, favoured armed resistance. The laity, on the whole, preferred to await developments, fearing the consequences of war with the British. The Amban probably supported the lay party, in the hope that if the mission were defeated by unaided Chinese effort, Chinese prestige would benefit, and in the knowledge that independent Tibetan action might so easily become uncontrollable. But by June 1886 the monks had won the day. They proposed that if the Maharaja of Sikkim was unable to prevent the advance of the British mission, they would have to take more drastic action. The first step was the sending of a Tibetan official to Lingtu, to meet the mission and try to persuade it to turn back. As a second line of defence troops were gathered in Chumbi commanding the passes from Sikkim. In early July, when the mission still had not advanced, some troops were moved forward to Lingtu, which place they fortified. News of the abandonment of the mission then reached Lhasa; and, with the crisis passing, the Tibetans began to withdraw the bulk of their force from Sikkim, leaving but a token garrison at Lingtu by September 1886; and even this was due to return to Tibet within a month or two.[10]

In October 1886, however, the Chinese chose to rebuke the Tibetans for their opposition to a mission which the Emperor had authorized; and as a gesture of defiance to the Chinese, the Tibetans closed the passes from Chumbi to Sikkim and reinforced Lingtu. Through the Sikkim Durbar they intimated that this time they would not withdraw their troops until the British had agreed not only never to send a mission to Tibet, but also never to allow any European official to pass beyond Lingtu. The Indian Government could not ignore such a challenge. Yet the situation was definitely embarrassing. On the one hand, there was the undoubted fact that territorial rights along the Sikkim-Tibet frontier were very confused, with many Sikkim villages near the border paying dues to Tibet as well as Sikkim; on the other hand, if the Tibetans were allowed to challenge unanswered the status of British-protected territory in Sikkim, the fact was likely to have an adverse effect on the security of British treaty relations with Nepal and Bhutan. There seemed no way, however, of finding out what the Tibetan claims were, let alone of rebutting them,

144

without reference to China.[11]

Lord Dufferin delayed informing Sir John Walsham, the British Minister in Peking, of even the fact of the Tibetan advance to Lingtu until January 1887, and only then with some reluctance. Dufferin observed that it would be easy enough to drive the Tibetans out of Sikkim, but this might be taken by the Chinese to signify an attempt 'to force a passage into Tibet', or as 'an inadequate execution of the Burma Convention'. Yet the Tibetans were stopping trade and unsettling the people of Sikkim and the Darjeeling District. Could Sir John persuade the Chinese to oblige their Tibetan subjects to withdraw from Sikkim, provided that

> any request for the withdrawal of the Tibetans should not be based on their being within the limits of Sikkim, nor even that Your Excellency should mention the fact that their position is in Sikkim; because any mention of the boundary might give rise to a specific assertion of China's suzerainty over Sikkim, which it is very desirable to avoid?[12]

The Indian Government, in fact, was still hoping that if the Tibetans were left alone and shown that they had nothing to fear from the British, they would withdraw of their own accord.

By May 1887 the Tibetans were still at Lingtu; they were levying taxes on the local population and showed no signs of departure. The Indian Government resolved to secure a new treaty from the Maharaja of Sikkim which would define more clearly the status of that state. He was summoned to Darjeeling for this purpose; but in June it became clear that even the suspension of his subsidy would not induce him to leave his retreat in Chumbi. It was discovered, moreover, that in the Maharaja's absence the government of Sikkim had been entrusted to an official of notoriously Tibetan sympathies.[13]

Masterly inactivity had failed completely, and it was a failure which was arousing comment in England, where the India Office and the Foreign Office continued to receive memorials from the Chambers of Commerce pointing out the value of the Tibet trade, regretting the abandonment of the Macaulay Mission, and remarking that if the British did not hurry up and secure an opening in Tibet they might well find themselves forestalled by another nation. Questions on the fate of the Macaulay project were asked in Parliament.[14] There was also comment in India. The Darjeeling merchants were grumbling, and the presence of the Tibetans had caused much alarm to the tea-planters of British Bhutan and Sikkim, who feared for their considerable investment in territory the title of which might soon be in dispute.[15] By October 1887 Lord Dufferin had made up his mind that the Tibetans must be expelled, come what may. He told Sir John Walsham that as no reply had been received to his query in January, he would take it that there was no objection to this course by the Chinese, and that he could go ahead with expulsion with no more delay.[16]

Walsham had, in fact, made tentative approaches to the Yamen on this matter, but as he had been asked by Dufferin not to say where the alleged aggression had taken place, he could produce no convincing reply to Chinese denials that there had been any aggression.[17] Only after he had heard that Dufferin meant to go ahead with expulsion did he mention the word Sikkim to the Yamen, who were unable to find any such place marked on their maps. They begged that nothing decisive should be done until they could receive a report on the situation from Lhasa, which Walsham thought reasonable enough,[18] despite Dufferin's growing impatience to get the expulsion over before winter should postpone it until the following spring.[19] In deference to the Viceroy, however, Walsham did persuade the Yamen to send orders to the Amban to instruct the Tibetans to withdraw, if it should prove that they were indeed trespassing on Sikkim soil.[20]

On 17th October the Yamen received a report from Lhasa. The Tibetans had indeed built a fort at Lingtu, 'with a view to protecting their country'; but 'not only was the place not subject to India, but it was a long way from Darjeeling', and consequently 'if the Viceroy of India takes upon himself to send a military expedition, his act will certainly affect the friendly relations between our two countries'.[21] The Indian Government refused to agree that there existed any doubts as to the Sikkim-Tibet frontier and emphasized that this could not be a subject for a discussion.[22] However, in the face of requests for delay from China, and because the campaigning season was now so far advanced, they were prepared to make a virtue of necessity and to put off any action until the following spring, but they made it clear that this was their last word.[23]

In December a letter was sent to the Lingtu garrison informing them that unless they withdrew by March the 15th, 1888, they would be expelled forcibly. In February 1888 the Viceroy wrote to the Dalai Lama outlining the British case, repeating the ultimatum, and emphasizing that whilst the British could not tolerate the presence of foreign troops in a state under their protection, they entertained no aggressive designs on Tibet, a country for which they had nothing but the friendliest sentiments.

Neither letter reached its destination since the Tibetans at Lingtu refused to accept or transmit any communications from the Indian Government.[24]

Throughout the winter of 1887-88 the Chinese, both through the Yamen and through the Legation in London, fought hard for the delay in the expulsion of the Tibetans.[25] In March 1888 they tried the expedient of suddenly dismissing one Amban and then asking for time for a successor to reach Lhasa.[26] Sir Halliday Macartney, the Secretary of the Chinese Legation in London, explained to the Foreign Office that the Chinese felt that the withdrawal of the Tibetans should be secured 'by the pacific action of the Suzerain power rather than by the Indian Government having recourse to arms', since the latter course would be highly damaging to Chinese prestige in Lhasa.[27] But the Viceroy, the Secretary of State and Sir John Walsham were now united in the conviction that further delay would be a sign of British weakness.[28]

There seems to be little doubt that the Chinese were very concerned at the direction in which the situation in Tibet was moving. In October or November 1887, Edward Goschen, then serving in Peking, had a frank conversation with Li Hung-chang who appeared to be 'greatly preoccupied' with the Tibetan question. Referring to the promises of the Yamen that the Tibetans should be ordered to withdraw, Li said:

The Yamen may promise what they like – but it is quite impossible in the present state of relations between China and Tibet for them to carry out their promise. People talk of China's influence in Tibet – but it is only nominal, as the Lamas are all powerful there, and the Yamen would only be able to carry out their promise by sending a large and costly expedition there, which it wouldn't suit them at all to do.

Li was most anxious to know what the Indian Government would do if the Chinese made no move at all in this matter.[29]

Influence in Lhasa, in fact, was of some considerable importance to the Chinese. In the first place, it was seen to be of value in keeping the peace in Mongolia where Tibetan Buddhism was very powerful. As a Manchu official once remarked: 'to tame the Mongols with the Yellow Religion is China's best policy'.[30] Writing in 1878, W. F. Mayers noted that

in furtherance of their policy of ensuring the control of the Mongolian tribes by means of ecclesiastical influences, the

147

> Chinese sovereigns of the reigning dynasty have been profuse
> in the establishment of Lamaist places of worship and official
> dignities in Peking and throughout the adjacent region.[31]

The support of the Lama hierarchy was one of the most valued
props of the alien Manchu Dynasty. Following the establishment
of direct Chinese control over Tibet in the eighteenth century, so
Grousset remarked, 'l'Eglise Jaune entra . . . dans les cadres de
l'administration chinoise'. It was in their capacity as protectors of
the Buddhist Church that the Chinese intervened in the Himalayas
in 1792.[32] In the second place, the trade between Szechuan and
Tibet provided much revenue for Szechuan Province which
would naturally resent its loss to the British.[33] Finally, Chinese
opinion was becoming alarmed at the decline of Chinese strength
in Central Asia. For signing the Treaty of Livadia with Russia in
1879, which surrendered portions of Chinese Turkestan, Ch'ung-
hou barely escaped with his life; and with this example before
him, no Chinese official was going to shoulder the responsibility
for the loss of Tibet.[34]

It must have been clear to the Chinese that they could not hope
to retain much influence in Lhasa in competition with the British
once the latter had sent their own representative there. The
Tibetans were bound to exploit such a situation to their own
advantage, and Tibetan interests now no longer seemed to
coincide with those of China. A new spirit of Tibetan independence was abroad. The 13th Dalai Lama had been chosen without
recourse to the Golden Urn, and the signs which influenced his
selection were particularly clear ones. These facts seem to have
encouraged greatly the Tibetans in the belief that soon they would
be free of Chinese control; and one may, perhaps, be permitted to
interpret the events of 1886 in this light. Another example of this
trend may well be detected in the Tibetan attack on and
destruction of the French Catholic mission at Batang in 1887.[35]

It would not be unreasonable to suppose, in these circumstances,
that the Chinese were most eager that the Tibetans should
withdraw from Lingtu before the British drove them out. But the
Yamen well knew that it was powerless to enforce such a
withdrawal by mere instructions to the Amban; and until it could
devise a method of coercing the Tibetans without appearing to
have surrendered to the British, the objective of the Yamen was,
no doubt, to postpone any decisive action for as long as possible.
Meanwhile it strove to acquire better intelligence on Tibet, and to
expedite the flow of information from Lhasa to Peking. In the
summer of 1887 Li Hung-chang sent a personal envoy, Chi Chih-

wen, to visit and report on the Sikkim-Tibet frontier;[36] and in January of that year Chengtu, the capital of Szechuan Province and the seat of the Provincial Government responsible for Tibet, was joined to Peking by telegraph.[37] The Amban, moreover, did not fail to tell the Tibetans to abandon Lingtu, so reports reaching Bengal indicated; but the Tibetans refused to listen and did all they could to prevent the Amban from visiting the disputed frontier.[38]

Walsham was inclined to accept, with reservations, the good faith of the Chinese, but the Indian Government was clearly unconvinced. Since Walsham felt that with the best will in the world the Amban would not persuade the Tibetans to withdraw, and Dufferin was impatient to have this irritating trouble spot on an obscure frontier cleared up, it was decided to go ahead with the expulsion of the Tibetans as planned.[39] In March 1888 a force of 2,000 men under Brigadier-General Graham drove out the garrison from Lingtu with little difficulty.[40] But the Tibetans, despite their primitive equipment and incomplete leadership, were not dismayed by this show of force. In May they attempted a surprise attack on the British camp at Gnatong and nearly succeeded in capturing the Lieutenant-Governor of Bengal, who was visiting the frontier; they were repulsed with severe losses.[41] There was a feeling among British officers and Bengal officials that this attack justified an invasion of Tibet itself, but the expeditionary force was strictly ordered not to enter Tibet territory unless it was essential on military grounds to do so.[42] In September a further Tibetan concentration near Gnatong was dispersed. This time the attackers were pursued into the Chumbi Valley, and for one day the village of Chumbi was occupied by British troops. Among the spoil on this occasion was a Tibetan map of Sikkim which showed the whole Darjeeling District in that part of Sikkim claimed by Lhasa.[43]

The active policy seemed to produce tangible results. When, after these defeats, the Tibetans approached the Tongsa Penlop of Bhutan for assistance, he refused on the grounds that if he gave help the British would cut off his subsidy.[44] Reports were received that many villagers in Chumbi were now openly seeking British protection and declaring that they no longer wished to remain subject to the tyranny of Tibet.[45] No sooner had the Expeditionary Force entered Chumbi than news reached Darjeeling that the Amban, despite Tibetan opposition, was on his way down from Lhasa to the frontier.[46] Even the Maharaja of Sikkim now announced that he was ready to come down to Darjeeling to talk things over with the Lieutenant-Governor.[47] Above all, the

149

Chinese had not actively intervened on behalf of their tributary. When the Yamen first learned of the success of the Expeditionary Force - they had hitherto placed great faith in the power of the Tibetan army, with its spiritual support from the monks - they were greatly alarmed. Some extremists seriously considered seeking Russian help in arms and ammunition and sending Chinese troops to aid the Tibetans. But moderate elements, helped, no doubt, by the strong advice of Sir Robert Hart and Sir Halliday Macartney, prevailed. Hart was firmly convinced that had he not brought the weight of his influence and wisdom to bear upon the Yamen, 'India and China would have come to blows in Tibet'. The Yamen were made to see that only by negotiating with the British could they preserve any vestige of influence in Tibet, though this did not prevent them from protesting vigorously against the violation of the Tibetan frontier by British troops.[48]

But one consequence of this success was not so pleasing to the Indian Government. With the news that the Amban was on his way down to the frontier it realized that it would be faced with negotiations of the very kind it wished most to avoid. The expedition had been planned to deal with a specific problem, the removal of the Tibetans from Sikkim, and not to bring about a general settlement of the frontier. This could well be arranged later by a treaty with the Maharaja of Sikkim, without reference to the Chinese. The crossing of the Tibetan frontier on to what was technically Chinese territory was, therefore, a mistake, for it gave the British action in Sikkim an international significance and weakened the argument that it was only a local police action. In these circumstances it was not possible to refuse to talk with the Amban. A. W. Paul, who had accompanied the expedition as Political Officer, was authorized to hold conversations with the Chinese, though it was emphasized that on no account was he to discuss the Sikkim frontier. He was soon joined by the Indian Foreign Secretary, H. M. Durand, assisted by Ney Elias and Desgodins, the French Missionary, as interpreter and adviser on Tibetan affairs.

The Indian Government was very conscious of its dignity. Durand did not go up to the frontier until he was certain that the Amban had arrived; he was not going to have it thought that he was waiting for a Chinese official. That talks were being held at all was only out of appreciation for the fact that 'the Chinese Government have shown a very conciliatory spirit towards England throughout the course of the Tibetan difficulty'. Durand was to accept an agreement only if it formally recognized the

British position in Sikkim, and was entered into by the Tibetans as well as the Chinese. There was no need for a definition of the Sikkim-Tibet frontier; this was already established and not open to question. A formal trade agreement was not to be insisted on, but Durand should do his best 'to secure an opening in this quarter for our commercial enterprise'.[49]

Durand found little satisfaction in his first talks with the Amban in December 1888. The Amban refused to admit that the Tibetans had any part in the dispute. Tibet was part of the Chinese Empire and its rights and interests were the rights and interests of China. The Sikkim frontier was very much open to question; Sikkim was a Tibetan dependency and therefore subordinate to China. The Amban then went on to argue, and this annoyed Durand more than anything else, that the Chinese could not possibly consider allowing foreign traders to visit Tibet, since the Tibetans would certainly attack and possibly kill them, and the Chinese were not strong enough to offer any protection. The Chinese position was quite clear; they would insist on the control of Tibet, but would never allow a situation to arise in which that control was put to the test. They were willing to accept the *de facto* British position in Sikkim but would insist on the preservation of the signs of its *de jure* dependence upon Tibet and China; the Maharaja must continue to pay his traditional homage to the Amban and be permitted to retain the rank and insignia conferred on him by the Emperor. These symbols of the dependence of Sikkim upon China and Tibet, which were to be referred to as 'the letters and presents', were as follows: the Maharaja of Sikkim could wear the hat and button of Chinese official rank; he was to send complimentary letters and presents to the Amban on his arrival at his post and at the New Year; he was to send similar letters and presents at intervals to the Dalai and Panchen Lamas; and he was to pay his respects to a number of Tibetan functionaries, lay and spiritual.[50] The Amban, moreover, showed as little conciliation in his actions, for he was in secret communication with the rulers of Sikkim and Bhutan. He had summoned a Bhutanese delegation to meet him on Sikkim territory, and he was planning to visit Rhenok on the border between Sikkim and British India with an accompanying escort of Tibetan troops. Durand could not let these actions go unremarked; he felt obliged to send a stiff letter to the Maharaja of Sikkim, summoning him once more to return from Tibet, and to impose a temporary suspension of the Bhutan subsidy.[51]

The Chinese terms were unacceptable. On no account could a British feudatory be allowed to pay homage to a foreign power.

Durand was prepared to make certain concessions; the Maharaja, on the pattern of the Burma agreement, might be allowed to pay spiritual tribute to the Dalai Lama, and, out of courtesy to the Chinese he could be permitted to wear the insignia of Chinese rank, the hat and button, during his life-time, but this practice should cease on his death. To the Amban he could send purely complimentary letters. Durand did not think that the homage question was a trivial one. He observed that·

> if we give way in respect to Sikkim, we must be prepared to do so, at some future time, not only with regard to Bhutan and Nepal, but with regard to Kashmir and her feudatories, such as Hunza and Nagar, and with regard to any of the smaller Himalayan states which may have committed themselves. We might even have China claiming suzerain rights over Darjeeling and the Bhutan Dooars, which we acquired from her so-called feudatories.

Durand refused to give in on this point, and when the Chinese would not listen to any compromise, such as the fiction that the Maharaja should pay homage for his estates in Chumbi and not as ruler of Sikkim, Durand, on 10th January 1889, informed the Amban that the discussions were now at an end.[52]

From the outset Durand had felt that these talks would be fruitless. In his opinion the Amban was frightened of the Tibetans: he had once said that he was 'only a guest in Lhasa - not a master - and he could not put aside the real masters'. He had no power over the Tibetans and Durand thought that his sole interest was to save 'face'. He had even gone so far, on one occasion, as to try to frighten Durand by threats of war. When Durand, however, pointed out the result of the last war between England and China and remarked that a war about Sikkim would be fought and decided elsewhere, the Amban 'shut up like a telescope' and profusely apologized for what was only intended as a harmless joke. The Amban, he felt, had neither the power to coerce the Tibetans nor the authority to make any concessions to the British.[53]

In Durand's opinion the Indian Government could take one of two courses of action. The policy favoured by Durand was to present the Amban with terms on a take it or leave it basis. If nothing came of this, the British should then enforce a settlement on the Tibetans without further reference to China by occupying the Chumbi Valley up to Phari, which should suffice to bring the Tibetans to their knees. This was a course which had recommended itself to many concerned with the Sikkim War of 1888, not only as a lever on the Tibetans but also as a just recompense for the million pounds which the war had cost. The outcome of such a policy, Durand noted, would be that

> we should put an end once and for all to our troubles with Tibet, and to our exclusion from that country, which would then be opened to our trade. We should entirely break the influence of the Tibetans, not only in Sikkim, but also in Bhutan: and we should greatly raise our reputation in the Himalayan States.

There were, of course, a number of disadvantages to any such plan: the Chinese might resent or resist it - Durand and his advisers doubted this; it might prove unpopular in England; it might cost more than was warranted by the prospects of Tibetan trade. If the Indian Government should feel these objections to be valid, then a milder policy suggested itself. The British could make a simple declaration of their position in Sikkim, threaten strong action if their rights were again violated, and let the whole question drop for the time being. A permanent official stationed at Gangtok in Sikkim, and paid for out of the Sikkim subsidy, would ensure that the Maharaja kept in line. After all, the Tibetans had been forced to withdraw, the war had been ended, and no one could doubt the ability of the British to enforce their rights. The Indian Government would lose nothing. If the trade question again arose, it could be discussed directly with the Tibetans and unhampered by any prior agreements with the Chinese.[54]

This alternative would be a logical conclusion to the Sikkim War. When the Macaulay Mission was abandoned, the Government of Lord Dufferin also abandoned all idea for the present of opening Tibet to Indian trade and diplomacy. The war was an unfortunate necessity, but it in no way invalidated the consider-ations which had decided the rejection of Macaulay's project. The object of the Sikkim Expedition had been to drive the Tibetans out of Sikkim, not to secure a far-reaching agreement on Anglo-Tibetan relations. Had the Indian Government been left to its own devices, there can be little doubt that the Tibetan question would have died a quiet and unmourned death.

The Chinese, however, realized that unless they secured an agreement at this time, they could not prevent, in any future dispute on this frontier, direct Anglo-Tibetan contact without Chinese participation. Such contact, they felt, would constitute a severe, if not fatal, blow to their influence in Lhasa. This had been the opinion of Sir Robert Hart, and it was as a result of his advice that at the very moment when Durand had broken off negotiations on the frontier the Yamen announced that James Hart, Sir Robert's younger brother and heir-apparent, had been instructed to proceed to Gnatong to assist the Amban in his discussions with Durand. Sir Robert Hart, at least, was sincere in his desire to reach a settlement, for he hoped that the talks on the frontier would so enhance his brother's reputation as to put beyond question the succession to the post of Inspector-General of the Chinese Maritime Customs.[55]

Durand strongly opposed reopening the talks unless the Amban and James Hart had something new to offer. He did not approve of Hart's appointment. It was futile, he thought, to send a man on such a task with no powers, no instructions and no knowledge of the questions at issue.[56] When Durand met Hart in Darjeeling he was confirmed in this opinion since he seems to have taken an instant dislike to this Irishman in Chinese service.[57] Lord Lansdowne, who had now succeeded Dufferin as Viceroy, agreed with Durand. He could not see how the Chinese could come to any agreement, and was still interested in the possibility of further military action against the Tibetans, who, it was reported somewhat vaguely in March 1889, had just encroached on British soil in Garwhal in the western Himalayas.[58]

It was the Foreign Office in London, more concerned with the future of Anglo-Chinese relations than with the Indian border, which urged that the talks be renewed, and said that it was disturbed by the 'unreasonable' and 'hasty' action of the Viceroy in refusing to listen to the new Chinese proposals.[59] Lord Salisbury could not understand, so he said, the attitude of the Viceroy. The dispute appeared to him to be more one of form than of substance, and he suggested to the India Office that if the Indian Government continue to refuse to talk to Hart, then another attempt should be made to deal with the Chinese diplomatically, either through Walsham or through the Chinese Legation in London. In any event, 'it would seem more prudent to keep the negotiations alive and to make some small concessions in regard to Sikkim, rather than to disturb our relations with the Chinese Government'. After all, concessions of the type under discussion had been made in the case of the Burmese Decennial Mission to China; matters of 'face' only were involved; no ill effects seemed to have followed conciliation over Burma and they need not over Sikkim. Lord Cross at the India Office concurred, and the Viceroy was instructed accordingly.[60]

In April 1889 talks were reopened. A. W. Paul was the British delegate and James Hart represented the Chinese. Hart produced as a basis for discussion this formula:

Sikkim and Tibet boundary to remain as before, and British to act on Sikkim side in accordance with Treaty with Raja, and Raja to send letters and presents as usual. China to engage that Tibetan troops shall neither cross nor disturb Sikkim frontier, and England to engage that British troops shall similarly respect Tibetan frontier.

This proposal was not, as it might at first seem, a restoration of the *status quo ante* with safeguards added to prevent further trouble. There was a great difference between the Maharaja sending letters and presents to the Ambans unknown to the British and his doing so with explicit British consent. Hart maintained that Sikkim, though a British protected state, had never been annexed by the British, and consequently the Chinese could hardly be expected to enter into a treaty 'ignoring relations formerly and still existing', which the British had not destroyed and the Chinese not consented to annul. He was prepared to make several amendments agreeable to the Indian Government, but on the crucial question of letters and presents he would not move. Lord Lansdowne was convinced that the renewed negotiations would not solve this impasse. Further discussions on the status of Sikkim would probably produce repercussions in Kashmir and elsewhere.[61] Nor did he show any enthusiasm for the plan to entrust the matter to the tender mercies of Sir John Walsham: 'negotiations in Peking would, we fear, end in the sacrifice of Indian interests, and do serious harm'.[62] Once again it was Lord Salisbury who kept the negotiations alive. In July the Foreign Office informed the India Office that:

Lord Salisbury would greatly deprecate anything like an abrupt rejection of the Chinese proposals, or an absolute denial of rights to which, however shadowy in their nature, the Chinese Government are found to attach so much importance. Such a denial is almost certain to lead to their re-assertion in some inconvenient manner.[63]

But Lord Salisbury did not rule out altogether direct action with the Tibetans, or against them should a suitable excuse be found or should the Tibetans once more encroach on British territory.[64]

In August 1889 Hart came up with fresh proposals. But once

again he maintained that Sikkim was protected but not annexed by the British, and that the letters and presents should go on as before;[65] and once again the Indian Government was unable to accept an agreement which, Lord Lansdowne said,

> would have remained on record as formal evidence of the success of the Chinese whose reputation, already inconveniently great among our ignorant feudatories, we could not have afforded to increase in this way at our own expense. From one end of the Himalaya to the other we should have weakened our influence. In India it is essential for the stability of our rule that we should permit no attempt at interference by Foreign Powers with any portion of the Empire.[66]

It seemed as if the negotiations were dead, and even the Foreign Office was prepared to accept this fact. Sir Thomas Saunderson minuted that the talks appeared to have closed in a friendly enough way so that the Chinese had no legitimate grounds for offence, and 'I do not think that any action on our part is called for unless the Chinese themselves raise the question at Peking'.[67]

In November 1889, however, Saunderson noted that 'the Chinese, seeing that they could not get any hold on Sikkim, have preferred at least to get recognition of their authority in Tibet', and seemed ready for a compromise.[68] The Chinese feared that if some agreement was not soon reached the British would try to deal directly with the Tibetans. The Emperor, moreover, so Walsham reported, was displeased at the delays in securing a settlement. And the Amban was not only under pressure from Peking to come to terms; the Tibetans were also complaining at the way the negotiations were dragging on. The Yamen therefore, informed Walsham through Sir Robert Hart of a new set of proposals, the chief of which gave

> recognition of India's sole protectorate . . . [over Sikkim] . . . accompanied by a formal assurance that this is held to mean that the external relations of the protected state will be solely conducted by India and that consequently the practice of presents and letters to the Tibetan Government will virtually cease.[69]

This formula was skilfully designed to save face all round. The Chinese had not actually surrendered the 'letters and presents'; the British had sole control over the foreign relations of Sikkim, and were under no obligation to permit the continuance of the 'letters and presents' if they did not want to. This was the implication of the phrase 'will virtually cease'. Lansdowne, who naturally welcomed a settlement of the status of Sikkim in British favour, agreed to reopen negotiations on this basis, and the India Office felt that the new Chinese formula promised to 'give all we want'.[70] Perhaps a pointed memorial from the Leeds Chamber of Commerce, with a suggestion that if the British did not come to some sort of agreement about Tibet in the near future the Russians might do so, which would be 'a serious injury to British Trade',[71] suggested that it would be politically advisable to make some rapid gesture to prove that, as far as Tibet was concerned, 'H.M.G. are fully alive to its importance as regards British interests'.[72] In December 1889 the British submitted draft proposals to Hart and the Amban;[73] and these became, with little change, the Sikkim-Tibet Convention which was signed in Darjeeling on 17th March 1890 by Lord Lansdowne and the Amban Sheng Tai.

This document defined the Sikkim-Tibet frontier as the watershed between the Tista river system in Sikkim and the Tibetan Mochu and the rivers flowing northwards into Tibet (Art. I). It admitted sole British control over the internal and external affairs of Sikkim (Art. II), and left three questions for future settlement. These were the question of Tibetan grazing rights in Sikkim (Art. V), which was of minor importance now that the status of Sikkim had been settled, the method whereby communication between the Indian Government and the authorities in Tibet was to be conducted in future (Art. VI), and the problem of trade across the Tibetan frontier (Art. IV). The Convention laid down that within six months of its ratification a joint Anglo-Chinese commission should be constituted to discuss these outstanding questions.[74]

The Sikkim-Tibet Convention settled the immediate problems arising from the Tibetan advance to Lingtu in 1886 and the consequent Sikkim Expedition of 1888. It did not, however, deal with the questions of trade and the future conduct of relations between the Indian Government and Tibet. These, and the minor question of pasturage along the Sikkim-Tibet frontier, were left for settlement in some future instrument. Provision for such discussion had existed since 1886 in the phrase in the Burma-Tibet Convention referring to Trade Regulations, 'should it be practicable'. The negotiations leading up to the Sikkim-Tibet Convention had nothing to do with trade; as Lansdowne wrote to Lord Cross in January 1889, there was no use in considering the trade question at that time when the pressing matter of British prestige on the frontier was at stake.[75] Trade and the other topics only arose when the Indian Government had obtained the Convention and had determined to extract the maximum benefit from such favourable circumstances.

During 1891, 1892 and 1893 Paul and Hart argued about pasturage, communications between the Indian Government and the Chinese in Tibet, and trade. The pasturage question presented little enough difficulty. In view of the British.position in Sikkim as set out in the Convention there could be no argument against the fact that the British could make such regulations as they saw fit concerning this and any other matter on their side of the frontier. All the Chinese asked was that, since the distinction between Sikkim and Tibet had in the past been somewhat vague, no abrupt change should be made by the British in the pastoral economy along what was now the frontier region without giving warning some time in advance; and Paul could find no fault with this reasoning.[76] The problem of communication was also simple; there was to be no question of British relations with the Tibetans, but only with the Chinese. All that was required was some means of getting letters from the Indian Government to the Amban; such letters had been passing to and fro satisfactorily enough since the end of 1888. The difficulties arose over the bringing about an improvement in the conditions of Indo–Tibetan trade, as one would have expected, since this involved the two vexed questions of the right of British subjects to travel in Tibet and to sell Indian tea in that country.

Paul made it clear that the British Government would never be completely satisfied with the conditions of trade in Tibet until it was freed from all restrictions on the travel of British merchants; as a concession to the Chinese, however, it would accept the limitation of access to a single, suitably placed mart. Phari would be an acceptable site for such a mart; Gyantse would be much better, of course, but the Indian Government would not embarrass the Chinese by pressing for the latter place. Phari had certain advantages. It had long been the place where the Tibetans had taxed goods to and from the south. The location of the trade mart there would enable the British to develop a road through Chumbi, which provided a route, so some Himalayan experts were suggesting at this time, for a railroad up to the edge of the Tibetan plateau.[77] Moreover, the right of British officials to travel to Phari, so far into Tibet, would provide the means for a constant reminder to the Tibetans of the existence and power of the British. Phari was not only the gateway to Lhasa and Shigatse, but also to Bhutan, whose traders came there frequently. Thus

158

Paul argued that Phari was the least for which he could ask. The Chinese, however, would not agree to Phari at any price; it was quite clear that they would never be able to get the Tibetans to accept the right of Europeans to travel so far into their country. They offered Yatung, in the Chumbi Valley thirteen miles from the Jelep La, and this the British had to accept, fully aware though they were of its shortcomings. There was only one road through a narrow valley by which Tibetans could reach Yatung, and this could easily be blocked without the British having any means of ascertaining where the stoppage was or of breaking the blockade. The Indian Government consoled itself by stating that Yatung was accepted only as a temporary concession and that eventually it would press for the removal of the mart to Phari.[78] The Chinese, it is to be presumed, were only too glad to have such contentious matters postponed for a while.

The Chinese fought hardest over the question of the import of Indian tea into Tibet. Since the middle of the nineteenth century this subject had been discussed and by the 1890s its literature had attained an impressive volume. It was one thing to write about the Tibetan tea market, however, and another to attempt to exploit it in practice. Up to 1893 the Indian tea trade with Tibet still remained no more than a theoretical possibility. The Indian Government had obtained samples of Szechuan brick tea along with information on the methods of its preparation which it had commissioned Baber and the French Missionary, Desgodins, to collect. Men like Campbell, Cooper, Hodgson, Edgar, Baber, Hosie and Macaulay had all written glowing accounts of the profits to be made here; but few tea producers had done anything for themselves. Few planters, indeed, outside the districts of Darjeeling and British Bhutan took much interest in the Tibetan market, and it was possible for a planter like Barker, writing in 1884, to survey various remedies for the ills then afflicting the Indian tea industry without once mentioning the word Tibet.[79] One firm is recorded to have tried to exploit the Tibetan market, and its experiences were instructive: in 1884-85 Cresswell and Co. of Darjeeling set themselves the task of preparing brick tea in imitation of that of Szechuan and found that they could not master the secret of the Chinese product.[80] By the 1880s, in fact, some observers seem to have concluded that the best way of tapping the Tibetan tea market was with Chinese tea shipped to Lhasa by way of Calcutta and Darjeeling.[81] It is significant that the Indian tea industry played little part in the agitation behind the Macaulay Mission; this was confined mainly to English Chambers of Commerce who saw Tibet either as a market for the manufactured goods of England, or as a source of high-quality wool for the looms of Yorkshire. In the 1890s, however, the Indian tea industry began to suffer from a depression brought about by overproduction and a drop in world prices.[82] The Indian Tea Association then began to take a more active interest in the Tibetan question; but this was at a time when the Indian Government had ceased to attach much importance to the commercial possibilities of its northern neighbour when balanced against the peace of the frontier.

The Chinese were determined to exclude Indian tea from their Tibetan dependency for a number of substantial reasons. They knew that the great Tibetan monasteries, who held much of the existing trade in this commodity in their hands, would resent such a development, and the Chinese could not afford to ignore so important a factor in the Tibetan political scene. The Chinese themselves used the tea trade to finance much of their government in Lhasa: the Amban raised cash from the monasteries in return for documents freeing monastic traders from the payment of an equivalent amount of *likin* at Tachienlu. The Tibetan tea trade was an important element in the economic life of Szechuan Province. Many thousand of porters in the border regions of Western Szechuan and Eastern Tibet depended upon it for their livelihood. The Provincial Government raised from it annually at least £38,000 in *likin*. The tea grown in Szechuan for the Tibet market was of a special kind which could not possibly find much sale elsewhere; and thus the Viceroy of Szechuan refused to take responsibility for the reaction of the Szechuan tea producers were their chief market opened to foreign competition.[83] As the Yamen said to O'Conor, it 'could not open to competition the one small country in the world where the consumption of China tea was still appreciated'.[84]

The Indian Government understood the Chinese position in this question, and it was willing to compromise. It agreed that Indian tea was not to be imported into Tibet for a five-year probationary period on the understanding that all other goods, except, of course, arms, narcotics and intoxicants, should cross the Indo-Tibetan border free of all duty. At the end of five years the whole question of the tariffs on the trade between British India and Tibet was to be re-examined. Tea was then to be admitted at a duty not higher than that charged in England on Chinese tea. This agreement was a little vague. The Indian Government understood it to mean that Indian tea *would* be allowed into Tibet in five years' time; and the Indian Tea Association expressed its satisfaction at this.[85] The Chinese fairly certainly meant no more than that Indian tea *might* be permitted to enter Tibet at the end of this period, and they presumably hoped to have discovered fresh grounds for procrastination by that time.

A document embodying the results of three years of discussion, the Regulations regarding Trade, Communication and Pasturage to be appended to the Sikkim-Tibet Convention of 1890, was signed at Darjeeling on 5th December 1893 by A. W. Paul for the Indian Government, and by James Hart and Ho Chang-jung for the Chinese. Pasturage was dismissed in one short article (Art. IX) empowering the Indian Government to regulate as it chose the conditions under which Tibetans might graze their flocks and herds across the Sikkim-Tibet border. An arrangement was made for the transmission of despatches from the Indian Government to the Ambans (Arts. VII and VIII), but not, be it noted, to the Tibetans, who were mentioned neither in the Convention nor the Regulations. The greater part of the Regulations dealt with trade. A trade mart was to be established at Yatung, just inside the Chumbi Valley, where merchants, native and European, could come to trade, could reside and could establish godowns. The Chinese were to protect the lives and property of British subjects, and to provide a suitable residence for the British official who might be appointed to supervise the working of a new mart, which was to come into operation on 1st May 1894 (Arts. I and II). Certain goods were not to be imported into Tibet such as armaments, intoxicants and narcotics (Art. III). Trade in all other goods was to be free of duty for the first five years following the opening of the mart, after which period a tariff might be jointly decided upon if found to be desirable. During this period Indian tea was not to be imported into Tibet, but its importation was to be allowed on the expiry of the five-year term subject to a rate of duty not exceeding that at which China tea was imported into England (Art. IV). All goods passing through the mart were to be registered at the Customs Station to be established there (Art. V). Any disputes arising in Yatung were to be settled by personal consultation between the Political Officer for Sikkim and the Chinese Frontier Officer (Art. VI).[86]

The terms of the Trade Regulations were moderate indeed: but concessions on such matters as tea and the location of the trade mart should cause no surprise. The negotiations which followed the Sikkim Expedition of 1888 were really concerned with the status of Sikkim and, by implication, with the status of all those other British-protected states with a common border with the Chinese Empire or with its dependencies. As J. D. Cunningham

161

had observed a half-century before, it was not fitting that the great British Empire in India should share the allegiance of its dependents with other powers. It has already been seen that the British negotiators of the Sikkim-Tibet Convention had more than Sikkim before their eyes, and that the precedents established on this small piece of hill frontier had a wide application. Kashmir possessed a common border with both Tibet and Chinese Turkestan. The political consequences of this fact, already noted at the time of Gulab Singh's invasion of Western Tibet, were once more called to mind by the bringing under British protection in 1891-92 of the two small states of Hunza and Nagar in the Karakoram, each with loyalties both to the Maharaja of Kashmir and to the Chinese authorities in Kashgaria. The forthcoming frontier demarcation in the Pamirs, a development of the Panjdeh crisis of 1885, also promised to raise knotty problems of divided allegiance of territory with borders on Russia, Afghanistan, China and British India. Burma, likewise, was affected by the decisions which might be reached on the Sikkim-Tibet frontier. The Burmah-Tibet Convention of 1886 had specified that the Burmese could send a purely spiritual mission once every ten years from the head of the Burmese Buddhist Church to the Chinese Emperor. The Indian Government had not been too happy about this provision, and it was anxious, now that the first of the Decennial Missions was about to fall due, lest the Chinese seize this opportunity to revive their Burmese claims. It was glad indeed, in 1895, to take advantage of a Chinese disregard of treaty obligations in ceding to France a strip of land in the neighbourhood of Tonkin, 'to get rid of the preposterous Decennial Mission proposition,' as Sir J. G. Scott put it.[87] All in all, as Lord Lansdowne wrote,

> there is a good deal to be said for coming to terms with the Chinese and not allowing the negotiations to end in nothing. We shall probably before long be engaged in other and far more important negotiations respecting the Pamirs, in which our interests and those of China will be in many respects identical. We shall very shortly have to deal with the Burmah Decennial Mission – an exceedingly awkward question. It has, therefore, appeared to us worthwhile, under the circumstances, to stretch a point in order to avoid a miscarriage in regard to the Sikkim-Tibet Convention, and we are disposed to regard the arrangement which has now been arrived at . . . as of importance not so much on account of the commercial interests involved, but as an outward sign

of neighbourly good-will prevailing between the two Empires.[88]

With the signing of the Regulations the Indian Government felt that it had successfully weathered the storms of the Tibetan problem, and could now look foward to a long period of calm on that frontier. The Sikkim Gazetteer, published in 1894, gives a fair picture of the official view of Tibet at this time. Riseley, its editor, observed that Tibet 'lies on the other side of a great wall, which we, as the rulers of India, have not the slightest ambition to climb over'. He scoffed at the supposed commercial prospects of Tibet and laughed at those who were still saying 'there lies the modern Brynhilde, asleep in her mountain top', and who called on the Viceroy to 'play the part of Siegfried and awaken her from the slumber of ages'. It was true that in Tibet there were still unsolved mysteries of great interest to the anthropologist, ethnologist, botanist, zoologist and geographer, but, Riseley concluded, 'who will deny that it would be a piece of surpassing folly to alienate a possible ally in China by forcing our way into Tibet in the interests of scientific curiosity, doubtfully backed by mercantile speculation'.[89]

It was in this frame of mind that the Indian Government hoped to settle the future relations to the Tibetans. Thus it was that the Shata Shape, one of the four members of what can only be described as the Tibetan cabinet, was ignored when he came down to Darjeeling in 1893 to keep an eye on the signing of the Trade Regulations. The Shata Shape, far from being wooed by the Indian Government, was permitted to suffer an insult in the Darjeeling streets which, so it is said, embittered him against the British for the remainder of his life. One version of the story is that while walking through the Darjeeling bazaar he failed to make way for an English lady and that this fault was observed by a party of English subalterns who considered that such an insult to a Memsahib should not go unpunished. They seized the unfortunate Tibetan by the scruff of his neck and threw him into a fountain which lay conveniently to hand.[90] Another version has it that the subalterns, noting that the Shata Shape failed to 'salaam' them, pulled him off his pony and manhandled him on the public highway.[91] Perhaps both incidents took place.[92] They should not have been possible had the Indian Government been at all aware of the importance of this person, the most senior Tibetan official to come down to India on business of state since the British first established themselves in Bengal. By ignoring the Tibetans unofficially, even though obliged to do so officially, the Indian

Government only increased its reliance on Chinese mediation in any future dealings with Tibet. The Sikkim-Tibet Convention and the Trade Regulations gave British recognition to Chinese authority over a people whom the Chinese had not the power to control, and bound the British in any future crisis along this frontier to deal with a government which was disliked and weak in Lhasa.

Note on the Maharaja of Sikkim: After his return to Sikkim from Chumbi in December 1887 the relations between Maharaja Thutob Namgyal and the Indian Government in general and J. C. White in particular became very strained. During the 1889-90 Anglo-Chinese negotiations the Maharaja was obliged to leave Sikkim and live more or less under house arrest in Kalimpong. He was allowed to return to Sikkim in early 1891, from which, in March 1892, he endeavoured to escape accompanied by the Maharini and at least one of his children. The motives and destination are not clear; but the chosen route passed through Nepal where the Maharaja was arrested by the Nepalese and handed over to the British. Meanwhile his eldest son and heir Tchoda Namgyal remained in Tibet. In February 1899 the Indian Government recognized a change of succession and the permanent exclusion of Tchoda Namgyal. The new heir, Sidkeong Namgyal, became a good friend of the British over the next fifteen years. See: Rao, *India and Sikkim*, op. cit., pp. 109-23.

VIII

YATUNG

·

1894 – 1898

SIR ERIC Teichman has remarked that the 'Tibetan Question' came into being with the signing of the Sikkim-Tibet Convention.[1] The idea of a mission to Lhasa, accepted by the Chinese in the Separate Article of the Chefoo Convention and abandoned by the British in Article Four of the Burma-Tibet Convention of 1886, was replaced by the hope that British requirements with regard to Tibet could be satisfied by the provisions of the Sikkim-Tibet Convention of 1890 and its ancillary Trade Regulations of 1893. The Convention of 1890 was not, strictly speaking, a development of the Separate Article of the Chefoo Convention of 1876; rather, it was a settlement of the situation arising from the Tibetan advance to Lingtu in 1886, made between the British and China, the suzerain power in Tibet. It was designed to determine the status of Sikkim and to regulate the Sikkim-Tibet frontier; British trade across that frontier was dealt with in the Regulations of 1893. By the instruments of 1890 and 1893 Anglo-Tibetan relations, theoretically, could not exist since a mechanism had been established by which the British were only able to discuss matters relating to Tibet with the Chinese. The Tibetans had taken no part in the negotiating of these two agreements, and no provision had been made for their participation in any discussion which might arise from them. It was a state of affairs which the Indian Government, which had from time to time shown itself desirous of establishing some kind of relationship

165

with the Dalai and Panchen Lamas, would have preferred to avoid; it was only accepted under pressure from London, where it was thought desirable to humour China as a possible future bulwark against Russian expansion. Before the century was out, the need for direct Anglo-Tibetan relations began to be apparent; the Tibetan Question, in great measure, resolved itself into the problem of how to establish such relations in face of the shackles which the British had attached to themselves in 1890 and 1893.

The absence of Anglo-Tibetan relations was of little significance provided the Chinese were able to exercise some measure of effective control over the Tibetans. Frontier policy, Lansdowne noted in 1894 to the Calcutta Chamber of Commerce, demanded that there should exist along the Indian borders no power vacuums, no 'border Alsatias', which could be filled by the expansion of other powers. He cited Sikkim as an example of such an area, now safely brought back into the British fold.[2] Tibet was not mentioned; the British had recognized it as forming an indisputable part of the Chinese Empire. It was a part of that Empire, however, over which the hold of the Chinese was visibly slipping, a fact upon which scarce a traveller who made the attempt to reach Lhasa in the 1890s failed to remark. Captain Bower, for example, who made a west-to-east crossing of the Tibetan plateau in 1892 with the support of British Military Intelligence, described the Chinese in Tibet in these words: 'a power which is incapable of protecting anyone or applying the most insignificant rules of police, does not deserve the name of a Government'. It was only in the extreme difficulty of the country in Northern Tibet that Bower saw any reasonable guarantee that Tibet would not soon fall into Russian hands.[3] Tibet did not seem to be a dangerous 'power vacuum' because of its geography.

After the outcome of the Sino-Japanese War in 1895 even the Foreign Office in London, which had managed to retain some degree of faith in the strength of the Chinese Empire up to this period, and which had dismissed the opinions of men like Bower as being 'somewhat crude',[4] could no longer maintain that the Chinese were likely to be much longer the masters of Lhasa. In 1895 a significant change in the climate of British official opinion about the status of Chinese Central Asia was apparent. Reputable observers of the Chinese scene began to advocate a British annexation of Tibet in the event of the collapse of China.[5] Chinese relations with states on the British side of the Himalayas, never welcomed by the Indian Government, began to be challenged with greater force. Thus in 1895 the Nepalese Tribute Mission, which the British had accepted since 1792 as part of the political framework of the northern frontier of India, was re-examined; and O'Conor told the Yamen that the British did not look on it as 'an acknowledgement of vassalage on the part of Nepal to China'.[6] The Sino-Japanese War had this result; in any future crisis on the Indo-Tibetan border the Indian Government would not find itself so much hampered by a need to conciliate China as it had been before 1895.[7]

The trade mart at Yatung came into operation on the eve of this change of opinion. Many in India, above all in the Bengal Government, had disapproved strongly of the leniency which had been shown to Tibet after the Sikkim campaign of 1888; they agreed with Waddell that some territorial benefits, the annexation of the Chumbi Valley for example, should have come to the British as compensation for the expenses of the campaign and as a warning to the Tibetans against further encroachments on to British territory.[8] The majority of the officials who came into daily contact with Tibetan and Chinese diplomacy at Yatung and who were responsible for the working of the Convention and the Trade Regulations were of this opinion. From the moment that Yatung was opened in May 1894 they began to find fault with the existing state of Anglo-Tibetan relations and to urge revision of the instruments upon which those relations were based. The obvious weakness of China in Central Asia was to lend much strength to their arguments.

Thus, in May 1894, when J. C. White, Political Officer for Sikkim, went up to Yatung to supervise the opening of the trade mart, he reported most unfavourably on its operation and prospects. He thought that its site was quite unsuited to the purpose; Yatung was situated in a narrow valley just within Tibetan territory and there was only one road leading out of it into Tibet. The Tibetans had built a wall across this road beyond which they allowed no foreigner, Indian or European, to pass. Even Mr. Taylor, the Chinese customs officer sent to supervise the mart on behalf of the Chinese Government, was unable to pass into Tibet beyond Yatung and had been obliged to travel to his post by way of British India. This was to be expected; but White was surprised to find that Tibetan traders were also denied free access to the trade mart; such traders approaching from the north, so White reported, were stopped at Phari at the head of the Chumbi Valley. At Phari a 10 per cent. *ad valorem* duty was imposed by the Phari Jongpens. All goods passing southwards beyond this point could only be carried by the Tromos, or natives of Chumbi, who were exploiting this transport monopoly to the full.

White saw much else in the functioning of the mart with which to find fault. For example: accommodation at Yatung was supposed to have been provided for White by the Tibetans; this had been done by the construction of a house so ramshackle and draughty as to be unworthy of the dignity of an official of the Indian Empire. White did not blame the Chinese too severely for the state of Yatung; they were friendly and courteous and evidently doing their best to honour the Convention, but they were frightened of the Tibetans, whom they found themselves powerless to control. White considered that the Tibetans 'repudiate the treaty and assert that it was signed by the British Government and the Chinese, and therefore they have nothing to do with it'. He thought that the least the Indian Government could do was to request the Amban to have the mart moved a little further up the valley, perhaps to Rinchingong.

White was personally in favour of a stronger line. The Jelep La should be closed; Yatung abandoned; and every effort made to open up an alternative route through northern Sikkim by way of the Lachen Valley, giving access to the Tibetan town of Khambajong, whose population had shown some signs of friendliness towards the British. Loss of trade might bring the inhabitants of Chumbi, at least, to a more reasonable frame of mind, and perhaps, also, the authorities at Phari. The only value of Yatung as at present constituted that White could discern, was as a look-out post on the affairs of Bhutan and Tibet.[9] He thought that not only had the Convention and the Regulations not improved Indo-Tibetan trade, but also that they had failed completely to solve the frontier problem out of which the Sikkim Campaign and the consequent instruments had emerged. The Tibetans, far from learning their lesson in the war and respecting the frontier as laid down by treaty, had established a military post at Giaogong in the extreme north of Sikkim, a few miles south of the watershed.[10]

The Indian Government did not accept White's conclusions on Yatung, observing that the obstructions about which White complained might have some justification, that the mart had only just opened and must be given a fair trial, and that 'it has always been recognized that the utmost patience is necessary in dealing with the Tibetans';[11] but it was unable to ignore the reported Tibetan transgression of the Sikkim-Tibet frontier. It proposed to the Amban that future frontier violations might be avoided if that frontier were demarcated on the ground by a joint Anglo-Chinese Commission.[12] The Amban agreed readily to this suggestion. He even improved on it. He had discussed the question with Lhasa and reported that Tibetan delegates were willing to join the Commission provided, he emphasized, it was understood that on no account should British Commissioners set foot on Tibetan soil. On this basis it was agreed that the joint Commission should start demarcation in May 1895.[13]

In 1894 a number of points had already emerged which were to play later a great part in the public presentation of the Tibetan question. Tibetan obstruction, it was said, was turning the Yatung mart into a travesty of that envisaged by the British negotiators of the Regulations. It seemed clear that the Tibetans did not intend to respect the Sikkim-Tibet frontier as laid down in the Convention. These points tended to be magnified in their gravity by the administrative machinery through which the British executed policy on the Sikkim-Tibet border. Yatung was a long way from Simla or Calcutta, and the Indian Government saw the progress of Anglo-Tibetan relations through the eyes of a hierarchy of Bengal officials – the Political Officer for Sikkim, the Commissioner of the Rajshahi Division, the Bengal Secretary and the Lieutenant-Governor – who were generally in favour of a more radical Tibetan policy than that approved by India during the administrations of Dufferin, Lansdowne and Elgin. This difference of opinion between Bengal and India was natural enough; to Bengal the Tibetan question was a local frontier matter while in India it was viewed in the light of wider Imperial policy. This machinery was bound to magnify the complications which would certainly arise from the decision to demarcate the frontier with the Tibetans and Chinese. If White was correct in his estimate of the Tibetan attitude to the Convention, and there was no evidence to the contrary, then the proposed demarcation could only result in a revival by the Tibetans of claims to Sikkim territory which it had been the chief object of the Convention to put to rest. The Indian Government should have known better than to have taken the Amban's ready acceptance of the idea of demarcation at its face value. As Lord Curzon told the University of Oxford in 1907; 'in Asiatic countries it would be true to say that demarcation has never taken place except under European pressure and by the intervention of European agents'.[14] By embarking on demarcation, which was not provided for in the Convention, the Indian Government was involved in a course of action which was unlikely to result in a success peacefully achieved, and from which it could not withdraw without loss of prestige.

That demarcation would be far from easy was apparent from the start. When White arrived at the frontier in April 1895 he learnt from the Chinese Commissioner, Major Tu, that the Tibetans had refused to provide the Chinese Commission with any transport. There was no sign of the Tibetan Commission. Major Tu begged White to delay demarcation for a while to give the Tibetans a chance to show up, but White refused.[15] On the Jelep La and neighbouring passes into the Chumbi Valley there was no dispute as to the location of the frontier: here, despite protests from the Chinese in Yatung, he put up boundary pillars without the assistance of the Tibetan and Chinese Commissioners. This repudiation of the principle of joint demarcation as proposed by the Viceroy to the Amban was approved by the Bengal Government.[16]

There now remained the disputed northern border, lying across White's proposed alternative trade route, in which the Tibetan encroachments had been reported. Sir Charles Elliott, the Lieutenant-Governor, felt that White should now make his way to this zone of contention; if the Chinese and Tibetan Commissioners still failed to put in an appearance, then White should proceed to demarcate on his own; if any Tibetans were found on British protected territory, they should be made to leave, by force if persuasion failed.[17] The Bengal Government considered the presence of Tibetans at Giaogong as a challenge to the validity of the Convention and to British prestige on the Sikkim-Tibet frontier. It was, therefore, more important to teach the Lamas a lesson than to observe with nicety the protocol of joint demarcation. The Indian Government, however, ordered restraint. It noted that demarcation had not been provided for in the Convention and that, to date, no serious political inconvenience had resulted from the fact that the frontier had not been demarcated. In its eyes the presence of a few Tibetans in a remote corner of Sikkim did not constitute a major crisis. White was instructed to take no further action without the participation of the Chinese.[18]

In June 1895, however, White was able to report a fresh development. On the 4th of that month the pillar which he had erected on the Jelep La frontier was knocked down and the numbered plaque attached to it removed. White immediately urged that an apology be demanded from the Amban for this outrage, and that demarcation in the Giaogong area, some distance from the Jelep La, should go ahead at once.[19] India, very properly, wished to know whether this had been the act of Tibetan officials or of 'ignorant common people'.[20] Despite White's assertion that the destruction of the pillar was a deliberate act of Tibetan policy,[21] it counselled moderation and friendly

170

consultation with the Amban;[22] advice which it did not modify when White reported the destruction of two more pillars, at the Donchuk and Doko Passes, on 11th June.[23] As Lord Elgin remarked; the Amban 'has hitherto displayed a friendly spirit in his communications and dealings with the Government of India'; he should not be embarrassed by complaints about the Tibetan action, which could only suggest that he had no control over the Tibetans. 'It is desirable', Elgin observed, 'that our local officers should not adopt any action on the border which might increase the Resident's difficulties.' White and his escort were told to return to Gangtok and the Viceroy wrote to the Amban to explain to him the present situation in the most friendly terms.[24]

Before he had completed his arrangements for his return to Gangtok White reported that he had heard that the Amban had just received orders from Peking to demarcate without delay and to insist on Tibetan participation. White was, accordingly, allowed to remain on the frontier to await the outcome of this new development.[25] It soon became apparent that this report was without foundation.[26] White applied himself to devising further arguments in support of a more forceful British policy. The Amban, he wrote in July, had no influence on the situation in Tibet. While the bulk of the Tibetan population favoured a settlement with the British, the obstacle to satisfactory Anglo-Tibetan relations lay with the monks of the three great Lhasa monasteries of Sera, Drebung and Gaden, whose influence dominated Tibetan politics. In Lhasa British weakness could only be interpreted as a resounding victory for the policy of the monastic party; but if the British were resolute and pressed on with demarcation the monastic opposition would collapse, since 'there is no doubt that the Tibetans are most anxious to avoid any conflict with India'.[27] These views were welcomed in Bengal. Sir Charles Elliott thought that further delay in demarcation would only encourage the Tibetans and lead to loss of British prestige. He felt that were it not for the need to pay some regard to China he would have no hesitation in advising Lord Elgin to make it plain to the Amban that unless demarcation were speedily carried out the Chumbi Valley would be occupied by British troops. With China in mind, he suggested that the Yamen should be pressed to permit the temporary occupation of Chumbi by the British, if need be, 'without any detriment to the Chinese suzerainty, but with the object of assisting them to establish their authority more firmly at Lhasa'.[28] To this piece of disingenuous argument Lord Elgin would not agree. He ordered that demarcation be put off until the summer of 1896.[29]

In November 1895 White and his immediate superior, Nolan, had talks at Yatung with the Chinese and with a Tibetan delegate, one Tenzing Wangpu, who was thought to enjoy the confidence of the Dalai Lama; and a clearer picture of the Tibetan case emerged. It was clear that the obstructions caused by the Tibetans at Yatung, about which White had already complained, did not, in fact, violate the letter of the Trade Regulations. The 10 per cent. duty at Phari, for example, was found to be no innovation; it was applied at other points on the Tibetan frontier, including Tachienlu, and was imposed on Nepalese, Bhutanese and Chinese traders as well as those from British India; it could not, therefore, be described as a specific attempt to obstruct Indian trade at Yatung. Similarly, the prohibition of Tibetan merchants from passing beyond Phari to visit Yatung was perfectly compatible with the letter of the Regulations which said no more than that British and Indian traders should be allowed to attend the trade mart. It was equally clear that the Tibetans did not like the Trade Regulations, which had been made without their consent, and that they were going to do nothing active to make the Regulations a success. Nor did there seem to be any prospect, at the end of the five-year period, of the Tibetans allowing Indian tea to be brought into their country; rather than permit this, they had stopped all trade in Chinese brick tea with India and deprived Sikkim and other hill areas where lived Tibetan populations of a cherished commodity.[30]

As a result of these talks, however, the Bengal Government was able to argue that whilst by hair-splitting the actions of the Tibetans might be justified, no sensible person could fail to conclude that 'by their systematic obstruction the object of the treaty with China is frustrated'.[31] The Indian Government was not moved by this reasoning. It noted that the object of the establishment of the mart at Yatung was to improve trade. The figures indicated that there had been an improvement, which Government attributed to its policy of 'moderation and patience' and not to a rise in the price of Tibetan wool in British India – trade at Yatung was assessed by value.[32] The figures did, in fact, show a rise. In 1885-86, the first year in which any attempt was made to separate trade with Tibet from that with Sikkim, Bengal imported from Tibet to the value of Rs. 3,72,735, and exported to the value of Rs. 2,45,714. In 1888-89, the year of the Sikkim Expedition, trade between Bengal and Tibet virtually disappeared, imports dropping to Rs. 3,168 and exports to Rs. 4,181. Thereafter a revival took place, and in 1893-94, on the eve of the establishment of Yatung, the figures were imports Rs. 3,58,799, and exports Rs. 3,31,613. With the opening of the Yatung mart a definite rise can be observed, with imports at Rs. 7,01,348 and exports at Rs. 4,47,802, though it is hard to say how much this increase was due to the greater accuracy of the collection of statistics at the trade mart. Between 1894 and 1905, with the exception of the years 1898 to 1900 when both imports and exports exceeded Rs. 10,00,000, the figures generally fluctuated between Rs. 7,00,000 and Rs. 3,00,000 for both exports and imports. These figures, it is worth noting, were not much higher than those for trade between Bengal and Bhutan, and almost insignificant when compared with the figures for the trade with Nepal. In 1895-96 Bengal imported goods worth Rs. 1,23,60,815 from Nepal and exported Rs. 1,04,37,062. The greater part of Bengal imports from Tibet was made up of wool; in 1892-93 wool made up Rs. 2,48,930 out of a total of Rs. 3,51,519. Of the exports to Tibet, European fabrics, generally not of British manufacture, made up the bulk, in 1892-93 Rs. 1,31,290 out of a total of Rs. 2,29,117, and the remainder was made up of the extraordinary variety of articles that somehow still find their way to the bazaars of Central Asia.[33]

One fact that can be learnt from a study of the figures for the trade between Bengal and Tibet - and this applies as well to the figures for such trade from Assam and the Punjab. In the years after the abandonment of the Macaulay Mission the trade between India and Tibet made up so small a portion of India's foreign trade as to be of serious interest only to the Local Governments concerned. Lord Elgin was not very interested in the theories that Bengal based upon the Yatung trade returns: he was far more concerned at what British officials at Yatung and in Sikkim had to say about Tibetan politics and the Tibetan attitude to the Sikkim-Tibet Convention.

Nolan concluded from his talks with Tenzing Wangpu in November 1895 that the Tibetan outpost at Giaogong symbolized a spirit of Tibetan nationalism, greatly reinforced by the recent coming of age of the 13th Dalai Lama. The Tibetans, Tenzing Wangpu said, did not feel bound by a treaty which had been negotiated on their behalf by Britain and China, and they would not discuss the frontier as defined in that treaty. They were willing, however, to discuss the frontier with reference to Tibetan maps; but Tenzing Wangpu emphasized that 'Tibet would not give up land merely because required to by the Convention'. It followed that demarcation in conjunction with the Tibetans would mean the renegotiation of the Sikkim-Tibet Convention and the revival of those Tibetan claims over Sikkim which the

173

British had found so distasteful during the years 1886 to 1890. Since Nolan could see little chance of the Chinese enforcing the Convention of 1890 on the Tibetans – he thought that they would have liked to have done so if they could – he could only suggest that the British should demarcate the frontier alone in 1896 and drive the Tibetans from Giaogong if they persisted in their claim to that remote portion of Sikkim.[34] To this Sir Charles Elliott agreed with a further proposal that should the Tibetans not honour the newly demarcated frontier the Chumbi Valley should be annexed. These arguments in favour of a stronger policy disturbed Lord Elgin. He did not feel that a piece of land as unimportant as Giaogong, and to which he was inclined to believe the Tibetans had claims with some merit, justified a course of action which could only damage the already insecure position in Tibet of the Chinese with whom the British were bound by treaty to deal as the Sovereign Power in Tibet. But did the manifest failure of the Chinese to exercise their authority in Tibet necessitate a drastic revision of the mechanism of Anglo-Tibetan relations? Lord Elgin was most anxious to hear Lord Salisbury's views on this question.[35]

Lord Salisbury thought that the Giaogong problem could be solved easily enough. The British ought to 'assert our claim to the boundary in question, not by a permanent occupation, but by periodically knocking down the erections of the Tibetans, walls and edifices', and 'this should be done as cheaply as possible'.[36] As Lord George Hamilton, the Secretary of State for India, put it:

> It is annoying to have to waste money and men even to the small extent involved in determining this question, but there seems now no alternative but to make the Tibetans understand that, if they insist on ignoring the Treaty, they will be punished.[37]

This was also the view of Sir N. O'Conor, who saw Chinese co-operation as 'proportionate to their opinion of the Indian Government's earnestness in the matter'.[38] In fact, by the end of 1895 and after the outcome of the Sino-Japanese War the opinion of Bower – dismissed in 1893 by the Foreign Office as 'somewhat crude' – that in dealing with Tibet China was not worth bothering about, was now widely accepted in London. .

Lord Elgin, however, partly because he wished to give neither the Chinese nor the Tibetans any excuse to open fresh discussions on the nature of the Sikkim-Tibet frontier, and partly because he appreciated that the exertion of any force against the Tibetans at

Giaogong would almost certainly result in a total stoppage of the trade at Yatung in which such commercial bodies in England as the Bradford Chamber of Commerce still showed interest,[39] adhered to his moderate policy. In March 1896 he informed Bengal that the point to which he attached most importance was the continuation of trade; and that 'the policy to be adopted towards the Tibetans should, therefore, be one of conciliation, and all action likely to produce friction should be carefully avoided'. He added, moreover, that in Giaogong 'the Tibetans probably possess claims which it would not only be impolitic but inequitable to ignore'.[40] He suggested to the Amban that in return for a sympathetic hearing for Tibetan claims to Giaogong the Tibetans might be persuaded to co-operate in the matter of trade at Yatung. As an initial step he proposed that the Tibetan claims should be examined at a meeting of British, Chinese and Tibetan representatives.[41] Lest this should be taken by the Tibetans as a symptom of British weakness, Elgin told White to point out, during the proposed meeting, how easy it would be for the British to expel the Tibetans from Giaogong; to give point to this warning he instructed that the construction of a good road up the Lachen Valley, the approach to Giaogong, be put in hand at once.[42] The Home Government accepted this plan, but with the significant proviso that no territory should be ceded to the Tibetans without a final demarcation and settlement of the frontier.[43]

In March 1896 the Chinese dismissed the Amban and requested that the British should take no action on the Sikkim-Tibet frontier until his replacement reached Lhasa.[44] This was agreed to largely because the new Amban, Wen Hai, 'has the reputation of being a comparatively honest official, and is favourably contrasted in this respect with Kwei Huan, his predecessor in Tibet'.[45] Despite protests by Bengal, Lord Elgin persisted in his policy of moderation; not only was there to be no further action on the frontier until the new Amban should arrive, but also the armed police post, which had been maintained at Gnatong, just on the Sikkim side of the Jelep La Pass leading into the Chumbi Valley, since the negotiating of the Convention, should be withdrawn as a demonstration to the Tibetans that the British had no aggressive designs.[46] Elgin's policy was clear enough; as he wrote in December 1896:

> We are not hopeful of any great advance in trade on this frontier, and we should, we think, rest content with that gradual development which may be expected to follow the

175

restoration of confidence on the border and the opening of such trade routes on our side of the frontier as can be constructed and kept in order at a reasonable cost.[47]

Giaogong, Elgin noted, was 'a worthless piece of territory';[48] and for so long as the figures of trade through Yatung continued to rise a little, and thus provide some sort of answer to queries from the English Chambers of Commerce, he was content.

The new Amban did not reach Lhasa until early 1898 - the disturbed state of Eastern Tibet had delayed him for over a year from arriving at his new post - and it was not until March 1898 that he suggested to Lord Elgin that demarcation, put off since 1895, should now take place; but, he added, the Tibetans should first be allowed to examine the disputed frontier so that they would have no excuse for 'holding back or reverting to old arguments'.[49] Elgin thought that the Amban sounded most conciliatory, and despite the usual protests from Bengal against any step which might lead to further delays, he was disposed to listen with sympathy to any proposal which the Amban might make.[50] It then transpired that the Amban envisaged a Tibeto-Chinese examination of the frontier without British participation, which would probably occupy the whole 1898 season, followed by Anglo-Chinese-Tibetan demarcation in 1899, 'always supposing, of course, that no point of disagreement crops up'.[51] Elgin, none the less, agreed to this further delay.[52]

The failure to demarcate in the 1898 season was destined to cost the Chinese and Tibetans a great deal. In 1899 Elgin was replaced by Curzon, thus bringing to the helm of the Government of India a man with a fresh and energetic mind and with strong preconceptions about the correct conduct of British policy in Central Asia. Curzon, moreover, was faced with the advocation by Bengal of an even more drastic approach to the Tibetan question than had been advanced to date, supported by an argument which could not fail to appeal to him.

In November 1898 White held discussions at Yatung with the Chinese frontier officer, Prefect Li, and the Tibetan representative, Tenzing Wangpu, in which it became clear that the plan to exchange Giaogong for better trading facilities at Yatung would not succeed. The Tibetans refused to see any connection between Giaogong and Yatung. Restoration of Giaogong, they felt, was no concession; it was their just due. Only after their rightful frontier was restored to them would the Tibetans consider discussing trade; and, in any case, not only was Tenzing Wangpu not empowered to deal with the trade question but also he quite failed to see in what way the conditions at Yatung required improvement.[53] Not only did the Tibetans refuse to compromise, but, White felt, they had deliberately insulted him by expecting him to sit in conference with two refugees from British justice whom the Tibetans were employing as English interpreters and advisers on British affairs.[54] These two men, Dhurkey Sirdar, who was wanted by the Darjeeling police for theft and for illegal political agitation, and Jampay, a former clerk who had run off with money belonging to the Darjeeling Improvement Trust, were destined to play a part on more than one occasion in the increasing tension on the Sikkim-Tibet border which followed the arrival of Lord Curzon.

By the end of 1898 White had renewed his vigour in urging a stronger policy towards Tibet, and with the arrival of Curzon, White was to receive more attention than he had under Elgin. He proposed that the price for the recognition of Tibetan claims to Giaogong should be raised from improvements at Yatung, or the removal of the mart to Rinchingong, one and one-half miles further into the Chumbi Valley, to the location of the mart at a completely new site, Phari, on the edge of the Tibetan plateau. In addition, the Tibetans should agree to an extradition treaty with the British which would preclude the future employment by the Tibetans of criminals escaped from British territory. Since there was little chance of such new terms being secured through the mediation of the Chinese, 'we should endeavour to negotiate direct with Lhasa'. White emphasized the urgent need for some such change in policy with a remark which foreshadowed a radical alteration in the nature of the Tibetan question, and which will soon be considered in some detail; 'the Russians', he warned, 'are making progress in the north, and have already, I am informed, tried to make their influence felt in Tibet. We should certainly be there before them, and not allow the Tibetan markets to be closed to English goods.'[55]

White, in effect, proposed two changes. Firstly, that in exchange for recognition of Tibetan rights at Giaogong the Tibetans should agree to the removal of the mart to Phari, where it would operate under the same conditions as those which should have been in force at Yatung. Secondly, that in Anglo-Tibetan relations the mediation of the Chinese should be dispensed with and direct contact established between the British and Lhasa. With minor, but significant, modifications of the proposed conditions under which the new mart at Phari should operate, these changes were approved by Bengal in February 1899, and by the middle of that year had become the policy of the Indian Government of

Lord Curzon, with the approval of the Home Government.[56] The acceptance of these changes was an acceptance of the thesis that the Sikkim-Tibet Convention and the Trade Regulations had failed to achieve their purposes and must be abandoned for what could only be a direct Anglo-Tibetan treaty, a step in contradiction to the principle of Anglo-Tibetan relations only through Chinese mediation which had been established in 1886 and reinforced in the Sikkim-Tibet Convention of 1890.

It is hard to see, if one confines oneself to the summary of the negotiations on the Sikkim-Tibet frontier from 1894 to 1898, why exactly the Indian Government returned to the policy of direct relations with the Tibetans which it had abandoned in 1886. The frontier negotiations, of course, had developed an impetus of their own so that each failure tended to bring about an increase in British demands. These negotiations, furthermore, were not very satisfying to the pride of those officials like White who were responsible for their conduct on behalf of the Indian Government; and the first of the Tibet Blue Books tries hard to show how intolerably humiliating was the attitude of the Chinese and Tibetans on this frontier during these years. Much was made of Tibetan obstruction to trade at Yatung. The case of the boundary pillars and of the Tibetans at Giaogong is presented in a way that suggests that it was of a gravity comparable to the Tibetan advance to Lingtu in 1886. An examination of these incidents, however, can only lead to the conclusion that they were trivial indeed. From the end of 1898 the impetus behind British policy towards Tibet was being provided not by events on the Sikkim-Tibet frontier but by the apparent development of Tibet into another field for that Anglo-Russian competition which dominated so much of Asian history in the nineteenth century.

How obstructive were the Tibetans during these first few years of the trade mart at Yatung? Much was made of the destruction of boundary pillars which White had put up on some of the passes leading into Chumbi. But it should be remembered that demarcation of the Sikkim-Tibet frontier had been agreed to by the Chinese in 1894 on the understanding that it should be carried out jointly by British and Chinese commissioners with Tibetan observers in attendance. White had put up his pillars - there were only three of them - without Chinese consent and in the face of Chinese requests for delay until their commissioners were ready. White, moreover, never produced any satisfactory proof that the destruction of the pillars was due to deliberate Tibetan policy: as the Indian Government noted after the first pillar had been knocked down, 'there is, however, at present no evidence that the mischief is to be directly attributed to Tibetan officials'.[57]

Considerable doubt also existed, as Lord Elgin admitted, about the rights and wrongs of the Tibetan position at Giaogong. The map which Markham printed in 1876 along with his edition of Bogle, and which was drawn by Trelawney Saunders, the chief cartographer at the Indian Office, extended the Sikkim frontier to a point nearly twenty miles to the north of Khambajong, and thus located Giaogong well within Sikkim.[58] Other maps, however, were not so definite. Of two British maps published in 1894, one, which Riseley included in his Gazetteer of Sikkim, placed Giaogong in Sikkim, while the other, in Louis' *Gates of Tibet*, located Giaogong three miles within Tibet. Giaogong is a plateau about 16,000 feet high. It overlooks the east bank of the Lachen River and lies slightly north of the line of the highest peaks of the Sikkim Himalaya. It leads on to the Tibetan plateau, and in 1902 White described it as the natural gateway to Shigatse.[59] Geographically, there can be no doubt that Giaogong falls into the area of the Tista system and is thus on the southern side of the watershed; but this fact only emerges after an accurate survey of a kind quite beyond Tibetan comprehension. The concept of a watershed is a product of modern geographical science and, like the concept of a frontier defined by geographical features without reference to the economy and history of the peoples on either side, quite foreign to the Tibetan mind which, as Eden had noticed in 1861, did not take very seriously minor frontier transgressions and could never understand British susceptibilities on this point.[60] Had the Tibetans possessed the scientific knowledge to define theoretically their frontier, they would probably have said that it followed roughly the 15,000-foot contour line.

Flocks and herds from both Sikkim and Tibet were grazed at Giaogong. When White visited this area in 1902 he found that there were about six times as many animals from Tibet grazing there as there were from Sikkim.[61] Since no one lived at Giaogong this fact must add considerable strength to the Tibetan claims which were already well fortified with historical argument. Hooker, and others, had in the past located the Sikkim-Tibet frontier well south of the watershed; Hooker described it as actually crossing the Tista River tributary, the Lachen River, and he placed the Kangra Lama Pass, in later maps within Sikkim, on the frontier itself.[62] The Tibetans claimed that the frontier south of Giaogong had been marked by the Chinese with stone pyramids in 1795 and inspected by Chinese and Tibetan frontier officials in 1821, 1844 and 1851. After each inspection a wooden tablet had been posted, later removed by the Tibetans for safe

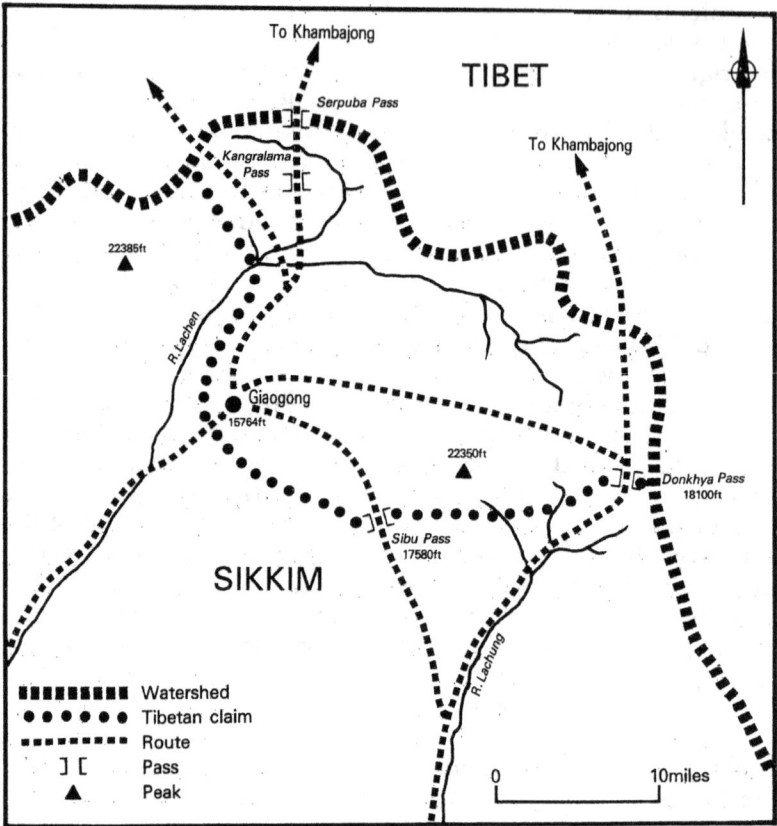

Sketch map of Giaogong and the disputed portions of the
Sikkim–Tibet frontier

keeping. These tablets were shown to White in 1898, but he
refused to attach any importance to them as they were not *in situ*.
In 1888 the Tibetans were reported to have built a wall at
Giaogong.[63] The report of their presence there in 1894, which
White made to Bengal, gives no indication as to how long they
had been occupying this piece of territory. It does not read like the
reports of the Tibetan advance to Lingtu in 1886; rather, it seems
as if White was recalling a long-established fact as additional
ammunition for his argument that the Sikkim–Tibet Convention
had failed. There is no evidence against the suggestion that the
Tibetans had been in occupation of Giaogong for centuries; and
the inference might well be that White had only just noticed in
1894 that this area lay technically within the Sikkim frontier as

defined on paper in 1890. It would be too much of a coincidence to suppose that the traditional frontier corresponded exactly with the watershed, which, as has been noted, was adopted by the British in 1846 as a convenient formula for settling boundaries in the Himalayas, and was based on expediency, not history.

The case against the Tibetans at Yatung likewise, on a closer examination, resolves itself into a conflict between the Trade Regulations and traditional Tibetan rights and practices. The 10 per cent. duty at Phari, as has already been noted, the British were soon obliged to admit was a generally applied Tibetan tax, and was not specifically designed to frustrate the mart at Yatung. It is probable that the difficulties which White and Nolan claimed the Tibetans were putting in the way of their own merchants who might wish to visit and trade at Yatung had a similar traditional basis. In a sense Phari was the Tibetan frontier town divided from India by the Chumbi Valley, a district which differed in many important respects from Tibet proper. Its inhabitants, the Tromos, seem mainly to have been descended from Bhutanese settlers. In their valley the Pön religion, containing many elements predating Buddhism, and sometimes called the Black Sect, predominates. While under the general control of the two Phari Jongpens, the Tromos at this time enjoyed an appreciable measure of autonomy under their village councils.[64] The valley was closely connected with Sikkim; the Maharaja of Sikkim, indeed, preferred to live there when he could. It is probable that the people of this valley had enjoyed the monopoly of the carrying trade through their land for many years before the establishment of Yatung, and had no wish to give up that valuable right on account of the trade mart. Yatung, like Phari, was the terminus of that section of the road over which goods were carried by Chumbi ponies. The real markets, where goods were bought and sold, were inevitably, Darjeeling, Kalimpong and the towns of Central Tibet, and not the dismal frontier post at Yatung.

Strict observance of the Convention and the Trade Regulations, as the British understood them, involved surrender by the Tibetans of what they clearly considered to be long-established rights. But why should the Tibetans be prepared to make such a surrender on the basis of a treaty imposed on them by the Chinese and in the negotiating of which they had taken no part? The British answer was, because China was the Suzerain Power in Tibet. Events in the 1890s, however, were rapidly removing much force from this reply.

The Chinese position in Tibet, which had been steadily declining for several decades, took a marked turn for the worse in the years following the outbreak of the Sino-Japanese War. The weakening of her hold on the periphery of her Empire was apparent to most observers. After 1894, for example, the impending Russian annexation of Mongolia and Sinkiang was widely discussed.[65] In 1895 a rebellion of 'formidable proportions' against Manchu rule in Kansu and North-West China erupted.[66] In Lhasa, where the result of the war with Japan was well known,[67] the Dalai Lama, in 1895, openly flouted the authority of the Amban by refusing to accept appointments made by the Chinese and by punishing on his own authority Chinese citizens in defiance of requests from the Amban that they should be handed over to him.[68] In 1896 it was reported in Chungking that there had been anti-Chinese riots in the Tibetan capital, and risings against the Chinese among the tribes of Eastern Tibet. The Government at Chengtu had hoped to extend the telegraph to Lhasa, the better to control Tibetan affairs, but was unable to construct the line beyond Tachienlu in the face of marauding tribesmen.[69] It was this disturbed state which prevented the new Amban, Wen Hai, who had set out from Peking in late 1896, from reaching Lhasa until the spring of 1898.[70] The Chinese tea trade with Tibet was also affected by the troubles in Eastern Tibet, and there was much economic distress in the tea-growing district of Yachou in Szechuan, which the local authorities blamed on the British; anti-British demonstrations ensued in 1896.[71] In that year the Censor Wu Kuang-k'uai memorialized the Throne to the effect that unless the Chinese Government made haste to incorporate Tibet into China proper they would lose it to either Britain or Russia; he strongly advised that official encouragement be given to the settlement of Chinese peasants in Eastern Tibet after the pattern already established in Mongolia;[72] and Chao Erh-feng was to follow such a policy in Eastern Tibet between 1905 and 1911. The Amban, in these circumstances, with inadequate funds and his escort below strength, was unable to make much impression on the Tibetan authorities. Lhasa was virtually a punishment posting and all too often the Amban tried to recompense himself for the discomforts of the task he had been assigned by resorting to every variety of 'squeeze'. In 1895, for example, O'Conor reported that Amban K'uei had behaved so corruptly that he had become a victim of blackmail on the part of the Tibetan Government, over whom, in consequence, he had no influence at all. His successor Wen Hai possessed a reputation for honesty, and presumably wished the Tibetans to show less intransigence towards British demands as the only alternative to direct Anglo-Tibetan relations, perhaps imposed by force, and hardly beneficial to the Chinese position in Lhasa.[73] But, like his predecessors, he had not the power to coerce the Tibetans; if pressed too hard in Lhasa, the monks might rise; the Amban and his entourage would then either be slaughtered or driven out of Tibet to face an unpleasant fate at the hands of the Government in Peking.

In 1895 the Tibetans acquired a focal point for their aspirations of independence in the person of an adult Dalai Lama. Since the death of the 8th Lama in about 1804 at the age of forty or so, no Dalai Lama had assumed the full powers and responsibilities of his office. The 9th Lama had died in 1815, with foul play suspected. The 10th Lama was said to have been murdered in 1838 and the 11th Incarnation met the same fate in 1855. The 12th Lama, who died in mysterious circumstances in 1875, was the last of this unfortunate series. The 13th Lama came of age either in or just before 1895, and he managed to frustrate the usual plots against his life with such success that he found himself in a more powerful position in Lhasa than had been his predecessors since at least 1792.[74] As Chinese officials at Yatung freely admitted, 'the Dalai Lama's coming of age would probably increase the power of the Tibetans'.[75] One result was immediately apparent. The years after 1891 saw yet another crisis on the Tibeto-Nepalese border, on this occasion arising out of a dispute over the rate of exchange between Tibetan salt and Nepalese rice. The crisis reached its height in 1895-96, when it produced British and Chinese reactions like those to the similar crises in the 1870s and 1880s. The Tibetan reaction, however, differed in two important respects. Firstly, the Tibetans were far more reluctant to accept Chinese advice to come to terms than they had ever been before; and, secondly, they began to give serious thought to putting their own defences on a sounder footing. In 1895 or 1896 the Dalai Lama, for instance, founded an arsenal at Lhasa where it was intended to manufacture rifles of a modern pattern.[76]

The Tibetans, it is clear, looked on the Convention and the Trade Regulations as having been imposed upon them by the Chinese; they saw, when it was explained to them that Giaogong lay within Sikkim territory as defined by the Convention, that acceptance of the Convention implied acceptance of the Chinese right to cede to a foreign power territory belonging to Tibet. To such a cession, in the prevailing spirit of Tibetan independence, and in the face of evident signs of the decline of Chinese power, the Government of the Dalai Lama was not prepared to agree; all the more so as it seems to have been under the misapprehension that the Convention and Trade Regulations would expire in 1899 and that all that was needed to prevent a crisis was to avoid any decisive action until that date.[77] There were other grounds for Tibetan unwillingness to co-operate with the British. The Lhasa monasteries saw that the opening of Tibet to Indian trade would eventually result in the import of Indian tea to the detriment of the revenues of those institutions which were based to a large extent on the monopoly of the import of Chinese tea from Szechuan. The Dalai Lama and his advisers, moreover, shared a suspicion which had been common in Tibet at least from the period following the Sikkim War of 1861 when the British started building roads up to the Sikkim-Tibet border, that the British had designs on Tibetan territory. The behaviour of White, with his refusal to accept Tibetan evidence as to the ownership of Giaogong and his frequently arrogant or minatory attitude towards Tibetans, like Tenzing Wangpu, who held discussions with him, coupled with the hostile opinions of men like the Shata Shape and Dhurkey Sirdar, can only have led Lhasa to believe that the British intended to swallow up Tibet as they had absorbed, one by one, other states in the Indian subcontinent. The British insistence on frontier demarcation, for which no provision had been made in the Convention, can only have confirmed the Tibetans in this interpretation of British intentions, for which, in Tibetan eyes, ample evidence already existed in the history of the Macaulay Mission and in the entry into Tibet for a few hours by British troops in 1888.

There is some evidence to suggest that in 1895, or shortly after, the Dalai Lama had come to the conclusion that in order to free Tibet from Chinese control and to prevent it from being swallowed up by the inexorable expansion of the British power in India some outside assistance was necessary. Of the two European Powers in a position to give such help, France and Russia, France was ruled out because of its aim to convert Tibet to Roman Catholicism; this could be the only conclusion to be drawn from French missionary activity in West China and Eastern Tibet. It must have seemed to the young and inexperienced Dalai Lama that the Russians alone neither wished to annex Tibet nor to convert it to a new religion and destroy that Buddhist faith in which all Tibetans take such pride. Russia was known to the Tibetans. Russian merchants of Asiatic origin were trading in Tibet when Bogle visited the Tashi Lama. Many Russian subjects, especially amongst the Buriat mongols of Lake Baikal, were Buddhist; there were frequent contacts between these Buddhist communities and Lhasa. Many young Buriats studied in the Lhasa monasteries and some remained there for the rest of their lives.

Some Buriat monks rose to high positions in the Tibetan monastic hierarchy. One such man, later to achieve a certain measure of international fame, Dorjieff by name, had by 1895 acquired considerable influence over the Dalai Lama, and was doubtless advising him to look to St. Petersburg for his political salvation.[78] Dorjieff, and the significance of his presence in Lhasa, will be discussed in greater detail in the next chapter.

The Indian Government had no Dorjieff at its disposal who might present the British case to the Dalai Lama. Indeed, its means of acquiring intelligence about Tibet and of intriguing in the Tibetan capital were quite inadequate for any serious competition with Russia or any other foreign power; and it must be remembered that in the 1890s the French, from their base in Western China, were showing an interest in Tibet which caused some alarm, at least to British consuls in Szechuan Province. M. Haas, the French Consul-General in Szechuan, who in 1884 was thought by some observers to be about to lead Upper Burma into French protection, was in the 1890s reported to be doing his best to coerce the Szechuan authorities into opening Tibet to French missionary enterprise. In 1896 a mission from the Lyons Chamber of Commerce visited Tachienlu and showed a keen interest in Tibetan commerce. In 1898 M. Bonin, one of many French travellers to venture into Tibet at this period, was investigating the minerals of Eastern Tibet. It looked as if Tibet might be a logical end of French expansion from Indo-China through Yunnan, as Francis Garnier had noted as long ago as 1872.[79] Thus Litton, the British Consul in Chungking, remarked in 1898 that 'I cannot think the time is very far removed when we shall see a forward move on the part of the French in these parts'.[80] As the nineteenth century drew to a close the northern frontier of India began to seem less secure than it had been since the time of Gulab Singh's invasion of Western Tibet. Until the arrival of Lord Curzon, however, the Indian Government did surprisingly little to safeguard itself against surprise in Tibet.

By the end of the nineteenth century it seemed as if no European stood much chance of making his way to Lhasa unless escorted there by an army. The failure of explorers of many nationalities stood in proof of this conclusion. For the British, moreover, the difficulties of Tibetan travel were increased by the Burma-Tibet Convention of 1886 and the Sikkim-Tibet Convention of 1890, whose terms prevented the Indian Government from attempting anything which might be interpreted as an official mission to the Tibetan capital. While the Indian Government did not forswear all unofficial attempts to penetrate

Tibet – the journeys of Bower in 1892, Welby in 1896 and Deasy in the same year all had some backing from Military Intelligence,[81] Bower, for instance, having been asked to look into the truth of rumours of Russians travelling 'in the neighbourhood of Ladak'[82] – in general it frowned upon the plans of Englishmen to travel without permission beyond the mountain frontiers of India, and strove to avoid giving cause for Chinese protests. Bower's journey of 1892 produced just such Chinese protests, to the concern of Sir John Walsham, who noted that Bower did not have a passport valid for Tibet – the Chinese had given him permission to travel in Sinkiang, which was quite another matter – and feared lest the Yamen should blow up this affair into an excuse to prevent all British officers from journeying in Sinkiang in the future.[83] This point had already risen on a number of occasions in the past: in 1884, for instance, in reply to a request from India for a Chinese passport for A. D. Carey of the Bombay Civil Service which would be valid for Tibet as well as Sinkiang, Sir Harry Parkes had written that

> the inclusion of Thibet within the scope of travel proposed by Mr. Carey occasioned me some embarrassment, as I knew that if I asked for a passport for that region it would be declined by the Chinese Government on the grounds of insecurity, and a refusal once made might create an inconvenient precedent for the future.[84]

After 1886 this point was reinforced by the terms of the Burma-Tibet Convention. Thus it should cause no surprise that in 1889 Dr. Lansdell, who had a letter from the Archbishop of Canterbury to the Dalai Lama, was refused permission to cross the Tibetan border by Lord Lansdowne's Government,[85] and that in that year Francis Younghusband, who was later to lead a British army to Lhasa, was not allowed to try to make his way into the heart of Tibet in the disguise of a Turki merchant.[86] The Indian Government was most unsympathetic to travellers like Lt. Gaussen in 1896,[87] and A. H. Landor in 1897, who entered Tibet without permission and then suffered at the hands of Tibetan frontier guards.

The Landor affair aroused considerable interest in England, and the failure of the Indian Government to turn it into an 'incident' is significant. Landor crossed into Tibet from Kumaon in May 1897 without permission either from Government or from the Chinese. With an entourage of thirty-one servants, most of whom deserted him soon after he entered Tibet, he hoped to make his way to

Lhasa. Near Lake Manasarowara Landor was arrested by a Tibetan patrol along with his few remaining servants. He was beaten, tied up, deprived of most of his possessions, made to travel in bonds for several days and finally released when he had reached a state of physical collapse. Many of his belongings were later returned by the Tibetans, but there was no denying that his treatment had been most harsh. Landor came back to India in a fury over what the Tibetans had done to him. But the Indian Government, far from sending a punitive expedition into Tibet, did no more than send home full details of what had happened to Landor so that the India Office would not be taken by surprise when that irate traveller burst into print. Lord Elgin remarked that

> it would probably be undesirable as well as futile to endeavour to obtain any redress. It is possible, however, that a public statement may elicit much sympathy for the sufferer, and perhaps give rise to a movement in favour of demanding reparation.[88]

Lord Salisbury was, in fact, addressed on this subject, and Landor wrote privately to Curzon, then Under-Secretary of State for Foreign Affairs. In view of his future part in the Tibet question, Curzon's reaction is of interest. He felt that there was no case for demanding reparation from the Chinese or the Tibetans; 'Tibet is not open to foreigners,' he observed, 'and anyone attempting to enter the country does so at his own risk entirely'.[89]

The Indian Government, of course, did sometimes allow Europeans to cross over into Tibet. The journeys of Bower, Welby and Deasy have already been noted. Generally these journeys, like those of Major-General Channer in 1894 and 1896, were for purposes of sport - no political consideration seemed sufficient to prevent officers of Her Majesty's Army from going off in pursuit of *Ovis ammon*. But it was stipulated that these ventures should take place in the remoter regions of Western Tibet, and not along the Sikkim-Tibet border. It was emphasized that there must be no trouble with local Tibetan officials; and for this reason Channer took care to bring all his supplies with him so that he would not have to come into contact with Tibetan villages, the potential scene of disputes.[90] But these secret dashes across the Tibetan border in pursuit of wild sheep were hardly calculated to be of much political value or to add much to British knowledge of Tibet.

Of not much greater political value were the travels in Tibet of native agents in the employ of the Indian Government. During the second half of the nineteenth century the Survey of India sent native explorers, the 'pundits' as they came to be known, into the deepest recesses of Central Asia. They often travelled in disguise, and their adventures make exciting reading. They paced out the roads of Tibet, counting their steps with the aid of special hundred-beaded Buddhist rosaries; they took bearings with compasses which they carried concealed in Tibetan prayer wheels; but they achieved very little of any political value. Most of the 'pundits' were humble men travelling in the disguise of humble men. They were not likely to preserve their anonymity once they tried to contact senior Tibetan officials. An exception must be made, however, in the case of Sarat Chandra Das, the prototype, it has been said, of Babu Hurree Chunder Mookerjee in Kipling's *Kim*. Das was employed on undoubted political work, and his part in the planning of the Macaulay Mission had already been noted. But by 1886 Das' value as a secret agent had gone. He was known in Lhasa; he could not visit Tibet; and he was closely watched by Tibetan spies in Darjeeling who intercepted many of his letters to Tibetan friends, as the Japanese traveller Kawaguchi was to discover to his cost in 1902. The most likely people for Tibetan secret service were men like Ugyen Kazi, the Bhutan Vakil at Darjeeling, or some of the Ladakis who were accustomed to visit Lhasa at regular intervals on one of the traditional missions. But, as the Indian Government had discovered in the 1840s with Anant Ram, such persons were extremely unwilling to compromise themselves in Tibetan eyes and could not be trusted to carry out the orders of their British employers.[91]

For its knowledge of what went on in Tibet the Indian Government was forced to rely on three main sources. Firstly, British officials in Sikkim and on the Sikkim-Tibet frontier – and to a much smaller extent on other points of territorial contact between India and Tibet – could collect bazaar gossip, question traders down from Tibet, and report occasional conversations with minor Tibetan and Chinese frontier officials. From such sources a surprising amount of general information was extracted, though its evaluation was a very difficult task. Secondly, the British Resident at Katmandu learnt about events in Tibet both from local gossip in that town which many traders from Tibet visited, and from the Nepalese Government, who maintained a Resident in Lhasa and who were willing, sometimes, to transmit portions of his reports to the British Resident. This information was even harder to evaluate; and there was a strong suspicion that what the Nepalese Durbar chose to tell it did so for reasons of its own. Finally, from the British Legation in Peking and from the British Consuls in Western China flowed a fairly steady stream of news of Tibetan affairs. Sometimes letters between the Amban and his superiors in Peking or in Chengtu were intercepted. The French Fathers in Szechuan and Eastern Tibet continued to pass on facts - and, all too often, fancies - about Tibet. A like office was performed by British missionaries, travellers and merchants like Archibald Little, who was doing his best to exploit the trade of Western China. Here again it was very hard to separate truth from rumour, and nothing can better illustrate the unreliability of information from the Eastern Tibetan frontier than the story of the British mission to Lhasa of 1878, which has already been noted.

In 1898, one may conclude, the Indian Government knew less of what went on in Lhasa and Shigatse than it did at the time of Warren Hastings. There was nothing to compare with the detailed and accurate narratives of Bogle and of Turner. This was a serious matter in a period when the signs were pointing towards Tibet becoming a field for Anglo-Russian competition. Much of Russian activity in Tibet first came to the ears of the Indian Government through the Russian press, and to a man of Lord Curzon's cast of mind this was an alarming fact. To others, of course, the very vagueness of such information, and the inherent unreliability of the sources from which it was derived, indicated that there was no cause for anxiety. Lord Elgin, for example, had received a number of indications that something · was afoot in Lhasa. In 1894 the Russian press reported the visit to the Tibetan capital of two Russian subjects, Menkujinov and Ulanov by name.[92] In the following year O'Conor reported from· Peking that he had heard the following story, which is so typical of this sort of intelligence that it deserves quotation at length:

A medical gentleman [O'Conor wrote] who is on intimate terms with several Chinese officials told me this afternoon (4 June 1895) that he had lately seen the Assistant to the Chinese Amban in Tibet, Kuei Ta-jen, who had returned to Peking and from whom he had heard the following story.

Some time ago some Russian officers had been in communication with the Tibetan authorities - my informant was unable to state even approximately the date - and impressed upon them the importance of maintaining friendly relations with the Russians who were alone able to protect them against the ambitious designs of the English who evidently coveted possession of Tibet. If difficulties arose

189

between England and Tibet the Russians would come to the assistance of the Tibetans and they handed them two letters, the first to be sent to the nearest Russian official in case of any disagreement and the second in case the British menaced their independence in any way. Upon receipt of the second letter the Tibetans could count upon Russian assistance.

These letters were given to the Dalai Lama from whose hands they passed into the hands of the Chinese Amban.

My informant was so vague as to the time when this occurred that I almost hesitate to report it, but in case it should coincide with other information in Your Lordship's possession, I mention it for what it may be worth.[93]

Elgin clearly thought such information, behind which, in fact, there was more than a grain of truth, was worth nothing at all. Curzon would have thought differently, and in this difference one may find one of the main changes which the coming of Lord Curzon brought about in the Tibetan question.

The altered state of Anglo-Tibetan relations which becomes apparent in 1899 cannot, of course, be blamed entirely on the new Viceroy. The great changes in the attitude of the Powers to the Chinese Empire which followed upon the Sino-Japanese War and accelerated with the outbreak of the Boxer troubles in 1900, played a far more important part in this. Indications of and suggestions about Russian interest in Tibet had arisen from time to time in the past, and a history of them must go back to the mission of George Bogle. One such indication was provided by Sir Thomas Wade in 1876 in a Chinese Imperial Decree of 1860, 'beyond doubt authentic', outlining a Russian proposal to the Chinese to set their Gurkha dependents upon the British flank, a plan which the Chinese wisely decided to ignore.[94] At the time of the Macaulay Mission and the Sikkim Expedition of 1888 a number of British observers had given thought to the possibility of the establishment of Russian influence in Lhasa. In 1889 Curzon had written that the first Russian exploring party to reach Lhasa would no doubt return home with some sort of treaty in its leader's pocket.[95] Two years earlier Ney Elias had observed that undoubtedly the Russians were attracted to Tibet as the back door to intrigue with Nepal, and that it would be a major triumph to Russian policy if it could make British relations with Katmandu as unsettled as they were with Kabul. Elias, however, taking note of the failure without exception of every exploring party to reach Lhasa, was able to write that 'as long as Lhasa remains closed to us, it will also remain closed to Russia'.[96] The Russians, in fact, were worse placed for reaching the Tibetan capital than were the British, for unlike the latter they had no territory in direct contact with Tibet, their approach lying through Chinese Turkestan and, moreover, across the barren wastes of the highlands of the north of Tibet. In the last years of the nineteenth century, however, Chinese Turkestan did not seem such a barrier. Nor did the cold and arid expanse of Northern Tibet. The Littledales,[97] and others, showed that it could be crossed easily enough by a few people, and it was clear that not many Russians were needed in Lhasa, provided their bags of gold were large enough, to unsettle the entire Himalayan frontier of India. The belief in the military barrier provided by the wastes of Northern Tibet, which was to revive again after 1904, demonstrated, it is interesting to note, a deep ignorance of Tibetan history; for in 1717 Lhasa was captured by a force of Dzungar tribesmen, some 6,000 strong, after a surprise march across this very region from their base at Khotan.[98]

Sir John Ardagh, who had charge of the Intelligence Division of the War Office in 1896-98, certainly thought along these lines. It seemed to him that Chinese Turkestan must soon fall to Russia and that the British had better prepare themselves for this event. The Kashgar region was already toppling, and before Russia absorbed it,

> we should endeavour to secure a frontier which will keep her as far away as possible, lest, when the time for actual demarcation arrives, we may find the Russians as inconveniently near to us on the Taghdumbash and the Karakoram as they now are on the north of Chitral.
>
> The same reasoning applies to Tibet as a buffer region. Unless we secure the reversion of Lhasa, we may find the Russians there before us.[99]

Tibet, in fact, was becoming a 'power vacuum' of the type which Lord Lansdowne wished to avoid. The significance of this development, and of Lord Curzon's attitude towards it, must be left to the next chapter. It should be noted here, however, that whatever change might take place in the motives behind British interest in Tibet, the means whereby the Indian Government could carry out a Tibetan policy were to a very great extent determined by the history of many years of effort to establish closer relations with Tibet. Tibetan suspicions, the result of a long process of misunderstanding British intentions, would not disappear overnight. The Indian Government was unable to escape from the petty disputes with China and Tibet over the Sikkim-Tibet frontier and the trade mart at Yatung. These disputes were to continue; but, while up to the arrival of Curzon the real issues involved were local frontier policy and the development of trans-frontier trade, after Curzon's arrival they became inextricably involved with the much wider question of Anglo-Russian rivalry in Asia. Curzon used the three boundary pillars, the Tibetan encroachments at Giaogong and the obstructions imposed on trade at Yatung, as well as every insult, real or imagined, which British officers had received from Chinese or Tibetan functionaries, as weapons in his armoury for that epic struggle.

IX

CURZON'S TIBETAN POLICY

.

1899 – 1902

L ORD CURZON, who became Viceroy in January 1899, decided to act on the proposals which White had made at the end of 1898. The trade mart, he agreed, must be removed from Yatung to Phari, and some attempt must be made to establish direct contact with the Government of the Dalai Lama. There were two reasons why Curzon should adopt this more forceful policy towards Tibet which Lord Elgin had resisted since 1894. Firstly, Lord Curzon was a man of extraordinary energy and was hardly likely to tolerate, as a new broom in the highest office in the British Empire, the continuance of this irritating frontier dispute. Secondly, Curzon had strongly-held views about the dangers inherent in any further Russian advance, be it of Russian rule or merely of Russian influence, towards India's borders. Many years of study of the politics of Asia had convinced Curzon· that sooner or later Britain would have to make a stand against the Russian threat to dominate the whole of that huge continent. As he wrote in October 1901:

As a student of Russian aspirations and methods for fifteen years, I assert with confidence - what I do not think any of her own statesmen would deny - that her ultimate ambition is the dominion of Asia. She conceives herself to be fitted for it by temperament, by history, and by tradition. It is a proud and not ignoble aim, and it is well worthy of the supreme moral and material efforts of a vigourous nation. But it is not to be satisfied by piecemeal concessions, neither is it capable of being gratified save at our expense. Acquiescence in the aims of Russia at Teheran or Meshed will not save Seistan. Acquiescence in Seistan will not turn her eyes from the Gulf. Acquiescence in the Gulf will not prevent intrigue and trouble in Baluchistan. Acquiescence at Herat and in Afghan Turkestan will not secure Kabul. Acquiescence in the Pamirs will not save Kashgar. Acquiescence at Kashgar will not divert Russian eyes from Tibet. Each morsel but whets her appetite for more, and inflames the passion for a pan-Asiatic dominion. If Russia is entitled to these ambitions, still more is Britain entitled, nay compelled, to defend that which she has won, and to resist the minor encroachments which are only a part of the larger plan.[1]

Curzon was not the man to ignore indications that Russia was establishing its influence in Lhasa; and by the middle of 1899 several signs that this was happening had come to light. White's remark of November 1898 that 'the Russians are making progress in the north' was based upon rumours then circulating on the frontier, and these were to become more substantial in the months to come. By April 1899, for example, the Amban was able to threaten that if the Indian Government continued to demand a trade mart at Phari the Tibetans 'would fall back on the support of Russia who had already offered them assistance'.[2] Rumours of the visit to Lhasa by a Russian mission found their way into the English-language press in India. In May 1899 Paul Möwis, a Darjeeling resident and self-styled Tibetan expert who had contributed to the *Simla News* on this subject, informed the Indian Foreign Office that stories about the visit to Lhasa of a party of Russians under the command of one Baranoff were going the rounds of the Darjeeling bazaar. Möwis thought that Baranoff, *Sbaranuff* in Tibetan spelling, had been at one time secretary to the great Russian explorer Prjevalski.[3]

None of this could be called intelligence of the first order; yet it undoubtedly made a profound impression on the new Viceroy. On 24th May 1899, the day after Möwis made his report, Curzon wrote privately to Hamilton, the Secretary of State for India, that

the Lamas there [Tibet] have found out the weakness of China. At the same time they are being approached by Russia. There seems little doubt that Russian agents, and possibly even someone of Russian origin, have been at Lhasa, and I believe that the Tibetan Government is coming to the conclusion that it will have to make friends with one or other of the two great Powers. That our case should not be stated in these circumstances, and that judgement should go against us by default, would be a great pity. Inasmuch as we have no hostile designs against Tibet; as we are in a position to give them something on the frontier to which they attach great importance and we none; and as the relations that we desire to establish with them are almost exclusively those of trade, I do not think it ought to be impossible, if I could get into communication with the Tibetan Government, to come to terms.[4]

The new policy towards Tibet was designed to ensure that Tibet would decide to ally herself with the British and not with the Russians. It was a policy both of pressure and of persuasion. Pressure would be applied in the matter of the trade mart, which, so Curzon informed the Amban in March 1899, was to be moved to Phari.[5] Persuasion was to be applied in two ways: by a demonstration of British moderation in the matter of the Phari mart, which was not to be open to European visits save that of the British officer in charge of the frontier trade, and by establishing relations directly with the Dalai Lama. This last measure was by far the more important, for Curzon had decided that the old method of dealing with Tibet only through China was 'most ignominious' and 'an admitted farce'.[6]

It was a measure of the extent to which China had fallen in the estimation of the Foreign Office that Lord Salisbury found little fault with this plan to disregard – and secretly, for the Amban was not to be informed of any letters between the Viceroy and the Dalai Lama – the provisions of the Burma-Tibet Convention of 1886 and the Sikkim-Tibet Convention of 1890. Salisbury agreed that 'if the Chinese ever had any authority in Tibet, they certainly have none now'.[7] But this did not mean, so Sir Claude Macdonald, the British Minister at Peking, thought, that it would be wise to 'ignore the Chinese Government altogether',[8] and so it was decided to carry out attempts to solve the Tibetan problem both by the old method of discussions with the Chinese, and by the new policy of approaching the Dalai Lama directly and in secret.

How was Curzon to get in touch with the Dalai Lama? It seemed unlikely that any European could get through to Lhasa at all, and he certainly could not do so without the Chinese finding out. This consideration would have ruled out Paul Möwis, who had offered his services as he was proposing to visit Lhasa in 1900 as part of a Buddhist mission which was to be jointly financed by Mr. Walter Rothschild, the *New York Herald* and the *Calcutta Englishman,* had not Bengal already decided that 'Mr. Möwis cannot be recommended for such service' because of his known unreliability and suspected lunacy. There was little prospect of any Tibetan frontier officer transmitting a British letter to his superiors in the Tibetan capital, as many such attempts in the past had demonstrated. A native agent would have to be entrusted with this delicate task. But where was such an agent to be found? S. C. Das, the obvious choice, could not be used because he was so well known in Tibet as a British agent. A likely person, though it was hoped that he would not be the only possibility, was Ugyen Kazi, the Bhutanese Vakil in Darjeeling. Ugyen Kazi had the entrée to the Tibetan capital. His loyalty to the British seemed to be ensured by the fact of his possession of much land in the Darjeeling District. It seemed unfortunate that he could not speak English, but this was a very minor disadvantage.[9]

Ugyen Kazi had already been tried out in this role in 1898. In July of that year he went up to Lhasa bearing gifts for the Dalai Lama from the Tongsa Penlop of Bhutan, and the Bengal Government had taken this opportunity to send a present of their own, a horse, to the Tibetan ruler. It seems likely that Ugyen Kazi had also been asked to investigate discreetly the attitude of the Tibetans in Lhasa towards closer relations with British India. On his return to India, at any rate, he had given White a long report on this subject. He had, so he said, warned the Tibetans of the danger of continuing to annoy the British, whereupon the Dalai Lama had asked him to act as a sort of unofficial peacemaker between Lhasa and Calcutta, a request which he refused on the grounds that he was already a servant of Bhutan and could not with propriety serve two masters. He concluded that the atmosphere in Lhasa was favourable to the reception of British overtures. One of the four Shapes had suggested that he might find out whether the British would be willing to receive a Tibetan of rank and to negotiate with him. The Tibetans, said Ugyen Kazi, 'did not like the Chinese yoke' and were quite willing to talk with the British provided that it did not appear that they were doing so on orders from China. Relations between the Dalai Lama and the Amban were strained at this time. The Lama was doing his utmost to lessen Tibetan dependence on China; he had, for example, established an arsenal in Lhasa, supervised by Indian Muslim craftsmen, in which he hoped to make Martini-Henry rifles to equip a national Tibetan army. All this Bengal found very interesting, though they were inclined to take what Ugyen Kazi said with a grain of salt.[10]

Bengal did not trust Ugyen Kazi to the point of handing to him secret correspondence without further trials. In September 1899 he was due to return to Tibet on private business. He was asked to write to the Dalai Lama from Phari, using his own words, and inform him of the British willingness to receive a Tibetan official. On the success of this experiment depended the decision whether to entrust Ugyen Kazi with a letter from the Viceroy to the Lama which had already been prepared. When Ugyen Kazi returned to India in November 1899 he reported that he had written to the Dalai Lama as instructed, but that the Lama's reply was very cautious and in no way indicated that he wished to enter into a clandestine correspondence with the British which might invite Chinese retribution. Bengal thought it was 'useless to make any further endeavour at present to open direct communications through an agent, with the Tibetan authorities'.[11]

India, however, wanted another trial to be made of Ugyen Kazi, who wrote once more to the Dalai Lama in December 1899. His language was on this occasion less general. He mentioned the British desire to open a 'bazaar' at Phari and noted that 'should the Viceroy in Calcutta lose patience it will not be well for you'; and he added that a settlement with the British would be good protection against Chinese or Russian influence.[12] The Lama's reply, which arrived in India in March 1900, still gave no hint of any willingness to deal directly with the British. As for Russian encroachment, said the Lama, 'on no account will we let them in. . . . They have repeatedly, with the orders of China, wished to come within our boundary. . . . We will not allow them on any occasion to come, and on this we are united, both lamas and laymen.' He promised to discuss the matter with the new Amban, and this the Bengal Government considered to be encouraging.[13]

In January 1900, before the answer to Ugyen Kazi's second letter had been received, the Indian Government cast its net for other agents on other sections of the Tibetan frontier. There were three possibilities; Nepal, Burma and Kashmir. Nepal was ruled out at once because the British Resident in Katmandu thought that no attempt could be made from this direction without the knowledge of the Nepalese Durbar, which, in view of the need for secrecy, was undesirable. A likely agent was spotted in Burma in the person of Taw Sein Ko, the Adviser on Chinese Affairs to the Government of Burma, who might perhaps be sent to Lhasa by way of Yunnan and Szechuan in the guise of a Chinese merchant. But the Government of Burma thought that Taw Sein Ko was quite unsuitable; he could not be spared; he was

Chinese, but having lived in Burma all his life, he did not speak Chinese as his mother tongue, and could not pass unsuspected as a Chinese; finally, 'he is very fat, and would probably be unequal to the hardships involved in a journey to, and residence in, Lhasa'.[14]

Kashmir, alone, seemed hopeful, by virtue of the relations existing between its province of Ladakh and Tibet. Sir Adelbert Talbot, the Resident in Kashmir, agreed with the Indian Government that some use might be made of the triennial *Lapchak* Mission from Leh to Lhasa to carry a letter to the Dalai Lama. Unfortunately, Talbot wrote, the obvious man to carry such a letter, Chirang Palgez, who had headed the *Lapchak* on several occasions, and who had no financial interest, at present, in the traditional trade between Lhasa and Ladakh and in consequence had no personal reason for discouraging direct Indo–Tibetan trade and relations, had lately been ensnared by the charms of *chang*, the Tibetan beer.[15] Thus Curzon's survey of the Indian Empire disclosed but three persons who could conceivably be used as intermediaries with the Dalai Lama; a minor Bhutanese official, a fat Chinese and a bibulous Ladaki.

Even if Chirang Palgez was now a broken reed, the way through Ladakh to Lhasa still possessed certain obvious advantages. Ladakh was connected to the Tibetan trade centre of Gartok, under the rule of the two Garpons, or Governors, by a complex of traditional trading missions. The sparse population in Western Tibet made it relatively easy for European travellers to penetrate a considerable distance into Tibetan territory before they were stopped and turned back by Tibetan officials. In the years before the Sikkim campaign of 1861 Gartok had seemed the obvious gateway to Lhasa and in 1898 it was again considered that this might be the case. In that year Captain Chenevix Trench, Assistant to the Resident in Kashmir for Leh, and Mr. Gracey, Deputy Commissioner at Almora, argued strongly in favour of a 'forward policy' in the direction of Gartok. Gracey, whose responsibility for the Kumaon–Tibet frontier had frequently brought him into contact with Tibetan officials, felt that they were 'hopeless conservatives to deal with', but would see reason quickly enough at the crack of a whip.[16] In 1899 Chenevix Trench's successor, Captain R. L. Kennion, again turned his mind to the possibilities of Western Tibet. He visited the Tibetan centre of Rudok, and the success of this journey convinced him that he might profitably open some sort of negotiations with the Garpons at Gartok. The nature of the relations existing between Ladakh and Tibet, which he subjected to a searching examination, provided ample excuse for communication or negotiation with the

Garpons. A British proposal to abolish the *Lapchak* Mission, for example, would surely induce the Garpons to receive a British envoy to discuss the question. In the *jagir* of Minsar, an enclave of Kashmir, and hence British feudatory, territory in Tibet near the sacred lakes, Kennion saw an admirable excuse to justify a British official in crossing the Tibetan frontier. Minsar, Kennion wrote, was 'the weak spot' in the Tibetan 'armour'; there could be little objection, in theory at least, to a British official accompanying a mission to collect revenue from the territory of a British tributary state.[17]

In May 1900, when Kennion learnt that the Indian Government was searching for agents to carry a letter to Lhasa, he took the opportunity to review his arguments of the previous year. It was useless, he wrote, to send a native on such a mission. No Buddhist could be trusted to maintain a regard for British interests in the presence of the supreme Pontiff of his faith. The only non-Buddhists who could be used on such a task, the Argun traders of Ladakh, Muslim Ladaki half-castes, were hardly more suitable. It was doubtful whether an Argun would ever obtain an audience with the Dalai Lama. Even if he did have an audience, 'it would be trying his honesty rather high to expect him to do his utmost to open a trade to outsiders of which he and his clan have hitherto had the monopoly'. Kennion thus ruled out both Chirang Palgez, a Buddhist, and the chief Argun trader, Haji Wazir Shah, who had headed the trading part of the *Lapchak* Mission of 1899. The only remaining possibility was that a British official should act as intermediary between the Indian Government and a responsible Tibetan official. Kennion proposed that he be authorized to visit Gartok, perhaps using the *jagir* of Minsar as an excuse for crossing the Tibetan frontier, and to persuade the Garpons (or Urkhus, as they were often called) to transmit a letter from the Viceroy to the Dalai Lama. Kennion felt that while he was at Gartok he might well open negotiations with the Garpons on Indo-Tibetan trade and on future correspondence between British and Tibetan officials.[18]

In July 1900 Kennion was authorized to visit Gartok and to entrust to the Garpons a letter from the Viceroy to the Dalai Lama if he felt it had a reasonable chance of reaching its objective. He was not to initiate discussions on Anglo-Tibetan relations at Gartok, since 'the whole object of the Government of India is to get into touch with the Dalai Lama', and was certainly not to get involved in protracted and, in all probability, futile discussions on another section of the Tibetan frontier. Kennion was not to suggest that the Tibetans might be punished by an abolition of the *Lapchak* Mission. If he used the *jagir* of Minsar as an excuse for crossing the frontier, he should do so without consulting the Kashmir Durbar, since Government had no wish to explain to the Maharaja of Kashmir the object of Kennion's mission. Government did not share Kennion's general distrust of native intermediaries. If the *Lapchak* was of little use, might not the *Chapba*, the Tibetan return for the *Lapchak*, include 'individuals who might be able to render assistance by communicating with Lhasa'?[19]

Kennion agreed that the .*Chapba* had its possibilities. The *Chapba* Mission, he noted, visited Leh from Lhasa every year, bringing tea and returning with saffron. Its head, known in Leh as the *Chapba* or 'tea man', was, in fact, an important Tibetan monk or layman holding the office of personal trader to the Dalai Lama. The office of *Chapba* was held for a three-year term. Its holder visited Gartok for all three years of his tenure of office, but only visited Leh in the third and last year. The *Chapba* (or *Zungston* as he was known in Tibet) Kunga came to Leh during the winter 1899–1900, so his successor would not be in Leh again until the winter of 1902–03. A new *Chapba*, however, would be in Gartok in September 1900, and Kennion would meet him when he went to Gartok. He thought the *Chapba* might well prove a more suitable agent for the transmission of the letter to the Dalai Lama than the Garpons.[20]

A letter to the Dalai Lama was duly prepared and translated into Tibetan by S. C. Das.[21] It was friendly and quite free from threats. The British only wished 'to facilitate trade between India and Tibet, to the mutual advantage of both countries, and to foster that direct and friendly intercourse which should subsist between neighbours'. The British had no territorial designs on Tibet. They hoped that the difficulties outstanding between the two countries would soon be settled by the deputation of a responsible Tibetan official to the Viceroy, who would only be too glad to receive him.[22]

In September 1900 Kennion set out for Gartok, brushing aside some twenty-five mounted Tibetan frontier guards who protested against his entry into their country. Twelve miles from Gartok he was met by a larger Tibetan force which insisted on his retiring for a mile or so. Some soldiers, to emphasize the point, grabbed the bridle of Kennion's pony. As 'it was not part of my object to force my way to Gartok', he reported, 'I accordingly turned back', and pitched camp. The next day representatives of the Garpons called upon him, bringing presents of sheep and yak, and showing nothing but friendliness. They insisted, however, that a

British official could not be allowed to visit Gartok. A few days later the Garpons came out to Kennion's camp in person. They said that they regretted that their orders prevented them from enjoying more frequent meetings with British officers, and they readily agreed to send on the letter to the Dalai Lama. The meeting ended cordially in a group photograph. Kennion also met the new *Chapba*, a young relative of the previous incumbent, Kunga, who seemed more intelligent and friendly than the normal Tibetan and who promised to provide a fairly sure means of communication with Lhasa for the next three years if Government chose to make use of him. Kennion was fairly confident that the Garpons would, in fact, send on the letter to Lhasa, though the great distance between Gartok and the Tibetan capital meant that no reply could be expected until at least February 1901.

> Whatever may be the direct effects of my mission [Kennion wrote to Government] I venture to think the indirect results cannot fail to be good. Friendly meetings with Tibetan officials and straightforward discussions must tend to clear their minds of the suspicion against foreigners in which they are steeped, and to disabuse them of prejudices engendered by centuries of isolation.

In the *jagir* of Minsar Kennion detected a way to bring about such meetings. The Garpons disputed that Kashmir enjoyed anything more than usufructory rights in Minsar, but they seemed unsure of their ground and could produce no documentary proof of their assertion. He suggested that Government should acquire from the Kashmir Durbar the rights over Minsar so that British officers, with a suitable escort, could visit it periodically, and *en route* to Minsar could call on the Garpons at Gartok. He thought that the presence of no more than twenty sepoys would remove all Tibetan objections to such visits.[23] Sir Adelbert Talbot and Government, however, felt that consideration of such ambitious projects should be postponed until a reply had been received to the letter to the Dalai Lama.[24]

In March 1901 Kennion heard from the Garpons. They returned the Viceroy's letter, which they said they had sent to Lhasa, whence it had been sent back unopened, with the comment that the Tibetan Government saw no need for any communication with the British. Kennion noticed, however, that the seals on the letter had been broken and it had evidently been read.[25] In April the Garpons again wrote. They now denied that the letter had ever been sent on to Lhasa; they had only agreed to send it on to avoid argument; they had not sent it on because were it ever to become known in Lhasa that they had been entertaining overtures from the British their lives would have been forfeit. Kennion felt that this second letter had been written on the orders of Lhasa as a device whereby the Tibetan Government could escape the onus of having refused to accept the letter. He knew, from other sources of information, that the Viceroy's letter had in fact been sent on as the Garpons had promised. It was possible, of course, that it may never have reached the Dalai Lama, having been intercepted by some high Tibetan official, but he had no doubt that someone in the Tibetan capital had read it.[26] Curzon, however, did not accept this argument. He had no doubt that his letter never left Gartok, and he thought that further attempts to get into touch with the Dalai Lama by way of Western Tibet would be so much effort wasted. Kennion's plans for using the *Chapba* and for exploiting the *jagir* of Minsar as an excuse for closer contact with the Garpons were shelved. Ugyen Kazi thus became the only channel between the Indian Government and Lhasa of any promise.[27]

The Dalai Lama had just purchased two elephants, two peacocks and a leopard, and had asked Ugyen Kazi to escort this menagerie up to Lhasa in June 1901. It was decided to entrust the Bhutan Vakil with a revised version of the letter from Curzon to the Dalai Lama which the Bengal Government had been holding since 1899, and which they still seemed to be reluctant to entrust to a messenger who did not enjoy entirely their confidence. Ugyen Kazi was told to hand the letter to no one except the Dalai Lama, and to do so with the greatest secrecy. He was to request the Lama to give him a reply to this letter to bring back to Bengal. 'He will be rewarded', Curzon said, 'according to the degree to which these instructions are observed and to the results achieved.'[28] This letter was more strongly worded than the one which Kennion had carried. If the Tibetans did not start negotiating with the British in the near future, Curzon wrote, 'my Government must reserve the right to take such steps as may seem to them necessary and proper to enforce the terms of the Treaty, and to ensure that the Trade Regulations are observed'.[29] Curzon did not consult London on the phrasing of this letter, and both Hamilton and Lansdowne were a bit worried at what would happen next when the Dalai Lama rejected what was to all intents and purposes an ultimatum.[30]

In October 1901 Ugyen Kazi returned from Lhasa with the Viceroy's letter unopened and its seals intact. He said he had handed the letter to the Dalai Lama, who had refused to accept it on the grounds that tradition forbade him to have any dealing with foreigners except in consultation with the Amban. Even if he had been able to negotiate with the British he would not have done so since there was nothing at fault with the present state of Anglo-Tibetan relations. In all this the Lama showed no personal animosity towards the British.[31] Bengal was satisfied that Ugyen Kazi had done his best.[32] But it soon became apparent that Ugyen Kazi's account of his visit to Lhasa did not agree in all respects with other reports reaching Darjeeling. Das thought that not only had he not handed the letter to the Lama, but he had not even mentioned its existence to him.[33] Ugyen Gyatso heard that Ugyen Kazi had told the four Tibetan chief ministers, the Shapes or Khalons, about the letter – thus disobeying his instructions as to secrecy – and that he had been dissuaded from presenting it to the Dalai Lama.[34] Not only did it seem that Ugyen Kazi had not carried out the mission entrusted to him, but also it soon came to light that he had behaved so indiscreetly as to have been forbidden ever again to enter Tibet. He had, it would seem, made an enemy of that Dhurkey Sirdar to whom White had so objected, and who held a position of great influence in the Chumbi Valley.[35] By November 1901, at any rate, Curzon had decided that Ugyen Kazi was a most unfortunate choice for a British secret agent. 'I do not believe', he wrote to Hamilton, 'that the man ever saw the Dalai Lama or handed the letter to him. On the contrary, I believe him to be a liar, and, in all probability, a paid Tibetan spy.'[36] For this choice Curzon blamed Bengal, which was a bit unfair since Bengal from the start had expressed reservations as to Ugyen Kazi's reliability.

When Curzon set out to open direct relations with the Dalai Lama he believed that Russian agents had already made their way to Lhasa. But he did not think, in 1899, that the Tibetans had yet joined the Russian camp. They were seeking the friendship of a European Power and, if the matter were presented to them in the correct light, they would probably decide to ally themselves to the British, who were so close to their borders, rather than to the distant Russians.[37] Even in November 1900, when, as will be seen shortly, much more had been learnt of Russian attempts to cultivate Tibetan friendship, Curzon was still able to write to Hamilton that 'I cherish a secret hope that the communication which I am trying to open with the Dalai Lama may inaugurate some sort of relations between us'.[38] The failure of Kennion's mission and the suspected duplicity of Ugyen Kazi were, therefore, serious blows to a policy which aimed to keep the Dalai Lama from deciding to throw in his lot with Russia. If the Russians could send their agents to Lhasa while the British could not even get a letter into the hands of the Dalai Lama, how was Curzon to counter Russian influence in Tibet? By July 1901, even before Ugyen Kazi's failure was known for certain, Curzon concluded that a more forceful Tibetan policy was needed.[39] The suspected duplicity of Ugyen Kazi - and Curzon did not doubt that these suspicions were well founded - could but confirm this conclusion. It was beyond the power of the Indian Government to put its case before the Dalai Lama by peaceful means. No wonder that Curzon felt that the Bengal Government, which was responsible for the discover of Ugyen Kazi as a possible agent, had let him down badly.[40]

While the attempts to get a letter to the Dalai Lama were in progress, the Sikkim-Tibet frontier was the scene of talks between British and Chinese officials of very much the same pattern of such talks since 1894. British terms were stiffer, of course, with Curzon's offer to the Amban of the removal of the trade mart to Phari, instead of to Rinchingong, in exchange for British concessions at Giaogong.[41] The Chinese refusal of these terms was also couched in stronger language, with the observation that if the British did not make over Giaogong to the Tibetans forthwith, the latter 'would fall back on the support of Russia who had already offered them assistance'.[42] It seemed that both the Tibetans and the Chinese had concluded that the British would never do anything about Giaogong, and there seemed little point in their making needless concessions. It was clear enough that no progress was to be made here unless the British adopted a more forceful policy. It was inevitable that sooner or later the Tibetans would have to be expelled from Giaogong just as they had been expelled from Lingtu in 1888, for British prestige demanded some indication that the Indian Government could not be flouted with impunity. As soon as the failure of Ugyen Kazi's mission was known for certain, Curzon began to take steps for the application of pressure on the Sikkim-Tibet frontier, steps which he had been considering since July 1901.[43] These measures, useful to the maintenance of British prestige in the Himalayas, would probably have been taken even if no fresh evidence had come to light since 1899 of Russian interest in Lhasa. With the emergence of such evidence, however, and with the British discovery that their means of acquiring intelligence about the politics of Lhasa and the intrigues of Russian agents there was quite inadequate for a period of active Anglo-Russian competition, an even more forward policy towards Tibet became inevitable. As will be seen, the discovery from late 1900 onwards of more and more indications that the Russians were further advanced in their plans to win the friendship of the Dalai Lama than Curzon could have dreamed possible in 1899 provided a dynamic force which rapidly brought the Viceroy to the conclusion that a British mission must make its way to Lhasa.

In October 1900 Russo-Tibetan relations became a matter for comment in the world press. On 2nd/15th October the *Journal de St. Petersburg* reported that on 30th September the Tsar had received at Livadia one 'Ahambra-Agvan-Dorjiew', an official of the Government of the Dalai Lama.[44] The report took the Indian Government by surprise.[45] The Chinese seemed to be no better informed.[46] No one appeared to know what the arrival of this man, hereafter referred to as Dorjieff, portended. Hardinge, Chargé d'Affaires at St. Petersburg, reported that Dr. Badmaev, the recognized authority on Tibetan affairs in the Russian capital, 'who has succeeded in maintaining some sort of connection with the Dalai Lama', considered that Dorjieff had come on an official mission, and not one of a complimentary nature. Hardinge doubted this; he thought that Dorjieff had come to settle some religious matter between Lhasa and the Russian Buriats and Kalmuks, who were largely Buddhist. He was certain, however, that 'whatever may be the object of the Lama's Mission, the Russian Government are quite certain to make what capital they can out of it'.[47] The Russian press certainly used Dorjieff's arrival to point out how natural it was for Asiatics to seek shelter under the benevolent protection of the Tsar. As the *Novoe Vremya* of 4th/17th November 1900 remarked:

Present events in China are quite sufficient to explain this attempt on the part of Tibet to seek a rapprochement with Russia, if such it really be. It is only natural, considering the actual state of the Chinese Government, that Tibet should seek Russia's protection. Russia has gained such renown by her peoples of Central Asia, who, like Bokhara, have fallen under her power or appealed to her protection, that it would be perfectly natural if not only Tibet, but all the other regions of Northern and Western China, contiguous with the Russian dominions, were to begin to take steps to obtain peace and tranquility under the aegis of the Czar.[48]

Curzon, it is interesting to note, did not take Dorjieff very seriously at this time. Das knew nothing of any embassy of the kind described in the Russian press; had there been any political mission from the Dalai Lama to the Tsar, he would surely have heard of it. The reports, Das said, must refer to some Embassy from Mongolia.[49] Curzon, still hopeful that he would soon get in touch with the Dalai Lama, was inclined to agree with Das. As he wrote to Hamilton in November 1900:

We are inclined to think that the Tibetan Mission to the Tsar is a fraud, and does not come from Lhasa at all. That the Russians have for a long time been trying to penetrate that place is certain; that a Russian Tibetan, or Mongolian Embassy may have conceivably been there and may have opened negotiations is also. possible; but that the Tibetan Lamas have so far overcome their incurable suspicion of all things European to send an open Mission to Europe seems to me most unlikely. Tibet is, I think, much more likely in reality to look to us for protection than to look to Russia, and I cherish a secret hope that the communication which I am trying to open with the Dalai Lama may inaugurate some sort of relations between us.

For this reason Curzon was 'not much disturbed' by the reports in the Russian press.[50] It was Hamilton at the India Office who showed more concern. While doubting that there could be much. truth in the reports, he did note that they 'had set a good many tongues wagging here, and letters are already beginning to be written to the press, as to the intrusion of Russian influence into Tibet'.[51]

Between June and August 1901 Dorjieff again visited Russia, and was once more received by the Tsar, to whom, it was said, he had brought complimentary letters from the Dalai Lama.[52] The omniscient Dr. Badmaev, whose name was closely linked in St. Petersburg with Russian policy towards Tibet, announced that the Tibetans were now seeking help from Russia in the event of British aggression.[53] The Chinese Chargé d'Affaires in St. Petersburg, while doubting Badmaev's story, still thought that Dorjieff's business was political, in that he had come on behalf of the Dalai Lama to beg the Tsar to restrain his subjects from exploring in Tibet.[54] Count Lamsdorff, the Russian Foreign Minister, not surprisingly, denied that the Mission had any political significance whatsoever,[55] and a number of observers in India, including the Rev. Graham Sandberg, agreed that this new Mission, like the one of 1900, was concerned solely with religious matters.[56]

By the autumn of 1901, however, Curzon had discovered enough about Dorjieff and his friends to inform Hamilton that 'I am afraid it cannot be said that the Tibetan Mission to Russia only represents Monasteries'. Dorjieff, Curzon learnt, was a Buriat Mongol of Russian nationality, who held the post, of 'Professor of Buddhist Metaphysical Philosophy', in Drebung Monastery. It was likely that Dorjieff had visited Russia and other European countries in 1899 following the arrival in Lhasa of that party reported by Paul Möwis, whose Baranoff was almost certainly the same person as Dr. Badmaev.[57] The following story, which could have given Curzon little pleasure, had also come to light.

In March 1900, shortly after Dorjieff had returned to Lhasa from Russia by an overland route, a rather mysterious Mongolian arrived at Calcutta by steamer from Marseilles. He put up for four nights at the Hotel Continental, where he signed the register with the name M. Hopityant, giving his nationality as Russian Asiatic. On 10th March he took a train for Darjeeling, where he was, for some unspecified reason, questioned by the local police. Darjeeling was the railhead on the road from India to Lhasa and there was nothing improbable in his story that he was a merchant from Peking who was taking some trade goods to Lhasa by the easiest route. This was confirmed by his baggage, some thrity-six cases of an innocent content. He now gave his name as Obishak. The Darjeeling police, however, were not quite satisfied with his story. They questioned him further, with the result that he was induced to provide a third account of his name and movements. He admitted, finally, that he was called Norzunoff. He had come from Marseilles and not from Peking, a discrepancy which he explained as resulting from a confusion of his present journey with one he had made some time before. He produced a passport to confirm his identity – no one had so far asked to see it – and also two letters of introduction from the Presidents of the Geographical Societies of Paris and St. Petersburg which described him as travelling 'to Tibet both on a religious pilgrimage and in the interests of science and commerce'. He said that he was taking up his cases of trade goods on behalf of a Mongolian Lama resident in Lhasa, a certain Darjilicoff. This Lama, he said, had visited Europe and had lived in Tibet for over fourteen years. To the Darjeeling police the name Darjilicoff, clearly the same as Dorjieff, meant nothing at all.

Norzunoff, alias Obishak, alias Hopityant, was not allowed to go on to Lhasa; but no obstacle was placed in the way of his sending letters to his patron in the Tibetan capital, who shortly came down to Darjeeling. Norzunoff and Dorjieff both stayed a while with the Lama Serap Gyatso, Abbot of Goom Monastery near Darjeeling, on whom the British relied greatly for information on the many Tibetans who came to visit the Darjeeling markets.

They were met here by Sarat Chandra Das. Neither Serap Gyatso nor Das made, at this time, any report on these two men, though, as was later to become clear, they had a shrewd idea as to what they were. In August 1900 Norzunoff was sent down to Calcutta and deported from India to Odessa 'on the ground that it is undesirable that a Mongolian or quasi-Russian adventurer with several aliases should trade with Tibet through British India', and that, while his baggage seemed to be harmless enough, 'his intentions might be the reverse'. Government paid his fare back to Russia. The matter was not reported to Curzon until some months later. Dorjieff did not return to Lhasa after his friend had been deported, but likewise made his way to an Indian port and took ship for Russia. No watch was kept on his movements in India, and the first that Curzon heard of him was through the Russian press in October 1900.

In March and April 1901 Dorjieff, having returned to Lhasa overland from his first mission to St. Petersburg, once more came down from Tibet into British India, this time by way of Nepal. Accompanied by Norzunoff and two or three other Mongolians he made his way to Bombay, where he boarded a ship bound for China. The British Military Attaché in Peking, Colonel Browne, met him in Peking at the end of April 1901, when he was staying with the Russian postmaster there, a fellow Buriat. In May Browne said that he had left for Chita and the Trans-Siberian Railway. As in 1900, no news of all this reached Curzon until after the Russian press had announced Dorjieff's arrival, this time at Odessa.[58]

Curzon was not sure whether Dorjieff was in fact a Russian agent carrying out the policy of the Tsar, but he strongly suspected that he was.[59] It was certain that British intelligence had failed dismally on the Tibetan border and that something would have to be done to prevent this sort of thing happening again. Curzon laid the blame squarely on Bengal, and saw in these failures, in the two unreported journeys of Dorjieff and in the duplicity of Ugyen Kazi, 'one of the most eloquent results of handing over political functions to Local Governments who have no aptitudes, no taste, no experience and no men for the job'.[60] He resolved to take the control of Anglo-Tibetan relations into his own hands, and to ensure that all information of events on the Tibetan border reached him immediately.[61] One result of this decision was the weekly Darjeeling Frontier Report which summarized rumours and facts on Tibet in a most ill-digested manner, and was sent directly to the Viceroy from July 1901 onwards. Some of the information in these reports and in those -

originating from Yatung was strange, to say the least. The following example should make this clearer. It was reported on 30th April 1902 that

> there is a rumour that the Dalai Lama is secretly cohabiting with a high bred nun, and that, if a male child is the result, he will be openly declared heir to the country and be proclaimed King; the Tibetans claiming from the Chinese the independence of the land. Also that the present Dalai Lama is the last incarnation. It is also said that the above is not true.[62]

The effect of the news of the Dorjieff Missions, together with the knowledge that British intelligence on Tibet was incompetent and that no means seemed to exist by which the Indian Government could present its views to the Dalai Lama, was, inevitably, to confirm Curzon in his opinion that a more forceful Tibetan policy was needed. As more evidence emerged of Russian activity in or about Tibet, so did Curzon's idea of what that Tibetan policy should be develop towards the final form of a British armed mission to Lhasa. In this process the crucial problems faced by British diplomacy throughout the world played their part. The first years of the twentieth century saw dangers to British security in many parts of the globe. The Boxer rebellion threatened to bring about the complete disintegration of the Chinese Empire. The advance of Russia in Asia seemed to be about to enter a fresh era of accelerated progress with the Russian occupation of Manchuria and with the signs of unhealthy Russian interest in Korea, Mongolia and Chinese Turkestan. Trouble was threatening on the Afghan frontier and a third Afghan War seemed not improbable. There were threats to the British position in Persia and the Gulf. Anglo-French tension was approaching a climax in Africa. In South Africa Britain was at war with some of her subjects. British relations with Germany were steadily deteriorating. These factors, and many more, played their part in the history of the Tibetan question, both in creating in England a profound reluctance to run any risk of more military commitments, and in India an accentuated awareness of frontier dangers; but the detailed consideration of their significance is beyond the scope of this work.

Curzon's Tibetan policy was to a great extent the reflection of his conviction that the Russians not only would like to establish their influence in Tibet - which he never doubted for one moment - but also that they were on their way to achieving this ambition. In June 1901, for instance, Curzon thought that, judging from the present rate of progress, a Russian protectorate over Tibet was perhaps ten years off, unless the British carried out some effective counter-action. The Tibetan situation, therefore, was not critical, though this did not mean, of course, that it could be ignored. Russia in Tibet might not pose a serious military threat to the Indian Empire for many years to come, but it might well have more immediately unsettling effects on Nepal, Sikkim and Bhutan. The Russians should certainly be kept out of Tibet. Direct relations with the Dalai Lama, had they proved practicable, would have been the best measure of prevention; but they had not been successful to date, and there was no reason to suppose that they would prove any more successful in the future unless the British acted with more vigour; the only way to stop Russia was 'by being in advance ourselves'. If the Tibetans could not be brought into direct relations with the British by friendly letters, they must be frightened into such relations, and Curzon proposed a plan of gradually increasing pressure on the Sikkim-Tibet frontier. First of all the Tibetans should be driven out of Giaogong, and the pillars along the border should be rebuilt and guarded. If the Tibetans resisted expulsion, or tried to return to Sikkim, or attempted to knock down the newly erected pillars, then the Chumbi Valley up to Phari should be occupied by British troops. By this time the Tibetans would certainly be frightened and would offer to negotiate, whereupon Curzon would say 'yes, but only at Lhasa'. 'I need hardly say', Curzon added, 'that I would not dream of referring to China in this matter. Her suzerainty is a farce, and is only employed as an obstacle. Our dealings must be with Tibet and Tibet alone.' This policy, Curzon emphasized, did not imply any idea of annexing Tibet. As he wrote privately to Hamilton on 11th June 1901:

> It would be madness for us to cross the Himalayas and occupy it. But it is important that no one else should seize it; and that it should be turned into a sort of buffer between the Indian and Russian Empires. If Russia were to come down to the big mountains she would once again begin intriguing with Nepal; and we should have a second Afghanistan on the north. I have not put this very clearly. What I mean is that Tibet itself and not Nepal must be the buffer state that we endeavour to create.[63]

What was worrying Curzon was not the first Dorjieff Mission to Russia but the potential danger created by the British failure to establish relations with the Dalai Lama and to keep an eye on what was going on beyond the Himalayas.

At this time the very idea of a mission to Lhasa was unthinkable in London. The India Office said it would only drive Tibet into Russian arms, as would an increase of pressure on the Tibetan border to the extent which Curzon proposed. Moreover, the Nepalese would object and so would the Chinese, who might so resent such a blatant disregard for their Tibetan suzerainty as to resist any settlement of the claims arising from the Boxer troubles. In any case, with the South African War in progress, it would be folly to embark on further military adventures, however minor.[64] Finally, Hamilton doubted that a Russian protectorate over Tibet was at all likely, and he advised Curzon to go on trying to get a letter through to Lhasa.[65]

After the second Dorjieff Mission, however, both in India and in London the Tibetan situation seemed far more threatening. Curzon thought it must surely damage British interests,[66] and the India Office considered, so Sir Arthur Godley informed the Foreign Office in August 1901, that it had created a situation essentially similar to that brought about by the Amir Sher Ali in 1876, 'when he refused to receive a Mission from the British Government whilst carrying on negotiations with the Russian authorities in Central Asia'. He proposed that a stiff note, which the Foreign Office thought it wise to tone down, be addressed to the Russian Government to the effect that England would never accept an alteration in the status of Tibet.[67] By the late summer of 1901 both the India Office and Curzon were agreed that some sort of situation was developing in Lhasa. They disagreed, however, both as to its gravity and as to the methods which should be adopted to counter it. Curzon had become convinced that only direct Anglo-Tibetan discussion could provide a solution to the problem of Tibet, and that, since the Dalai Lama refused to accept British letters, he must be made to talk with a British mission, in Lhasa if need be. The India Office disliked any scheme which involved sending British officers beyond the Indian frontier. They could not, so Younghusband later remarked, rid themselves of the memory of the murder of Colonel Cavagnari in Kabul in 1879 and of its consequences.[68] They did not wish to run any risk of finding themselves involved in a war on the Tibetan plateau at such a critical period in British history. With the whole vista of British Foreign policy before him, Hamilton told Curzon in August 1901 that 'the Tibetans are but the smallest of pawns on the political chess-board, but castles, knights and bishops may all be involved in trying to take that pawn'.[69] Hence the India Office was constantly on the lookout for some easier method of dealing with the Tibetans. Might not Nepal, for instance, be persuaded to invade Tibet and force a settlement on the Dalai Lama? In this way, at least, British troops would not be involved, or so reasoned Sir William Lee-Warner and Sir Alfred Lyall in July 1901.[70]

Curzon, of course, shuddered at the thought of making use of Nepal in this way since he was unwilling to encourage any increase in the spirit of Nepalese independence. Thus he was left with only one policy towards Tibet which seemed to have any prospect of success, and that was to increase pressure on the Tibetan border. This, of course, had been implied in 1899, when it was proposed to request the removal of the trade mart to Phari; but nothing much had been done while attempts to get a letter through to the Dalai Lama were in progress. After the failure of these attempts had become apparent beyond doubt, with the return of Ugyen Kazi from Tibet in October 1901, there was no reason why Curzon should not bring about some settlement of at least the two issues of the demarcation of the frontier between Sikkim and Tibet and of the continued presence of the Tibetans at Giaogong.

Curzon outlined a policy along these lines in February 1902. The Chinese, he said, should be informed that White would be going up to the Sikkim–Tibet frontier to put up boundary pillars and either to drive the Tibetans out from Giaogong or to exact a tax on them if they persisted in remaining there. Should the Tibetans oppose White, or should they go on knocking down frontier markers, then 'they would only have themselves to thank for any collision that might ensue'. White, who would need a small escort, would forcibly expel the Tibetans from Giaogong if they agreed neither to go nor to pay any tax. If, after such an expulsion, the Tibetans should still seem hostile, then the Indian Government would have to give serious thought to the possibility of occupying Chumbi and of holding it until 'the Tibetans had signified their willingness to come to terms, and to open negotiations at Lhasa'. Whatever happened, the Tibetan policy of isolation, which 'from its own point of view it may not be difficult to comprehend', must be ended 'with as little delay and commotion as possible'. It was, Curzon concluded

> the most extraordinary anachronism of the 20th Century that there should exist within less than three hundred miles of the borders of British India a State and a Government, with whom political relations do not so much as exist, and with whom it is impossible even to exchange a written communication.[71]

The India Office, to whom these proposals looked very much

like an attempt to provoke the Tibetans into providing an excuse for a mission to Lhasa, obliged Curzon to make certain modifications. No fresh boundary pillars were to be erected; they would only tempt Tibetan irresponsibility. There was to be no question of an occupation of the Chumbi Valley, for such an action would, in the eyes of the Foreign Office, constitute a violation of Chinese territorial integrity, and thus throw the question of the Sikkim-Tibet frontier into the arena of international diplomacy. Not that the Foreign Office cared very much about Chinese rights as such; but, as Sir F. Bertie minuted, 'there comes the question of Russia taking up the cudgels for China for her own benefit, and is the present a safe opportunity for raising the question of Tibet? That seems to be a matter for Cabinet discussion.'[72] There seemed to be no objection, however, to the expulsion of the Tibetans from Giaogong - the alternative of taxing them had now been dropped - and Curzon could go ahead with this as soon as he saw fit.[73]

In June 1902 White went up to Giaogong with an escort of one hundred troops under the command of Major Iggulden, and drove the Tibetans from this long-disputed tract of hill country. There were only forty Tibetans there, and it needed but a few light blows from White's and Iggulden's canes to set them moving towards Tibet. The expulsion over, the two British officers settled down in this reconquered British territory to celebrate the coronation of King Edward VII. The ease with which Giaogong was cleared of Tibetans was an anticlimactic ending to eight years of discussion, and it rather suggested that had Lord Elgin not been so patient and moderate, and had he decided to treat this matter as a local police action, this frontier dispute would have been ended in 1894.[74]

The Tibetan reaction to the expulsion was very mild. Trade at Yatung did not suffer. Tibetan officials headed by Dhurkey Sirdar, who said he had been appointed a special frontier commissioner by the Dalai Lama, came down to talk to White. White, however, refused as he had in the past to have any dealings with Dhurkey Sirdar, or to consider any discussion of the frontier beyond a demarcation of the watershed, unless he was approached by a Tibetan delegate with written credentials from the Dalai Lama empowering him to make decisions on frontier questions. And even if the Tibetans did send such a delegate, said White, any discussions would have to take place at Lhasa or some large Tibetan town, and not on the frontier, where further talks would be 'a mere waste of time'.[75]

The Chinese were clearly impressed by the British action at

Giaogong. In July 1902 they appointed Ho Huang-hsi and the new Chinese Customs Officer at Yatung, Captain Parr, to discuss with White the outstanding questions of Tibetan trade and the Sikkim-Tibet frontier. The Chinese attitude seemed much more conciliatory than it had ever been before. They now admitted, for instance, that the Tibetans were wrong in their claims as to the line of the frontier, and that this was partly due to the Chinese, for Amban Sheng Tai had told the Tibetans in 1890 that Giaogong belonged to them. The Chinese were now ready to exchange Giaogong for better trading facilities. White thought, with some reason, that the Chinese were quite sincere in this fresh approach. Their prestige demanded some settlement soon, without which, moreover, the Anti-Chinese faction in Lhasa would gain strength from its ability to protect Tibet from British pressure. Had the frontier and trade been the only points at issue, White would have been quite unjustified in refusing to sit down with Dhurkey Sirdar or anyone else who might represent the Tibetans. But the Russian issue made it essential for the British not to permit themselves to be bogged down in a further series of protracted discussions on the frontier. Thus, in the forthcoming talks with Ho and Parr, which White could hardly avoid, he was instructed not to accept any terms which did not include the removal of the trade mart from Yatung to Phari.[76] As will be seen, to Curzon the trade mart was a political instrument of some importance even if no trade actually passed through it. A mart at Phari meant the right for a British officer to visit that town located on the very edge of the Tibetan plateau, and no Tibetan could fail to ignore the lesson of the presence of a British representative at this strategic point. Lhasa could shut its eyes to what happened at Yatung or at Giaogong, but it could hardly miss the significance of events at Phari. This was an argument which Curzon was soon to employ to justify a further advance of the mart to Gyantse. To borrow the chess simile of Hamilton, the mart was a pawn employed to protect the advance of the king, the symbol of British power.

By 1902 the issues of trade and the frontier had ceased to seem of much importance when compared to the need to convince the Dalai Lama of the dangers inherent in refusing to open relations with the rulers of British India. This fact gives an air of unreality to the discussions which took place on the frontier in the latter part of that year and in the first months of 1903. The Chinese, as usual, were very slow in beginning the discussions which they had suggested, and many excuses were advanced for these delays. In August Ho, the chief Chinese delegate, was busy in Lhasa consulting with the Dalai Lama's Government, and then he announced that he was ill and could not come down to the frontier for a while.[77] In December, a new Amban, Yu T'ai, was appointed with special instructions for the forthcoming talks, and it was necessary to await his arrival in Tibet.[78] But the India Office,[79] and the British officials on the frontier,[80] were disposed to think that this time the Chinese would like to achieve a settlement. They appreciated the delays, however irritating, were an inescapable part of diplomatic dealings with the Chinese; and there can be little doubt that if the Tibetan question had still been as simple as it was during the administration of Lord Elgin the year 1903 would have produced nothing more than a series of Anglo-Chinese discussions on the frontier, perhaps with a more serious intent than had been the case in the past, but with no essential difference from such discussions which had been taking place since 1894. But 1902 was not like 1894-98. Tibet had become a possible field for Anglo-Russian competition, and almost daily it was becoming more apparent in India that the Russians were making considerable progress in this region where the British had been unable to make their influence felt at all. Talks with the Chinese on the Sikkim-Tibet frontier were no answer to this situation.

By the beginning of 1902 it seemed reasonably certain to Curzon that Dorjieff was a Russian agent of some importance. He had been in Lhasa for many years, perhaps from 1886, and he had much influence over the Dalai Lama whom, many rumours were now suggesting, he had convinced of the friendship held by Tsar Nicholas II towards Tibet and the Buddhist faith.[81] He had, so reports from Nepal indicated, been busy making friends with the influential Lhasa monasteries by the distribution of gifts and money.[82] The general picture was that in Dorjieff the Russians had found the sort of agent whom Curzon would dearly have liked to possess, and that they were making use of Dorjieff in much the way that Curzon would have exploited any agent of his who had been successful enough to gain the friendship of the Dalai Lama. Curzon began to suspect that a Russian protectorate over Tibet was nothing like so distant an event as he had once supposed. Throughout 1902 rumours reached his ears from a variety of sources, from Katmandu, from the Sikkim-Tibet frontier, from St. Petersburg and from Peking, to confirm him in this suspicion. It was this flood of information, albeit much of it most unreliable, that provided the final stimulus to plans for sending a British mission to Lhasa, and for this reason the rumours and reports of 1902 deserve a detailed examination.

215

In February 1902 the Maharaja Chandra Shamsher Jang of Nepal told the British resident, Colonel Pears, of a conversation he had held in January with a Tibetan Lama who had come to Katmandu on religious business. The Lama reported that British activity on the Tibetan frontier had been so bitterly resented by the rulers of China, Tibet, Bhutan and Ladakh that they had formed an alliance for war against the British in India. The promise of Russian support had been secured and hostilities were due to commence in 1904. The allies had a cunning plan whereby British armies were to be enticed into the high passes of the Himalayas and then destroyed by bringing down the mountains on top of them with skilfully placed explosive charges. The Lama said that if the Nepalese wished to join the alliance he would speak to the Chinese authorities on their behalf; if they joined, he could promise the extension of their territory to Calcutta. In proof of his assertion that Russian help would be forthcoming he pointed to the two missions of Dorjieff, which, he said, came not from the Dalai Lama but from the Amban. In further proof he observed that there were three Russian engineers employed in the Lhasa arsenal supervising the construction, among other things, of a weapon which sounded suspiciously like a Maxim gun. While someone in the Foreign Office in London minuted that the Lama 'talked such nonsense that it is very likely it is not true', it is clear that the Nepalese were not laughing this information off as idle gossip.[83] Nonsense the Lama was certainly talking, but it could well have been nonsense with more than a grain of truth behind it. It was just this sort of bazaar gossip, so detrimental to British prestige, that Curzon wished to avoid; and how could he avoid it without some visible means of exercising British influence in Lhasa?

In April 1902 Reuters reported that the Russian Minister in Peking, M. de Lessar, had suggested to Prince Ch'ing that China should grant Tibet her independence, a request which many Chinese took to mean that Russia intended to acquire Tibet for herself in the near future. The Nepalese Durbar, which paid close attention to the English press, wondered what truth there was in this.[84] In the same month a Chinese merchant just come down from Lhasa told the Deputy Commissioner for Darjeeling that Russia had recently made a secret treaty with the Dalai Lama. He observed that a prohibition, on pain of severe penalties, had been placed on all discussion of this matter in the Tibetan capital.[85]

The stream of rumour and report of a Russian treaty about Tibet soon became a flood. In May 1902 Kang Yu-wei, the exiled Chinese reformer who had settled in Darjeeling, told Bengal that

Jung Lu, the head of the Chinese Grand Council and the most trusted of the advisers of the Empress Dowager, had just signed a secret treaty with Russia which gave that Power a protectorate over Tibet. The same story was heard by Captain Parr at Yatung.[86] In August Sir Ernest Satow reported that rumours of such a treaty had been appearing in the Chinese press, possibly originating in a Suchow newspaper. He thought that it was all a 'ballon d'essai' put out by the Russo-Chinese bank, but he did consider it more than probable that M. de Lessar had been hinting to the Wai-wu-pu, the successor to the Yamen which had been set up after the Boxer rising, that he would like to come to some agreement over Tibet.[87] Details of the alleged Russo-Chinese treaty were now emerging. Parr described it as an instrument of eleven articles: in return for Chinese cession to Russia of her rights and interests in Tibet, Russia would support China in the maintenance of her integrity; active assistance in China would begin as soon as the Russian position in Tibet was secure; Russia would then aid China in the suppression of internal risings; Russia was permitted to establish government agencies in Tibet; China would have the right to place consular representatives in Tibet; Russia would protect Chinese commercial interests in Tibet; China would be able to extradite criminals from Tibet; only very light duties would be charged on Chinese goods entering Tibet; Russia promised that her officials in Tibet would not oppress the local population; Christianity would not be introduced forcibly into Tibet; China would be allowed to participate in Russian mining and railway enterprises in Tibet.[88] Sir E. Satow sent home a version of this treaty culled from the *China Times* on 18th July 1902 identical with that provided by Parr except for the addition of a twelfth clause to the effect that Russian railway construction in Tibet would not lead to the desecration or destruction of temples and other sacred places. While Satow had no reason to believe that any such document had been signed, he did think 'it is reasonable to suppose that some sort of pourparlers of an unofficial kind have taken place between the Russian Legation and a member of the Grand Council on the international position of Tibet'.[89]

In October 1902 another, and to Satow highly probable, version of Jung Lu's dealings with the Russians came to the notice of the British Legation. An informant of the Legation claimed to have been shown by an agent of Jung Lu's, one Hsü, son of Hsü Ying-k'uei the Viceroy of Foochow, a draft agreement with the Russians bearing Jung Lu's seal. This document contained four articles: the Russians guaranteed to protect Jung Lu, his possessions and his family from any retribution by the Powers for Jung Lu's somewhat ambiguous role during the Boxer outbreak; in return the Russians were to be given a privileged position in China, with Tibet, Mongolia and Sinkiang as their special sphere of interest; the Russians would assist the Dynasty in quelling any internal revolutions; freedom of travel throughout the Chinese Empire was granted to Russian officials, merchants and missionaries. The agreement was made on Jung Lu's own authority. When the time came he would move the Throne to give it official sanction; but till then it would remain secret. This version certainly agreed with the opinion of Kang Yu-wei and Yuan Shih-k'ai that Jung Lu had come to terms with the Russians to save himself from the consequences of his position during the Boxer troubles.[90]

Yet another version of a Russian agreement about Tibet emerged from St. Petersburg in November 1902. Hardinge, the Chargé d'Affaires, reported that he had heard from a secret but, he believed, reliable source that an 'arrangement' now existed between the Russians and the Dalai Lama whereby in return for certain religious privileges for Russian Buriat Buddhists the Dalai Lama had agreed to the Russians stationing an agent in Lhasa, and permitted the entry into Tibet of Orthodox, but not, of course, Roman Catholic, missionaries. An agent, whose position was to be kept secret lest the British should demand the same right, had already been selected, a certain Badengieff. This story had also appeared in the *Osservatore Romano*, and its publication was said to have caused 'consternation' in Russian ministerial circles.[91] Younghusband later had no difficulty in identifying Badengieff with Dr. Badmaev.[92] Hardinge's story was curiously paralleled by a report from Satow at Peking enclosing the translation of a telegram which was said to have been sent by the Amban to Jung Lu announcing that the Dalai Lama had approved the deputation to Tibet of a Russian officer accompanied by a mining engineer and an escort of Cossacks.[93]

In March 1903, apparently from a source in the Chinese Government, there emerged yet another account of a Sino-Russian treaty over Tibet. It was said to have been signed in Lhasa on 27th February 1903 by the Amban and a Russian representative whose name, no doubt much distorted, was given as Licoloff. The British Intelligence in China reported that a party of five Russians had gone from China to Lhasa early in 1903 for the purpose of negotiating this instrument. As reported in the *North China Herald* of 26th March 1903, this treaty contained eight clauses, all dealing with the granting of Russia of mining rights in

Tibet. The Treaty was to remain valid, so the first article ran, in the face of protests from the Powers. It permitted to Russia the conduct of a geological survey of Tibet to be financed by the Russo-Chinese Bank. A 10 per cent. royalty was to be paid to China on the profits of Russian mines in Tibet. A limit of 2,000,000 taels was imposed on Russian investment in Tibet. Provisions existed for the settling of disputed mining claims. The Chinese were not to tax the import into Tibet of mining machinery and equipment. All prospecting in Tibet, whether by Chinese or by Russians, required written Chinese authority. The Chinese were to be consulted on every mining venture which the Russians proposed to initiate in Tibet.[94] This was the last of the Sino-Russian treaties to be reported. On 11th April 1903 Jung Lu died. Both Kang Yu-wei and Francis Younghusband thought that with Jung Lu's death the Russo-Chinese agreement over Tibet would pass into oblivion.[95]

The rumours of the various treaties by which Russia was said to have obtained for herself a special position in Tibet were, as will be seen in the following chapter, noted by the British with far more alarm than were the stories of the Dorjieff missions. The Tibet Blue Books have not made much of the stories of the treaties because their compilers had adopted a deliberate policy of trying to minimize the diplomatic complexity of the Tibet crisis. While aimed generally at justifying British action in Tibet, the first Blue Book (Cd. 1920 of 1904) was intended specifically to 'place on record that we have received satisfactory assurance from Russia', and to show 'that our procedure towards China has been strictly correct'.[96] As it will be seen shortly, neither of these objectives could have been achieved if anything like the full story of the secret treaties and the British reaction to them was made public. It should be clear from what has already been said that neither were the Indian Government satisfied with Russian assurances such as that of Lamsdorff of July 1901 that the second Dorjieff mission had no political significance, nor was the British attitude towards China without its disingenuous elements.

It was hard to argue in open diplomacy that the Dorjieff missions were not as innocent as Lamsdorff said they were. The mere fact that a Russian national had been to Lhasa meant little in an age when travellers of all nationalities were trying to reach that mysterious city. Although the Russians were in the van in these attempts - with the exploring venture of Kozlov and the visit of Lhasa to Tsybikoff, who returned to Russia from that place in 1901 with a very fine collection of photographs for which he was awarded the Prjevalski Medal by the Imperial Geographical Society of St. Petersburg[97] - they had but to point to the Tibetan ventures of Englishmen like the Littledales, Frenchmen like Bonvalot, Dutreuil du Rhins, Grenard, Henri d'Orleans, Americans like Rockhill, Dutchmen like Rijnhardt, Germans like Schlagintweit, and Japanese like the monk Kawaguchi, to show they were not alone in trying to reach Lhasa. The last decade of the nineteenth century saw a most remarkable intensification of Tibetan exploration, and it would be an invidious task to draw a distinction between bona fide geographical discovery and political intrigue. The British suspected that many of the French and Russian explorers had been entrusted with political commissions by their Governments but there was nothing that could be done about them.[98]

The reported treaties, however, fall into a somewhat different category. If proved true, the British could protest diplomatically against such treaties. Even if no such proof were forthcoming, the British could, and should, attempt counter-action. The stories had much to suggest their veracity. They referred continually to the Russo-Chinese Bank, which was known to be the financial spearhead of Russian imperialism in the Far East. They emphasized Russian interest in Tibetan minerals, by which, of course was understood gold; and it was well known that Mongolor, a subsidiary of the Russo-Chinese Bank then engaged in the exploitation of Mongolian gold, was interested in fresh fields for its enterprise, and Tibet was a logical enough step from Mongolia. M. von Groot, a Russian formerly in the service of the Chinese Customs, was managing Russian gold mining in Mongolia, and it might have been significant that in November 1902 he was reported to have sought from the Chinese a concession for the construction of an extension of the Trans-Siberian into Tibet, it is presumed to tap the gold of that region.[99] In October 1903 Spring Rice at St. Petersburg described von Groot as 'the chief organizer of Russian influence in Mongolia and Tibet'.[100]

Warren Hastings had been interested in Tibetan gold, and in the latter part of the nineteenth century that interest had revived with the visit of a native explorer to the gold-producing regions of Western Tibet in 1867.[101] By the last decade of the nineteenth century the British were convinced that one of the objectives of Russian explorers in Tibet was to prospect for Tibetan gold. Sven Hedin was suspected of acting on behalf of the Russians in such an enterprise, and the India Office assumed that Kozlov's Tibetan expedition of 1899 to 1901 had the same end in view. Interests in the City of London - the name Rothschild was whispered in this connection – were also attracted by Tibetan gold mines. In 1899, under the cover of a Mr. Miller, they approached the India Office for help in exploiting these riches, and they hired Sir Thomas Holdich to lead a survey party.[102] Curzon opposed the scheme,[103] and nothing seems to have come of it, though at the time of the Younghusband Mission of 1904 these same interests were looking for gold mining concessions in Eastern Tibet.[104] It is interesting that it was gold, which is not mentioned in the Blue Books, and not tea, which inspired British commercial interests to take some definite action in the years before the Younghusband Mission. No one who knew about this project of the Rothschilds could deny that a profit might well be made from Tibetan gold were political conditions favourable to its exploitation. The reported Russo-Chinese and Russo-Tibetan treaties created such conditions and they could only seem, if true, to be eminently reasonable measures. Even those who saw the Russian threat to India as a product of a fevered imagination could hardly deny that the Russians would exploit a potential gold field if they could.

Note on Ugyen Kazi and Lord Curzon's letter to the Dalai Lama. When he arrived in India in early 1910 as a refugee from the Chinese invaders of Central Tibet, the Dalai Lama was questioned by Charles Bell on this point. Had Ugyen Kazi actually delivered the Viceroy's letter? The Dalai Lama then said that in fact Ugyen Kazi had delivered the letter which the Dalai Lama had accepted but had declined to open because in 1901, he explained, he had still been following the instructions of the Chinese that he have no contact with foreign countries except through the mediation of the Amban. See *The McMahon Line. A Study in the Relations Between India, China and Tibet 1904 to 1914*, 2 vols (London 1966), by A. Lamb, vol. 1, pp. 200–1.

X

THE
YOUNGHUSBAND
MISSION

·

1903 – 1905

THE REPORTS of the secret Russo-Chinese treaty or treaties about Tibet were taken seriously enough by the British. Satow, in Peking, while not convinced that a formal instrument had been signed, was sure that the Russo-Chinese Bank and certain influential Chinese, among whom Jung Lu should be numbered, had been discussing the future of Tibet.[1] Lord Lansdowne, at the Foreign Office, had concluded by October 1902 that 'the story of the Russo-Chinese agreement as to Tibet is supported by a good deal of evidence'.[2] At the India Office Hamilton, so he told Curzon privately in August 1902, was sure that the Russians had signed such a treaty, and as the year went on nothing came to light to make him change his mind.[3] The India Office reaction to the reports of this treaty was that 'we cannot tolerate this'. Curzon, of course, had no doubt at all that something was afoot. In November 1902 he described himself as 'a firm believer in the existence of a secret undertaking, if not a secret treaty, between China and Russia about Tibet'. He considered it his 'duty to frustrate this little game while there is yet time'.[4]

It was not only the British who took these reports seriously. The Tibetans, if reports of interviews with Tibetan merchants on the frontier were any guide, now felt that their country possessed a powerful bulwark against British aggression. Three such interviews, which Lt.-Col. Ravenshaw, Resident at Katmandu, described to Government in January 1903, illustrated well this attitude.[5] A Chinese merchant in Katmandu, recently from Lhasa, said that

Tibet has now sought the protection of Russia, and China also has loosened her grasp on Tibet. The Tibetans who were at Kalimpong used to say that the Russians will commence building a big palace at Lhasa this year.

A Tibetan monk said that

there is talk at Lhasa that the Tibetans can now rest at ease and should have no fear either of the British or Nepal.

And a Tibetan merchant told this story:

From last year the Potola Lama [Dalai Lama] has sought the protection of Russia, so that Tibet is now a protégée of Russia. China has also arranged with Russia to let away Tibet. The Russians will come to Lhasa, and this they will do before the ensuing year of Sambat 1960 [1903] is over, if practicable. I got the above information from the talk of some big men at Lhasa.

These were but three examples of the hundreds of such pieces of intelligence which were reaching the Indian Government at this time from Katmandu, Darjeeling and Yatung. They did not prove that the Russians had come to an agreement with the Chinese and with the Dalai Lama, but they provided good evidence that the Tibetan people were convinced that such agreements had been made; and this was a fact not likely to make the Tibetans more amenable to coming to terms with the British.

The Nepalese were, or at least said they were, very worried at what would happen once the Russian protectorate over Tibet became effective. Such a protectorate, the Nepalese Prime Minister said to Colonel Ravenshaw, could only result in an increase in Tibetan military strength. The Tibetans, he added, were eager to revenge themselves on Nepal for the defeat they had suffered at Gurkha hands in 1856, and 'a well-armed and powerful Tibet and an ill-armed Nepal would be a very depressing sight and an unequal match'.[6] Curzon did not believe that the Nepalese were as worried as they said, but he was sure that the Nepal Durbar was watching events in Tibet with a keen interest. Its attitude to such events, Curzon said, was divided. One party was hoping that 'should Russia at any time come down into Tibet' it might be able 'to hold the scales between the Russians and the English'. Another party disliked the idea of Russia in Tibet, since they hoped that they themselves would annex one day a substantial portion of Tibetan territory. Both parties, Curzon concluded, saw in the Tibetan situation an admirable opportunity for the increase of Nepalese independence and for the strengthening of the Gurkha army through arms purchased from British India. In the present situation the British would find it very hard to refuse a Nepalese request for permission to buy arms and ammunition. An increase in the size of the Gurkha army, apart from its inherent undesirability as a threat to the peace of the frontier, might well result in a reduction in the number and quality of Gurkha recruits available for British service.[7]

Thus the Foreign Office, the India Office and the Viceroy all seemed to be in agreement that the reports of the Russo-Chinese treaties could not be ignored. They did not agree, however, on what measures should be taken to mitigate the ill effects of these alleged instruments. Lord Lansdowne advocated the tried diplomatic method of a declaration to the Chinese and the Russians that Great Britain would not tolerate an alteration of the status of Tibet. Satow approached the Chinese on this subject in September 1902 and Hardinge did likewise to the Russians in October. Both the Chinese and the Russians denied categorically that any alteration in the status of Tibet was then being contemplated, and the Russians added a counter protest that the British had themselves designs on Tibet and were planning to build a railway line to Lhasa.[8]

The India Office agreed with Curzon that 'a policy and a plan' for Tibet were needed, and that much more was involved in the Tibetan question than the trifling matters of frontier demarcation and trans-frontier trade: but they still could not accept, at the end of 1902, the idea of a British mission to Lhasa which might give rise to British military commitments on the Tibetan plateau at a period when the British were still involved in the South African War. Such a mission, moreover, would give rise to embarrassing Russian protests, and it might prove harmful to the negotiations then in progress with China over the abolition of *likin* which would bring more benefit to Indian commerce than ever would the opening of Tibet.[9] What alternative was there to a mission to Lhasa? The answer to this, so the India Office seemed to think, lay in the use of Nepal. Sir William Lee-Warner had worked out a plan for this in September 1902 which promised to bring pressure to bear on the Tibetans without committing British troops or compromising British diplomacy elsewhere. Lee-Warner had discovered that by the Tibeto-Nepalese Treaty of 1856 the Nepalese had agreed, in return for the Tibetan subsidy, to assist Tibet 'if the troops of any other Raja invade that country'. The Nepalese could therefore, with perfect justice, ask the Tibetans, through their Agent in Lhasa, whether the Russians had been establishing any relations with the Dalai Lama, since this was a matter which directly affected Nepalese interests. The British could inform the Chinese that they entirely sympathized with this request, and would support the Durbar in any action it might see fit to take. If the Nepalese did not receive a satisfactory answer from the Tibetans, 'might not Nipal be urged to send a force to Lhasa and demand from Tibet an assurance that it would permit no Russian troops to enter its country?'[10] The Political Committee and Hamilton approved;[11] and Lansdowne wrote of Lee-Warner's 'Note on Tibet' which outlined this argument, 'I think he is right. . . . The Nipalese are friendly and would fight.'[12] On 6th January 1903 Lee-Warner's scheme was adopted by the India Office as its final solution to the Tibetan question.[13]

The War Office alone in England saw a mission to Lhasa as an acceptable solution to the problem of Russia in Tibet. In October 1902 Lt.-Col. Robertson of the Mobilization and Intelligence Department expressed his conviction that 'Russia is actuated by a desire to establish a footing of some kind in Tibet'. While it was most improbable that Russia would ever invade India from a Tibetan base, a few Russian agents in Lhasa could easily upset the tranquillity of the states along the Himalayan frontier. Gurkha soldiers, whose services to the Indian Army were 'practically indispensable', might be diverted from British to Russian service, and this consideration alone was sufficient to make it impossible for the British to tolerate a Russian protectorate over Tibet. The remedy lay in the establishment of a British Resident at Lhasa. He could be placed there with the deployment of no more than a single brigade, and the cost would be nugatory. Lord Roberts, the Commander-in-Chief, approved of these arguments, and the words of that great soldier deserve quotation:

Russia's predominance in Tibet would not be a *direct* military danger to India, but it would be a very serious disadvantage. It would certainly unsettle Nepal, and would, in all probability, interfere with our Gurkha recruiting, which would of itself be a real misfortune. I consider it out of the question Russia being permitted to obtain a footing in Tibet; we have had, and shall still have, quite enough trouble owing to Russia being so near us on the N.W. frontier of India - that we cannot avoid; but we can, and ought to, prevent her getting a position which would inevitably cause unrest all along the N.E. frontier.[14]

To Curzon there was only one sound solution to the Tibetan situation; an Anglo-Tibetan treaty negotiated in Lhasa. The folly and danger of Lee-Warner's Nepalese plan, which would only create another Afghanistan on India's northern flank, he would not consider for one moment. He would act in consultation with the Durbar, and he had the assurance of Nepalese co-operation, but on no account would he let Nepal deal with Tibet alone.[15] His proposals were set out in a long despatch dated 8th January 1903, which, as one of the crucial documents in the history of Anglo-Tibetan relations, deserves careful attention. There was nothing new in his proposals, which he had suggested many times in his private letters to Hamilton, but he supported them in this despatch with a brilliant review of the history of the Tibetan question, from which he argued with majestic logic that there was but one feasible solution.[16]

Curzon's basic assumption was that without some bargaining card further talks with the Chinese and Tibetans on the frontier would be quite futile, even if no more than questions of trade and the frontier were involved. He saw no promise in the new Chinese overtures. But the Tibetan question had now become one in which the very status of Tibet was at issue. The 'constitutional fiction' of Chinese suzerainty and the policy of Tibetan isolation had only been tolerable to the Indian Government so long as they carried 'no elements of political or military danger'. The possibility of a Russian protectorate over Tibet demanded a completely new approach. The Chinese should be told that the British were prepared to open talks in the spring of 1903, but that the venue was to be Lhasa, not Yatung or some other point on the Sikkim frontier, and that a properly qualified Tibetan representative should take part. The present was a particularly suitable time to enter into negotiations with the Tibetans since for the first time in over a century there was a Dalai Lama 'who is neither an infant nor a puppet'. Curzon proposed that the talks in Lhasa should deal not only with 'the small question of the Sikkim frontier, but the entire question of our future relations, commercial and otherwise, with Tibet', and 'should result in the appointment of a permanent Consular or Diplomatic representative in Lhasa'. The British mission to Lhasa should be provided with an escort adequate to defend it in case of attack by the Tibetans. Nothing should be done without consulting the Nepal Durbar. The proposed mission was to be described to the Chinese and Tibetans as a purely commercial one, and assurances would be given that no British protectorate over, or annexation of any part of, Tibet was contemplated. Unless these proposals were agreed to by the Cabinet, Curzon was not prepared to answer for the consequences.

In this despatch Curzon criticized those who had been responsible for the abandonment of the Macaulay Mission in 1886. Was Curzon's project but a renewal of that of Macaulay? Macaulay's mission had been commercial in object; he had mentioned political objectives, but only in the most general terms as an additional argument in support of his contention that the opening of Tibet to British commerce would bring untold benefit. Curzon described his mission as commercial while making it quite clear that the trade question was of the most trivial importance. In his mind was the conviction that some form of Russian protectorate over Tibet had been, or was about to be, established, and that it was his duty to prevent such a development. In his private letter to Hamilton of 13th November 1902, in which he paved the way for his great despatch of 8th January 1903, there is no mention of commerce. In it he showed his certainty that the presence of Russian influence in Tibet to an extent harmful to British interests was no longer a mere possibility; it was an accomplished fact. When Ho failed to come down from Lhasa to Yatung on the grounds of ill health, and when the Wai-wu-pu delayed the opening of negotiations until a new Amban could arrive, he saw no signs of a Chinese acknowledgement of responsibility for the affairs of Tibet: rather 'my impression is that the Russians have told the Chinese on no account to negotiate with us or to allow us to come to close quarters with the Tibetans'. He regarded the situation in Tibet created by the Sino-Russian agreement, which was a fact not a rumour, 'as very serious', and 'unless we take steps promptly and effectively to counteract it, we shall rue the day for years to come'.[17] It is quite clear that Curzon was not trying to use the rumours of a Russian treaty about Tibet as an excuse to justify the opening by force of the Tibetan market to Indian tea out of deference to the wishes of the Indian Tea Association. The first of the Tibet Blue Books, as Lord Rosebery remarked in the House of Lords in February 1904, could well give the impression that 'the whole object of the policy of the Indian Government . . . was to make people drink Indian tea who did not like Indian tea and did not want Indian tea'.[18] The India Office, of course, was under no such illusion. Lord Curzon's

Tibetan policy was not primarily concerned with trans-frontier trade. As Sir D. Fitzpatrick of the Council of India minuted in April 1903, this trade was 'not worth the very big candle, and I need not say that it is not of this trade Lord Curzon is thinking'.[19]

Curzon's despatch of 8th January 1903 made a profound impression upon the India Office. Lee-Warner's Nepalese scheme, unanimously adopted by the Political Committee a bare fortnight earlier, was forgotten. Some sort of mission to Tibet seemed to be essential even 'if it seems only too probable that we should in the end be forced to declare a protectorate and maintain a garrison at Lhassa'.[20] Hamilton agreed that unless the British acted in Tibet at this time, 'it seems to me perfectly hopeless for Great Britain to attempt to arrest Russia's progress in any part of Asia'.[21] Hamilton had to admit, albeit with reluctance, that some sort of mission to Tibet was required by the circumstances as Curzon had described them in his despatch. The question now was not whether there should be a Tibet mission, but, so Hamilton wrote to Curzon privately, 'can we establish a good international case for the course of action you suggest?'[22] Without such a case, Hamilton said, 'the Cabinet will probably hesitate and delay, until it may be too late to send an expedition this year'.[23]

What the India Office had to persuade the Cabinet to accept was this. To the question 'even if Russia establishes her influence in Tibet, how will that cause any danger, given the defence and organization of the Indian Empire', the Cabinet would have to be made to see that the answer was that 'apart from considerations of Asian politics, Nepal is unfortunately outside those defences and that organization', and that 'with Russia in Tibet, it may become a second Afghanistan; whereas with British influence paramount at Lhasa, there is no need to interfere with the independence of Nepal as it exists at present'.[24] At the Cabinet of 19th February 1903 Hamilton was not able to bring Balfour and Lansdowne to accept this reasoning, with its clear implication of a British mission to the Tibetan capital. Balfour feared lest a British mission should be construed by the Powers as 'an attack on the integrity of China', and lead to a further round of claims for compensating advantages. Lansdowne wanted to keep the Tibetan question on a diplomatic level; he was negotiating with the Russians for a declaration that the Russian Government had no interest in Tibet; he was prepared to tell the Russians that were they to establish an agent in Lhasa, the British would press for equal rights; but so long as he was carrying on diplomatic discussions a British mission to Lhasa would certainly be regarded by the Powers as an example of the 'sharp practice' to be expected from perfidious Albion. The Cabinet, in effect, rejected Curzon's proposals for the time being; and all Hamilton could do was to tell Curzon to go on with negotiations on the Sikkim–Tibet frontier and to insist on the presence at these talks of a properly accredited Tibetan representative.[25] The main weight of the British counter-attack to Russian advances in Tibet, in fact, was to be borne by Lansdowne in discussions with the Russian Ambassador in London, Benckendorff.

Lansdowne discovered that diplomatic conversations with the Russians held their own dangers to the chances of a successful achievement of British requirements in Tibet. If the British could protest at the rumoured gains which the Russians appeared to be making of late in Lhasa, the Russians could also object to reports of British plans to force their way into Tibet. Thus on 11th October 1902 the Russians, through Baron Graevenitz, their Chargé in London, protested at reported British plans to push a railway from India to Lhasa under cover of a British invasion of Tibet.[26] In December Graevenitz asked Lansdowne whether there was any truth in the story that the Indian Government was planning a military expedition to Lhasa.[27] In February 1903 the Russian Embassy in London turned again to this report, which had now grown with time into the story that British forces had reached Komba-Ovalenko (?Khambajong) on their way to Lhasa from the Chumbi Valley, and pointed out that were there any truth in this report, the Imperial Government might find itself obliged to take steps to safeguard its interests in Tibet.[28] Lansdowne, in fact, was finding himself forced into a position where he had either to admit, in order to justify British interests in Tibet, that the Russians too had interests in that region, or to propose a self-denying ordinance to the effect that neither Russia nor Great Britain had any cause to alter the status of the roof of the world. Rather than give the Russians a diplomatic foothold in Tibet, Lansdowne was inclined to accept the alternative position if he had to. On 8th April 1903 Lansdowne and Benckendorff exchanged denials of any intention to alter the status of Tibet; but on this occasion, as in subsequent conversations on 11th and 18th February, Lansdowne managed to obtain Benckendorff's agreement that the British, as the possessors of a common frontier with Tibet, had the right to ensure that the Tibetans respected their treaty obligations to the Indian Government, and to do so by force if need be.[29] But these were informal talks, and the Russian Government in St. Petersburg did not seem so ready as Benckendorff to make a specific yes or no answer to the question 'whether there was or not a Secret Agreement between

Russia and Tibet'.[30] Even Benckendorff, who was only too willing to deny that Russia had any intention of altering the status of Tibet, seemed a bit shifty when asked whether there was any truth in the story of Badengieff that Hardinge had reported in November 1902.[31]

Hamilton was inclined to be content with Benckendorff's assurances. They seemed to provide a sufficient guarantee that the Russians would do nothing too drastic in Tibet for a few months at least, and thus the British mission to Tibet seemed a little less urgent. Negotiations could well begin on the frontier without the prelude of a mission, but 'that could be done later if the Tibetans proved recalcitrant'.[32] Provided that the British did nothing that could not be said to arise out of an attempt to implement the Sikkim-Tibet Convention or the Trade Regulations or the Chinese agreement to demarcate the frontier, and provided that 'we stop short of a protectorate or annexation', Hamilton observed, Benckendorff's assurances 'give us an absolutely free hand in Tibet'.[33] Hamilton thus saw that British policy towards Tibet, now concerned mainly with the prevention of the establishment of Russian influence in Lhasa, would have to be based on, and justified by, the old issues of frontier demarcation and trans-frontier trade. This was the immediate consequence of Lansdowne's diplomacy.

Curzon refused to give up his immediate Tibetan mission without further argument. Benckendorff had said nothing to suggest that the Russian danger was now any less than it had been when Curzon drafted his despatch of 8th January. 'If you ask me', he wrote to Hamilton, 'whether Benckendorff's apparently categorical reply removed my suspicions, I say emphatically no.' It was inconceivable that all the evidence from Nepal, China, Tibet and Russia could be entirely without foundation; and the telling of a deliberate lie by an official of the Russian Government was not without precedent. Curzon thought that the Russians had indeed been about to declare a protectorate over Tibet but had been frustrated by the speed and intensity of the British reaction; H.M.G. had good cause to be thankful that the Russians had been 'a little premature'. That Russia, however, would now drop her Tibetan ambitions was an absurdity. She would merely keep them secret in future, while continuing to spread her influence by secret missions, by gifts of money, and by building up the military potential of Tibet by supplying materials of war and technicians to work in the Lhasa arsenal. A mission to Lhasa was as necessary now as it had ever been.[34]

In his despatch of 8th January 1903 Curzon had proposed that a mission to Lhasa should be the opening move in the renewed discussions of the Tibetan question in 1903. As a result of the Cabinet's attitude he saw this proposal would never be sanctioned on the basis of the arguments then at his disposal. Therefore, since he had no doubt that such a mission was essential, it must develop logically from the reopened negotiations. While the correspondence between Curzon and Hamilton on this matter is somewhat circumspect - and not surprisingly so, since many of the letters concerned found their way into all sorts of places outside the India Office - they leave no doubt of what was in Curzon's mind. Hamilton later described Curzon's new Tibetan plan as one 'for asserting our political influence in Tibet for the future on the basis of extended trade operations',[35] a plan dependent upon the exploitation of British treaty relations with China concerning Tibet for purposes other than those for which the original treaties were intended. The India Office was willing for Curzon to go ahead with this scheme so long as he did not create a situation which it could not defend to the Cabinet. The India Office disliked the idea of the mission to Lhasa, but it was under no illusion that Curzon did not mean what he said when he remarked that when the situation presented itself for the British to request the Chinese to allow their advance into Tibet, 'to Lhasa they shall go'.[36]

We have seen that following White's expulsion in June 1902 of the Tibetans from Giaogong the Chinese gave many signs of willingness to open fresh talks with the Indian Government on the frontier. Preliminary correspondence and discussion between junior officials had been going on since the summer of 1902, but for a number of reasons the opening of the actual negotiations had been delayed, and this fact can hardly have displeased Curzon as it must have seemed to him a welcome breathing space while the fate of his stronger Tibetan policy was being decided. For this reason, when the Chinese Commissioner, Ho, at last turned up at the Sikkim-Tibet frontier in January 1903, the Indian Government deputed no official to meet him, and Ho felt both hurt and alarmed. Without instruction, White refused to talk with Ho.[37] Curzon's justification for this unco-operative British attitude was that there seemed to be no point in starting anything until the new Amban should arrive, and he was not expected until at least June 1903.[38] Where in the past it had been the British who had tried to hurry the dilatory Chinese, now, in April 1903, the tables seemed to have been turned and the Chinese were trying to get the British down to a conference table as quickly as possible. No doubt they appreciated from the British reaction to the alleged

231

Russo-Chinese agreements of 1902 that a drastic change of policy was in the air. Whatever the cause, on 6th April 1903 the old Amban in his eagerness to get talks started gave Curzon the opportunity for which he was looking and out of which the whole structure of the Younghusband Mission to Lhasa of 1904 was to emerge. After some mild rebukes at the tardy way in which the British were taking notice of the presence of Chinese delegates at Yatung, the Amban said that

> the Deputy appointed by Your Excellency can either come to Yatung or the Chinese Deputies will proceed to Sikkim or such other place as may be decided upon by Your Excellency.[39]

What did 'such other place' mean? The Amban, no doubt, understood it to mean Darjeeling or some other town in British India, and he probably considered the expression of his willingness to visit foreign territory an abundant sign of his good-will. Curzon, however, interpreted this ambiguous phrase to mean somewhere in Tibet, and he proposed on the strength of it that talks should now take place at the Tibetan town of Khambajong.[40]

Curzon said that Khambajong was suited in many respects as the venue for such talks as were now contemplated. It was not far inside Tibet, being situated some twenty-five miles to the north of Giaogong, but this was far enough to allow of no doubt that it was on Tibetan soil that the British now proposed to negotiate. Its proximity to Giaogong had, moreover, an obvious lesson for the Tibetans. Reasonable communications through Sikkim linked Khambajong to British India. The town lay on main routes to Lhasa and Shigatse, which towns could not so easily ignore what went on here as they could talks at Yatung. Khambajong lay within the territory of the Panchen Lama, who had, ever since the days of Bogle and Turner, showed himself to be better disposed towards the British than his colleague in Lhasa, and whose officials might prove to be useful links between the British and Lhasa in the forthcoming talks. If, however, Khambajong proved to be unsuitable as a location for such talks; if, for instance, Chinese and Tibetan delegates did not turn up – and nothing was to be done this time without the equal participation of fully accredited Tibetan representatives – then the scene of the talks would be advanced to Gyantse or Shigatse. Curzon further proposed that the British delegation, with an escort of about two hundred men, should consist of J. C. White and Major Francis Younghusband, then Resident at Indore, as Joint Commissioners.

Younghusband was new to negotiations on the Sikkim–Tibet frontier, but Curzon took especial pride in his selection. He had, Curzon told Hamilton, travelled widely in Central Asia and written a book about it.[41] He understood better than anyone else in the service of the Government of India the nature and motives of Russian intrigue; and he knew the Oriental, especially the Chinese, 'by heart'.[42] Younghusband and White – and it is clear from the subsequent development of the Tibetan question that White was no longer a person of much importance – were to present the Chinese and Tibetans with even stronger terms than Curzon had put to the Amban in 1899. The Indian Government were no longer satisfied with Phari as the new site for the trade mart; only Gyantse would do.[43]

The Home Government softened Curzon's proposals. There was to be no advance beyond Khambajong without a further review of the whole question in London. The removal of the mart to Gyantse was approved, though reluctantly, but Curzon was clearly informed that there was to be no question of establishing a British Political Agent there.[44] The Cabinet, in fact, were hardly more sympathetic to Curzon's scheme 'for asserting our political influence in Tibet for the future on the foundation of extended trade operations' than they had been to his plan for an immediate mission to Lhasa. They were so obsessed with the dangers inherent in recent occurrences in Manchuria, Aden, and Somaliland that they were unable to consider the Tibetan question on its merits. They refused to consider what would follow if and when the talks at Khambajong failed. But, as Hamilton pointed out,

> it is self evident that if the negotiations break down, and the Tibetans still decline to give effect to the obligations they have entered into, we must express our disapproval, and that disapproval can but take shape, with little inconvenience and certainly no risk of future complications, of either a blockade or the occupation of the Chumbi Valley.[45]

It is interesting, moreover, that at this stage Lord Lansdowne, when approached on this question, saw nothing in a British occupation of Chumbi to conflict with his assurances to Russia. He thought, indeed, that too much attention could be paid to Russian objections.[46]

Hence Curzon, despite the coolness of the Cabinet, held a strong hand. If the talks failed, a further advance of some sort was inevitable; there was a limit to the tolerance even of the Cabinet. If the talks were successful, Curzon would get a trade mart at

Gyantse, and according to the Trade Regulations of 1893 the British had the right of stationing a commercial officer at the mart, and the distinction between a commercial officer and a political one was not very rigid.[47] But Curzon, despite his assurances that the Tibetans would readily agree to a mart at Gyantse,[48] can hardly have expected to obtain this by negotiation after the failure during so many years of the Indian Government to secure the smooth functioning of the minimum demand of the mart at Yatung. The chief significance of the mission to Khambajong must have been that the Home Government had accepted the necessity for some form of British mission on to Tibetan soil; if Khambajong failed, the only direction that mission could possibly move was forward.

Both the Tibetans and the Chinese showed that they considered the advance of a British mission on to Tibetan soil to be quite unjustified, but they did not oppose it with force when it crossed the frontier in July 1903, though Tibetan frontier guards did most politely ask White and Younghusband to turn back to Sikkim.[49] The Amban, however, did not come down to Khambajong, and the Tibetans only sent delegates who were not properly accredited in the sense demanded by Curzon, that they should be plenipotentiaries duly authorized in writing by the Dalai Lama to make agreements with the British which were binding on the Tibetan Government.[50] By November 1903 it was abundantly clear that talks at Khambajong would be no more successful than they would have been at Giaogong or Yatung. It might have been possible to have obtained an exchange of Giaogong for improved trading conditions at Yatung, terms which would have amply satisfied Lord Elgin, but this would not be enough to counter the Russians. The penalty which Curzon had to pay, and it was a penalty inherent in the Cabinet's refusal to follow his advice of 8th January, for his policy of carrying out political objectives under the guise of settling trade and the frontier, was that he was obliged to take steps which could never be justified by the triviality of their ostensible objects. Somehow the excuse must be found for an advance of the mission, and the only excuse possible within the imposed limits of the scope of the discussions at Khambajong was that the Tibetans had shown themselves openly hostile to the British.

A case of sorts was built up along these lines. It was based in part on the attitude of the Tibetan delegates who came to Khambajong and who had shown themselves neither more nor less hostile to the British than had the Tibetans since 1894. It was based in part on the failure of the Amban to come down to

Khambajong; but as one Amban was at the very end of his term of office, and his replacement was still on his way out to Tibet from China, not too much could be made of this fact. Other arguments had emerged from the fruitless stay of the mission at Khambajong. They were trivial, but they were to be the basis for a request by the Indian Government for a further advance of the mission into Tibet. Firstly, in July 1903 the Tibetans arrested two men from Lachung in Sikkim while travelling towards Shigatse. These men were certainly information gatherers for the British, if not spies, and they were, it was later to transpire, treated reasonably enough by the Tibetans. But rumour had it that the two Lachung men were outrageously maltreated in a Lhasa gaol – some went so far as to say that they were put to death. Curzon made much of this, as he did of piteous petitions from their relatives in Sikkim. The Chinese, when approached to secure the release of these two men – sometimes the number was raised to three – found that they were indeed imprisoned at Lhasa, and that the Tibetans refused to release these British spies, as they called them, but that the Lachung men were in good health and being well treated. Curzon, who, incidentally, had refused to show any indignation when, as an Under-Secretary of State at the Foreign Office, he had to consider the ill treatment of A. H. Landor by Tibetan frontier guards in 1897, made himself out to be most outraged at the fate of the Lachung men, which he described as 'the most conspicuous proof of the hostility of the Tibetan Government, and of their contemptuous disregard for the usages of civilization'.[51]

While not so important as the case of the Lachung men, a second argument as to Tibetan hostility towards the British was found in this incident. In August 1903 the Nepalese sent a convoy of yaks to Khambajong to act as reinforcements for the baggage train of the British mission there. The Tibetans caused delay in the passage of these animals through their territory, and many yaks died. This was interpreted as deliberate Tibetan obstructions, though, as in the case of so many such frontier incidents, the circumstances were so obscure as to make any very definite judgment impossible.[52] A third argument arose from the fact that no sooner had the British mission entered Tibet from Sikkim than the Tibetans virtually closed the trade mart at Yatung.[53] Finally, as the mission continued to stay at Khambajong in fruitless discussions with the Tibetans or in unfulfilled expectation that the Amban would soon make his appearance, more and more rumours came to light of Tibetan preparation for an armed conflict with the British. Spies, one imagines, reported every group of Tibetan shepherds as Tibetan soldiers journeying towards an assembly point. By October 1903, at any rate, Younghusband said he was convinced that Tibetan troops had been concentrated in large numbers between Shigatse and Khambajong.[54]

These four arguments, of the Lachung men, the yaks, Yatung and Tibetan troop concentrations, were the public justification for Curzon's request for permission to move Younghusband further into Tibet. On 6th November 1903 permission was granted by the India Office for the British occupation, though most temporary, of Chumbi, and for the advance of a British mission to Gyantse, if need be, though it was to be understood that these steps were to result neither in the permanent occupation of Tibetan territory nor in the establishment of a permanent British mission in Tibet.[55] The policy of 6th November was justified by Lansdowne to Benckendorff in these words:

> Owing to the outrageous conduct of the Tibetans, who had broken off negotiations with our Representative, seized British subjects, and carried off the transport animals of a friendly state, it has been decided to send our Commission, with a suitable escort, further into Tibetan territory, but that this step must not be taken as indicating any intention of annexing or even of permanently occupying Tibetan territory.[56]

The fear of Russia in Tibet, which hardly appears in the published documents after the end of 1902, had not, of course, disappeared. Curzon wrote at length on this topic in a private letter to Hamilton of August 1903, which deserves quotation as being typical of the rumours of 1903:

> Our suspicions about Russia in Tibet are receiving fresh confirmation from every quarter. Captain Parr, the Chinese Customs Officer, and one of . . . [the Chinese] . . . representatives on the Mission (his name must on no account be breathed) has told Younghusband in confidence upon his arrival at Khamba Jong that he has good reason to believe that Russians are now actually on their way to Lhasa. Younghusband further telegraphs us that he finds the Tibetans very bumptious and confident, that they rely absolutely upon Russian support. The same reports reach us from Nepal and elsewhere and they are confirmed by a recent Reuter that several hundred Cossaks have been sent to Tibet.

I should like nothing better, for, as you know, I am firmly convinced of Russian *mala fides* in the matter, and should, after what Lansdowne said to Benckendorff, then be bound to take it up. The latest telegram of today from Younghusband rumours an intended attack by the Tibetans upon the British Camp which Younghusband was quite prepared to repel with a Maxim. No doubt there is a good deal of exaggeration in all these stories, and we must not be frightened. But, before we are through with this business, there will probably be strange developments.[57]

Younghusband occupied himself with the writing of memoranda on the Russian danger in which he subjected to a microscopic scrutiny every scrap of evidence that had to date come to light, such as the rumours which came in from a number of sources of Russian Cossacks on their way to Lhasa, to which Curzon referred in the above quoted letter.[58] At the end of 1903, Curzon and his man Younghusband were as much concerned with the possibility of a Russian advance in Tibet as they had ever been. In August 1903 Younghusband summed up the objects of his Tibetan policy in words of the greatest interest:

When we have obtained this access to Tibet, and acquired as much influence there as is required for keeping Russian influence at bay, we shall have averted an insidious political danger to India; we shall have put ourselves in a position which will have as a barrier between our frontier and the probable future frontier of Russia the whole breadth of the inhospitable Chang Thang plateau; we shall have prevented the junction of any possible future spheres of French and Russian influence north and south across Asia: and we shall, on the other hand, be in a position of support to our own efforts in Szechuan and for combining our strength from east to west.[59]

It is interesting that Younghusband took so seriously French interest in Tibet, which, he said, at one time nearly developed into a serious threat to British security, and might still do so in certain circumstances. Younghusband was very much impressed by what Dutrueil de Rhins had told him in Kashgar in 1891, and what Bonvalot had later expressed publicly, that the French ambition in this part of the world was to extend their sphere of influence from its Tonkin base right up to the Russian border, and thus give a solid demonstration of the Franco-Russian alliance at work in

Asia.[60] Curzon, of course, had hinted at this in his *Russia in Central Asia*, which was published in 1889.[61]

With the decision to abandon Khambajong and to advance further into Tibet, the Mission of 1903 was reconstituted. Younghusband became the sole political head, White having been dropped out, and Brigadier-General Macdonald was appointed commander of the military escort, which eventually swelled to over 8,000 men.[62] In December 1903 Younghusband and the advance guard of his escort marched unopposed over the Jelep La, up the Chumbi Valley and into the Tibetan frontier post of Phari on the edge of the Tibetan plateau. In January he moved forward a further twenty miles to Tuna, where he set up camp for three months while awaiting vainly for the arrival of Tibetan delegates and while the bulk of his escort set up winter quarters in Chumbi. In March, with the approach of spring, the mission renewed its advance, and a few miles to the north of Tuna, by the hot springs of Guru, it had its first armed clash with the Tibetans. In this engagement, which was little more than a massacre of Tibetans, with 700 casualties inflicted, and which took place after the Tibetans had agreed to give up their arms, the opposition in England to Curzon's Tibetan policy was to find valuable ammunition. After further clashes, in which the British force suffered less than ten casualties through Tibetan fire, Gyantse was reached on 11th April, and here Younghusband set up camp to await the arrival of Tibetan delegates. In May the Mission was attacked and besieged in its quarters below the walls of Gyantse fort, an event which, so Younghusband said, was a 'complete and sudden change in the situation in Tibet'.[63] Younghusband waited at Gyantse until the end of June. Tibetan delegates did appear from Lhasa, but Younghusband claimed that they lacked the proper written credentials from the Dalai Lama, and without these documents he would open no talks. On the expiry of an ultimatum, which demanded the production of such credentials giving the delegates full powers to discuss and make binding agreements as to trade and the frontier, the Mission was authorized to begin its final advance to Lhasa, a step which had certainly been contemplated from the outset, and which became inevitable after the attack on the Mission at Gyantse. Attempts by the Tibetans to persuade the Mission to return to Gyantse to await delegates who, it was assured, would this time have the desired credentials, were firmly ignored. After the crossing of the Tsangpo, when Major Bretherton, the officer whose brilliance had been largely responsible for the solution of the many logistic problems involved in an operation across the Himalayas, lost his life, the Mission reached Lhasa on 3rd August and entered the city on the following day. A month of negotiations ensued, at the end of which, on 7th September, Younghusband signed a treaty, the Lhasa Convention, with Tibetan representatives - the Dalai Lama had fled his capital before the arrival of the British. On the following day a Separate Article was added to the Convention. On 22nd September, having failed to persuade the Amban to append his signature to these two documents, the contents of which are described a little further on, Younghusband and his escort left Lhasa and returned to India. While the Tibetans had opposed the British advance with a determination which surprised many observers, in defeat they proved to be so docile and well disposed as to give rise to a renewed spate of argument based on the old theory that the Tibetan people would welcome deliverance from the oppressive rule of their overlords, both Chinese and monastic. Thus Rawling, in a military report of 1905, was able to write:

It appears to be the general wish of the inhabitants of that country [Tibet] that they should come under British adminis-tration. The people are discontented with the hard laws under which they live at present, and have no patriotism or love for their country; only staying there because they cannot exist at lower altitudes. Continually hearing from traders of the gentleness and justice of the British administration, they often talk of how they would welcome the rule under which India flourishes.[64]

While one should not take this kind of argument too seriously, it is a fact of some significance that only one incident, the attack on two British officers by a mad monk, disturbed the peace after Younghusband had entered Lhasa, and from that time the line of communication between the Mission and India was quite peaceful. It is clear that the spirit of Tibetan patriotism was hard to arouse: but events in Tibet in the 1950s would seem to indicate clearly enough that the Chinese Communists aroused it in a way that Younghusband never did.

Younghusband's expedition was in many ways a remarkable exploit. To bring a force of more than brigade strength, and largely composed of troops quite unused to mountain warfare, on to the Tibetan plateau in winter and then to lead it to Lhasa and back - the distance from Phari to Lhasa is 230 miles - involved the solution of extremely difficult problems of supply and communi-cations. To carry out a military action at over 19,000 feet, as

Gurkhas and Sikhs did at the Karo La, was to perform a feat unique in the annals of the British Army. The exploration of the road to Lhasa, the study of Tibetan Buddhism, the detailed description of the buildings of the Tibetan capital, the journeys by British officers around Lake Yamdok and up the Tsangpo, or Upper Brahmaputra, to Gartok and the Sutlej, all these added much to the knowledge of the geography of Tibet and the way of life of its people. That so much was achieved with so little loss of British life is due to a great extent to the inspiration which Younghusband provided for his staff, and no one can deny that he deserves the place that he acquired in the history of exploration.

The achievements of the Younghusband Mission, however, should not be allowed to obscure its failures. From the start the Mission was affected by a quarrel between Younghusband and the military commander of the expedition, General Macdonald. As Younghusband was Curzon's choice and Macdonald owed his appointment to Lord Kitchener, this quarrel on the Tibetan plateau was to have its repercussions in India and in England. Several times, on the way to Lhasa, Younghusband threatened to resign.[65] Macdonald's letters to his superiors cannot be said to have been full of praise for the political leader of the expedition, whose policy was represented as involving the British in a campaign beyond the Himalayas which might drag on for two or more years.[66] The quarrel between the civil and military sides of the Mission was only a prelude to the arguments that arose on Younghusband's return to India.

Instead of being treated as a hero, as Mrs. Younghusband told Ampthill he should be,[67] he found himself almost in disgrace over the terms of the Lhasa Convention and over what both Ampthill, who was acting as Viceroy in Curzon's absence on leave in England, and St. John Brodrick, who had taken over from Hamilton as Secretary of State for India after the palace revolution of September 1903 had expelled the Chamberlain faction from the Balfour Government, considered to be a blatant disregard of his instructions. Nor did Younghusband's subsequent behaviour, his attempt to appeal to the King and his dealings with Curzon over Ampthill's head, meet with much approval.[68] The Younghusband controversy was a reflection of the differences that existed between the views of the Cabinet and of Lord Curzon as to what the mission to Tibet was about, and Younghusband's failure lay in the fact that he forced the Cabinet to insist that its Tibetan policy, rather than that of Curzon, should prevail. His Lhasa Convention seemed in London to be an attempt to present the Home Government with a *fait accompli*, and this it could not tolerate.

240

There can be little doubt that by 1903 Curzon was convinced that the Tibetan problem could only be solved by a mission to Lhasa. Younghusband was also of this opinion, if not at the moment when he was selected to go to Khambajong, then certainly after a few days of lingering on the windswept edge of the Tibetan plateau. No one more ardently demonstrated the Russian threat in Tibet than did Younghusband while he was at Khambajong; he wrote what amounted to a book on the subject.[69] And it was clear to him that just as British influence in Kabul was the answer to the Russian threat to Afghanistan, so was a British representative in Lhasa the only rational counter to the Russian menace to Tibet. He never believed that anything would be achieved at Khambajong. Nor did some members of the Cabinet, for that matter, take Khambajong very seriously. To Lansdowne, who by September 1903 was trying to convince Balfour of the need for an advance to Gyantse, the mission to Khambajong was no more than a demonstration to the Russians of British moderation.[70]

Brodrick, who took over from Hamilton at the India Office, had no illusions as to what the Viceroy was about, which was certainly not the settlement of problems arising out of the conditions of Indo-Tibetan trade. Thus, when the move to Gyantse was being discussed, Brodrick saw that it implied a yet further advance to Lhasa. In a memorandum of 4th November 1903 Brodrick put his finger on the crucial problems arising from this final advance to Lhasa. The Indian Government, he noted, said that it could be achieved at little military expenditure and no military risk. But, Brodrick asked, was it worth at this time committing any troops at all to Tibet to forestall this highly problematical Russian threat? Would the mission into the heart of Tibet rather increase the Russian threat by presenting to St. Petersburg on a silver platter an example of British aggression which Russian diplomats could exploit to their heart's content? Could the British afford to risk a war, even a very small war indeed, when things were looking so threatening in Somaliland and the Far East?[71] These remained Brodrick's fears throughout the Tibetan crisis, and many of his colleagues in the Cabinet agreed with him. The only answer from India was to demonstrate that the Russian threat did justify some risks at this critical period, and such a demonstration Younghusband did his best to provide throughout his advance to Lhasa. Every tittle of evidence that the Russians were behind the Tibetans was carefully noted. The stubborn nature of Tibetan resistance on several occasions was attributed to Russian leadership.[72] Much was made of the capture of a rifle and some revolver ammunition of Russian manufacture.[73] Supporting arguments for the conclusion that it was worth the while of the British to establish a lasting influence in Tibet were brought forward. Tibetan gold, the one item of Tibetan commerce then arousing much interest in England, was mentioned.[74] The Tibetan people, it was said, were very friendly and would welcome the presence of the British, which would, moreover, have a most salutary effect on the loyalty of the Bhutanese.[75]

It was clear to Younghusband that a mission to Lhasa was not enough by itself. The treaty which it secured would have to guarantee the continuance of British influence in Tibet for many years to come. Thus, as he argued in May 1904, a British Resident, with an escort, should be established in the Tibetan capital; the Chumbi Valley should be occupied (permanently, it would seem) and the British should make a 'sustained intervention in Tibetan affairs'.[76] Curzon agreed. It was no use dashing to Lhasa, imposing a treaty, knocking down, perhaps, a few forts, and then pulling out in the hope that this demonstration would suffice to keep the Russians from ever meddling in Tibetan affairs in the future. As he wrote to Ampthill in July 1904:

> My point is that, with no one to keep the Tibetans straight at head-quarters, they may begin a hostile and Russophile policy again the moment our backs are turned. Forts may be rebuilt. Dorjieffs may multiply. Trade may be prohibited. Our man (if we have one) sitting in Gyantse will be quite powerless: for of one thing we may be sure – that no Government that we can contemplate for a long time to come will send another mission or another expedition to Lhasa.[77]

The Home Government, however, was deaf to arguments of this sort, and refused to consider a Resident in Lhasa on any terms. It would seem, so Brodrick said again and again, like the establishment of a British protectorate over Tibet in the face of contrary promises to the Russians. No protectorate and no annexation of Tibetan territory was to result from the Younghusband mission. So the Home Government had declared on 6th November 1903 in the telegram to Curzon on which, Curzon somewhat bitterly remarked:

> Brodrick in particular has pinned his faith in so many Parliamentary answers and Primrose League speeches that it has attained in the eyes of Government to an almost canonical sanctity.[78]

Thus, long before he reached Lhasa Younghusband must have realized that he would have to carry out his policy by indirect means, and on his own, for in April 1904 Curzon went to England on leave and did not return to India until December. During the crucial period of the final advance to Lhasa Lord Ampthill, a far from Curzonian character, was at the Indian helm.

The gains of the mission to Lhasa, whatever they might be, would have to be embodied in some sort of treaty between Younghusband and the Tibetans, preferably with Chinese adhesion. The Indian Government had no previous experience of Anglo-Tibetan treaties, and did not know whether the Dalai Lama was, in fact, able to conduct treaty relations at all. Younghusband solved this particular dilemma in the summer of 1903 by bringing to Government notice the *Tsongdu*, the Tibetan National Assembly, whose very existence had been unsuspected until now, and who could, it was hoped, supersede the authority of the Dalai Lama in temporal matters.[79] When the Dalai Lama fled from Lhasa, along with Dorjieff, as the British approached his capital, the *Tsongdu*, whatever might be its legality, was the only body remaining in Lhasa with whom Younghusband could deal. The Dalai Lama, it is true, left a regent behind him, the Ti Rimpoche, to act in his absence. But the Amban, apparently at Younghusband's instigation, had deposed the Dalai Lama, and what were the powers of the representative of a deposed ruler?[80] The Dalai Lama also left behind him one of his Great Seals, the one he used for documents of religious import – and, it would appear, of no value for temporal documents such as a treaty.[81] The Panchen Lama also remained, and Younghusband gave some thought to setting up the Incarnation of Tashilhunpo in place of that of Lhasa, but technical difficulties prevented him from playing the part of Lama maker.[82] In the end the Lhasa Convention, as Younghusband's treaty came to be called, was negotiated with the deposed Dalai Lama's representative, adorned with his spiritual seal, and ratified by the *Tsongdu*, a body of doubtful constitutionality. The Amban did not affix his signature to this document, surely one of the oddest treaties in the history of British diplomacy.

The Lhasa Convention of 7th September 1904 was a document of nine articles. It recognized the Sikkim-Tibet frontier as laid down in 1890 (Art. I); it opened two new trade marts, Gyantse and Gartok, to operate under the conditions established for Yatung in 1893, which meant that a British trade agent could reside at the marts (Art. II); it reserved questions of tea and tariff for subsequent discussion (Art. III); it provided for free trade for articles not subject to the tariffs to be mutually agreed later (Art. IV); it obliged the Tibetans to keep open the roads to the new marts, and to transmit letters from the British Trade agent to the Chinese and Tibetan authorities (Art. V); it imposed on the Tibetans an indemnity of Rs. 75,00,000 (£500,000), payable in 75 annual instalments (Art. VI); as security for the payment of the indemnity and for the proper operation of the trade marts, the Chumbi Valley was to be occupied by the British until the indemnity had been paid (Art. VII); the Tibetans were to raze all fortifications between the British frontier and Gyantse (Art. VIII); the Tibetans agreed to have no dealings of any kind with any Foreign Power without British consent (Art. IX).[83] Appended to the Convention was a separate agreement permitting the British Trade Agent at Gyantse to visit Lhasa if and when he saw fit.[84]

Articles VI, IX and the Separate Article were to cause the British a considerable amount of trouble. While Younghusband was not responsible for the wording of Article IX, the significance of which will be discussed later, he was certainly responsible for Article VI, with its details of the indemnity which the Tibetans were expected to pay, and for the Separate Article which authorized the Trade Agent at Gyantse to visit Lhasa. The indemnity article was not objected to so much because of the size of the sum demanded, which was far less than the cost of the Tibetan campaign to the Indian Government, as because the method of its payment by the Tibetans involved a British occupation of the Chumbi valley for 75 years, and this was tantamount to an annexation as forsworn in the famous telegram of 6th November 1903. The Separate Article, of course, was a veiled way of getting a British Resident to Lhasa, and it deceived no one for a moment. Had Curzon been in India at the time when the treaty was signed, both these provisions might have survived the storm of protest they aroused. As it was, with Curzon on leave, there was no one in India to fight for what Younghusband had achieved. The Separate Article was abandoned at once; as Brodrick said, 'the FO feel that otherwise it could not prevent the sending of a Russian commercial agent to Lhasa'.[85] Ampthill, on his own authority, reduced the indemnity to Rs. 25,00,000 and the period of payment to three years.[86]

Younghusband certainly knew that these two provisions would cause trouble. He had been told on several occasions to do nothing which might possibly be construed as an attempt to establish a British Residency at Lhasa. He had been told quite firmly not to extract any indemnity from the Tibetans larger than they could pay off in three years.[87] Both these instructions he had ignored, and in a rather obvious way to boot. No sooner had the Lhasa Convention been signed than a virtual silence fell on Lhasa. Younghusband was most reluctant to answer telegrams from India, or even to acknowledge them until after 22nd September and the departure of the Mission. At this point of course, he claimed that it was too late to make any alterations in the Convention without a serious loss of face.[88] Younghusband was rather hurt that he was not welcomed as a conquering hero on his return by his superiors in India and in London, and that he was awarded the niggardly K.C.I.E. instead of the more prestigious K.C.S.I. But, as Brodrick said, Younghusband had behaved in a way which would have guaranteed the recall of any diplomatist in this age when Stratford Cannings were no longer tolerable.[89] Brodrick was thankful that Ampthill was in India during the final advance to Lhasa, and not Curzon, as the following extract from one of his private letters to Ampthill shows clearly enough:

The Tibet papers have caused some little stir here, though it is subsiding very rapidly. For your private eye, and not for transmission to Curzon, I may say that I think the line you took has met with a great deal of sympathy in our Party. In all probability, if you had been likely to be permanent, and there had been no Curzon, the Cabinet would have been less insistent than they were on my sending as vigorous despatches as I was forced to do. Of course I accept the entire responsibility of everything I had to write, but I always anticipated and told the Cabinet that, with prevailing feeling with regard to Russia and annexations on our frontier, the public would not be inclined to deal harshly with a man who had done as good service as Younghusband. But the truth is that Curzon's whole attitude about this and about Afghanistan frightened the Cabinet to death. Whereas you on your own motion saw the necessity of reducing the indemnity, I believe that Curzon would have declared a protectorate over Tibet without a moment's hesitation.[90]

There can be little doubt that Younghusband knew that he was disobeying the letter of what instructions he had in securing the indemnity payable in 75 instalments, and in obtaining permission for the British Trade Agent at Gyantse to visit Lhasa. It was no excuse that the Tibetans and the Amban had not objected to these provisions, and that the 75 instalments made the payment of the indemnity less of a burden on the Tibetan people.[91] The objections to these provisions were diplomatic, and the feelings of the Tibetans and the Amban carried no weight in London. But it would be unfair on Younghusband not to admit that he had acted in a difficult situation in a way which seemed to him to offer the only solution of the Tibetan problem. In the face of conflicting concepts of his superiors as to what the Tibetan problem was about, Younghusband must have felt that he was better entitled to use his own discretion than he would have been on a more conventional diplomatic mission.

From the correspondence of 1904 one may well derive the impression that there were at least three Tibetan policies, if not four, in existence at the same time. Brodrick saw the mission to Lhasa as nothing more than a demonstration of British might on this section of the frontier of India. As he wrote to Ampthill in July 1904:

> Our main point is to re-establish our prestige, and to make it clear to Russia that we will not surrender predominance in – Tibet to her. In our judgement the mere fact of a British force marching to Lhasa and slaughtering a great number of Tibetans on the way ought even without a treaty to establish our claims and show our power.[92]

Curzon and Younghusband saw that only by the establishment of some permanent mechanism for the exercise of British influence in Tibet could Russia be kept out. As Curzon wrote in May 1904:

> The Cabinet are very much against a permanent agent at Lhasa or anywhere. But I have said that I do not see how they can avoid it in some form or other; although steps may be required to qualify the appearance.[93]

Lansdowne saw in Tibet both a diplomatic danger and, perhaps, if properly exploited, a diplomatic weapon of some strength. Thus, in the early summer of 1904 while Younghusband was being besieged at Gyantse, Lansdowne was hinting to the Russians that he might be prepared to make some modifications in British claims as to the status of Tibet, which the Younghusband Mission could not fail to alter in practice if not in theory, in exchange for Russian acceptance of the principles of the recent Anglo-French agreement over Egypt. Lansdowne's attitude made Curzon exclaim: 'Good God! Such is the wisdom with which we are governed!'[94]

As a possible fourth Tibetan policy one may well classify the feeling amongst members of the Bengal, Punjab and other Local

Governments having a direct interest in the Indo-Tibetan border, that the Younghusband Mission should not only result in the frustration of Russian schemes, but also in a settlement of some of the outstanding problems of the frontier. Something should be done to improve the position of Indian trade in both Eastern and Western Tibet, areas neglected since the concentration of British attention on the Sikkim route. Trade marts should be opened at Gartok and, perhaps, at Rima in Eastern Tibet. There were a number of minor Indo-Tibetan border arguments which required settlement. For example: since the 1860s the Kashmir Durbar had been arguing with the Gartok authorities over a small area north of the Panggong Lake; in 1888-9 there arose an Anglo-Tibetan conflict of jurisdiction south of the Niti Pass on the Garwhal border; and as late as 1897 it was still clear that the Tibetan authorities at Taklakot differed a little from the British authorities in Kumaon as to the proper border alignment and demarcation of administration. Some such issues were to be the subject of Anglo-Tibetan discussion after 1920, yet the border was not, it would seem, a matter to which Younghusband gave high priority; and his abrupt departure from the Tibetan capital prevented any consideration of such matters which the Local Governments were just beginning to suggest to the Viceroy as suitable topics for Anglo-Tibetan talks.[95] It was hoped that some discussions might arise from the reduction of the indemnity, which, Ampthill suggested, might be made conditional upon the granting of a further trade mart at Zayul and, perhaps, of the transfer of the control of the customs at Yatung and other marts from Chinese to British hands.[96] But this was ruled out on diplomatic grounds. The only direct concession to considerations of local Indian trade to be detected in the Lhasa Convention was the new mart at Gartok - the Gyantse mart, of course, being a purely political device to get a British official stationed in the heart of Tibet. That Gartok was included at all must be attributed to the enthusiasm of Sir Louis Dane, the Indian Foreign Secretary, whose tenure of the posts of Resident in Kashmir from 1901 to 1903 and of Chief Secretary to the Punjab Government from 1898 to 1901 had given him a strong interest in Western Tibet and a desire to remove all traces of Tibetan influence in Ladakh and other British-protected areas along that frontier. In June 1904 Ampthill told Curzon that

> Dane is mad keen to extend the Indian frontier to the Kuen Luen Mountains, thus annexing Western Tibet, and to establish a trade mart at Gartok. I have been obliged to pour much cold water on these ambitious designs.[97]

The Gartok mart was a gesture to Dane.

The Mission to Lhasa took place in the year of the outbreak of the Russo-Japanese War, and it has been a temptation to later critics of Curzon's Tibetan policy to point out some connection between these two events. The records of the India Office and the Foreign Office have nothing to suggest that the decision to send Younghusband to Tibet was in any way influenced by the fact that Russia's attention was now distracted by her war with Japan. On the contrary, the Russo-Japanese War seemed to provide strong arguments for a postponement of the Mission, as Younghusband was quick to perceive.[98] The effect of the Japanese victories from May 1904 onwards was to suggest that it might not be advisable to take steps which might result in further strains on the already critical state of Anglo-Russian relations. In May 1904 Hardinge was advocating a more conciliatory attitude to Russia over Tibet,[99] and in June Ampthill was wondering whether the British should not, now that Germany was becoming such a threat, give serious thought to making friends with Russia. Had the British been fair in their judgement of Russian expansion, he asked Brodrick, and

> is it altogether unreasonable to suppose that her expansion of territory has been forced upon her in much the same way as the growth of our Empire has been due to circumstances over which we had no control?

He urged that success in Tibet be not obtained 'at the cost of implacable Russian hostility'.[100] In other words, the fear of Russia was waning, and the basis of the Younghusband Mission was once more in danger of being challenged by the Home Government. Younghusband, who saw nothing to convince him that the danger of Russia in Tibet had decreased, must have appreciated that he must act quickly and on his own if he were to obtain the crucial element of his plan to keep Russia out of Tibet, the British Agent in Lhasa.

The Home Government felt itself obliged to modify Younghusband's Lhasa Convention. The Separate Article, despite Younghusband's urgent pleading that such a step would damage severely British prestige, was renounced.[101] The indemnity was reduced from Rs. 75,00,000 to Rs. 25,00,000 and it was made payable in three annual instalments instead of the original 75. Provided the indemnity was paid British forces were not to remain in Chumbi beyond 1908.[102] The only lasting guarantee that Russia would not once more begin to exert her influence in Tibet lay somewhat insecurely in Article IX of the Convention, which read as follows:

> The Government of Tibet engages that, without the previous consent of the British Government:-
>
> (a) no portion of Tibetan territory shall be ceded, sold, leased, mortgaged or otherwise given for occupation, to any Foreign Power;
>
> (b) no such Power shall be permitted to intervene in Tibetan affairs;
>
> (c) no Representatives or Agents of any Foreign Power shall be admitted to Tibet;
>
> (d) no concessions for railways, roads, telegraphs, mining or other rights shall be granted to any Foreign Power. In the event of consent to such concessions being granted, similar or equivalent concessions shall be granted to the British Government;
>
> (e) no Tibetan revenues, whether in kind or in cash, shall be pledged or assigned to any Foreign Power, or the subject of any Foreign Power.[103]

The wording of this Article was ambiguous. What was meant by 'a Foreign Power'? Was China to be included in this category? Were the British to be considered to have excluded themselves from Tibet on the same footing as other Powers? Clause (d), in fact, could well be construed to mean that the British had given themselves an exclusive position in Tibet, and this construction could be reinforced by the fact that the Lhasa Convention gave the British a Trade Agent at Gyantse while other Powers, it might well seem, were prevented from establishing their own such agents by clause (c).

Article IX, in fact, was open to attack from many directions. The Chinese claimed that it ignored their historical rights to Tibetan suzerainty, and on this count they refused to adhere to the Lhasa Convention.[104] The Russians protested that the Convention constituted the establishment of a British Protectorate over Tibet, and in proof they pointed to Article IX as it was reported in *The Times* of 17th September 1904.[105] This report in *The Times*, unfortunately, phrased Article IX slightly differently from the original so as to create the impression that the British were excepted from the prohibitions of this Article.[106] The Russians also pointed to the British occupation of Chumbi, even if only for three years, and to the British construction of a telegraph line from the Indian border to the trade mart at Gyantse, which measures, they argued, proved that Britain considered that Article IX did not apply to herself.[107]

The Germans took exception to Article IX, on the grounds that it gave the British the status of Most Favoured Nation in Tibet, and some said that the German Minister in Peking, Baron Mumm, had been doing his best to persuade the Chinese to oppose the Lhasa Convention.[108] A statement to this effect in *The Times* brought on a flurry of protests from Berlin.[109] The United States, France and Italy, through their Peking representatives, also remarked pointedly on the Most Favoured Nation implications of the Convention; and Satow reported that the Chinese were very worried lest their acceptance of Younghusband's treaty should give rise to German claims in Shantung, Japanese in Fukien and French in Yunnan. The Chinese, Satow said, wanted the British to modify Article IX in such 'a manner as to provide a complete answer to foreign Powers who might found on it similar claims to predominance in parts of China proper'.[110]

The entire episode of the Younghusband Mission raises one question above all others. What were the real motives behind it? Had Tibet ever, in fact, been a place in which the Russians had taken a serious interest? Had the Tsar ever intended to place the land of the Dalai Lama under his protection? A complete answer to these questions would require a study of Russian primary sources which is beyond the scope of this work. From what has been published one gathers the impression that since 1893 the Tsar and some of his advisers - for the Imperial Government was one in which the right hand was all too often unaware of the activities of the left hand - had been considering the possibility of using Tibet as a means of bringing to Russian allegiance the Buddhist subjects of the Chinese Empire. Tsar Nicholas II was influenced in his views on Tibet by one Dr. P. A. Badmaev, a Buriat Mongol, who had served as an expert on Mongol affairs in the Russian Foreign Ministry from 1875 to 1893, and who later became a physician to the Tsar. It was Badmaev, so Witte records in his memoirs, who produced in 1893 for the inspection of the Tsar (Alexander III) a grand design for the construction of a railway line from Kiachta to Peking, which was to coincide with a pro-Russian revolt of the Tibetan and Mongol peoples against the Manchu Dynasty. The Tsar, Witte said, agreed to finance Badmaev to the tune of 2,000,000 roubles to pave the way for the revolt by sending Buriat agents into Mongolia and Tibet,[111] and Badmaev seems to have had little difficulty in winning Alexander's successor Nicholas over to such schemes. The two Russians, presumably Buriats, who visited Lhasa in 1894 may have been part of this plan since it would not be unreasonable to suppose that one of them, Oulanov (or Ulanov), was the same person as 'le Captaine en second Oulanow' who was Russian interpreter to Dorjieff's party in Russia in 1901, and as the Cossack officer Ulanov whom the Tsar sent to Tibet shortly after the Younghusband Mission.[112] Dorjieff, likewise, was an associate of Dr. Badmaev, and what we know of his career leads to the conclusion that he was a political agent who enjoyed the confidence of the Imperial Government.[113] While the story of the Japanese traveller Kawaguchi, who lived in Lhasa from 1900 to 1902, and who described with a wealth of detail the efforts of Dorjieff during these years to persuade the Tibetan monks that the Tsar was their best friend, may not be entirely trustworthy[114] - Kawaguchi was a Buddhist pilgrim, but he may also have been a Japanese agent - there can be little doubt that Dorjieff was more than a mere Buddhist monk. In 1915, for instance, we hear of this strange character acting as a propagandist among the Buriat peoples on behalf of the Russian war effort.[115] In 1924 the German Tibetan traveller Filchner produced a very detailed account of Russian intrigue in Tibet at the time of the Younghusband Mission, and he introduced a further Russian agent, a subordinate of Dorjieff's named Zerempil. According to Filchner, Zerempil was in charge of the Lhasa arsenal and commanded Tibetan troops in a number of engagements with the advancing escort of Younghusband. His adventures, however, seem to have been too true to Kipling's concept of the 'Great Game' to be credible, and there is no record of him in British documents; though this last point need not, of necessity, be conclusive.[116]

Several responsible Russian officials have testified to the Tsar's Tibetan ambitions in the years before 1904. In 1903, in an often quoted remark, Kuropatkin, the Russian Minister of War, told Witte that:

> our Sovereign has grandiose plans in his head; he wants to seize Manchuria and proceed towards the annexation of Korea; he also plans to take Tibet under his rule.[117]

The Russian diplomat Korostovetz noted that sometime before the Younghusband Mission set out along the road to Lhasa the Tsar had promised his support to the Dalai Lama in the event of a British invasion of Tibet.[118] In 1901 the Russian Finance Minister remarked upon the value of the Dalai Lama's friendship to Russian policy in Mongolia.[119] The thesis of Lobanov-Rostovsky, that the Tsar only became seriously interested in Tibet after the

251

Younghusband Mission, cannot be accepted.[120]

And what of the various secret treaties about Tibet? Did they ever take place? Younghusband did not come across much documentary evidence on this point when he entered Lhasa, but he did see a draft treaty between Russia and China in which both parties agreed to protect Tibet, and the Russians promised to provide instructors to train a Tibetan army. The Amban admitted to Younghusband, moreover, that Russia had provided the Tibetans with a number of rifles which arrived in Lhasa so rusted as to be useless; but Younghusband did not see these weapons for himself.[121] Indeed, very few weapons of Russian manufacture were found in Lhasa, and these, so Candler remarked, 'were weapons that must have drifted into Tibet from Mongolia, just as rifles of British pattern found their way over the Indian frontier into Lhasa'.[122] The rifles made in the Lhasa arsenal were Martini-Henrys of English pattern. The Younghusband Mission, in fact, brought back no evidence of great value to confirm the rumours of Russian arms being supplied in bulk to the Tibetans, rumours which are accorded the status of fact in the pages of Kawaguchi.[123]

Towards the end of 1904 some fresh evidence from a good source came to light in Peking when T'ang Shao-yi, the Chinese official deputed to negotiate with the British on Chinese adhesion to the Lhasa Convention, made this interesting statement to Satow:

> Mr. T'ang informed me that it was not long after the signature of the Convention of 1890 that the Dalai Lama obtained written assurances from Russia of her readiness to protect Tibet against India. These documents, three in number, had been obtained from him by the Amban Sheng Tai, but at some time during the stay of the latter his subordinates had been bribed to give them up, and subsequently it was found that they had disappeared. It was believed that the Dalai Lama had them in his possession at this moment, and the Chinese Government would not feel at ease until they were recovered and destroyed.

On this Satow remarked that

> if this remarkable story is true, it shows that Russian intrigue at Lhasa dates from a much earlier period than has hitherto been known.[124]

This story is probably the same as that which O'Conor reported to Lord Elgin in 1895, 'for what it is worth'.

There can be no doubt that there had emerged by 1903 a great deal of evidence to suggest that the Russians were up to something in Tibet; and both Curzon and Younghusband were absolutely convinced that this was the case. Oddly enough, neither seems to have appreciated a particular item of intelligence which was available since 1900 when the Russian Buriat Norzunoff was deported from India and which could perhaps throw some light, albeit rather hazy, upon the whole situation. Norzunoff had in his possession a letter of introduction signed by the President of the Imperial Russian Geographical Society, one Prince 'Outomoky'. Prince 'Outomoky' was, in fact, Prince E.E. Ukhtomsky, a very important Russian indeed.[125]

Ukhtomsky was not only interested in Buddhist matters and a person who moved in the same circles as Dr. Badmaev, but he also occupied a position of influence in the centre of Tsarist Russian policy making in Asia in the years culminating in the crisis of the Russo-Japanese War. Ukhtomsky was a close friend of Tsar Nicholas II, whom, shortly before his accession, he had accompanied on a journey round the world. He was extremely wealthy and had many business interests including the ownership of a newspaper and a Directorship of the Russo-Chinese Bank. He was what would today be called a 'hawk' in Tsarist policy in Asia, urging Russian advances in the direction of Korea and Manchuria (in which he was an ally of Witte). In 1896 he had played an active part in the negotiations with Li Hung-chang during the Chinese statesman's Russian visit which culminated in a Russo-Chinese treaty which, among other features, was of great benefit to the Russo-Chinese Bank. At this time Ukhtomsky was still associated with what might be called a 'hard' line towards Afghanistan, where he saw no harm in a more active Russian competition with British influence. Moreover, he never concealed his belief that it was Russia's destiny to rule, or at least dominate, all of Asia including the Indian subcontinent.

Prince Ukhtomsky's name barely appears in the standard histories of Russia; but his career certainly deserves a close scholarly examination. Lacking such research, one can only speculate. It is possible that the Dorjieff missions had their direct origins less in official Tsarist governmental policy than in the inspiration provided by Ukhtomsky and his friends and associates. Their motives, just as those of the figures behind the Russian adventures in Manchuria and Korea which precipitated the conflict with Japan in 1904, combined patriotism with profit.[126] It is unlikely, for example, that men of affairs like Prince Ukhtomsky had overlooked the great potential which was then detected in the gold fields of Tibet.

Official Russian interest in the Dorjieff missions, whoever may have been responsible for their actual operation, probably was directed towards two considerations. First: the general thrust of Russian Far Eastern policy which was evolving at this period was towards regions where Buddhism was of great importance; and here the good will and support of the Dalai Lama could well prove to be of the greatest value. Second: there is a distinct possibility that in Tsarist diplomatic eyes the Dorjieff missions were really concerned as much with Afghanistan as with Tibet. In 1899-1900 there began a fresh phase of activity in Russian interest in Afghan affairs. The completion of a Russian railway to the northern Afghan border was accompanied by new attempts to establish some formal mechanism of direct Russo-Afghan diplomatic relations of the kind which the British had spent so much energy during the course of the nineteenth century to prevent. The Russian case *vis à vis* Afghanistan was strong. Afghanistan was now in direct contact with an extensive tract of Russian territory; and it seemed reasonable that the Russians should have some measure of contact with events across that common border. What about such matters as the joint use of water supplies and the joint control of disease and locust swarms? In all this there were close parallels between the Russian interest in Afghanistan and the British interest in Tibet, a region in direct contact with British territory where British diplomatic penetration was at that time prevented by obstacles not of British making. Clearly implicit in the Dorjieff missions was the possibility of a bargain of some kind in which the Russians might assist the British over Tibet in return for a more co-operative British approach to Russian requirements in Afghanistan.

Curzon, of course, was perfectly aware of all this. The obvious British counter to any such attempt to bring about a trade-off between Tibet and Afghanistan would be to remove the Tibetan card from the negotiating table or, at least, change its face value. Something like this would have to be done before any useful diplomatic results could be achieved from a British mission to the new Amir Habibullah (who succeeded Abdur Rahman to the Afghan throne in late 1901 and with whom the old Amir's agreements with the British might well have to be renegotiated). In this sense the Younghusband Mission could well be interpreted as a necessary preliminary to the Dane Mission to Afghanistan which finally reached Kabul in December 1904. Whatever Younghusband may or may not have achieved in Lhasa, there can be no doubt that his venture on to the Tibetan plateau did have a profound impact upon the subsequent shape of British relations with Afghanistan, if only because it guaranteed that in any attempt to bring about a settlement of Anglo-Russian differences in Asia, such as was made in 1907, the questions of Tibet and Afghanistan should find themselves placed side by side on the agenda. [127]

As a concluding observation to this chapter it is, perhaps, worth commenting on Younghusband's subsequent career following the Tibetan adventure. After his return from Lhasa, Younghusband spent some months in England. He was appointed Resident in Kashmir in 1906; and he remained in that comfortable and well-paid post until his retirement in 1909 at the age of 47. He took no further part in the conduct of British policy towards Tibet, at least at a level which shows in the documents, even though Kashmir was in fact adjacent to both Tibet and Sinkiang and very much an element in British Central Asian policy. In 1917 he was given the K.C.S.I. which he thought he ought to have received in 1904. Shortly after his retirement in 1909 the position of the Chinese was greatly augmented in Central Tibet by the arrival in Lhasa of Chao Erh-feng's troops. Younghusband chose this moment to publish his own account of the whole Tibetan adventure, *India and Tibet*, a work of the greatest value in explaining Younghusband's own outlook. It is quite clear that Younghusband considered the presence of a permanent British representative in Lhasa to have been a minimum requirement for the preservation of British prestige to the north of the Himalayas.

XI

THE AFTERMATH

·

1905 – 1910

THE YOUNGHUSBAND Mission transformed the Tibetan
problem. Up to the arrival of Lord Curzon as Viceroy in 1899
the question of relations between British India and Tibet could by
no stretch of the imagination have been described as occupying
one of the front row seats in the theatre of British policy
formulation. The matters of trans-border trade, contacts between
British and Tibetan officials on the frontier, minor disputes over
jurisdiction in remote tracts (as, for example, on the Tibet-
Kumaon border in the neighbourhood of the Niti Pass), and even
the complex Sikkim border problem which evolved since the
proposed Macaulay Mission of 1885, none of these had by 1904
assumed an importance which would have justified a British
military expedition to Lhasa. They would have continued to be
short footnotes in the history of the British Indian frontier had
Indo-Tibetan relations remained at the low level of intensity which
had obtained throughout the nineteenth century. What the
Younghusband Mission achieved was the addition to these
essentially local issues of a very wide international dimension.
Tibet became what a recent Indian writer has described as a piece

Note: The history of British relations with and concerning Tibet from
1904 to 1910 is examined in considerable detail in *The McMahon Line* by
Alastair Lamb, 2 vols (London 1966), Vol. 1, which will be referred to in
this chapter as *ML*.

256

'on the imperial chessboard'.[1] Thus, for example, the editors of *British Documents on the Origins of the War 1898-1914* devote a full chapter to Tibet: they certainly would not have done this if the central issue in the Tibetan question was the location of pillars along the Sikkim-Tibet border.[2]

The Curzon-Younghusband policy had been directed towards the exclusion or neutralization of Russian influence in Tibet by means of the establishment of an appropriate measure of British influence. In the very short term it was entirely successful. In August and September 1904 there could be no doubt that the British Indian Empire was powerful in Central Tibet. In practice, however, after Younghusband's departure from Lhasa not only did the original Russian issue remain unresolved but also a number of other matters requiring diplomatic attention became clearly defined in a way that they never had before.

The Younghusband Mission did not exclude the Dalai Lama from contact with the Russians. Indeed, on the eve of the British advance to Lhasa the Dalai Lama fled to Mongolia where he promptly established contact with the Russian Consulate at Urga and the Russian Legation in Peking.[3] That the Russians did not exploit this situation was the consequence of Russian policy then in the process of rapid change induced by the pressures of war with Japan, and not because of the presence (or potential presence) of a British army in Lhasa. Only Anglo-Russian diplomacy, presumably conducted in Europe, could determine what the Russians might or might not do in Tibet.

The Younghusband Mission did not decide the nature of Chinese relations with Tibet. The Lhasa Convention was not signed by the Chinese; and it is to be supposed that Younghusband interpreted this fact as a preliminary step in the freeing of Tibet from China. In the event it became clear that, in order to have any force, the Lhasa Convention required Chinese consent. Further Anglo-Chinese negotiations could not be avoided, and in these the Chinese status in Tibet could well be clarified to China's advantage.

Perhaps the most far reaching consequence, and that the least anticipated by the Government of India, of the Younghusband Mission was to bring out into the open the question of what exactly was Tibet, who had the final say in its affairs and what were its precise geographical limits. Throughout the period of Anglo-Tibetan contact from the age of Warren Hastings until the arrival of Lord Curzon there had existed a certain degree of ambiguity concerning such matters. From the middle of the eighteenth century the Chinese had operated in Tibet a system of the kind which the British in the late nineteenth century might have called 'indirect rule'. Day to day affairs were left in the hands of the traditional authorities. The Chinese Ambans at Lhasa for most of the time remained in the background. Only in moments of extreme crisis, as that which emerged from the Nepalese attacks on Tibet in the late eighteenth century, did the Chinese intervene directly in force. The Younghusband Mission, in Chinese eyes, constituted another such crisis; and the response of one section of the Chinese ruling establishment was a policy of direct intervention which culminated in the occupation of Lhasa by a Chinese army in early 1910.

From the point of view of British India in 1904 the word Tibet really meant the western sector of a wider geographical region in which lived Tibetan people and flourished the distinctive Tibetan civilization. The eastern portion of this region was of marginal importance at this time, though in subsequent years it was to become the subject of considerable British interest. From the point of view of China the situation was in some respects the reverse. The eastern part of the Tibetan world touched on Chinese provinces, Szechuan, Yunnan and Kansu. There had existed for centuries a marginal zone between China and Tibet proper where Tibetans lived under central Chinese rule or there were to be found Tibetan states with ties at least as close to Peking as to Lhasa. The western part of Tibet, the world of the Dalai Lama's theocracy, was very much on the outer frontier of the Chinese world. Only when it was threatened by military invasion, as in 1717 by the Dsungars, after 1788 by the Gurkhas, possibly in 1841 by the Dogras, and in 1904 by the British, did China under the Manchu Dynasty incline towards a policy of direct military involvement in Central Tibet. In the past it had sufficed to restore Chinese prestige and, perhaps, tighten up a bit the mechanism by which Chinese influence could be exerted, and then withdraw the expeditionary force. Here the post-Younghusband situation was rather different from those of the past. In Chinese experience, painfully acquired during the second half of the nineteenth century, it did not seem as if a body like the Government of British India could be treated in the same way as, say, the Gurkha Government of Nepal. Post-Younghusband Chinese policy in Tibet involved a fundamental restructuring in which the area of direct Chinese rule would be extended westwards, perhaps to incorporate Lhasa, perhaps even to embrace all territory that could be said to be in any way Tibetan. The outcome could well mean not only a dramatic expansion of the area of provincial China but also a quantum increase in the complexity of the definition of the dividing line between Tibet and British India. Indeed, one can make a strong argument to the effect that the actual, as opposed to latent, Sino-Indian boundary question begins at this time. That China might be looking at all of Tibet in this new light, as a region of direct rather than indirect rule, was rumoured to be the subject of official discussion in Peking by November 1904, so Satow reported.[4]

The full consequences of a Chinese dominated Tibet with their implications for the security both political and military of very long stretches of the northern borders of British India were not to become the subject of concentrated consideration by the higher echelon of the Government of India until after the Chinese military entry in force into Lhasa in early 1910. The issues presented to the Indian Government by the aftermath of the Younghusband Mission seemed less dramatic; but out of the various questions raised there were three categories which appeared to require fairly urgent answers. First: what was to be the pattern of day to day Anglo-Tibetan relations in the light of the new situation obtaining in Tibet? What were the practical implications for British officials in charge of Tibetan policy of the Lhasa Convention and the new trade marts? Was it at last possible to conduct direct relations between the Indian and Tibetan Governments of the kind which Curzon and Young-husband had hoped for when the Tibetan venture was being planned? Second: what now was the position of China in Tibet? How could the Lhasa Convention be reconciled with the general pattern of Anglo-Chinese treaty relations? Third: how would the new situation in Tibet be exploited by both the British and the Russians in the rapidly evolving understanding between these two nations who had for so long been rivals in the struggle for influence and power in Asia? These three issues dominate the Tibetan problem, at least on the British side, in the five and a half years which separate the departure of Younghusband's Mission from Lhasa in September 1904 and the arrival there of the Chinese army sent by the Chinese commander on the Szechuan-Tibet border, the so called Warden of the Marches, Chao Erh-feng, in February 1910.

Central to the Tibetan policy devised by Curzon and Younghusband was the establishment of some form of permanent British representation in the administrative centre of Tibet, there both to combat possible Russian intrigues and to conduct the normal business of relationships across a mutual frontier. The Separate Article to the Lhasa Convention was intended to achieve this by enabling the British Trade Agent in the newly established

Gyantse mart to visit Lhasa more or less at will. This was now prohibited. From the moment of Younghusband's return through the last months of Curzon's Viceroyalty there were frontier officials who argued, with apparent Viceregal support, that there might be an unofficial, but effective, alternative to the cancelled Separate Article. Men like J. C. White, still Political Officer in Sikkim, and W. F. O'Connor, the Trade Agent at Gyantse, advanced the proposition that the cancelling of the Separate Article may have excluded Lhasa; but it in no way limited the right of the Trade Agent to visit Shigatse, the seat of the Panchen Lama. Since at this moment the Dalai Lama was in exile and, moreover, had been declared by the Chinese to have been deposed, it was quite possible that the Panchen Lama was now the true repository of Tibetan sovereignty (however that concept might be defined). If so, relations with Shigatse could well turn out to be more useful than relations with Lhasa.[5]

O'Connor first visited Shigatse in October 1904 as a member of the expedition under Captain Rawling which Younghusband had despatched to explore the course of the Tsangpo river upstream to its sources and thence to investigate the Sutlej-Gartok route. He was able to meet the Panchen Lama, the 9th (or 6th) Incarnation then about 20 years old, and to open discussions of a distinctly political nature. By the end of 1905 the Panchen Lama had agreed to visit India to meet the Prince of Wales at a great Durbar to be held at Calcutta. In return White and O'Connor had effectively promised the Lama British protection against either the wrath of the Dalai Lama if and when he should return to Tibet or the hostility of Chinese officials who might interpret the Panchen Lama's dealings with British India as acts of treason. O'Connor expressed the policy behind all this in the clearest terms:

In a word, the policy which I would indicate for our adoption in Tibet is somewhat as follows: to seize the present favourable opportunity for cementing our friendship with the Tashi Lama, even going so far, if necessary, as to subsidize and protect him; to open, under the terms of the Lhasa Convention, a new Trade Mart at Shigatse: and to let it be clearly understood that any intrigues of other Powers at Lhasa would be met by a corresponding extension of our influence in the province of Tsang and Southern Tibet: and all this might be done without openly impugning or infringing Chinese suzerainty.[6]

It is extremely unlikely that the various negotiations with Shigatse escaped the notice of Lord Curzon during the final months of his term of office; but he said nothing about them and they aroused no great stir in the India Office.

The Panchen Lama arrived in India in late 1905 at the very moment when major changes were taking place in the formulation of British Indian foreign policy. Curzon had been succeeded by a new Viceroy, Lord Minto; and in London the Conservative Administration was in the process of making way for the Liberal Administration of Sir H. Campbell-Bannerman in which the Secretary of State for India, John Morley, certainly felt no urge to extend British influence to the north of the Himalayas. Morley was rather shocked by the Panchen Lama affair, which he interpreted (perhaps correctly) as a not too subtle measure by local frontier officers to get around prohibitions set out at the higher levels of Government. This he would not tolerate. By the end of 1906 it had become well established that British frontier officers were as effectively excluded from Shigatse as they were from Lhasa.

Even if British officials might not establish diplomatic relations with the authorities in Lhasa and Shigatse, was there any reason why British subjects should not travel all over Tibet? The Lhasa Convention did not prohibit such travel and, indeed, in its provisions relating to easy access to the Trade Marts it could be interpreted as permitting British subjects (including, no doubt, officials) from approaching the Trade Marts by routes which were not of necessity the shortest. Rawling's journey from Gyantse to Western Tibet was a good example of the kind of venture which might now be possible. The travellers, of course, did not have to be British. Curzon was perfectly willing to give every assistance to the Swedish explorer Sven Hedin, including the loan of Government of India surveyors and, even, a military escort under the command of a British officer.[7]

As in the case of the Panchen Lama affair, the Liberal Administration and its supervisor of Indian affairs, Morley, experienced no difficulty here in detecting the stratagems of frontier officers struggling to keep alive the Curzonian doctrine. In the light of diplomacy with both China and Russia this was not to be tolerated. Morley was able to use the case of Sven Hedin to bring to the notice of a very wide public indeed the fact that when he said that it was not British policy to interfere in the affairs of Tibet he meant exactly that. By the end of 1906 British India had ceased to be a convenient launching point for ventures of exploration into the Tibetan unknown. Sven Hedin was not the only would-be venturer on to the roof of the world who found that his ideas were no longer in fashion.

Morley's comments to his Viceroy, Lord Minto, on the Sven Hedin episode convey admirably the flavour of many aspects of Liberal policy in London towards the northern frontier of India and the land which lay beyond. He wrote on 7 June 1906 that:

> What may be our ultimate relations with Tibet, I do not venture to predict. But today? Is it not certain that our policy is to satisfy Tibet, China, and Russia - that we mean to keep our word - deliberately given to all three - that we mean no intervention or anything leading to intervention? Why else did we take such trouble, after I came to this Office, to procure the adhesion of China? Yet here, before the ink on the Chinese settlement is dry, and before we have even seen the text of it, here is a policy from Simla, of expeditions, explorations, and all the other provocative things - that, in case of Tibetan resistance would mean either another senseless Mission, or else humiliating acquiescence. What may be done in the way of exploration by and by, I repeat, I do not presume to say. But today!! Consider the language held by Spring-Rice to Lamsdorff only a few weeks ago - each of them solemnly and emphatically declaring that he would have nothing to do with intervention. Consider the row we made (very rightly) about the Buriat escort for the Dalai Lama. And now here we are, sending a whole squad of explorers in every direction, and Sven Hedin with a troop of Native Assistants, a force of Gurkhas, and a British Officer in charge. I cannot but think of this as Curzonism pure and simple.[8]

It is interesting that very shortly after arriving in India Lord Minto began to find himself agreeing to some extent with the frontier officers and regretting the tone adopted by Morley in communications of the kind quoted above. Thus after Curzon's departure a degree of Curzon's frontier outlook persisted in India, even in the mind of the Viceroy where it was continually reinforced by expert advisers whose outlook accorded far more closely to Curzon and Younghusband than to Morley. It was not easy to persuade the Government of India to abandon all efforts to retain some measure of British influence to the north of the Himalayas.

The most immediate problem confronting the Indian Government after Younghusband's return was that very document which he regarded as such a diplomatic triumph, the Lhasa Convention. The Lhasa Convention had been virtually emasculated by the decision of Lord Ampthill (acting as Viceroy while Curzon was away on leave) to cancel the Separate Article permitting the Gyantse Trade Agent to visit Lhasa and by reducing the Chumbi occupation from seventy-five to three years along with a two-thirds reduction in the size of the Tibetan indemnity against the payment of which Chumbi was to be held as security by the Indian Government. The Convention, however, in 1905 still retained a few elements which could be exploited to keep alive some key features of Curzon's Tibetan policy. First: if the Chinese could be manoeuvred so as to reject it entirely or refuse to put their signature to it in a form that the British could accept, then in effect it would have to stand on its own. As such, over time, it could well be converted into the charter for a Tibet free of Chinese control and able to enter into those relationships with British India which seemed so desirable to Curzon. Second: even if the Lhasa Convention were to be converted into a component in the fabric of Anglo-Chinese diplomacy, there still remained one element in it which might be turned into a channel for some special kind of direct Anglo-Tibetan contact. The Tibetans had agreed to pay an indemnity. The Tibetans, and no one else on their behalf, could be made to pay. Moreover, it could be argued that even though the Chumbi occupation had been reduced to three years the indemnity by being reduced two-thirds had, in fact, been reduced from seventy-five annual payments to twenty-five. Following this line of reasoning the Indian Government had acquired by the Lhasa Convention the right to put all sorts of pressure on, or establish various unspecified but direct links with, the Tibetan authorities over the indemnity question for the next two and a half decades, which was a very long time in frontier policy. If the indemnity could really be extracted from the economy of Tibet, rather than from the much larger revenues of the Chinese Government, there would be imposed a significant strain upon the resources of the Tibetan authorities in Lhasa. The reduction of the indemnity, or even its total abandonment, could well be exploited by the British as a bargaining card of formidable power: and, of course, all sorts of political advantage could be wrung from the non-payment of an instalment.

It is probable that one unspoken reason for Younghusband's rapid departure from Lhasa in September 1904 was to avoid having to discuss in that place with the Chinese the validity of the Lhasa Convention. Ampthill had, in fact, instructed Younghusband to remain in Lhasa to modify the Convention in the light of the decision to abandon the Separate Article and alter the terms of the

Chumbi occupation and the indemnity. In exchange for these modifications Younghusband was to seek a fourth trade mart, at Rima on the Lohit at the extreme eastern edge of the Assam Himalayas, as well as to discuss a number of detailed financial matters relating to customs duties and the payment of the indemnity. Younghusband managed to avoid receipt of these orders; but it is clear that the Chinese Government in Peking were under the impression that the British expedition would remain in Lhasa for a while longer. On 27 September 1904 the Wai-wu-pu told Satow that they had despatched to Tibet via India an extremely able official, T'ang Shao-yi, with powers to negotiate with Younghusband in Lhasa.

With Younghusband gone, the Indian Government decided that it was better, if any further discussions about the Lhasa Convention with the Chinese were unavoidable, that they should take place in India rather than in Peking. At least in India the interests of the Government of India could be supervised by its own officers, rather than by diplomats like Satow who appeared in British Indian eyes to be at times more pro-Chinese than pro-British. During most of 1905, the last months of Curzon's Viceroyalty, Anglo-Chinese talks took place in Calcutta, the Chinese being represented initially by T'ang Shao-yi and then by his secretary Chang Yin-t'ang.

The central issue of these discussions was the nature of the Chinese position in Tibet. T'ang and Chang were prepared to accept the greater part of the Lhasa Convention provided that it was understood that Chinese assent to it was required and that without such Chinese participation the Tibetans could make no binding international agreements. The Indian side, represented by the Indian Foreign Secretary S. M. Fraser, advanced what was, in the language of Anglo-Chinese diplomacy, an essentially new argument. Tibet was not like the rest of China. The Chinese were *suzerain* in Tibet, not *sovereign*. Quite what this meant was not clear. The implication, however, was that the Chinese position in Tibet was more ceremonial than effective, and that in the day to day conduct of affairs the Tibetans enjoyed a considerable degree of autonomy. Perhaps the analogy might be with the kind of position that the British had *vis à vis* Canada or Australia. T'ang Shao-yi would have nothing to do with this idea. Nor was he happy about another Indian suggestion, that the Chinese would agree that in Tibet, in contrast to China proper, they would deny themselves the right to employ European officials such as those who were in the service of the Chinese customs service then still under the command of Sir Robert Hart.

Had men of a Curzonian cast of mind been in charge of British affairs both in London and in India by the end of 1905 then the probability would have been that, once an impasse was reached between the British and Chinese delegates in Calcutta, the Anglo-Chinese negotiations would have been allowed to lapse and the Lhasa Convention would have remained by default the determining instrument in the subsequent shape of Anglo-Tibetan relations. Even after modification by Ampthill, the Lhasa Convention could still be construed to give the British a special position in Tibet which the Chinese, failing their adhesion to the agreement, could be argued not to enjoy. From this starting point something like a British protectorate over, Tibet could have evolved in due course. The Lhasa Convention was still, in late 1905, worth fighting for; and one of Curzon's very last communications as Viceroy of India was to argue that the British both in London and India now accept the validity of Younghusband's Convention (duly modified) without the necessity for Chinese adhesion. As he put it on 14 November 1905, three days before he handed over officially to Minto;

> In my opinion it now remains only for His Majesty's Government to intimate officially at Peking that they dispense with China's adhesion to the Lhasa Convention which they nevertheless have always regarded and still regard as in itself complete and of full validity and that they will themselves without reference to the Chinese Government take such measures as they may find necessary for the execution of its terms.[9]

In the real world, however, such an interpretation of the Lhasa Convention had not been possible from the moment of its signature by Younghusband. Apart from the existence of a corpus of Anglo-Chinese treaties going back to the Chefoo Convention of 1876 in which Tibet had been treated as being in some significant way Chinese, there was the fact that the Russians were watching closely for any British forward move in Tibet; and long before Younghusband reached Lhasa the Russian Government had been assured that the British had no intention of making any permanent alteration in the international status of Tibet. The whole Younghusband Mission was intended to solve some temporary local difficulties, and nothing more. With this background it was never possible to prevent the Chinese from having their say about the Lhasa Convention. Once the Calcutta negotiations broke down the Government of India was unable to prevent the transfer of the discussions to Peking. What the Conservative Government of Balfour in its last year would not have been able to resist (had it wished to do so) the new Liberal Government welcomed. In January 1906 negotiations were reopened in Peking between Satow and T'ang Shao-yi who was now a member of the Board of the Wai-wu-pu, the Chinese equivalent of Foreign Office. On 27 April 1906 a Convention was signed. By an exchange of notes appended to the Convention the Chinese, to show good will, even agreed to the exclusion of their own European employees from Tibet (but without defining what they in fact meant by Tibet).

The new Convention did not state in so many words that Tibet was part of China; but it left no room for doubt that the British had acknowledged that the Chinese were responsible for the conduct of external relations of Tibet. Article II could only be interpreted in this sense.[10] It declared that:

> The Government of Great Britain engages not to annex Tibetan territory or to interfere in the administration of Tibet. The Government of China also undertakes not to permit any other foreign State to interfere with the territory or internal administration of Tibet.

In Article I, moreover, the Chinese undertook, in effect, to assume those responsibilities which had been assigned to Tibet in the Lhasa Convention of 1904. In other words, should there be any modifications of the 1893 Trade Regulations, such as were suggested in Article III of the Lhasa Convention, these would now, the implication was clear enough, be negotiated with the Chinese rather than with the Tibetans. The argument that China was suzerain rather than sovereign in Tibet was not touched upon in the new Convention.

There can be no doubt that the Anglo-Chinese Convention of 1906 was a serious blow to the advocates of anything like a British forward policy in Tibet; and it was soon to be followed by further shocks from what hitherto would have been a rather unsuspected direction, St. Petersburg, in the shape of Anglo-Russian negotiations leading to the Convention of 1907, of which more later. The Indian officials concerned with the northern border, however, did not give up without a struggle. There still remained two arrows in their quiver, the manner of the payment of the indemnity and the negotiations of new trade regulations.

In the indemnity question, which became a matter for policy in late 1905 with the first instalment due, there were two issues.

First: who would pay it, the Tibetans or the Chinese? Second: would there be three instalments or twenty-five? The Chinese endeavoured to answer both questions at once. In November 1905 the Indian Government was informed that the Chinese Government, by way of the Hong Kong and Shanghai Bank, proposed to make a direct transfer to the Indian Treasury of the first instalment of the indemnity, which the Chinese indicated came to the sum of Rs. 8,33,333-5-4, or one-third of the Rs. 25,00,000 specified in the Lhasa Convention as modified by Ampthill. It was clear that there were only going to be three instalments after the payment of which the·indemnity question would be closed once and for all. The Indian Government could not fight this. They could, however, insist on a rather different manner of payment. A Tibetan official of rank would come down to Calcutta, collect the money, return to Tibet and hand over the instalment of the indemnity in Gyantse to the British Trade Agent there, thus demonstrating to all that some kind of direct Anglo-Tibetan relationship without any Chinese mediation existed. In the event the Gyantse charade was dispensed with, though for the first instalment the Indian Government managed to insist upon the visit to India of a senior Tibetan official, the Sechung Shape, who collected the cheque in Calcutta from an account opened for him by the Chinese and passed it on to the Indian Treasury. By the time this had been achieved the whole business had assumed some of the qualities of farce. For the 1907 instalment, despite an effort by Minto, Morley refused to countenance a repetition of these antics. The second and third (and final) instalments of the indemnity were paid from the Chinese to the Indian Treasury by direct telegraphic transfer.[11]

Even after all this the Government of India did not give up. In the negotiation of a new set of Trade Regulations specified in the Lhasa Convention, which opened in the summer of 1907, the British managed to ensure the presence of Tibetan as well as Chinese representatives.[12] The Tibetan delegation to Simla, headed by Tsarong Shape, became the subject of complex and not always amicable Anglo-Chinese discussion. The Chinese delegation, headed by Chang Yin-t'ang, wanted Tsarong Shape to be described as acting 'under the instructions' of the Chinese. The British side, headed by L. Dane (the Indian Foreign Secretary), sought for Tsarong Shape's status to be defined as 'fully authorized' representative of the Tibetan (and by implication fully sovereign) Government. Eventually a compromise was reached. Tsarong Shape was referred to in the preamble to the Trade Regulations as they were signed at Calcutta in April 1908 as, indeed, the fully authorized head of the Tibetan Government but a head who was in the negotiations to act 'under the direction of Chang', the chief Chinese delegate.[13]

The whole tone of the 1908 Trade Regulations gave support to the Chinese position as overlords in Tibet, though a certain number of ambiguities remained. In the final analysis, however, in such matters as the maintenance of law and order in Tibet it was recognized that the ultimate responsibility, and hence authority, was Chinese. In the Trade Regulations the British actually agreed to abandon their right to maintain a military presence with infrastructure of rest houses and telegraph lines in Tibet once the Chinese were in a position to assure security of persons, property and communications. The Trade Regulations of 1908 really confirmed the Chinese claim, which Chang Yin-t'ang had been asserting since his posting to Tibet after the abortive 1905 Anglo-Chinese Calcutta talks, that Tibet was under Chinese control. From the end of 1905 Chang had set out to demonstrate in practice this authority by undermining the status of the British Trade Agents in Tibet at Gyantse and in the Chumbi Valley. No doubt Chang's brief from Peking was to do all he could to pave the way for the incorporation of much of Tibet, if not all of it, into the Chinese provincial administrative structure in a way which hitherto had only been attempted in some districts along the Szechuan border with Eastern Tibet. He was, in the event, remarkably successful in that he had helped to eliminate by the end of 1909 any traces of the Lhasa Convention and the Younghusband Mission such as might be exploited in British India to frustrate a Chinese military occupation of Lhasa. The Chinese military presence in Central Tibet in force, it could even be argued, was in full conformity with the 1908 Trade Regulations which called upon the Chinese to ensure proper security at the Trade Marts.

Lord Minto, who started out in late 1905 with very un-Curzonian frontier attitudes, had by 1908 come to regard the escapades of Chang Yin-t'ang and his assistants in Tibet and during Anglo-Chinese discussions over Tibet with increasing distaste. Left to his own devices he would surely have drifted into some kind of forward policy leading to what might have looked very much like a second Younghusband Mission. Other things being equal, Minto might have proved as difficult to control by Morley as had Curzon by his Secretary of State. In the event, however, one diplomatic consideration above all others effectively tied the hands of the Indian Government in Tibet and provided the Chinese with a measure of assistance which they had certainly not anticipated from this quarter when the Younghusband Mission reached Lhasa in August 1904. This was the signing of the Anglo-Russian Convention relating to Persia, Afghanistan and Tibet in St. Petersburg on 31 August 1907. Probably more than any other factor this agreement constrained the British reaction to events along their northern border over the next crucial years. Long after the Russian regime which it represented had been overthrown by revolution the influence of this Convention persisted in British diplomatic attitudes if not in acknowledged British obligations in international law.

The idea of a rapprochement between Britain and Russia had been present in the minds of a number of influential diplomats on both sides since the very beginning of the twentieth century. The logic of the alteration in the European balance of power dictated the folly, when England and France were burying their differences, of continued hostility between England and France's major ally. By the time that Younghusband entered Lhasa it was already quite clear to the British Foreign Office in London that the local Indian advantages claimed for a forward policy in Tibet were outweighed by the damage it might do to the still fragile structure of Anglo-Russian dialogue. In order to preserve what had been achieved, in 1904 still little enough, the Conservative Administration of Arthur Balfour was quite prepared to abandon any apparent political gains on the northern borders of India which the Lhasa Convention might have secured for the British. The Liberal Administration of Campbell-Bannerman, which came to office in late 1905, was even more firmly wedded to such a course of action.

By late 1905, of course, there had been a major alteration in the perceived international status of Tsarist Russia. The war in the Far East with Japan both on land and on sea had turned out to be most unfortunate from the Russian point of view. The image of the Russian menace in Asia shrunk somewhat after 1905. In St. Petersburg there was a revived interest in the Balkans as a theatre for Tsarist imperial policy and a shift of the main focus of attention from the east to the west. In London it was now easy to dismiss talk of the Russian threat to the British position in the Indian subcontinent as unjustified scaremongering. In this more relaxed climate of opinion it became possible to contemplate some general elimination by treaty of the major causes of Anglo-Russian friction in Asia. A pattern for such a settlement had, indeed, long existed. For half a century there had been at work a process of Anglo-Russian diplomacy directed towards the definition of the limits and status of Afghanistan, a region which increasingly became the buffer between British India and the rapidly expanding Tsarist Empire in Central Asia. Despite interruptions during periods of crisis, the implications of this process as a whole were clear enough. Adequately defined boundaries either to sovereign territory or to political influence had to be established and, once established, respected. The need had originally arisen as much from the requirements of local imperial administration as from any general diplomatic consideration. With the change in attitudes in both London and St. Petersburg, however, it became possible to extrapolate the concepts behind the often rather pragmatic arrangements over Afghan borders into the idea of some general agreement covering a large number of zones of actual or potential conflict.

The shift in direction of policy, easy to detect in London and St. Petersburg, was not always so apparent in those tracts where British and Russian imperial interests approached each other. Russian officials in Turkestan still pressed for the establishment of some kind of formal diplomatic representation in Afghanistan, with which Russia now possessed a long common border the very existence of which generated trans-border problems, irrigation, plague control and the like. A total ban on any contact at all across the Russo-Afghan border was an administrative absurdity. Thus there was a steady Russian pressure for an alteration in the nature of Russian diplomatic contacts with the Afghan Government. This precipitated a crisis in 1904. After a number of more extreme measures were contemplated, Louis Dane was sent by Lord Curzon to Kabul on a mission to the Amir Habibullah.[14]

Within British India, and also, of course, among the band of former British Indian officials now in English retirement, there were many who saw no good reason why the British should be unduly sympathetic about Russian problems in the administration of the Russo-Afghan border. They saw no corresponding sympathy for British difficulties on the North West Frontier. A lifetime's experience, moreover, had convinced them of Russia's determination, agreements or no agreements, to advance in Asia until no further advance was possible. To these men it was obvious that the undermining of the stability of the British Indian Empire, the biggest single potential obstacle to Tsarist expansion, was a prime Russian objective. There might be times when it suited some Russian statesmen to speak with the tongues of doves; but it would be folly indeed to be lulled by this into the belief that the long term Russian goal had been abandoned. It had not. The Russians were always dangerous and never to be trusted.

This suspicion of Russian intentions, while it did not prevent the evolution of the policy which culminated in the Anglo-Russian Convention of 1907, certainly was a factor which the diplomats in Europe could not ignore. It was present not only in India but also in London. Not everyone in the India Office agreed with the new approach; and there were many Members of Parliament who were quite prepared to voice their doubts. Opposition to the rapprochement with Russia was sure to be widely reported in the press. It was, therefore, only with some caution that the Anglo-Russian agreement was brought into being. Its scope was narrower than would have been the case in the absence of such potential opposition; and, perhaps more importantly, the British Government, once committed to this policy, had to be extremely vigilant to ensure that some incident on the frontier would not be brought about by officials hostile to the new attitude towards Russia in order to undermine it.

At the time of the Younghusband Mission the three areas along the British India border most directly the subject of Anglo-Russian competition were Persia, Afghanistan and Sinkiang which, between them, flanked the entire north western corner of India from the Persian Gulf to the Karakoram mountains. In all three regions there had been a long history of Russian attempts to expand a diplomatic influence which, if unopposed, might well turn (as it had in the Central Asian Khanates) into Russian political control. By Curzon's day Russian influence in northern Persia was steadily increasing in a country where the stability of the ruling dynasty was certainly open to question. In Afghanistan Russian diplomatic influence was still excluded, but for how much longer it was impossible to say. In Sinkiang the power of the Russian Consulate-General in Kashgaria seemed to be as great, if not greater, than that of the Chinese whose territory this was; and in Sinkiang the British had yet to secure recognition for a Consular representative of their own.[15] The British failure in this respect, it was widely believed, was the result of Russian intrigue with the Chinese. Compared to these three regions, at least until the period of the Younghusband Mission, Tibet would have been considered to have been of but the most trivial importance.

One of the most significant consequences of the Dorjieff ventures and the British reaction to them was to make Tibet a central issue in the structure of Anglo-Russian relations. The advance of Younghusband to Lhasa had been the subject of Russian diplomatic enquiries which had resulted in British denials of any intention to establish a permanent presence in Tibet. At the same time, Younghusband had not, in fact, been able to prevent the continuation of some kind of public display of friendly relations between the Tsar and the Dalai Lama.

Before Younghusband reached Lhasa the Dalai Lama fled towards Mongolia where he established his base at Urga. Here he was in contact with Russian diplomats; and from here in early 1906 came Dorjieff once more on a mission from the Lama to the Tsar. Dorjieff brought ceremonial gifts. The Tsar, on 5 April 1906, replied by sending the Lama a telegram. There followed much publicity about a party of devout Russian Buriats who were proposing to provide a volunteer armed escort to take the Dalai Lama back to Lhasa. The Russians claimed it was all very innocent. Religious exchanges between Lama and Tsar were reinforced by the religious enthusiasm of individual Russian Buddhist Buriats. The British suspected that there was more to it than this. At the worst it might mean a Russian version of the Younghusband Mission was being planned; and, at best, it could be argued that the Russians were demonstrating that they had an effective answer to the recent British dealings with the Panchen Lama. In the event the situation was defused by the Dalai Lama's decision, under Chinese pressure, not to return just yet to Lhasa and, indeed, to leave Mongolia to the remote monastery of Kumbum in Kansu Province where he would be out of the public eye.[16]

These events in 1906 put Tibet very much on the agenda of the negotiations which were just beginning in St. Petersburg between Sir Arthur Nicolson and the Russian Foreign Minister, Alexander Isvolski. It is probable, indeed, that Tibet actually displaced Sinkiang as a topic for discussion and a counter in the resulting bargains. The structure of the negotiations was designed to remove some of the major Anglo-Russian points of friction in Asia by a set of balanced concessions.

The Russians were confirmed in a virtual protectorate over northern Persia, balanced by similar rights for the British in a tract of Persia adjacent to India along the Gulf (but not, interestingly enough, including the zone of the oilfields which were to be established in 1908). In Afghanistan the Russians were to have no diplomatic relations except through the mediation of the British. In Tibet the Russians could have Buddhist religious relations only: the British would have no direct political relations except through the Trade Marts as provided for by the Lhasa Convention of 1904 and the Anglo-Chinese Convention of 1906, neither would they annex any Tibetan territory or otherwise interfere in internal Tibetan administration; and they would send no representatives to Lhasa. All this was set out in a Convention which was signed by Nicolson and Isvolski in St. Petersburg on 31 August 1907.[17]

The portion of the Convention which dealt with Tibet contained a number of features, some created almost *en passant* and others contained in an exchange of notes appended to the Convention, which were to be of the greatest significance for the future conduct of British policy towards its northern border along the Himalayas. First: in Article II of the Tibetan section there was the following phrase: 'in conformity with the admitted principle of the suzerainty of China over Tibet, Great Britain and Russia engage not to enter into negotiations with Tibet except through the intermediary of the Chinese Government'. Here the status of Tibet was defined with a precision lacking in earlier instruments. Whatever 'suzerainty' might mean, and there was great room for argument over this, yet it was clear that it could not be construed to give Tibet the right to conduct international relations except through China. The fact that China was not a party to the Convention was not important: the Chinese position had been guaranteed by Britain and Russia in such a way that neither could disregard it without breaching the Convention. Second: in notes appended to the Convention both Britain and Russia agreed for a period of three years not to permit the passage from their respective territories into Tibet of 'scientific mission', of any kind whatsoever; and they further agreed to secure Chinese collaboration in this insulation of Tibet from such unofficial penetration. Among other consequences this rather strange provision meant that in early 1910 the British could not combat Chinese influence in Lhasa by arranging for a flood of visits to that place by 'unofficial' British explorers, at least not without much unwelcome preliminary diplomacy. Third: in an annexe to the Convention the British said that, once the three instalments of the indemnity imposed upon the Tibetans by the Lhasa Convention had been paid and the Trade Marts were operating properly, the British occupation of the Chumbi Valley should be terminated. If, for any reason, this did not happen, then there should be further Anglo-Russian discussions.

After the signing of the Convention the room for British manoeuvre in Tibet was severely limited. In theory both Britain and Russia could, through their Buddhist subjects, maintain relations with the Dalai Lama and other Tibetan religious figures of a purely spiritual nature, which meant, in effect, that Dorjieff could continue to come and go between Lhasa and St. Petersburg. In theory, of course, the British could use their own equivalent of Dorjieff; but, in practice, the Government of India was never able to find anyone who was completely satisfactory in this role. The British could use the Trade Marts as outposts of their influence

273

along the lines permitted in the Lhasa Convention; but here the necessity of dealing through the Chinese proved to be a severe limitation on their capabilities. Any attempt to go beyond the provisions of the Convention would involve further discussions with the Russians, who could well seek some most unwelcome *quid pro quo*.

It was against this background that Chinese policy towards Tibet was able to evolve. The Chinese Government had been seriously alarmed by the Younghusband Mission which had brought about a major challenge to the position in Tibet which it had maintained since the eighteenth century. Traditional Chinese policy was content in the absence of external threats to maintain a fairly low profile. Only in crisis, as has already been noted, did the Manchu Dynasty see fit to send troops in significant numbers to reinforce the Ambans and their escort of little more than ceremonial import. Younghusband's arrival in Lhasa and his negotiation with Tibetans (without Chinese signature) of the Lhasa Convention presented Peking with just such a crisis.

From the middle of the nineteenth century the position of the Manchu Dynasty seemed to many foreign observers to be insecure; and after the Boxer crisis of 1900 it looked as if it had entered a terminal stage. In fact, it was easy to underestimate the degree of patriotic determination that inspired many Chinese officials who were not of necessity enthusiastic supporters of the Manchus. The reconquest of Chinese Turkestan by Tso Tsang-t'ang in the 1870s and the conversion of the region into a Chinese Province, Sinkiang, showed what individual Chinese officials were capable of whatever the state of confusion which might be detected in the Imperial councils in Peking. After 1900 we see a similar Chinese attitude towards Tibet in which the Younghusband Mission, if it was not the sole inspiration, without doubt was a major warning that the old system of loose and indirect rule could no longer guarantee the continued presence of Tibet within the Chinese Imperial structure.

The Chinese were able to operate two distinct lines of policy on the new Tibetan problem. The first was what might be called 'diplomatic' in that it exploited the existing structure of Anglo-Chinese relations through the British Legation in Peking. The transfer of the negotiations concerning Chinese adhesion to the Lhasa Convention from India to Peking was a triumph of this approach; and in their subsequent activities in Tibet Chinese officials like Chang Yin-t'ang were building on this foundation. These men represented a new phenomenon in Tibet, at least in the experience of the British. They were representatives not of the

274

Lhasa Ambans, who continued to operate in their traditional way the old patterns of Sino-Tibetan relationships, but of the central Chinese Government in Peking. Whatever they did or happened to them was soon reported to the British Minister in Peking and became by this means the concern as much of the British Foreign Office as of the Government of India and the India Office. Through them the 1908 Trade Regulations were negotiated; and through them the impression was created in Central Tibet that the Chinese had assumed the greater part of the powers and advantages which the Lhasa Convention had conferred upon British India. Once the final instalment of the indemnity had been paid and the British occupation of Chumbi ended, there was little that the British, restricted as they now were by the Tibetan provisions of the Anglo-Russian Convention of 1907 (of which Chang Yin-t'ang and his colleagues were certainly well aware), could do to avoid Chinese mediation on the Tibetan plateau and deal directly and alone with the Tibetan authorities at the Trade Marts. Lhasa was quite beyond their reach. Indeed, it was with some difficulty that British frontier officers were able to counter Chinese overtures towards Nepal and Bhutan. One direct consequence of this new Chinese activity was the British decision to take formally Bhutanese foreign relations under their control through a new Anglo-Bhutanese treaty.[18]

The second line of Chinese policy had its base in Szechuan Province which had long been concerned with the conduct of relations between Provincial China and the states of Eastern Tibet. Eastern Tibet marked an extensive zone of transition between the Chinese Provinces of Szechuan, Kansu and Yunnan (of which the first was the most important in this particular context) and the region under the theocratic rule of the Dalai Lama. This zone, which in the past had served as a buffer between China and Central Tibet, the Chinese at the very beginning of the twentieth century had begun to incorporate into China proper, a process the necessity for which was emphasized by the Younghusband Mission. In 1905 the Eastern Tibetan policy came under the control of a Manchu General, Chao Erh-feng, who was in the next five years to bring about a fundamental alteration of the military position of China not only in Eastern Tibet but also in Central Tibet as well.[19]

By 1908 it was evident that both lines of policy were working very well. In Central Tibet the prestige of China, as opposed to that of British India, had been reestablished to a degree sufficient to overcome the lingering effects of the Lhasa Convention. Indeed, many Tibetans believed that with the new Trade

Regulations, the payment of the final instalment of the indemnity and the termination of the Chumbi Valley occupation, the Lhasa Convention had in fact been cancelled or had expired. In Eastern Tibet the Chinese position had been consolidated by Chao Erh-feng as far west as Batang, between which and the Szechuan border land was being brought under the direct administration of Chinese magistrates and opened to Chinese settlers (who, in the event, were very reluctant to venture into this area). In these circumstances the Chinese Government decided to permit the Dalai Lama, after visiting Peking and obtaining the forgiveness of the Manchu Dynasty, to return to Lhasa. The Lama finally arrived in his capital city in December 1909 and took up residence once more in the Potola.

The return of the Dalai Lama was followed immediately by the final stage of Chao Erh-feng's Tibetan advance. From his base in Chamdo Chao Erh-feng despatched a flying column of some 2,000 modern drilled troops to Lhasa, which they reached on 12 February 1910 (but Chao Erh-feng himself never visited Central Tibet). As the Chinese neared the gates of Lhasa the Dalai Lama took flight again, this time towards India. By the end of February he was on British territory and under British protection. The Chinese were now masters in both Eastern and Central Tibet. The London *Morning Post* in an editorial on 28 February 1910 summed up the situation well enough from the British point of view when it declared:

A great Empire, the future military strength of which no man can foresee, has suddenly appeared on the North-East Frontier of India. The problem of the North-West Frontier thus bids fair to be duplicated in the long run, and a double pressure placed on the defensive resources of the Indian Empire.

The men who advocated the retention of Lhasa have proved not so far wrong, whatever their reasons for giving the advice. The evacuation of Chumbi has certainly proved a blunder. That strategic line has been lost, and a heavy price may be extracted for the mistake. China, in a word, has come to the gates of India, and the fact has to be reckoned with. It is to be hoped that the Indian Government will do what they can to retrieve the position, and use the presence of the Dalai Lama [in India] as a lever for securing from the Chinese Government some concessions in frontier rectification.[20]

The *Morning Post* editorialist was right. China had indeed come to the gates of India. Her initial stay was to be brief, for the outbreak of revolution in China in late 1911 undermined her position in this remote outpost of her empire; and by the end of 1912 the Chinese had been forced to abandon Central Tibet. The Dalai Lama returned to Tibetan soil in the summer of 1912 but did not enter Lhasa until January 1913. The Chinese, however, were still present in strength in parts of Eastern Tibet whence, one day, they would probably return to resume what all factions in Chinese politics regarded as their rightful place on the roof of the world.

The Chinese occupation of Lhasa in early 1910 was followed by increasing Chinese activity along much of India's northern border. Apart from the implication for British prestige in Nepal and Bhutan of the new Chinese power, the most disturbing aspect of the situation from the British Indian point of view was that it created an entirely new border problem, compared to which the old question of the boundary markers along the Sikkim-Tibet border was trivial indeed, along a stretch of some 300 miles of the Assam Himalayas.[21] Here the British had, ever since they acquired this border by virtue of their annexation of Assam in 1826, considered the range of mountains stretching from Bhutan to Burma to provide an adequate buffer between British India and whatever power might lie to the north. The depth of the mountain belt, over fifty miles at the narrowest point, the absence of easy routes through them, and the fact that except in the Tawang tract they were occupied by tribes who did not usually welcome external influences, combined to make it appear unnecessary to annex the country. The official British border ran, where it ran at all, along the foot of the mountains on the northern edge of the Brahmaputra valley. Only along the Tawang tract, where the British considered that Tibetan authority in some form or other extended southwards all the way through the mountains, was there a frontier defined by some form of international agreement; and it lay not along the crest of the high mountains but down near the Brahmaputra River not far from its junction with the Ganges.

During the course of 1910 the Chinese began to show an interest in this mountain tract which British officials, particularly those concerned with the administration of Assam, found most disturbing. Chinese patrols penetrated the Assam Himalayas contacting tribes and planting boundary markers in a region which had hitherto been entirely insulated from international interest. Not only was China at the gates of India but it looked as if those gates might turn out to be located not in some remote and barren mountain range, where British strategists thought they ought to be, but actually at the very edge of the Indian plains. Here, as became clear after the Chinese had indicated that they considered that some at least of this Assam borderland belonged not to Tibet but to China proper as part of the newly proclamed Sikang Province, directly administered prefectures of metropolitan China (which in late 1911 changed from Empire to Republic) could well march with directly administered districts of the British Indian Empire.

British Indian frontier policy was presented with a challenge by these developments which it was never able to meet. The short duration of the first crisis, which was effectively defused by the Chinese collapse in Central Tibet in 1912, postponed the need for a solution for a while. Indeed, after 1914 the whole issue was more or less forgotten for two decades only to reappear again in the 1930s. The story of this problem is not the concern of the present book beyond observing that to a significant degree it emerged from the consequences of the Younghusband Mission.

Younghusband himself, in his *India and Tibet* which appeared in 1910, detected in the Chinese occupation of Lhasa evidence of the folly of the abandonment of the clauses of the Lhasa Convention which provided for a British representative with access to Lhasa and for a British military force permanently stationed at Chumbi on the edge of the Tibetan plateau. Could these provisions in fact have ever been exploited to exclude the Chinese from Central Tibet? If Tibet had remained in a diplomatic vacuum it is possible that something might have been achieved. In reality, of course, the Chinese had every right by Anglo-Chinese treaty to send troops in Central Tibet to maintain law and order; and the British, because of not only their treaties with China but also the Anglo-Russian Convention of 1907, were debarred from any counter. The Dalai Lama was now in their hands. It would be quite easy to show that the Lama had sought British aid to recover his lost capital and to reestablish his rule over his people. In theory it might be possible to use British bayonets to restore the Lama and drive the Chinese away. In practice it was quite impossible.

Apart from the distaste of the Liberal Administration for adventures on the fringes of Empire and the undesirability in the eyes of British diplomats outside India of any conflict with China which might damage British commercial interests in that country, there remained the fact of the Anglo-Russian Convention. A British intervention in Tibet would require Russian assent. It is interesting that Younghusband, who went to Lhasa in 1904 to keep the Russians out, was in 1910 seriously advocating the desirability of a joint Anglo-Russian expedition to Lhasa.[22] In theory such joint action was quite possible. In practice, however, the Russian price for agreeing to any modification of the Tibetan clauses of the Anglo-Russian Convention of 1907 would have been extremely high. Probably it would have involved some concession over Constantinople and the Straits so great as to bring about a revolution in the balance of power in the eastern Mediterranean. The alternative, to ignore the 1907 Convention and go ahead anyway without the Russians, arguing that the Tibetan situation presented a challenge to British national interest which could not be ignored, was not a course which would ever be countenanced by the Foreign Office in London. The 1910 crisis on the Indian northern border could not be made to justify risking the abandonment of the diplomatic balance in Europe by the alienation of Russia; and it is a fact that no senior British official seriously advocated such a policy.

There was an alternative policy open to the British. It would have been possible to give diplomatic assistance to the Chinese position in Tibet in exchange for effective (as opposed to symbolic) Chinese help in the conduct of the administration of the Indo-Tibetan border and of the trade which took place across it. Upholding Chinese territorial claims in Central Asia as a barrier against Russia was not a novel concept to the Indian Government. Something very like this had been attempted in western Sinkiang in the 1890s when the British tried to enlist active Chinese support in checking the Tsarist advance into and beyond the Pamirs.[23] The guaranteed continuation of a Chinese Tibet was probably the simplest way to avoid the emergence of a Tibet dominated by Russia: it involved, after all, no more than the confirmation of what had been more or less acknowledged to exist in the corpus of Anglo-Chinese agreements since the Chefoo Convention of 1876. Had the Chinese been able to maintain their hold over Central Tibet after 1912, then it is hard to see how the Government of India could have avoided eventually coming to some such agreement with China. In the process there would have had to be a definition of borders, not least in the Assam Himalayas; and the outcome could only have been beneficial to Sino-Indian relations in the 1950s and 1960s.

The major objection on the part of British Indian policy makers to admitting unqualified Chinese rights in Tibet was to be found less in logic than in the instinctive feeling that it would be undesirable for any Power, even one apparently as weak and disorganized as China, to be in a position of direct territorial contact with the Indian Empire where this could be avoided by the interposition of some kind of buffer. The confirmation of Chinese status, for example the formal acceptance of Chinese *sovereignty*, in Tibet would certainly reduce, if not eliminate entirely, those Tibetan buffer-like properties which had been a feature of the Indo-Tibet border for much of the nineteenth century.

There was another, more subtle, aspect of a fully Chinese Tibet which was not to the taste of the Government of India. If Tibet were treated as if it were a region of China proper, then Indo-Tibetan relations would form but part of the wider pattern of Anglo-Chinese policy which was directed from London rather than India. It would not be possible to conduct Tibetan foreign relations on the same basis as those of Afghanistan and Nepal, as the concern primarily of the Government of India. The accepted existence of a Chinese Tibet could only mean that the Foreign Office in London would acquire structurally an interest in the details of Indian border administration which the Government of India considered to be their own exclusive field.

For the Government of India there were two theoretically satisfactory solutions to the Tibetan problem. The ideal, probably, would be for Tibet to remain in that state of obscurity which had prevailed since at least the middle of the nineteenth century until the arrival of Lord Curzon, when it was not really necessary to have any formal structure of Anglo-Tibetan relations at all (though after 1885 the Indian Government found it increasingly difficult to leave well enough alone). If relations really were necessary, however, as they came to be seen to be with the reports of the Dorjieff missions and other signs of Russian interest, then it would be as well if Tibet became (at least in diplomatic terms) something like Nepal, with the Government of India possessing the final say in its contacts with any other Powers. A Nepal-like Tibet was, it is to be presumed, what Curzon and Younghusband hoped would emerge from the Mission to Lhasa in 1904.

The two possible lines of policy described above are the equivalents of what, on the Afghan frontier, were sometimes referred to as 'masterly inactivity' and the 'forward policy'. In Curzon's mind, and in that of Younghusband as well, while the Tibetan project was being planned there were ever present parallels between what had happened on the Indo-Afghan border and what might be about to happen along the Indo-Tibetan border. 'Masterly inactivity' was what had been going on ever since the expulsion of the Tibetans from Lingtu in 1888. It had not worked. It was time to switch to the 'forward policy'. The line of argument is not without force. The major problem arose from the differences in the nature of Tibet as opposed to Afghanistan. In practice Afghanistan could be treated as a sovereign state. Provided internal anarchy did not overflow on to British territory, and provided other Powers did not intervene in Afghan internal affairs, the country could be left to its own devices. If, however, it was necessary to take 'forward' action, there was the potential of a sovereign Afghan government against which to act. The Amir could be deposed and another put in his place. A binding treaty, which in the last resort could be enforced by British arms, could be negotiated with the Amir without the need to consult any third party.

In practice Tibet, unlike Afghanistan, from at least the time of the Chefoo Convention could not be treated as a sovereign state by the Government of British India. Without Chinese consent and, indeed, active participation, a binding treaty simply could not be obtained from the Tibetans. At the end of the day an effective 'forward policy' in Tibet or concerning Tibet had to be directed against the Chinese rather than any section of the Tibetan body politic. This would not have been easy for the British Government in London to do, had it ever so wished: it was beyond the powers of the Government of India. The Viceroy of India, for example, was quite unable on his own to send gunboats against a Chinese port.

In any case, it is not clear why at any stage in the Tibetan crisis since the abandonment of the Macaulay Mission, gunboats should, actually or metaphorically, bombard the Chinese. While the Chinese Government had not opened up the Tibetan plateau to Indian trade in the manner that some British enthusiasts had hoped for, it had participated in the conduct of the administration of relations along the Indo-Tibetan border to the degree necessary to enable the Indian Government to avoid major expenditure, not to say political problems at the hands of critics in London, arising from a series of trans-frontier expeditions. The Sikkim campaign of 1888 was quick, cheap and effective in that it did not call for a prolonged military follow up. Indeed, from 1888 until 1903 the Sikkim-Tibet border, despite all the arguments about boundary pillars and the operation of the trade marts, was policed on the British side with the absolute minimum of force. This happy state of affairs could, other things being equal, have gone on indefinitely. The Chinese, in other words, were on the whole proving to be not such bad neighbours in the Tibet of the immediate pre-Younghusband era.

The 'forward policy' which Curzon launched in the shape of the Younghusband Mission was not directed towards the Chinese at all. Curzon concluded that the Chinese position in Tibet was a 'fiction', and that the Chinese could do nothing to stop the Russians from establishing a special influence, harmful to British interests, with the Tibetans. The aim of the Lhasa Mission, therefore, was, first, to expel or exclude Russian influence and, second, to create a Tibet which was capable of continuing to keep the Russians out. Such a Tibet, in the last analysis, had to be an independent Tibet, certainly not a . Tibet hiding behind an ineffective Chinese presence; and it had to be a Tibet whose foreign policy, at least, was controlled through British India on the Nepalese model. This required something like a British Resident in Lhasa to monitor Tibetan politics and keep the Indian Government informed on what was going on beyond the Himalayas. To be effective, the Younghusband Mission would have to create a new kind of Tibet. In this respect the 'forward policy' of Curzon and Younghusband towards Tibet in 1904 was quite different from anything which had been seen before on the Afghan frontier.

With the benefit of hindsight it is now reasonable to say that Curzon and Younghusband mishandled the Tibetan situation in 1903 and 1904 in that they initiated a course of action which could not, given the general diplomatic trend of the times, achieve for the British the results which they sought. What could they have done instead?

The reports of the Dorjieff missions between Lhasa and Russia and the other Buriat activities, combined with items of intelligence from Peking and elsewhere, convinced Curzon that the Russians were planning something in Tibet. Whatever the Russian objectives might be, however, in 1903 the Russian methods still remained essentially diplomatic. Despite much rumour, there was no hard evidence of a significant Russian military presence in Tibet. Reports of the supply of Russian arms to the Tibetans were, at best, vague; and, in any case, the Tibetan army as it then was, even with some modern weapons, was no threat to the British Indian Empire. In 1903 the Russians still did not possess direct access to the Tibetan plateau; this would require a Russian advance into western Sinkiang which, while anticipated by many observers, had yet to take place. Until the Russians entered Kashgaria in force, an action which would immediately be reported to the Government of India, there were no overwhelming reasons why the British should abandon diplomacy.

Curzon agreed that by 1903 diplomacy had failed. In that he had not managed to bring about a revolution in Tibetan foreign policy, he might have been correct; but in that diplomatic means had no more to offer the British he was surely mistaken. There was much that diplomatic pressure on St. Petersburg could do to make the Russians clarify, and at the same time constrict, the nature of their interest in Tibet and their relations with the Dalai Lama. It is possible that greater effort by the Government of India, moreover, might have resulted in the discovery of at least one British subject to the Buddhist faith who could open some discussion with the Dalai Lama: somewhere in India, Burma, Ceylon or Malaya such a person probably existed. The discovery of a British Dorjieff might take time. Meanwhile, accompanied by constant British dialogue with the Russians in St. Petersburg, the local issues of the Sikkim-Tibet border and the Yatung trade mart in the Chumbi Valley might as well have been left to the kind of talks on the spot which had been going on since 1893. It might have been at times something of a charade; but it certainly was not going either to bring down the British Indian Empire or, for that matter, the British Government in London.

The policy behind the Younghusband Mission, which derived from the thoughts and experiences of Curzon, Younghusband and a band of Indian frontier specialists who had been brought up in the atmosphere of the 'Great Game', was in fact by 1904 out of date. The 'Game' was, if not ended, at least reduced to a minor league in the British diplomatic calendar. When competition was at its height there were strong arguments in favour of the 'forward policy': it was probably better, other things being equal, to get there before the enemy. When rapprochement was beginning, however, 'inactivity' was the key. Let the other side make the moves and then try to explain them. The side which held its fire would derive the greater diplomatic advantage. In this context the Younghusband Mission was a premature volley.

'Masterly inactivity' could have turned Tibet into a British diplomatic card of great value. In the Anglo-Russian discussions of 1906 and 1907, during which a wide spectrum of Russian and British interests in Asia were considered, a rather different balance of regional concessions and distribution of spheres of influence might have emerged than that which was actually negotiated under the shadow of the Younghusband Mission. Without any forward move into Tibet to explain, the British would have been in a much stronger position to exploit the Dorjieff adventures as arguments for Russian support for an improved British relationship with the Lhasa Government, so close to the borders of British India and so far from the territories of the Tsar. The resultant Convention might have looked something like this: Persia as in the actual Convention and likewise Afghanistan; Russia's special interest in Mongolia admitted against Britain's special interest in Tibet; a Russian special interest in western Sinkiang (Kashgaria) balanced against some kind of British dominated buffer strip along the northern slopes of the Karakoram and Kunlun mountains.

Once Russia had agreed to a special British position in Tibet, then it would have been far easier to negotiate with both the Chinese and the Dalai Lama on Indo-Tibetan questions. Both would know that Russian support against any escalation of British pressure in Tibet would not be forthcoming. After a Convention of this pattern it might well have been possible for the British to create with the authorities in Tibet a structure of treaty relations with and concerning that country which could have stood the test of time.

Following a course of events of this kind Tibet might have evolved *vis à vis* British India much as Outer Mongolia was developing under the influence of Tsarist Russia. In 1913 the Chinese Government, weakened as it was by Revolution, admitted the autonomy of Outer Mongolia and the right of the Russians to maintain direct contact with the Mongolian authorities in Urga. In 1915 the status of Outer Mongolia as defined in 1913 was further clarified in a tripartite Russian, Mongolian and Chinese treaty (signed at Kiachta 25 May/7 June 1915).[24] In theory China was the suzerain power in Outer Mongolia which was Chinese territory. In practice Outer Mongolia was autonomous with an internal administration declared free from Chinese interference. The Russians were confirmed in their ability to exert influence over Outer Mongolian external relations. From this base, in the achievement of which the Russians were in no way hindered by the Anglo-Russian Convention of 1907 (which was totally silent on Mongolia), a Russian protectorate over Outer Mongolia would have evolved fairly calmly had it not been for the traumatic impact of the Russian Revolution which provided an opportunity for other possible developments in Mongolian history. In the event, however, Outer Mongolia survived the revolutionary crisis as a state free from Chinese supervision and with the closest relations with Russia.

Tibet might well have evolved the same way had there been a correlation between Tibet and Mongolia in any Anglo–Russian agreement. Tibetan autonomy, nurtured by British India, would have sooner or later turned into Tibetan independence, at least in so far as Central Tibet was concerned. British military assistance would, moreover, have surely enabled a Tibetan army to defy attempts at a Chinese reversal of this state of affairs from the direction of Yunnan, Szechuan and Kansu. Since there was no British Revolution, there would have been a continuity of Anglo-Tibetan relations which would not have paralleled the turbulence in Mongolia. With the transfer of power in 1947 the new independent India would have taken over smoothly and without fuss the special relationship between India and Tibet. This would, at least, have given Tibet a reasonable chance of surviving the irredentist fervour of Communist China in the 1950s.

Perhaps none of this could ever have happened. The Young-husband Mission and its consequent effect on the shape of the Anglo-Russian Convention of 1907 guaranteed, however, that it would not. In these circumstances the long term beneficiary of Lord Curzon's Tibetan policy was neither India nor Tibet but China.

NOTES

I First Contacts: 1766-1792

1 H.E. Richardson refers to him as the 3rd Incarnation. See *The Karma-pa Sect. A Historical Note*, by H.E. Richardson (JRAS 1958), p. 161n.
2 *Economic Annals of Bengal*, by J.C. Sinha (London 1927),pp. 33-4. *The English Factories in India 1642-1645*, by Sir W. Foster (Oxford 1913),pp. 138.
3 Hodgson MSS (in the India Office Library, London), vol. I, f. 26. Sketch of the Relations between the British Government and Nepal, quoting Select Committee to Court 25 Sept. 1767.
4 The Kinloch expedition of 1767 is discussed in detail in *Anglo-Nepalese Relations from the Earliest Times of the British Rule in India till the Gurkha War*, by K.C. Chaudhuri (Calcutta 1960). See also: *Modern Nepal: Rise and Growth in the Eighteenth Century*, by D.R. Regmi (Calcutta 1961); *Nepal and the East Indian Company*, by B.D. Sanwal (Bombay and London 1965); *British India's Relations with the Kingdom of Nepal 1857-1947*, by Asad Husain (London 1970); *Political Relations between India and Nepal*, by K. Mojumdar (Delhi 1973).
5 Home Miscellaneous (in the India Office Library, London), vol. 219, f. 325, Court to Bengal 16 Feb.1768.
6 The Logan mission is examined in some detail in Chaudhuri, *Anglo-Nepalese Relations*, op. cit., pp. 34-9.
7 See: 'Some notes on the Intercourse of Bengal with Northern Countries in the second half of the 18th century' by S.C. Sarkar, *Proceedings of the Indian Historical Records Commission*, 41(Calcutta 1930).

8 Rennell's activities on the Bhutanese border from 1766 onward are outlined in *Major James Rennell and the Rise of Modern English Geography*, by C.R. Markham (London 1895), pp. 45-54. Scholarly attention to the political implications of Rennell's work was first drawn by A.R. Field, 'A Note Concerning Early Anglo-Bhutanese Relations', *East and West*, NS Vol. 13, No. 4, 1962.

Rennell's own field experience provided some material for his great geographical study, *Memoir of a Map of Hindustan*, of which the first edition appeared in London in 1773. Rennell, perhaps on the basis of his own experiences in 1766-71, concluded correctly that the great Tibetan river, the Tsangpo, flowed through the Himalayan range to join the Brahmaputra. The earlier Jesuit surveyors of the Chinese Empire, as represented by the French geographer D'Anville, had the Tsangpo running into the Irrawaddy in Burma.

9 *Frontier and Overseas Expeditions from India*, compiled in the Intelligence Branch, Division of the Chief of Staff, Army Head Quarters, India (Simla 1907), vol. iv, p. 128. *Treaties, Engagements and Sanads*, by C.U. Aitchison (Calcutta 1929), vol. ii, p. 189. *Narratives of the Mission of George Bogle to Tibet and of Thomas Manning to Lhasa*, edited by C.R. Markham (London 1876), p. lxviii.

See also: *British Relations with Bhutan*, by S. Gupta (Jaipur 1974), pp. 30-8, and *Bhutan and India. A Study in Frontier Political Relations (1772-1865)*, by A. Deb (Calcutta 1976), pp. 72-6. It is interesting that in neither book is there any reference to Rennell.

10 Markham, *Narratives*, op. cit., pp. 5-8.

11 Apart from Markham, *Narratives*, op. cit., there are fairly detailed accounts of the Bogle mission in: *Into Tibet. The Early British Explorers*, by G. Woodcock (London 1971), and *Tibet. A Chronicle of Exploration*, by J. MacGregor (London 1970). While in Tibet Bogle married a Tibetan lady, said to be a close relative of the 6th Tashi Lama; but Markham suppressed this fact in editing Bogle's narrative. See: *Tibet and its History*, by H.E. Richardson (London 1962), p. 65.

12 Markham, *Narratives*, op. cit., p. 202. Sinha, *Annals*, op. cit., p. 166.

13 Bogle Papers in the India Office Library (Eur. MSS E/226): Hamilton to Hastings 30 May 1776.

14 Markham, *Narratives*, op. cit., pp. 150-1.

15 Ibid., p. 203.

16 Markham, *Narratives*, p. 150.

17 'The Missions of Bogle and Turner according to the Tibetan Texts', by L. Petech (*T'oung Pao* 1949-50), vol. XXXIX, p. 339.

18 Markham, *Narratives*, op. cit. p. 203.

19 For both the narrative of Chapman's mission to Vietnam and the policy behind it, see: *The Mandarin Road to Old Hue. Narratives of Anglo-Vietnamese Diplomacy from the 17th century to the Eve of the French Conquest*, by Alastair Lamb (London 1970), pp. 57-137.

20 Straits Settlements Factory Records, vol. 2: Minute by Macpherson 13 Dec. 1786.

21 *John Company at Work*, by H. Furber (Cambridge, Mass.), 1951. See also 'Lord Macartney at Batavia, March 1793', by Alastair Lamb (*Journal of the South Seas Society*, Singapore 1958).

22 Bogle Papers: Extract from General Letter to Bengal 16 April 1777.

23 Indian National Archives: Bengal Public Consultation No. 7 of 19 April 1779.

24 'The Buddhist Monastery at Ghoosery' (*Bengal Past and Present*, vol. XXVI, pt. II). 'Notes on a Buddhist Monastery at Bhot Bagan', G.D. Bysack (*JASB*, vol. LIX, Calcutta 1890).

25 Indian National Archives: General Letter to Court 15 Jan. 1776.

26 Bogle Papers: Hamilton to Hastings 30 May 1776.

27 Bogle Papers: Hamilton to Hastings 22 July 1777.

28 Bogle Papers: Hamilton to Bogle 30 May 1776.

29 Bogle Papers: Tashi Lama to Hastings, received 22 July 1775.

30 Home Miscellaneous, vol. 219, f. 373: Bengal General Consultation of 19 April 1779. *Warren Hastings; Maker of British India*, by A.M. Davies (London 1935), p. 428. *Bengal Past and Present*, vol. XLI, p. 120.

31 Markham, *Narratives*, op. cit., pp. 207-10.

32 *Trade through the Himalayas*, by S. Cammann (Princeton 1951), pp. 76-80; *The Visit of the Teshoo Lama to Peking*, by E. Ludwig (Peking 1904): 'Bogle's Embassy to Tibet', by D.B. Diskalkar (*Indian Historical Quarterly*, vol. ix, 1933); 'The Panchen Lama's Visit to China in 1780', by S. Cammann (*Far Eastern Quarterly*, vol. ix, 1949).

33 *Warren Hastings' Letters to Sir John Macpherson*, ed. H. Dodwell (London 1927), p. 189.

34 Home Miscellaneous, vol. 219, f. 455: Bengal General Consultation of 9 Jan. 1783.

35 Turner, *Embassy*, op. cit., p. 373.

36 Home Miscellaneous, vol. 219, f. 469: Hastings to E. Wheeler 22 April 1784.

37 Turner, *Embassy*, op. cit., pp. 419-33. Home Miscellaneous, vol. 608, f. 33.

38 Home Miscellaneous, vol. 608, f. 33: Bengal Consultation of 26 Jan. 1876.

39 Bengal Despatches, vol. 16, f. 547: General Letter to Bengal 27 March 1787.

40 Indian National Archives: Bengal Public Consultation No. 17 of 13 Jan. 1790 enclosing Lt.-Col. R. Kyd to E. Hay 21 Dec. 1789. *Three Year's Wanderings in the Northern Provinces of China, etc.*, by R. Fortune (London 1847), pp. 197-8. 'The Instructions of the East India Company to Lord Macartney and his reports to the Company, 1792-4', ed. E.H. Pritchard (*JRAS* 1938), pp. 389, 501.

41 *The Chronicles of the East India Company Trading to China*, by H.B. Morse, vol. II (Oxford 1926), p. 162.

42 *The Crucial Years of Early Anglo-Chinese Relations, 1750-1800*, by E.H. Pritchard (Research Studies of the State College of Washington,

IV, Pullman, Washington 1937), p. 239.

43 Morse, *Chronicles*, op. cit., vol. II, p. 155.

44 Morse, *Chronicles*, p. 235.

45 CO/77/79 (a collection of miscellaneous letters relating to the Macartney Mission, preserved in the Public Records Office, London): Macartney to Dundas 25 March 1793.

46 For the somewhat confused history of the two Tibeto-Nepalese Wars, see BM Add. MSS No. 39,871 (Warren Hastings Papers, supp. vol., f. 51): Turner to Hastings 25 November, 1792; Home Miscellaneous (in the India Office Library, London), vol. 608, f. 33; which contains a useful summary of correspondence; Cammann, op. cit., chapters V and VI; *An Account of the Kingdom of Napaul*, by W. Kirkpatrick (London 1811), pp. 339-79; Turner, *Embassy*, op. cit., pp. 437-42; 'The Tibeto-Nepalese War of 1788-93', by D.B. Diskalkar (*Journal of the Bihar and Orissa Research Society*, vol. XIX, Patna, 1933); *An Authentic Account of an Embassy from Great Britain to the Emperor of China*, by Sir G. Staunton, Bart. (2 Vols., London 1797), vol. II, p. 211 et seq.; 'The Dalai Lamas of Lhasa, etc.', by W.W. Rockhill (*T'oung Pao*, vol. XI, 1910), pp. 60-3; 'Histoire de la Conquête du Népal, etc.', by M.C. Imbault-Huart (*JA*, Paris 1878).

47 Home Miscellaneous, vol. 608, f. 33; Bengal Consultation of 6 Jan. 1789 and 9 March 1789. Diskalkar, 'Tibeto-Nepalese War', loc. cit., pp. 367-9.

48 *Cornwallis in Bengal*, by A. Aspinall (Manchester 1931), p. 178.

49 *L'Eglise Jaune*, by R. Bleichsteiner (Paris 1937), p. 110.

50 Aitchison, *Treaties*, op. cit., vol. XIV, p. 56. Attempts were made by the British to revive this treaty in 1834 and 1836; but with no avail.

   Correspondence of Charles, First Marquis Cornwallis, ed. C. Ross (3 vols., London 1859), Vol. II, p. 551. Aitchison, *Treaties*, op. cit., vol. XIV, pp. 48-9. Home Miscellaneous, vol. 608, f. 35; Consultation of 14 Oct. 1792.

51 Kirkpatrick, *Nepaul*, op. cit., pp. 371-9.

52 Ibid., p. 372.

53 Ibid., p. 377.

54 *Some Account of the Public Life and a Selection of the Unpublished Writings of the Earl of Macartney*, by J. Barrow (2 vols., London 1807), vol. II, pp. 203-4.

55 Barrow, op. cit., pp. 228, 267. *The Instructions of the East India Company to Lord Macartney on his Embassy to China and his reports to the Company*, by E.H. Pritchard (JRAS 1938), p. 499.

56 Staunton, *Embassy*, op. cit., vol. II, pp. 229-30.

57 Ibid., vol. II, pp. 227-8.

58 *China Past and Present*, by E.H. Parker (London 1903), pp. 149-50. See also 'Letter from the Emperor of China to King George the Third', by E.H. Parker (*Nineteenth Century*, vol. XV, 1896); 'Nepaul and China', by E.H. Parker (*Imperial and Asiatic Quarterly Review*,

NOTES TO PAGES 22-31

Vol. VII, 1899); Morse, *Chronicles*, op. cit., vol. II, pp. 273-6; *The English in China*, by J.B. Eames (London 1909), pp. 129-30.

59 *China: an outline of its government, laws and policy*, by P. Auber (London 1834), p. 129.

60 BM Add. MSS No. 39,871 (Warren Hastings Papers, supp., vol. I, f. 51); Turner to Hastings 25 Nov. 1792.

II Nepal: 1792–1816

1 Board's Collections, vol. 9, Collection No. 720: Abdul Kadir Khan to Lumsden 6 Jan. 1796.

2 Cammann, op. cit., p. 125.

3 *The Private Records of an Indian Governor-Generalship; the correspondence of Sir John Shore . . . with Henry Dundas, . . . 1795-1796*, ed. H. Furber (Cambridge, Mass., 1935), p. 65.

4 *The Correspondence of David Scott*, ed. C.H. Philips (Royal Historical Society, Camden Third Series, vol. LXXV, London 1951), p. 57: Scott to Duncan 12 Jan. 1796.

5 Bengal Despatches, vol. 31, f. 705: Bengal Political Despatch 4 Oct. 1797.

6 Board's Collections, vol. 9, Collection No. 720: A.K. Khan to Lumsden 6 Jan. 1796 and Lumsden to Shore 22 Jan. 1796.

7 Board's Collections, vol. 9, Collection No. 720: Lumsden to Shore 22 Jan. 1796.

8 Loc. cit.: Political Letter from Bengal 30 June 1796.

9 Loc. cit.: Bengal Political Consultation 7 March 1796.

10 Board's Collections, vol. 162, Collection No. 2,804: Secret Letter from Bengal 31 Aug. 1801; Northey, *Gurkhas*, op. cit., pp. 43-4.

11 Board's Collections, vol. 162, Collection No. 2,804: Knox's instructions dated 31 Oct. 1801.

12 Sanwal, *Nepal*, op. cit., pp. 84-124.

13 *Summary of the Administration of the Indian Government*, etc., by the Marquess of Hastings (Edinburgh 1825), p. 13. Lord Moira, 2nd Earl of Moira in the Irish peerage, was created Marquess of Hastings in 1817, mainly as a result of his victory over the Gurkhas.

14 For the background to the war with Nepal, see: *Papers Relating to Nepaul*, printed for the Court of Proprietors of the East India Company (London 1824); *The Invasion of Nepal. John Company at War*, by J. Pemble Oxford 1971.

15 Markham, *Narratives*, op. cit., pp. clv-clxi and 213-94.

16 Board's Collections, vol. 421, Collection No. 10,366: Bengal Political Letter of 15 June 1813.

17 'Le Cas Moorcroft; un problème de l'exploration Tibétaine', by Robert Fazy (*T'oung Pao*, vol. XXXV, 1940), pp. 155-84. See also *Travels in Tartary, Tibet and China by Huc and Gabet*, trans. W. Hazlitt and ed. P. Pelliot (2 vols., London 1928), vol. II,

pp. 222, 253-5; *Abode of Snow*, by K. Mason (London 1955), pp. 65-7. Rachel Gibb, who has made a study of the life of Moorcroft on the basis of the Moorcroft MSS in the India Office Library, has suggested to me what is almost certainly the answer to the mystery of Moorcroft's death. Moorcroft died in Afghanistan. A number of native agents of his, however, possessed letters from him in his writing, and, very probably, English maps. At least one such agent was a Kashmiri with commercial connections with Lhasa - Mir Izzut Ullah - and someone like him may well have died in Tibet in or about 1835, leaving papers which could give rise to the rumour that he was Moorcroft in disguise.

18 Home Miscellaneous, vol. 646, f. 747. *Papers Relating to Nepaul*, p. 45: Buchanan to Adam 9 Aug. 1914.

19 *Papers Relating to Nepaul*, pp. 84-6: Moorcroft to Adam 14 Sept. 1814.

20 *Papers relating to Nepaul*, p. 556: Secret Letter from Lord Moira 11 May 1815. *Journal of a tour through part of the Himalaya Mountains*, J.B. Fraser (London 1826), p. 526.

21 *Papers relating to Nepaul*, p. 45: Buchanan to Adam 9 Aug. 1814.

22 *Papers relating to Nepaul*, p. 551: Secret Letter from Lord Moira 11 May 1815.

23 *Papers Relating to Nepaul*, p. 268: Memo on Sikkim by Dr. Buchanan and Adam to Scott 2 Nov. 1814. See also *History of Sikkim*, compiled by their Highnesses the Maharaja Sir Thutob Namgyal, K.C.I.E., and Maharani Yeshay Dolma of Sikkim, 1908 (in typescript, copies in the libraries of the India Office and the Royal Central Asian Society, London), p. 76.

24 *Papers Relating to Nepaul*, pp. 258, 266-9, 412.

25 *Papers Relating to Nepaul*, p. 412: Monkton to Latter 6 Dec. 1914.

26 *Papers Relating to Nepaul*, p. 924: Latter to Adam 19 Dec. 1815.

27 Morse, *Chronicles*, op, cit., vol. III, p. 258, quoting Lord Moira to Select Committee at Canton 15 June 1816.

28 *The Private Journals of the Marquess of Hastings*, edited by his daughter, the Marchioness of Bute (2 vols., London 1858), vol. II, p. 146.

29 Home Miscellaneous, vol. 650, f. 72: Scott to Monkton 20 Jan. 1815.

30 Board's Collections, vol. 552, Collection No. 13,383: Scott to Adam 24 Sept. 1816. For an account of Kishen Kant Bose's mission, see *Political Missions to Bootan* (Calcutta 1865).

31 *Papers Relating to Nepaul*, p. 721: Secret Letter from Lord Moira.

32 *A Short History of India and the Frontier States of Afghanistan, Nipal and Burma*, by J. Tallboys Wheeler (London 1889), p. 465.

33 Board's Collections, vol. 552, Collection No. 13,383: Gardner to Adam 19, 27 and 28 Aug. 1816.

34 Loc. cit.; Gardner to Adam 30 Aug. 1816.

35 Board's Collections, vol. 552, Collection No. 13,383: Adam to Gardner 14 Sept. 1816.

36 Loc. cit.: Lord Moira to Lord Amherst 14 Sept. 1816.

37 Loc. cit.: Latter to Adam 3 Sept. 1816 and 30 Oct. 1816; Adam to Latter 9 Nov. 1816.

38 Loc. cit.: Gardner to Adam 7 Oct. 1816 and Adam to Gardner 2 Nov. 1816.
39 *History of the Political and Military Transactions in India during the Administration of the Marquess of Hastings 1813-1823*, by H.T. Prinsep (2 vols, London 1825), vol. I, pp. 209-13. See also Hastings, *Journals*, op. cit., vol. II, pp. 137-9, 145; *The History of British India from 1805 to 1835*, by H.H. Wilson (in continuation of Mill) (3 vols., London 1846), vol. II, pp. 79-80; *China: Commercial, Political and Social*, by R.M. Martin (London 1847), p. 25.
40 Board's Collections, vol. 552, Collection No. 13,383: Scott to Adam 24 Sept. 1816.
41 *Journal of the Proceedings of the Late Embassy to China*, by H. Ellis (London 1817), p. 196.
42 *Papers Relating to Nepaul*, p. 272: Supercargoes to Lord Moira 5 Oct. 1814.
43 Morse, *Chronicles*, op. cit., Vol. III, pp. 258, 279.
44 *Papers Relating to Nepaul*, p. 996: Lord Moira to the Chairman of the East India Company 6 Aug. 1816.
45 Morse, *Chronicles*, op. cit., vol. IV, pp. 18-41.
46 Board's Collections, vol. 843, Collection No. 22,566: Supercargoes to India 26 Dec. 1822.
47 Loc. cit.: Bengal Political Letter 10 Sept. 1824. Despatches to Bengal, vol. 103: Commercial Despatch of 24 Oct. 1826.
48 *Papers Relating to Nepaul*, p. 926: Adam to Latter 13 Jan. 1816; p. 690: Political Letter to Bengal 13 Feb. 1817.
49 Aitchison, *Treaties*, op. cit., vol. XII, p. 58.
50 Prinsep, *Transactions in India*, op. cit., vol. I, p. 86. See also *A Geographical, Statistical and Historical Description of Hindostan and the Adjacent Countries*, by W. Hamilton (2 vols., London 1820), vol. II, p. 86.
51 Hastings, *Journals*, op. cit., vol. II, p. 146.
52 Board's Collections, vol. 552, Collection No. 13,385: Political Letter from Bengal 16 Nov. 1816 and Moorcroft to Adam 22 Sept. 1816.
53 *Papers Relating to Nepaul*, p. 241: Fraser to Adam 20 Oct. 1814.
54 *Papers Relating to Nepaul*, p. 761: Secret Letter from Lord Moira 2 Aug. 1815.
55 Hamilton, *Hindostan*, op. cit., vol. II, p. 655.
56 *Papers Relating to Nepaul*, p. 551: Secret Letter from Lord Moira 11 May 1815.
57 *Papers Relating to Nepaul*, p. 673: Secret Letter from Lord Moira 20 July 1815.
58 For Moorcroft's journey to Gartok, see Asiatic Researches, vol. XII (Calcutta 1816).
59 Board's Collections, vol. 552, Collection No. 13,384.
60 *Simla Past and Present*, by E.J. Buck (Bombay, 1925), p. 6, quotes Capt. Mundy, A.D.C. to Lord Combermere, writing in October 1828.
61 *Summary of the Administration of the Indian Government from October*

1813 to January 1823, by the Marquess of Hastings (London 1824),

III Western Tibet: 1816 – 1861

1 Board's Collections, vol. 552, Collection No. 13,384: Webb to Doyle 7 June 1816. Enclosures to Secret Letters, vol. 89, Enclosure No. 115: Cunningham to Clerk 3 Aug. 1842.
2 *The Great Plateau*, by C.G. Rawling (London 1905), p. 263.
3 *Asiatic Researches*, vol. XII, 1816, p. 449.
4 *Asiatic Researches*, vol. XI, 1810, p. 530.
5 FO 17 1109, Indian Foreign Letter No. 123 of 16 Aug. 1889. FO 17 1398, IO to FO 3 Jan. 1899. FO 17 13 445, IO to FO 22 Aug. 1900. FO 17 1447, IO to FO 3 Oct. 1900.
6 *Ladak, Physical, Statistical and Historical*, by Alexander Cunningham (London 1854), pp. 244, 248.
7 *Asiatic Researches*, vol. XII, 1816, p. 451.
8 Hamilton, *Hindostan*, op. cit., vol. II, p. 451.
9 Bengal Despatches, vol. 34: Bengal Commercial Despatch of 31 Oct. 1799.
10 *Asiatic Researches*, vol. XII, p. 451.
11 Ibid., p. 374.
12 Punjab States Gazetteer, vol. VIII, No. 2, Bashahr State, p. 8. Enclosures to Secret Letters, vol. 89, No. 38, Enclosure 114: J. Cunningham to Clerk 30 July 1842. *Report on the Trade and Resources of the Countries on the North-Western Boundary of British India*, by R.H. Davies (Lahore 1862), App. XXIV, pp. CCXXI-CCXXII.
13 *Narrative of a Journey from Caunpoor to the Boorendo Pass in the Himalaya Mountains etc. by Major Sir W. Lloyd and Captain Alexander Gerrard's account of an attempt to penetrate by Bekhur to Garoo and the Lake Manasarowara, etc.*, ed. G. Lloyd (2 vols., London 1840), vol. I, p. 174.
14 Davies, *Report*, op. cit., p. 61.
15 'Notes on Moorcroft's Travels in Ladak', by J. D. Cunningham (JASB, vol. XII, 1844), pt. I, p. 210.
16 *Travels in the Himalayan Provinces of Hindustan and the Panjab, etc.*, by W. Moorcroft and G. Trebeck, ed. H. H. Wilson (2 vols., London 1841), vol. I, p. 420. *A History of the Sikhs from the origin of the Nation to the Battles on the Sutlej*, by J.D. Cunningham, ed. H.L.O. Garrett (London 1918), p. 331.
17 Cunningham, *Ladak*, op. cit., pp. 10-12. *Travels in Kashmir and the Panjab*, by Baron Charles Hügel (London 1845), pp. 101-2. *Travels in Kashmir, Ladak, Iskardo, etc.*, by G.T. Vigne (2 vols., London 1842), Vol. II, pp. 333, 335, 375.
18 Board's Collections, vol. 1643, Collection No. 65,660.
19 Board's Collections, vol. 1642, Collection No. 65,650.
20 Cunningham, *Ladak*, op. cit., p. 331.

21 Bengal Despatches, vol. 68: India Political Despatch 6 Jan. 1815.
22 Moorcroft MSS (in India Office Library). Two letters from Moorcroft at Leh to George Swinton, both dated 17 Dec. 1821. One of these agents, Agha Mehdi, carried a letter of introduction from Count Nesselrode, the Russian Foreign Minister, to Ranjit Singh. See: *Ladakh and Western Himalayan Politics: 1819-1848*, by C.L. Datta (New Delhi 1973), pp. 204-5.
23 Moorcroft, *Travels*, op. cit., vol. I, pp. 358-9.
24 Ibid., vol. I, p. 256.
25 *Account of Koonawur in the Himalaya*, by Capt. A. Gerard, ed. G. Lloyd (London 1841), pp. 104-5. See also Hamilton, *Hindostan*, op. cit., vol. II, p. 662; *Voyage dans l'Inde*, by V. Jacquemont, vol. II (Paris 1841), pp. 276-7; *Travels in Ceylon and Continental India*, by W. Hoffmeister (London 1848), pp. 448-9.
26 Lloyd and Gerard, *Narratives*, op. cit., vol. II, pp. 91, 125, 155-6, 178.
27 Jacquemont, *Voyage*, op. cit., p. 340. See also JASB VIII, pt. II, p. 945.
28 Board's collections, vol. 1181, Collection No. 30,743: Bengal Political Letter of 3 July 1828. Cunningham, *Sikhs*, op. cit., p. 183n.
29 For Csoma de Körös see *The Life and Works of Alexander Csoma de Körös*, by T. Duka (London 1885).
30 Board's Collections, vol. 1639, Collection No. 65,571: Political Letter from India 28 Nov. 1836.
31 *The Founding of the Kashmir State*, by K.M. Pannikar (London 1953), pp. 74 et seq.
32 Ibid., pp. 76-77. *A History of Western Tibet*, by A.H. Francke (London 1907), p. 137.
33 JASB XIII, pt. I, 1844, p. 208.
34 Panikkar, op. cit., p. 80.
35 Enclosures to Secret Letters, vol. 75, No. 31: Clerk to India 25 Mar. 1841.
36 Enclosures to Secret Letters, vol. 79: Agra Letter 20-8-41, Erskine to Hodgson 21 July 1841.
37 JASB XIII, pt. I, 1844, p. 210.
38 Enclosures to Secret Letters, vol. 79, No. 76: Thomson to India 4 Sept. 1841.
39 Enclosures to Secret Letters, vol. 79, No. 76: Clerk to India 4 Sept. 1841.
40 Enclosures to Secret Letters, vol. 81: Agra Letter 21 Nov. 1841, Clerk to India 31 Oct. 1841.
41 Enclosures to Secret Letters, vol. 78, No. 65: Hodgson to India 6 June 1841.
42 *China, During the War and Since the Peace*, by Sir J.F. Davis, Bart. (2 vols., London 1852), vol. I, pp. 151, 315. See also Imbault-Huart, op. cit., pp. 375-6; 'Nepaul and China', by E. H. Parker (*Imperial and Asiatic Quarterly Review*, vol. VII, 1899), p. 80.
43 Enclosures to Secret Letters, vol. 79, No. 76: Clerk to India 4 Sept. 1841.

44 Enclosures to Secret Letters, vol. 79: Agra Letter 20 Aug. 1841, Erskine to Hodgson 21 July 1841.

45 Enclosures to Secret Letters, vol. 80: Agra Letter 21 Sept. 1841, Metcalfe to Thomason 6 Sept. 1841.

46 Enclosures to Secret Letters, vol. 79: Agra Letter 20 Aug. 1841, India to Lushington 17 Aug. 1841.

47 Enclosures to Secret Letters, vol. 80: Agra Letter 21 Sept. 1841, Hodgson to India 6 Sept. 1841.

48 Enclosures to Secret Letters, vol. 80: Agra Letter 21 Sept. 1841, India to Clerk 20 Sept. 1841. Enclosures to Secret Letters, vol. 81: Agra Letter 21 Dec. 1841, Clerk to India 20 Dec. 1841.

49 Enclosures to Secret Letters, vol. 80: Agra Letter 21 Sept. 1841, Clerk to Thomason 2 Sept. 1841.

50 Enclosures to Secret Letters, vol. 89, No. 38: Clerk to India 31 Aug. 1842. Enclosures to Secret Letters, vol. 82: Agra Letter 22 Jan. 1842, Hamilton to India 21 Jan. 1842. Enclosures to Secret Letters, vol. 88, No. 30: Cunningham to Clerk 29 June 1842.

51 Enclosures to Secret Letters, vol. 82, No. 8: Clerk to Cunningham 13 Dec. 1841.

52 Enclosures to Secret Letters, vol. 90: Secret Dept. Confidential News Letter No. 3 of 22 Jan. 1842.

53 Enclosures to Secret Letters, vol. 90, No. 52: Cunningham to Clerk 24 Sept. 1842.

54 Enclosures to Secret Letters, vol. 92, No. 31: Erskine to Clerk 1 April 1843.

55 Panikkar, op. cit., pp. 84-9.

56 FO 17 1109, Indian Foreign Letter No. 123 of 16 Aug. 1889.

57 FO 17 1445, Indian Foreign Letter of 2 Aug. 1900 in IO to FO 22 Aug. 1900.

58 Enclosures to Secret Letters, vol. 89, No. 38: Cunningham to Clerk 3 Aug. 1842.

59 Enclosures to Secret Letters, vol. III, No. 48: Erskine to India 19 July 1847.

60 Panikkar, op. cit., p. 90 et seq.

61 Cunningham, *Ladak*, op. cit., p. 12.

62 Enclosures to Secret Letters, vol. 106, No. 33: Henry Lawrence to Vans Agnew and A. Cunningham 23 July 1846.

63 Davies, Report, op. cit., p. 60. See also Cunningham, *Ladak*, op. cit., p. 13; Punjab District Gazetteers, vol. XXX A, Kangra District, pts. II-IV (Lahore 1918), p. 261; *The Himalayan Districts of Kooloo, Lahaul and Spiti*, by Capt. A.F.P. Harcourt (London 1871), p. 132.

64 Enclosures to Secret Letters, vol. III, No. 48: Erskine to India 19 July 1847.

65 Enclosures to Secret Letters, vol. 106, No. 33: H. Lawrence to Vans Agnew 31 July 1846.

66 Secret Letters from Bengal and India, vol. 31, f. 401: Hardinge to Court 14 Aug. 1846.

67 Enclosures to Secret Letters, vol. 106, No. 33: Edwards to

H. Lawrence 4 Aug. 1846.

68 Secret Letters from Bengal and India, vol. 32: Hardinge to Court 28 July 1847.

69 Cunningham, *Ladak*, op. cit., p. 14. Enclosures to Secret Letters, vol. 114, No. 36: Cunningham to Lawrence 29 Aug. 1847.

70 Enclosures to Secret Letters, vol. 114, No. 36: Strachey to Lawrence 26 Jan. 1848.

71 Cunningham, *Ladak*, op. cit., p. 15. Enclosures to Secret Letters, vol. III, No. 48: Erskine to India 19 July 1847.

72 Secret Letters from Bengal and India, vol. 32: Hardinge to Court 28 July 1847.

73 Enclosures to Secret Letters, vol. III, No. 48: India to Lawrence 10 July 1847.

74 Enclosures to Secret Letters, vol. III, No. 48: India to Cunningham 27 July 1847. See also *Western Himalaya and Tibet*, by Dr. T. Thomson (London 1852), p. 116.

75 Secret Letters from Bengal and India, vol. 32: Hardinge to Court 28 July 1847.

76 Enclosures to Secret Letters, vol. 114: Lawrence to Cunningham 16 July 1847.

77 Enclosures to Secret Letters, vol. 114: Sir J. Davis to Hardinge 12 Aug. 1847. See also *Chinese Miscellanies*, by Sir J. Davis (London 1865), pp. 47–8.

78 Board's Collections, vol. 2461, Collection No. 136,806: Dalhousie to Court 31 July 1851.

79 *Histoire Generale de la Chine*, by H. Cordier, vol. IV (Paris 1921), pp. 12–13. *Eminent Chinese of the Ch'ing Period*, ed. A.W. Hummel (2 vols., Washington 1943), vol. I, pp. 126–8. *L'Expulsion de MM. Huc et Gabet du Tibet: documents inédits*, by H. Cordier (Paris 1909).

80 Enclosures to Secret Letters, vol. 114, No. 36: Strachey to Lawrence 25 Sept. 1847.

81 Enclosures to Secret Letters, vol. 114, No. 36: Cunningham to Lawrence 20 Oct. 1847.

82 Punjab Government Records, vol. IV: Lahore Political Diaries 1847–1849, pp. 52, 254–5.

83 *The Physical Geography of Western Tibet*, by Captain H. Strachey (London 1853). See Board's Collections, vol. 2461, for the original MSS of Thomson's and Strachey's books.

84 Secret Letters from Bengal and India, vol. 33: Dalhousie to Court 2 May 1848. Board's Collections, vol. 2461, Collection No. 136,806: Dalhousie to Court 31 July 1851.

85 For example: *The Exploration of Tibet*, by G. Sandberg (Calcutta 1904), pp. 137–8.

86 Panikkar, op. cit., p. 107.

87 JASB, vol. XVII, pt. I, 1848, p. 295.

88 Enclosures to Secret Letters, vol. 114, No. 36: Strachey to Lawrence 26 Jan. 1848 and Sir F. Currie to India 22 March 1848. Secret

Letters from Bengal and India, vol. 33: Dalhousie to Court 2 May 1848.

89 Markham, *Narratives*, op. cit., p. 125.

90 *Essays on the Languages, Literature and Religion of Nepal and Tibet*, by B.H. Hodgson (London 1874), p. 94.

91 *Report on Bootan*, by R.B. Pemberton (Calcutta 1838), p. 172.

92 Board's Collections, vol. 2497, Collection No. 141m513: Minute by Lord Dalhousie 16 Feb. 1852.

93 *Imperial Gazetteer of India* (Oxford 1908), vol. VII, pp. 94-5.

94 Enclosures to Secret Letters, vol. 82, No. 8: Cunningham to Clerk 13 Nov. 1841.

95 India and Bengal Despatches, vol. 81, f. 169: India Foreign Letter No. 74 of 7 Dec. 1852. Accounts and Papers 1857, Session I, XI: Minutes and correspondence relating to the Hindustan-Tibet road, f. 275. Report on the Hindustan-Tibet Road by D. Briggs, 19 Dec. 1855.

96 India and Bengal Despatches, vol. 113: Public Works Dept. No. 21 of 29 June 1858.

97 Punjab States Gazetteers, VII, No. 2, p. 63n and App. I, p. vii.

98 Davies, *Report*, op. cit., App. A, p. 12.

99 Davies, *Report*, pp. 60-61.

100 Ibid., App. B, p. 21.

101 Ibid., p. 78.

102 Ibid., App. C, p. 33. *Journal of a Tour through Spiti to the Frontier of Chinese Thibet*, by P.H. Egerton (London 1864), p. 65. *Travels in Ladak, Tartary and Kashmir*, by Lt.-Col. H.D. Torrens (London 1862), App. III, pp. 364-7.

103 Egerton, op. cit., p. 44.

104 Ibid., p. 45.

105 Ibid., p. 67.

106 Ibid., p. 66.

107 Accounts and Papers 1867-68, L, f. 705: Correspondence . . . relating to the appointment of a Commercial Agent in Ladakh, and to his proceedings there.

108 Accounts and Papers 1871, LI, f. 619: Correspondence Relating to the Mission of Mr. Douglas Forsyth to Yarkand.

109 Report on the External Land Trade of the Punjab 1881-82 (Lahore 1882): Punjab to India Financial No. 1814 of 21 July 1882.

110 Report on the External Land Trade of the Punjab 1882-83. p. 2.

111 See pp. 198-201 below. For two accounts of the relations between Ladakh and Tibet, both somewhat coloured by considerations arising from the Sino-Indian boundary dispute of the 1950s and early 1960s, see: 'Tibet and Ladakh: A History', by Z. Ahmad, in *St. Antony's Papers No. 14. Far Eastern Affairs Number Three* (London 1963); *Himalayan Battleground. Sino-Indian Rivalry in Ladakh*, by M.W. Fisher, L.E. Rose and R.A. Huttenback (London 1963). A major study of the trade and foreign relations of Kashmir (including Ladakh), but

with its main emphasis on the period after 1860, is *British India's Northern Frontier 1865-1895*, by G.J. Alder (London 1963).

IV   The Opening of Sikkim: 1817 – 1861

1 *History of Sikkim*, op. cit., p. 84. *Darjeeling, Past and Present*, by E. C. Dozey (Darjeeling 1917), p. 2. *Dorjé-ling*, by H. V. Bayley (Calcutta 1838), pp. 3, 40-3, and App. AA. 'Particulars of a Visit to the Siccim Hills', by J. D. Herbert, *Gleanings in Science* (Calcutta 1830), p. 91.
2 *History of Sikkim*, op. cit., p. 87. Bayley, *Dorjé-ling*, op. cit., App. AA and p. 4. Board's Collections, vol. 1728, Collection No. 69,861. Board's Collections, vol. 1612, Collection No. 64,812: Fort William Political Consultation 23 Jan. 1835, India Political Letter 15 Feb. 1836. See also: *India and Sikkim (1814-1970)*, by P. R. Rao (New Delhi 1972).
3 India and Bengal Despatches, vol. 5, f. 655: Political Letter to India No. 31 of 22 July 1835. Board's Collections, vol. 1612, Collection No. 64,812.
4 Dozey, *Darjeeling*, op. cit., pp. 3-6.
5 Bayley, *Dorjé-ling*, op. cit., App. B and p. 53.
6 *History of Sikkim*, op. cit., pp. 90-2.
7 *Journals kept in Hyderabad, Cashmir, Sikkim and Nepal*, by Sir R. Temple (2 vols., London 1887), vol. I, p. 168.
8 *History of Sikkim*, op. cit., pp. 95-6.
9 Dozey, *Darjeeling*, op. cit., p. 3.
10 'Journal of a Trip to Sikkim in December 1848', by Dr. A. Campbell (JASB, XVIII, pt. I, 1849, p. 483).
11 JASB, XVIII, pt. I, 1849, p. 502. *Himalayan Journals*, by Dr. J. Hooker (2 vols., London 1855), vol. I, p. 107. *Report on a Visit to Sikkim and the Thibetan Frontier in October, November, December 1873*, by J.W. Edgar (Calcutta 1874), p. 9.
12 Hooker, op. cit., vol. I, p. 274.
13 JASB, XVIII, pt. I, 1849 pp. 482, 484, 509-10, 525. Hooker, op. cit. vol. II, p. 29.
14 Board's Collections, vol. 2484, Collection No. 139,963: Campbell's Diary, 25 Sept. 1849.
15 For the second journey to Sikkim of Hooker and Campbell in 1849 see Hooker, op. cit., vol. II. Board's Collections, vol. 2484, Collection No. 139,963: Campbell's Diary.
16 Aitchison, *Treaties*, op. cit., vol. XII, p. 52. *Frontier and Overseas Expeditions*, op. cit., p. 45. *Bhotan and the Douar Way*, by Surgeon Rennie (London 1866), p. 10.
17 India and Bengal Despatches, vol. 71: Political and Military Committee to India No. 28 of 30 July 1851.
18 Board's Collections, vol. 2415, Collection No. 130,437: Offg. Supt. Darjeeling to India 21 Nov. and 23 Nov. 1849.

19 Board's Collections, vol. 2415, Collection No. 130,438: Resident in Nepal to India 11 Dec. 1849.
20 Hooker, op. cit., vol. II, p. 212.
21 Ibid., vol. II, pp. 247-8.
22 *History of Sikkim*, op. cit., p. 96.
23 *Frontier and Overseas Expeditions*, op. cit., p. 45.
24 Ibid., p. 47. See also *Sikkim, with Hints on Mountain and Jungle Warfare*, by J. G. Gawler (London 1873).
25 Accounts and Papers 1862, XL, East India (Sikkim Expedition),p.519: India to Eden 28 Dec. 1860.
26 Aitchison, *Treaties*, op. cit., vol. XII, pp. 61-6.
27 Accounts and Papers, Sikkim Expedition, op. cit., pp. 558-69: Eden to Bengal 29 March and 8 April 1861.
28 Accounts and Papers 1865, XXXIX: Papers Relating to Bhutan, p. 139.
29 Board's Collections, vol. 1706, Collection No. 68,907: Jenkins to India 7 April 1837.
30 Loc. cit.: India to Jenkins 24 April 1837.
31 Loc. cit. Collection No. 68,908: Auckland to the Dalai Lama 7 Aug. 1837.
32 Loc. cit.: Jenkins to Macnaghten 23 May 1837.
33 Board's Collections, vol. 1706, Collection No. 68,908: Macnaghten to Pemberton 7 Aug. 1837.
34 Enclosures to Secret Letters, vol. 114, No. 36: Jenkins to India 19 Aug. 1847.
35 The history of the relations between the Assam Himalayan hill tribes and the British has been related in *History of the Relations of the Government with the Hill Tribes of the North-East Frontier of Bengal*, by A. Mackenzie (Calcutta 1884), continued in *History of the Frontier Areas Bordering on Assam from 1883-1941*, by Sir R. Reid (Shillong 1942).
36 *The McMahon Line*, by Alastair Lamb, 2 vols (London 1966), vol. 2, pp. 292-323.
37 Letters from India, vol. 48, ff. 1289, 1377.
38 *Tibet the Mysterious*, by Sir T. Holdich (London 1908), pp. 333-4.
39 *Letters and Journals of James, Eighth Earl of Elgin*, ed. T. Walrond (London 1872), pp. 455-9.
40 Elgin Papers in the India Office Library, London (Eur. MSS F/83): Beadon to Elgin 7 Aug. 1862.
41 For the history of Bhutan, see *Sikkim and Bhutan*, by J.C. White (London 1909). *Lands of the Thunderbolt*, by Lord Ronaldshay (London 1923). Pemberton, *Bootan*, op. cit. *Political Missions to Bootan* (Calcutta 1865). 'La Guerre du Bhotan', by H. Blerzy (*Revue de Deux Mondes*, Paris 1866). Rennie, *Bhotan*, op.cit. *Bhotan, the Unknown Indian State*, by G. Sandberg (Calcutta 1897). Accounts and Papers 1865, XXXIX: Papers Relating to Bhutan. Accounts and Papers 1866, LII: Further Papers Relating to Bhutan. *The Annexation of Assam*, by R. M. Lahiri (Calcutta 1954). *British Relations with*

Bhutan, by S. Gupta (Jaipur 1974). *Bhutan and India. A Study in Frontier Political Relations (1772-1865)*, by A. Deb (Calcutta 1976).

V The Sikkim Route: 1861 – 1874

1 *Notes on the Services of B. H. Hodgson, Esq.*, collected by a friend (for private circulation, no date), p. 48.
2 *Report on Darjeeling*, by W. B. Jackson (Selections from the Records of the Bengal Government, No. XVII, vol. IV, Calcutta 1854), App. I, p. ii.
3 Jackson, *Report*, op. cit., p. 25.
4 *Calcutta Review*, vol. LV, 1857, p. 29.
5 Bengal District Gazetteers: *Darjeeling*, by L. S. S. O'Malley (Calcutta 1907), p. 28.
6 *China Opened*, by C. Gützlaff (2 vols., London 1838), vol. I, pp. 279, 284.
7 *A Handbook of Darjeeling*, by J. A. Hathorn (Calcutta 1863), p. 95. Hoffmeister, *Travels*, op. cit., p. 473.
8 *The Phoenix II* (London 1871), p. 170. *History of the Expansion of Christianity*, K. S. Latourette, vol. VI (London 1945), p. 129.
9 Latourette, *Christianity*, op. cit., vol. VI, p. 265. *L'Expulsion de MM. Huc et Gabet du Thibet*, by H. Cordier (Paris 1909). *Le Thibet d'après la correspondence des Missionnaires*, by C. H. Desgodins (Paris 1885). *Histoire de la Mission du Thibet*, by A. Launay (2 vols., Lille and Paris 1904).
10 FO 228 299, India to Peking 21 May 1861, enclosing Smyth to Bowring 13 and 14 May, 1 and 7 Aug. 1860; Col. Baker to Dr. N Shaw 30 Nov. 1860.
11 Loc. cit., Aitchison to Smyth 9 April 1861.
12 FO 228 299, India to Peking 21 May, 21 June and 29 June 1861.
13 FO 228 301, Bruce to Blakiston 13 Nov. 1861. FO 228 299, Bruce to India 13 July 1861. *Five Months on the Yang-Tsze*, by T. W. Blakiston (London 1862), p. 302.
14 FO 228 299, Bruce to India 13 July 1861.
15 FO 228 299, India to Peking 21 May 1861, enclosing Ramsay to India 13 May 1861.
16 FO 228 341, India to Peking 18 Dec. 1863.
17 *Travels of a Consular Official in Eastern Tibet*, by Sir E. Teichman (Cambridge 1922), p. 5.
18 *Essays on the External Policy of India*, by J. W. S. Wyllie, ed. W. W. Hunter, (London 1875), pp. 192-3.
19 *Sketches from Nipal*, by H. A. Oldfield (2 vols., London 1880), vol. II, pp. 1-18. Northey, *Gurkhas*, op. cit., pp. 74-5. *History of Nepal*, by D. Wright (Cambridge 1877), p. 61. *Summary of Affairs of Government of India in the Foreign Department for 1864 to 1868*, by

G. J. Tallboys Wheeler (Calcutta 1868), pp. 217-18. FO 228 443, India to Peking 27 Aug. 1867. Secret Letters from India, vol. 7: Lawrence to India 10 Sept. 1870.

20 FO 228 443, India to Peking 27 Aug. 1867. FO 17 543, India Foreign Letter No. 91 of 17 March 1869 in IO to FO 8 May 1869. Launay, *Mission du Thibet* op. cit., vol. II, p. 53. Collections to India Political Despatches, vol. III, No. 37: Agnew to Bengal 22 Sept. 1869. FO 228 461, India to Peking 22 April 1868.

21 FO 228 443, India to Peking 27 Aug. 1867.

22 *Travels of a Pioneer of Commerce*, by T. T. Cooper (London 1871). *The Mishmee Hills*, by T. T. Cooper (London 1873).

23 Cooper, *Travels*, op. cit., p. 252.

24 FO 17 630, Wade No. 116 of 17 June 1872.

25 FO 17 531, Fraser to Alcock 17 March 1869.

26 FO 17 531, Fraser to Alcock 17 March 1869.

27 FO 17 519, Alcock No. 35 of 9 Feb. 1869.

28 Political Despatches to India, vol. 10: Despatch No. 20 of 7 Feb. 1867.

29 *Journal of an Overland Journey from China towards India*, by T. T. Cooper (Calcutta 1869). Report of Mr. T. T. Cooper's Journey from Sudiya through the Mishmee Country towards Bathang in Eastern Tibet, in Collections to Despatches, vol. III. Collections to Despatches, vol. 99, No. 161.

30 Collections to Despatches, vol. 80, No. 4: Capt. T. Lamb to Agent, N.E. Frontier 23 Feb. 1865.

31 FO 17 568, Haughton to Bengal 23 Oct. 1869 in IO to FO 26 Nov. 1870.

32 Collections to Despatches, vol. III, No. 33: Eden to India 15 Nov. 1869.

33 Collections to Despatches, vol. 117 No. 48: Eden to India 19 Jan. 1870.

34 Loc. cit.: India to Bengal 10 March 1870.

35 Political Despatches to India, vol. 13: India Political Despatches Nos. 33 of 24 March 1870 and 48 of 5 May 1870.

36 FO 17 568, IO to FO 26 Nov. 1870.

37 FO 228 497, Haughton to Bengal 22 July 1870 in India to Peking 20 Sept. 1870.

38 FO 228 497, India to Peking 20 Sept. 1870.

39 FO 17 553, Wade No. 152 of 18 Nov. 1870. FO 228 497, Wade to India 10 Nov. 1870.

40 FO 17 603, Haughton to Bengal 21 April 1871 in IO to FO 30 Nov. 1871.

41 Bengal Administration Report 1871-72 (Calcutta 1872), pt. II, p. 12. FO 228 517, Bengal to India 24 Nov. 1871 in India to Peking 7 May 1872. FO 228 507, India to Peking 21 Oct. 1871.

42 FO 228 517, Bengal to India 24 Nov. 1871 in India to Peking 6 July 1872.

43 Collections to Despatches, vol. 135, No. 101: Wade to Viceroy

17 June 1872.

44 FO 17 631, Wade No. 139 of 17 Aug. 1872.

45 Political Despatches to India, vol. 14: Political Despatches Nos. 147 of 6 Dec. 1871 and 47 of 27 April 1871. Political Despatches from India, vol. 13: Political Despatches Nos. 136 of 30 Nov. 1870 and 149 of 28 Dec. 1870.

46 Journal of the Society of Arts, vol. XXI, 1873, p. 433.

47 'Account of a visit . . . to Independent Sikkim', by W. T. Blanford (*JASB*, vol. XL, pt. II, pp. 367-415).

48 FO 17 603, Haughton to Bengal 21 April 1871 in IO to FO 30 Nov. 1871.

49 Secret Letters from India, vol. 7, f. 659: Lawrence to India 10 Sept. 1870. FO 17 602, Indian Foreign Letter No. III of 7 July 1871 in IO to FO 24 Aug. 1871. Secret Letters from India, vol. 15: Indian Foreign Letter No. 77 of 2 June 1873. Secret Letters from India, vol. 16: Indian Foreign Letter No. 170 of 2 Oct. 1873. FO 228 527, India to Peking 20 May 1873. Secret Letters from India, vol. 18: Resident in Nepal to India 18 May 1874, with minute by O. T. Burne. FO 228 545, Lyall to Wade 20 May 1874.

50 Bengal Administration Report 1872-73 (Calcutta 1873), pt. II, pp. 46-7. FO 17 692, Bengal to India 23 June 1873 in IO to FO 31 March 1874.

51 FO 228 527, Bengal to India 17 June 1873 in India to Peking 19 Sept. 1873.

52 FO 17 692, Edgar to Bengal 13 Aug. 1873 in IO to FO 31 March 1874.

53 FO 17 692, Edgar to India 16 Aug. 1873 in IO to FO 31 March 1874.

54 Edgar, *Report*, op. cit., p. 21 et seq.

55 Edgar, *Report*, op. cit., pp. 85-91. *A Statistical Account of Bengal*, by W. W. Hunter, vol. X (London 1876), pp. 158-63.

56 FO 17 671, To Wade No. 32 of 8 April 1874.

57 FO 17 674, Wade No. 144 of 14 July 1874.

58 FO 228 544, Wade to India 26 July 1874.

59 FO 17 674, Wade No. 144 of 14 July 1874.

VI   The Chefoo Convention and the Macaulay Mission: 1876 – 1886

1 FO 17 670, IO to FO 17 Oct. 1873.

2 'China via Tibet', by D. C. Boulger (*JRAS* (NS), vol. x, 1878), p. 113.

3 See p. 67 above.

4 'India, China and Tibet', by E. V. G. Kiernan (*Journal of the Greater India Society*, vol. XIV, No. 2, 1955), pp. 117-42. *The International Relations of the Chinese Empire*, by H. B. Morse, vol. II (London 1918), p. 283. *The Margary Affair and the Chefoo Convention*, by S. T. Wang (Oxford 1940). Accounts and Papers, 1876, LXXXII, 393:

Correspondence on the attack on the expedition to Western China and the murder of Mr. Margary. Accounts and Papers 1876, LXXXVIII, 171: Further correspondence. Accounts and Papers, 1876, LVI, 647: Papers on the development of Trade between British Burmah and Western China, and on the Mission to Yunnan of 1874-75. Accounts and Papers 1880, LXXVIII, 279: Correspondence on the Chefoo Agreement of 1876. Accounts and Papers 1882, LXXX, 147: Further Correspondence. FO 17 726, Wade No. 185 of 25 Aug. 1876.

5 FO 17 728, Wade separate and confidential of 23 Nov. 1876.
6 Home Correspondence India, vol. 20, f. 171: Wade to Lord Derby 14 July 1877.
7 FO 17 822, Question by Sir C. Dilke 15 Feb. 1879.
8 FO 17 809, Wade No. 29 of 10 July 1879. FO 17 810, Wade No. 56 of 9 Aug. 1879.
9 Home Correspondence India, vol. 23, f. 283.
10 *China and her Neighbours*, by R. S. Gundry (London 1893), p. 128.
11 FO 17 782, Fraser No. 129 of 7 Aug. 1878.
12 FO 228 608, Baber to Fraser 4 Jan. 1878.
13 FO 17 756, Fraser No. 142 of 16 July 1877.
14 FO 228 576, India to Peking 25 July 1876. FO 17 772, IO to FO 8 Oct. 1877. FO 17 809, Millbank to FO 24 March 1879. FO 17 829, Wade No. 10 of 16 Jan. 1880.
15 FO 17 782, Fraser No. 166 of 17 Sept. 1878 and No. 172 of 30 Sept. 1878. FO 17 783, Fraser No. 184 of 12 Oct. 1878 and Separate of 17 Oct. 1878; IO to FO 17 May 1879.
16 FO 17 783, Fraser to Viceroy 7 Dec. 1878 in IO to FO 17 May 1879.
17 Accounts and Papers 1878-79, LXXII: Report of Mr. Baber on his Journey to Ta-chien-lu. Accounts and Papers 1884-85, LXXX: Report by Mr. Hosie on a Journey through Central Ssu-Ch'uan. *Travels and Researches in Western China*, by E. C. Baber (RGS Supp. Papers, vol. I, London 1886). *Three Years in Western China*, by A. Hosie, 2nd Ed. (London 1897). FO 228 666, India to Peking 6 Feb. 1880. FO 228 627, Baber to Wade 4 March 1879. FO 228 698, Hosie to Grosvenor 6 Dec. 1882.
18 Report on the External Trade of Bengal with Nepal, Sikkim and Bhutan 1882-83 (Calcutta 1883). O'Malley, *Darjeeling*, op. cit., p. 30.
19 Aitchison, *Treaties*, op. cit., vol. XII, p. 54. *Gazetteer of Sikkim*, ed. H. H. Riseley (Calcutta 1894), p. vi.
20 *Report on a Mission to Sikkim and the Tibetan Frontier*, by Colman Macaulay (Bengal Secretariat Press, Calcutta 1885), p. 73. *Narrative of a Journey to Lhasa in 1881-82*, by S. C. Das (Bengal Secretariat Press, Calcutta 1885), pp. 78-84. See also *Journey to Lhasa*, by S. C. Das, ed. W. W. Rockhill (London 1904).
21 *Portrait of the Dalai Lama*, by Sir C. Bell (London 1946), p. 46. Rockhill, *Dalai Lamas*, op. cit., p. 71.

22 FO 17 968, IO to FO 11 Jan. 1884. *The Times*, 14 Nov. 1883. FO 17 923, Grosvenor No. 102 of 3 July 1883. Bell, *Dalai LKama*, op. cit., p. 254. FO 17 948, Parkes No. 15 of 21 Jan. 1884. FO 228 772, Parkes to Viceroy 14 Jan. 1884. FO 17 985, O'Conor No. 442 of 29 Oct. 1885. FO 17 986, O'Conor to Viceroy 24 Nov. 1885. FO 17 972, IO to FO 12 Nov. 1884. Li, *Tibet*, op. cit., p. 64.
23 FO 17 971, IO to FO 19 July 1884.
24 Letters from India, vol. 44, f. 827: Indian Foreign Letter No. 101 of 19 June 1885.
25 Riseley, *Sikkim Gazetteer*, op. cit., p. viii. Macaulay, *Report*, op. cit., p. 74.
26 Macaulay, *Report*, op. cit., p. 10.
27 Macaulay, *Report*, pp. 43-7.
28 Ibid., pp. 57-74.
29 Macaulay, *Report*, pp. 83-104.
30 FO 17 1002, IO to FO 23 July 1885.
31 Home Correspondence India, vol. 69: Dufferin to Kimberley 14 Jan. 1885.
32 Home Correspondence India, vol. 71: Parkes to Granville 24 Jan. 1885.
33 Macaulay, *Report*, op. cit., p. 59. FO 17 1002, IO to FO 23 July 1885.
34 Home Correspondence India, vol. 75: O'Conor to Dufferin 2 May 1885.
35 Home Correspondence India, vol. 76: IO memo to Indian Foreign Trade 1 Dec. 1884.
36 *The Times*, 24 Nov., 1, 2, 29 Dec. 1884.
37 FO 17 972, Burne to Godley 3 Dec. 1884.
38 *The Times*, 12 Dec. 1884.
39 FO 17 1002, Dewsbury C. of C. to FO 19 May 1885.
40 Home Correspondence India, vol. 76: Manchester C. of C. to IO 14 July 1885.
41 FO 17 1002, Birmingham C. of C. to FO 14 July 1885.
42 FO 17 1002, Memo by C. Macaulay 16 July 1885.
43 FO 17 1002, IO to FO 23 and 31 July 1885.
44 Home Correspondence India, vol. 75: Minute by Sir Owen Burne 22 July 1885.
45 FO 17 983, O'Conor No. 379 of 11 Aug. 1885.
46 Home Correspondence India, vol. 75: Memo by W. G. Pedder 10 July 1885.
47 Home Correspondence India, vol. 77: Macaulay to Burne 21 Aug. 1885.
48 Home Correspondence India, vol. 76: Macartney to Burne 17 Aug. 1885. Home Correspondence India, vol. 75: Memo on an interview between Macartney and Burne 20 July 1885. *Life of Sir Halliday Macartney*, by D. C. Boulger (New York 1908), p. 242.
49 FO 228 813, Durand to O'Conor 24 Aug. 1885.

50 Home Correspondence India, vol. 79: Macaulay to Burne 13 Oct. 1885.
51 FO 17 984, O'Conor No. 423 of 10 Oct. 1885.
52 FO 17 985, O'Conor No. 433 of 17 Oct. 1885.
53 FO 228 813, O'Connor to Viceroy 17 Oct. 1885.
54 FO 17 985, O'Conor No. 443 of 29 Oct. 1885.
55 FO 17 986, O'Conor No. 455 of 16 Nov. 1885.
56 FO 17 986, O'Conor to Viceroy 30 Nov. 1885.
57 *The Englishman in China during the Victorian Era*, by A. Michie (2 vols., London 1900), vol. II, pp. 309-10. *Indian Pandits in the Land of Snow*, by S. C. Das, ed. N. C. Das (Calcutta 1893), pp. vii-viii.
58 Gundry, *China*, op. cit., p. 342. FO 17 1062, O'Conor No. 164 of 16 May 1886.
59 FO 228 840, O'Conor to Viceroy 12 Feb. 1886.
60 FO 17 1061, O'Conor No. 67 of 28 Feb. 1886.
61 FO 17 1061, O'Conor to Viceroy 27 Feb. 1886.
62 FO 17 1062, Tel. Viceroy to Sec. of State 2 March 1886.
63 FO 17 1062, IO to FO 24 April 1886.
64 FO 17 1062, IO to FO 26 May 1886.
65 FO 17 1062, O'Conor No. 154 of 11 May 1886.
66 FO 17 1063, O'Conor No. 177 of 30 May 1886.
67 FO 17 1063, O'Conor No. 184 of 1 June 1886.
68 FO 17 1021, Tel. to O'Conor No. 27 of 28 May 1886 with minute by Sir P. Currie.
69 FO 17 1063, O'Conor No. 178 of 31 May 1886.
70 FO 17 1063, Tel. Viceroy to Sec. of State 1 June 1886.
71 FO 17 1063, Tel. O'Conor No. 28 of 4 June 1886.
72 FO 17 1063, O'Conor No. 189 of 5 June 1886.
73 FO 17 1063, O'Conor No. 195 of 9 June 1886.
74 FO 17 1063, Tel. Sir J. Walsham of 16 June 1886.
75 FO 17 1064, Sir J. Walsham No. 214 of 12 July 1886.
76 FO 17 1021, Sir J. Walsham Tel. No. 40 of 8 July 1886.
77 FO 17 1064, Secret IO memo on Chinese claims to Suzerainty over Burmah 31 July 1886.
78 FO 17 1053, Halifax C. of C. to FO 8 Jan. 1887; Huddersfield C. of C. to FO 10 Jan. 1887; London C. of C. to FO 20 Jan. 1887. FO 17 1038, Manchester C. of C. to FO 30 Dec. 1886.
79 FO 228 856, India to Peking 3 Feb. 1887.
80 FO 228, India to Peking 3 Feb. 1887.
81 *China, Tibet, Assam*, by F. M. Bailey (London 1945), p. 11.
82 *The Gates of Thibet*, by J. A. H. Louis, 2nd Ed. (Calcutta 1894), p. 83. Das, *Indian Pandits*, op. cit., App. 1
83 FO 17 1021, Tel. to O'Conor No. 27 of 28 May 1886 with minute by Sir P. Currie. Boulger, *Macartney*, op. cit., p. 425.
84 Home Correspondence India, vol. 79: Macaulay to Burne 3 Nov. 1885.
85 *The Life of the Marquess of Dufferin and Ava*, by Sir A. Lyall (2 vols.,

London 1905), vol. II, pp. 132-6. *The Marquess of Dufferin and Ava,* by C. E. D. Black (London 1903), p. 261.

86 FO 17 983, O'Conor No. 357 of 18 July 1885. *Hart and the Chinese Customs,* by S. F. Wright (Belfast 1950), pp. 558-617.

87 *British Diplomacy in China: 1880-1885,* by E. V. G. Kiernan (Cambridge 1939), p. 300. *History of British India,* by P. E. Roberts (Oxford 1952), pp. 481-2. *The Trade and Administration of China,* by H. B. Morse (London 1921), p. 368. *Treaties Between Great Britain and China,* by G. E. P. Hertslet (2 vols., London 1908), vol. I, pp. 85-7. FO 17 983, O'Conor No. 379 of 11 Aug. 1885. FO 17 1062 generally. Home Correspondence India, vol. 75, f. 735; Memo by W. G. Pedder 10 July 1885.

For the work of Ney Elias, see: *Ney Elias. Explorer and Envoy Extraordinary in High Asia,* by Gerald Morgan (London 1971); *Anglo-Russian Rivalry in Central Asia 1810-1895,* by Gerald Morgan (London 1981); Alder, op. cit.

VII   The Sikkim-Tibet Convention and the Trade Regulations:
1886 – 1893

1 FO 17 1055, D. M. Wallace 16 May 1887, enclosing report on Tibet by N. Elias 5 May 1887.

2 Letters from India, vol. 48: Indian Foreign Letter No. 180 of 11 Oct. 1886.

3 Letters from India, vol. 48: Indian Foreign Letter No. 180 of 11 Oct. 1886.

4 Letters from India, vol. 48: Indian Foreign Letter No. 180 of 11 Oct. 1886 with IO minutes attached.

5 *History of Sikkim,* op. cit., p. 101.

6 *Sikhim and Bhutan,* by J. C. White (London 1909), p. 24. Riseley, *Sikkim Gazetteer,* op. cit., p. 126 et seq.

7 FO 17 984, O'Conor No. 447 of 2 Nov. 1885. FO 17 1020, Walsham No. 295 of 29 Oct. 1886 and No. 303 of 15 Nov. 1886. FO 17 1014, IO to FO 2 Jan. 1886 and O'Conor No. 18 of 21 Jan. 1886. FO 17 1099, Walsham No. 11 of 7 Aug. 1890.

8 Riseley, *Sikkim Gazetteer,* op. cit., p. 126.

9 For the history of Sir Ugyen Wangchuk, see White, *Sikkim and Bhutan,* op. cit.; Ronaldshay, *Lands of the Thunderbolt,* op. cit.; 'Travels in Bhutan', by Lt.-Col. F. M. Bailey (*JCAS,* XVII, 1930).

10 FO 228 856, India to Peking 9 June 1887.

11 FO 17 1054, Indian Foreign Letter No. 180 of 11 Oct. 1886 and Indian Foreign Letter No. 15 of 1 Feb. 1887.

12 FO 228 856, India to Peking 20 Jan. 1887.

13 FO 17 1056, Indian Foreign Letters No. 73 of 3 June 1887 and No. 111 of 22 July 1887.

14 FO 17 1054, Leeds C. of C. to FO 22 March 1887; Manchester C. of

C. to FO 1 April 1887; Questions by Gerald Balfour 7 March 1887 and R. Lethbridge 2 May 1887.

15 Riseley, *Sikkim Gazetteer*, op. cit. pp. XV-XVI.

16 FO 17 1043, Dufferin to Walsham 7 Oct. 1887.

17 FO 17 1043, Walsham No. 77 of 12 Nov. 1887.

18 FO 17 1043, Walsham to Yamen 12 Oct. 1887 and Yamen to Walsham 17 Oct. 1887; Tel. Walsham to Dufferin 22 Oct. 1887.

19 FO 17 1043, Tel. Walsham to Dufferin 17 Oct. 1887.

20 FO 17 1043, Walsham No. 77 of 12 Nov. 1887.

21 FO 17 1043, Yamen to Walsham 17 Oct. 1887.

22 FO 17 1043, Tel. Dufferin to Walsham 29 Oct. 1887.

23 FO 17 1044, Walsham to FO 19 Dec. 1887.

24 FO 17 1108, Indian Foreign Letter No. 22 of 7 Feb. 1888.

25 FO 17 1108, Minute by Sir P. Currie on call by Sir H. Macartney 28 Feb. 1888. Tel. Walsham to FO 12 March 1888.

26 FO 17 1108, Tel. Walsham to FO 12 March 1888.

27 FO 17 1108, Memo by Sir H. Macartney 12 March 1888.

28 FO 17 1108, IO to FO 14 March 1888; Tel. Walsham to FO 15 March 1888.

29 FO 17 1056, E. Goschen to Sir P. Currie 8 Dec. 1887.

30 'Wei Yuan on the Mongols', by E. H. Parker (*JNCBRAS* NS, XXII, 1887), p. 101.

31 *The Chinese Government*, by W. F. Mayers (Shanghai 1878) p. 112.

32 *Histoire de l'Extrême Orient*, by R. Grousset (2 vols., Paris 1929) vol. II, p. 541.

33 Mayers, *Chinese Government*, op. cit., p. 102.

34 Kiernan, *British Diplomacy*, op. cit., pp. 38-57.

35 Bell, *Dalai Lama*, op. cit., p. 377. Wright, *Hart*, op. cit., p. 618. *Diary of a Journey across Tibet*, by Captain H. Bower (London 1894), p. 224.

36 FO 228 847, Walsham to Dufferin 20 March 1887.

37 FO 228 850, Bourne to Walsham 10 Feb. 1887.

38 FO 17 1108, Indian Foreign Letter No. 128 of 21 July 1888.

39 FO 17 1108, IO to FO 7 March 1888.

40 FO 17 1108, Tel. Viceroy to Sec. of State 23 March 1888.

41 FO 17 1108, Indian Foreign Letter No. 128 of 21 July 1888.

42 *The 2nd Battalion Derbyshire Regiment in the Sikkim Expedition of 1888*, by Capt. H. A. Iggulden (London 1900), p. 52.

43 Ibid., pp. 75-90. Riseley, *Sikkim Gazetteer*, op. cit., p. VIII.

44 FO 17 1108, Indian Foreign Letter No. 152 of 8 Sept. 1888.

45 *Among the Himalayas*, by L. A. Waddell (London 1899), p. 280.

46 FO 17 1108, Tel. Viceroy to Sec. of State 10 Oct. 1888.

47 The Maharaja had returned from Chumbi to Sikkim in December 1887.

48 Wright, *Hart*, op. cit., pp. 618-19. FO 228 862, Tel. Cockburn to Walsham 13 Sept. 1888. FO 228 876, Cockburn to Walsham 1 Feb. 1889.

49 FO 17 1109, Indian Foreign Letter No. 3 of 8 Jan. 1889 and Indian

Foreign Letter No. 28 of 12 Feb. 1889.

50 FO 17 1109, Memo on the course of the negotiations by H. M. Durand 1 Jan. 1889.

51 FO 17 1109, Indian Foreign Letter No. 28 of 12 Feb. 1889.

52 FO 17 1109, Indian Foreign Letter No. 28 of 12 Feb. 1889.

53 *Sir Mortimer Durand*, by Sir P. Sykes (London 1926), pp. 163-6.

54 FO 17 1109, Indian Foreign Letter No. 3 of 8 Jan. 1889.

55 FO 17 1109, Tel. Walsham to Viceroy 15 Jan. 1889. FO 17 1122, Wade to Sir T. Saunderson 15 July 1891.

56 FO 17 1109, Indian Foreign Letter No. 28 of 12 Feb. 1889.

57 FO 17 1109, FO memo on the course of the negotiations 26 April 1889.

58 FO 17 1109, Tel. Viceroy to Walsham 20 April 1889. Lansdowne Papers in the India Office Library, London (EUR. MSS D/555), IX, vol. I: Lansdowne to Cross 13 March 1889.

59 FO 17 1109, FO memo 26 April 1889.

60 FO 17 1109, FO to IO Immediate and Confidential 26 April 1889 and IO to Viceroy 29 April 1889.

61 FO 17 1109, Godley to Saunderson 12 July 1889.

62 FO 17 1109, Tel. Viceroy to Sec. of State 28 June 1889.

63 FO 17 1109, FO to IO 28 June 1889.

64 Lansdowne Papers, IX, vol. I: Lord Cross to Lansdowne 6 June 1889.

65 FO 17 1109, Tel. Viceroy to Sec. of State 13 Aug. 1889 and Indian Foreign Letter No. 128 of 23 Aug. 1889.

66 FO 17 1109, Lansdowne to Cross 23 Aug. 1889.

67 FO 17 1109, Memo by Sir T. Saunderson on Indian Foreign Letter No. 128 of 23 Aug. 1889.

68 FO 17 1109, Minute by Sir T. Saunderson 11 Nov. 1889.

69 FO 17 1109, Walsham Tel. No. 28 of 9 Nov. 1889.

70 FO 17 1109, Tel. Viceroy to Sec. of State 24 Nov. 1889. FO 17 1109, Minute by Sir T. Saunderson 11 Nov. 1889.

71 FO 17 1109, Leeds C. of C. to Lord Salisbury 26 Nov. 1889.

72 FO 17 1109, FO to Leeds C. of C. 3 Dec. 1889.

73 FO 17 1109, Tel. Viceroy to Sec. of State 27 Dec. 1889.

74 Papers Relating to Tibet 1904 (Cmd. 1920), pp. 6-7.

75 Lansdowne Papers, IX, vol. I: Lansdowne to Cross 8 January 1889.

76 FO 17 1168, Indian Foreign Letter No. 134 of 4 July 1893 in IO to FO 10 Aug. 1893.

77 Waddell, *Himalaya*, op. cit., pp. 279-82.

78 FO 17 1168, Indian Foreign Letter No. 134 of 4 July 1893 in IO to FO 10 Aug. 1893.

79 *A Tea Planter's Life in Assam*, by G. M. Barker (London 1884), concluding chapter.

80 Report on the External Trade of Bengal with Nepal, Sikkim and Bhutan 1884-85 (Calcutta 1885).

81 FO 228 862, Cockburn to Walsham 4 July 1888.

82 O'Malley, *Darjeeling*, op. cit., p. 36: *India's Foreign Trade since 1870*, by P. Ray (London 1934), p. 202.
83 FO 228 1111, O'Conor to Lansdowne 7 March 1893. FO 17 1168, Indian Foreign Letter No. 134 of 4 July 1893 in IO to FO 10 Aug. 1893.
84 FO 228 1111, O'Conor to Lansdowne 27 Feb. 1892.
85 FO 17 1168, Indian Foreign Letter No. 134 of 4 July 1893 in IO to FO 10 Aug. 1893.
86 Papers Relating to Tibet 1904, pp. 21-3.
87 *Burma*, by Sir J. G. Scott (London 1924), p. 361.
88 FO 17 1168, Indian Foreign Letter No. 134 of 4 July 1893 in IO to FO 10 Aug. 1893.
89 Riseley, *Sikkim Gazetteer*, op. cit., pp. XII-XIII.
90 *The Unveiling of Lhasa*, by E. Candler (London 1905), p. 26.
91 *Lhasa and its Mysteries*, by L. A. Waddell (London 1905), p. 49.
92 Or, perhaps, neither did. Lt.-Col. F.M. Bailey told the author that he did not believe that either version was true.

VIII   Yatung: 1894 – 1898

1 *Affairs of China*, by Sir E. Teichman (London 1938), p. 222.
2 *The Administration of the Marquis of Lansdowne; 1888-1894*, by G. W. Forrest (Calcutta 1894), p. 52.
3 FO 17 1167, Some Notes on Tibetan Affairs by Capt. H. Bower in IO to FO 18 May 1893.
4 FO 17 1167, FO minute on IO to FO 18 May 1893.
5 FO 17 1252, Sir. E. Hornby to Lords Rosebery and Kimberley 18 March 1895. *Peoples and Politics of the Far East*, by H. Norman (London 1895), pp. 316, 403.
6 FO 228 1186, O'Conor to Elgin 23 Nov. 1895.
7 Private Correspondence India, pt. I, vol. I: Hamilton to Elgin 28 Feb. 1896.
8 Waddell, *Himalayas*, op. cit., pp. 280-2.
9 Papers Relating to Tibet 1904, pp. 27-30: White to Nolan 9 June 1894.
10 Ibid., pp. 26-7: Bengal to India 25 June 1894.
11 Ibid., p. 31: Indian to Bengal 9 Aug. 1894.
12 Ibid., p. 32: Viceroy to Amban 9 Aug. 1894.
13 Ibid., pp. 33-4: Amban to Viceroy 4 Oct. 1894 and Viceroy to Amban 6 Dec. 1894.
14 *Frontiers*, by Lord Curzon (Romanes Lecture, Oxford 1907).
15 Papers Relating to Tibet 1904, p. 37: White to Nolan 11 May 1895.
16 Ibid., p. 38: White to Nolan 19 May 1895.
17 Ibid., p. 36: Bengal to India 20 May 1895.

18 Ibid., p. 39: India to Bengal 30 May 1895.
19 Papers Relating to Tibet 1904, p. 39: Bengal to India 5 June 1895.
20 Ibid., p. 39: India to Bengal 5 June 1895.
21 Ibid., p. 39: Tel. Bengal to India 7 June 1895.
22 Ibid., p. 40: Tel. India to Bengal 10 June 1895.
23 Ibid., p. 40: Tel. Bengal to India 12 June 1895.
24 Ibid., pp. 40-1: India to Bengal 13 June 1895.
25 Ibid., p. 42: Bengal to India 17 June 1895.
26 Ibid., pp. 47-8: Amban to Viceroy 3 July 1895. FO 228 1186, O'Connor to Viceroy 16 July 1895.
27 Ibid., pp. 45-6: White to Nolan 6 July 1895.
28 Ibid., pp. 44-5: Bengal to India 22 July 1895.
29 Ibid., p. 49: Tel. India to Bengal 10 Aug. 1895.
30 FO 17 1288, Nolan to Bengal 24 Nov. 1895 in Indian Foreign Letter No. 56 of 18 March 1896 in IO to FO 17 April 1896.
31 Papers Relating to Tibet 1904, pp. 53-4: Bengal to India 7 December 1895.
32 FO 17 1255, India to Bengal 17 Aug. 1895 in Indian Foreign Letter No. 175 of 3 Sept. 1895 in IO to FO 24 Sept. 1895.
33 Reports on the External Trade of Bengal with Nepal, Sikkim and Bhutan, 1885-1905.
34 FO 17 1288, Nolan to Bengal 24 Nov. 1895 in Indian Foreign Letter No. 56 of 18 March 1896 in IO to FO 17 April 1896.
35 Private Correspondence India, pt. I, vol. I: Elgin to Hamilton 26 Nov. 1895.
36 Loc. cit.: Hamilton to Elgin 20 Dec. 1895.
37 Private Correspondence India, pt. I, vol. I: Hamilton to Elgin 26 Dec. 1895.
38 Private Correspondence India, pt. II, vol. I: Elgin to Hamilton 2 Dec. 1895.
39 FO 17 1289, Bradford C. of C. to IO 21 Nov. 1895 in IO to FO 30 July 1896.
40 Papers Relating to Tibet 1904, p. 58: India to Bengal 4 March 1896.
41 Ibid., p. 59: Viceroy to Amban 4 March 1896.
42 FO 228 1219, Eastern Section Intelligence Summary of Oct. 1896 in India to Peking 26 Nov. 1896.
43 FO 17 1287, IO to FO 28 Feb. 1896.
44 FO 17 1288, Tel. Peking to India 2 April 1896 in Indian Foreign Letter No. 113 of 9 June 1896 in IO to FO 30 June 1896.
45 Loc. cit.: Beauclerk to Viceroy 30 March 1896.
46 Bengal under the Lieutenant-Governors, by C. E. Buckland (2 vols., Calcutta 1901), vol. II, p. 975. Louis, Gates of Tibet, op. cit., p. 65.
47 Papers Relating to Tibet 1904, p. 72: Indian Foreign Letter No. 198 of 23 Dec. 1896.

48 Private Correspondence India, pt. II, vol. I: Elgin to Hamilton 26 Nov. 1895.
49 Ibid., pp. 76-7: Amban to Viceroy 11 March 1898.
50 Ibid., p. 77: Viceroy to Amban 2 June 1898.
51 Ibid., pp. 78-9: Amban to Viceroy 11 Aug. 1898.
52 Ibid., p. 80: Viceroy to Amban 28 Oct. 1898.
53 FO 17 1401, Bengal to India 23 Nov. 1898 in Indian Foreign Letter No. 60 of 30 March 1899 in IO to FO 4 May 1899.
54 Papers Relating to Tibet 1904, p. 60: White to Nolan 23 November 1898.
55 Ibid., pp. 95-7: White to Nolan 9 Dec. 1898, but omitting the passage on the Russians, for which see FO 17 1401, IO to FO 4 May 1899.
56 Ibid., p. 99: Viceroy to Amban 25 March 1899. FO 17 1401, FO to IO 15 May 1899.
57 FO 17 1254, Indian Foreign Letter No. 125 of 25 June 1895 in IO to CO 15 July 1895.
58 Markham, Narratives, op. cit., p. 294.
59 FO 17 1450, White to Bengal 15 Aug. 1902 in India to Peking 24 Oct. 1902.
60 Accounts and Papers, Sikkim Expedition, op. cit., p. 569: Eden to Bengal 8 April 1861.
61 FO 17 1401, White to Nolan 23 November 1898 in IO to FO 4 May 1899.
62 Hooker, op. cit., vol. II, p. 98.
63 FO 17 1401, White to Nolan 23 November 1898 in IO to FO 4 May 1899.
64 Bell, Tibet, op. cit., pp 73-81.
65 FO 17 1149, Russia in Asia Intelligence Summary for Nov. 1894. FO 17 1278, Sir C. Macdonald No. 198 of 19 Aug. 1896.
66 FO 17 1239, O'Conor No. 387 of 10 Oct. 1895. FO 228 1186, India to Peking 14 Sept. 1896.
67 FO 228 1186, India to Peking 5 Aug. 1895. FO 17 1288, Nolan to Bengal 24 Nov. 1895 in IO to FO 17 April 1896.
68 FO 228 1186, India to Peking 5 Aug. 1895. Papers Relating to Tibet 1904, pp. 54-6: Nolan to Bengal 24 Nov. 1895.
69 FO 228 1225, Chungking Int. Report Feb.-April 1896. Teichman, Travels, op. cit., p. 6.
70 FO 228 1253, Chungking Int. Reports Nov. 1896-Jan. 1897, May-July 1897, Aug.-Oct. 1897.
71 FO 228 1225, Chungking Int. Report May-July 1896.
72 FO 228 1225, Chungking Int. Report Aug.-Oct. 1896.
73 FO 228 1186, O'Conor to Viceroy 20 May 1895.
74 Rockhill, Dalai Lamas, op. cit., pp. 46-73.
75 FO 17 1288, Nolan to Bengal 24 Nov. 1895 in IO to FO 17 April 1896.
76 FO 17 1288, Indian Foreign Letter No. 101 of 19 May 1896 in IO to

FO 8 June 1896: Tel. Viceroy to Sec. of State 17 April 1896 in IO to FO 17 April 1896. FO 17 1287, Tel. Viceroy to Sec. of State 25 Feb. 1896 in IO to FO 25 Feb. 1896 with minute by F. Bertie. FO 228 1225, Chungking Int. Report Feb.-April 1896. FO 228 1219, Eastern Section Int. Summary Aug. 1896.

77 FO 228 1186, India to Peking 5 Aug. 1895. FO 17 1255, IO to FO 24 Sept. 1895.

78 On Russia and the Buriats, see 'Mongolian Nationalism', by R. Rupen (*JRCAS* 1958), pp. 171-3.

79 *La Geste Française en Indochine*, by G. Taboulet (2 vols., Paris 1955), vol. II, p. 704.

80 FO 228 1225, Chungking Int. Report Aug.-Oct. 1896. FO 228 1284, Chungking Int. Report May-July 1898: Litton to Macdonald 31 May 1898.

81 *Through Unknown Tibet*, by M. C. Welby (London 1898). *In Tibet and Chinese Turkestan*, by H. H. P. Deasy (London 1901). FO 17 1289, Mil. Int. to FO 17 July 1896.

82 FO 228 1060, India to Walsham 14 Jan. 1891.

83 FO 17 1144, FO to IO 7 July 1892, IO to FO 22 July 1892, IO to FO 10 Sept. 1892.

84 FO 17 952, Sir Harry Parkes No. 236 of 27 Oct. 1884.

85 *Chinese Central Asia*, by H. H. Lansdell (2 vols., London 1893), vol. II, pp. 359, 372.

86 *India and Tibet*, by Sir F. Younghusband (London 1910), p. 96.

87 FO 228 1219, India to Peking 18 Nov. 1896. *To the Forbidden Land: Tibet*, by A. H. Landor (2 vols. London 1898). FO 17 1356, Indian Foreign Letter No. 163 of 16 Dec. 1897 in IO to FO 14 Jan. 1898.

88 FO 17 1356, Indian Foreign Letter No. 163 of 16 Dec. 1897 in IO to FO 14 Jan. 1898. 'Great Figures of Nineteenth-Century Himalayan Exploration', by K. Mason (*JRCAS*, 1956).

89 FO 17 1330, Broadfoot Vaughan to Lord Salisbury 13 Nov. 1897, with views of Curzon attached. Landor published an account of his experiences: see *To the Forbidden Land: Tibet*, by A. H. Landor (2 vols., London 1898).

90 FO 228 1219, India to Peking 18 Nov. 1896.

91 On the work of the 'pundits' see Holdich, *Tibet*, op. cit.; Sandberg, *Exploration of Tibet*, op. cit.; *Memoir of the Indian Survey 1878-1890*, by C. E. D. Black (Calcutta 1891); *Abode of Snow*, by K. Mason (London 1955).

92 FO 228 1149, Eastern Section Int. Summary Oct. 1894. FO 228 1186, Eastern Section Int. Summary Jan. 1895.

93 FO 228 1186, O'Conor to Viceroy 4 June 1895.

94 FO 17 721, Wade No. 120 Confidential of 24 May 1876, enclosing Wade to Lord Northbrook 24 May 1876.

95 *Russia in Central Asia*, by G. N. Curzon (London 1889), p. 251.

96 FO 17 1055, Report on Tibet by Ney Elias 5 March 1887.

97 Holdich, *Tibet*, op. cit., pp. 281-4.

98 Petech, *China and Tibet*, op. cit., pp. 25-41.

99 FO 17 1361, Ardagh to FO 18 July 1898. See also 'Some Notes on Russian Intrigue in Tibet', by Alastair Lamb (*JRCAS*, 1959).

IX   Curzon's Tibetan Policy: 1899 – 1902

1 Letters from India, vol. 139, No. 1376: Minute by Lord Curzon on Russian Ambitions in East Persia 28 Oct. 1901.
2 FO 17 1407, Le Mesurier to Nolan 30 April 1899 in IO to FO 22 Nov. 1899.
3 Loc. cit., India to Bengal 24 May 1899.
4 Private Correspondence India, pt II, vol. XIII: Curzon to Hamilton 24 May 1899.
5 Papers Relating to Tibet 1904, p. 99: Curzon to Amban 25 March 1899.
6 Private Correspondence India, pt. II, vol. XIII: Curzon to Hamilton 23 March 1899.
7 FO 17 1401, FO to IO 15 May 1899.
8 FO 17 1403, FO to IO 24 July 1899.
9 FO 17 1407, India to Bengal 23 May 1899 and Bengal to India 8 July 1899 in IO to FO 22 Nov. 1899.
10 FO 17 1407, Bengal to India 23 Jan. 1899 in Indian Foreign Letter No. 198 of 26 Oct. 1899 in IO to FO 22 Nov. 1899.
11 Papers Relating to Tibet 1904, p. 119: Bengal to India 22 Dec. 1899.
12 Ibid., p. 120: White to Rajshahi Division 20 March 1900.
13 Ibid., p. 119: Bengal to India 23 April 1900. FO 17 1508, IO to FO 21 Aug. 1901.
14 FO 17 1445, IO to FO 22 Aug. 1900.
15 Loc. cit., India to Talbot 25 Jan. 1900 and Talbot to India 19 Feb. 1900.
16 FO 17 1398, Trench to Kashmir 17 Sept. 1898 in IO to FO 3 Jan. 1899.
17 FO 17 1445, Kennion to Talbot 8 Nov. 1899 in IO to FO 22 Aug. 1900.
18 FO 17 1445, Kennion to Talbot 30 May 1900 in IO to FO 22 Aug. 1900.
19 FO 17 1445, India to Talbot 25 July 1900 in IO to FO 22 Aug. 1900.
20 FO 17 1447, Kennion to Talbot 10 Aug. 1900 in IO to FO 3 Oct. 1900.
21 FO 17 1445, India to Bengal 25 July 1900 in IO to FO 22 Aug. 1900.
22 Papers Relating to Tibet 1904, pp. 120-1: Curzon to Dalai Lama 11 Aug. 1900.
23 FO 17 1508, Kennion to Talbot 7 Oct. 1900 in IO to FO 21 Aug. 1901.
24 FO 17 1508, Talbot to India 17 Oct. 1900 and India to Talbot 31 Oct. 1900 in IO to FO 21 Aug. 1901.
25 FO 17 1508, Kennion to Deane 13 March 1901 in IO to FO 21 Aug. 1901.

26 FO 17 1508, Kennion to Deane 5 April 1901 in IO to FO 21 Aug. 1901.
27 FO 17 1508, India to Deane 15 May 1901 in IO to FO 21 Aug. 1901.
28 FO 17 1511, IO to FO 4 Dec. 1901. Papers Relating to Tibet 1904, p. 121: India to Bengal 8 June 1901.
29 Ibid., pp. 121-2: Curzon to Dalai Lama 8 June 1901.
30 Home Correspondence India, vol. 196: Godley to Hamilton 9 July 1901. FO 17 1508, Minute by Lansdowne on IO to FO 21 Aug. 1901.
31 Papers Relating to Tibet 1904, pp. 129-30: Tel. Bengal to India 31 Oct. 1901.
32 FO 17 1745, Bengal to India 25 Nov. 1901.
33 FO 17 1745, Darjeeling Frontier Report 7 Dec. 1901.
34 FO 17 1745, Darjeeling Frontier Report 17 July 1902.
35 FO 17 1745, Darjeeling Frontier Report 20 Sept. 1902.
36 Private Correspondence India, pt. II, vol. XXI: Curzon to Hamilton 5 Nov. 1901. See note on p. 221 below.
37 Private Correspondence India, pt. II, vol. XIII: Curzon to Hamilton 24 May 1899.
38 Private Correspondence India, pt. II, vol. XVIII: Curzon to Hamilton 18 Nov. 1900.
39 Private Correspondence India, pt. II, vol. XX: Curzon to Hamilton 10 July 1901.
40 Private Correspondence India, pt. II, vol. XXI: Curzon to Hamilton 5 Nov. 1901.
41 Papers Relating to Tibet 1904, pp. 105-6: Amban to Curzon 22 April 1899.
42 Ibid., pp. 104-5: Le Mesurier to Nolan 30 April 1899.
43 Private Correspondence India, pt. II, vol. XX: Curzon to Hamilton 10 July 1901.
44 FO 65 1601, Hardinge No. 340 of 17 Oct. 1900.
45 FO 17 1506, India to Bengal 12 Nov. 1900 in IO to FO 1 July 1901.
46 FO 65 1601, Hardinge No. 352 Conf. of 22 Oct. 1900.
47 FO 65 1601, Hardinge No. 365 of 31 Oct. 1900.
48 Home Correspondence India, vol. 191, No. 2468.
49 FO 17 1506, Bengal to India 14 Nov. 1900 in IO to FO 1 July 1901.
50 Private Correspondence India, pt. II, vol. XVIII: Curzon to Hamilton 18 Nov. 1900.
51 Private Correspondence India, pt. I, vol. V: Hamilton to Curzon 24 Oct. 1900.
52 FO 65 1621, Sir C. Scott No. 165 of 13 June 1901.
53 FO 65 1621, Sir C. Scott No. 183 of 1 July 1901.
54 FO 65 1622, Sir C. Scott to Lansdowne 7 Aug. 1901.
55 FO 65 1621, Sir C. Scott No. 194 of 10 July 1901.
56 FO 17 1506, Note on the alleged Tibetan missions to Russia 3 Dec. 1900. FO 17 1551, Bengal to India 6 July 1901 in IO to FO 3 July 1902.
57 FO 65 1601, Hardinge No. 365 of 31 Oct. 1900. FO 17 1551, IO to FO 3 July 1902.

58 FO 17 1551, IO to FO 3 July 1902. The enclosure of this letter is a summary of all the available information on the Dorjieff Missions up to this date.
59 Private Correspondence India, pt. II, vol. XXI: Curzon to Hamilton 11 Sept. 1901.
60 Private Correspondence India, pt. II, vol. XXI: Curzon to Hamilton 5 Nov. 1901.
61 Letters from India, vol. 136, No. 986: India to Bengal 29 July 1901.
62 Letters from India, vol. 144, No. 770: Transfrontier Diary 30 April 1902.
63 Home Correspondence India, vol. 196, No. 2151: Extract from Private Letter from Curzon to Hamilton 11 June 1901.
64 Home Correspondence India, vol. 196: Memo by Sir W. Lee-Warner of 9 July 1901 on Curzon to Hamilton 11 June 1901; Memo by Sir A. Lyall 17 July 1901.
65 Private Correspondence India, pt. I, vol. VI: Hamilton to Curzon 11 July 1901.
66 Private Correspondence India, pt. II, vol. XXI: Curzon to Hamilton 11 Sept. 1901.
67 FO 17 1507, Godley to FO 25 July 1901.
68 *India and Tibet*, by Sir F. Younghusband (London 1910), pp. 76-7.
69 Private Correspondence India, pt. I, vol. VI: Hamilton to Curzon 22 Aug. 1901.
70 Home Correspondence India, vol. 196, No. 2151.
71 Papers Relating to Tibet 1904, pp. 125-7: Indian Foreign Letter No. 32 of 13 Feb. 1902.
72 FO 17 1745, Minute by Sir F. Bertie on IO to FO 14 March 1902.
73 Private Correspondence India, pt. I, vol. VII: Hamilton to Curzon 13 March 1902.
74 FO 17 1745, Tel. Bengal to India 3 July 1902 in IO to FO 1 Sept. 1902.
75 FO 17 1450, White to Bengal 15 Aug. 1902 in India to Peking 24 Oct. 1902.
76 Papers Relating to Tibet 1904, p. 162: Tel. India to Bengal 29 Aug. 1902.
77 Papers Relating to Tibet 1904, p. 164: White to Mandarin 27 Aug. 1902. Ibid., p. 176: Amban to Viceroy 28 Nov. 1902.
78 Ibid., p. 146: Townley Tel. No. 372 of 6 Dec. 1902.
79 Ibid., p. 148: Tel. Sec. of State to Viceroy 17 Dec. 1902.
80 Ibid., p. 173: Tel. India to Bengal 22 Oct. 1902.
81 FO 17 1551, Darjeeling Frontier Report 15 Sept. 1901 in IO to FO 3 July 1902.
82 FO 17 1745, PM of Nepal to Col. Pears 18 Nov. 1901 in IO to FO 8 Jan. 1902. FO 17 1546, PM of Nepal to Col. Pears 25 Dec. 1901 in IO to FO 11 Feb. 1902.
83 FO 17 1745, Col. Pears to India 13 Jan. 1902 in IO to FO 24 Feb. 1902.
84 FO 17 1745, PM of Nepal to Lt.-Col. Ravenshaw 27 April 1902 in

IO to FO 11 June 1902.

85 Letters from India, vol. 145, No. 926: Darjeeling Frontier Report 27 May 1902.

86 FO 17 1551, Tibet Transfrontier Diary 27 May 1902 in IO to FO 26 July 1902.

87 FO 17 1745, Sir E. Satow Tel. No. 230 of 2 Aug. 1902.

88 FO 17 1745, White to India 20 Aug. 1902 in IO to FO 16 Sept. 1902.

89 FO 17 1745, Sir E. Satow No. 217 of 5 Aug. 1902.

90 FO 17 1745, Sir E. Satow No. 289 Conf. 8 Oct. 1902. Kang Yu-wei to Curzon 22 Aug. 1902 in IO to FO 21 Oct. 1902. Tel. Viceroy to Sec. of State 12 Nov. 1902 in IO to FO 14 Nov. 1902.

91 FO 17 1745, Hardinge No. 349 of 10 Nov. 1902.

92 FO 17 1746, Younghusband to India 3 June 1903 in IO to FO 8 July 1903.

93 FO 17 1745, Sir E. Satow Tel. No. 361 of 20 Nov. 1902.

94 FO 17 1746, Indian Foreign Letter No. 88 of 2 July 1903 in IO to FO 23 July 1903, Hosie to Townley 1 May 1903. 'How the Tibetans Grew', by E. H. Parker (*Imperial and Asiatic Quarterly Review*, vol. XVIII, Oct. 1904), p. 255.

95 Letters from India, vol. 154, No. 798: Walsh to Bengal 30 April 1903. FO 17 1746, *Memo on our Relations with Tibet*, by F. E. Younghusband (Simla 1903), p. 25.

96 FO 17 1747, IO to FO 24 Dec. 1903.

97 FO 17 1746, Sir C. Scott No. 147 of 25 May 1903.

98 FO 17 1746, Younghusband to India 8 July 1903 in IO to FO 8 July 1903.

99 FO 17 1745, Sir E. Satow Tel. No. 361 of 20 Nov. 1902.

100 FO 17 1746, Spring Rice No. 335 of 15 Oct. 1903. *The International Position of Outer Mongolia*, by G. M. Friters (Dijon 1939), p. 35.

101 Markham, *Narratives*, op. cit., p. xxiv.

102 Home Correspondence India, vol. 182, No. 1021. Private Correspondence India, pt. I, vol. IV: Hamilton to Curzon 8 June 1899. Private Telegrams India, vol. I: Hamilton to Curzon 18 April 1899.

103 Private Correspondence India, pt. II, vol. I: Curzon to Hamilton 17 May 1899. Private Telegrams India, vol. I, 27 April 1899.

104 FO 17 1750, Indian Foreign Letter No. 120 of 30 June 1904 in IO to FO 26 July 1904.

X   The Younghusband Mission: 1903 – 1905

1 FO 17 1535, Sir E. Satow Tel. No. 266 of 8 Sept. 1902.

2 FO 17 1554, Minute by Lansdowne in IO to FO 1 Oct. 1902.

3 Private Correspondence India, pt. I, vol. VII: Hamilton to Curzon 27 Aug. 1902.

4 Private Correspondence India, pt. II, vol. XXIV: Curzon to Hamilton

13 Nov. 1902.

5 FO 17 1745, PM of Nepal to Ravenshaw 20 Jan. 1903 in IO to FO 19 Feb. 1903.

6 Letters from India, vol. 150, No. 1551a: PM of Nepal to Ravenshaw 6 Oct. 1902.

7 Letters from India, vol. 150, No. 1551a: India to Ravenshaw 28 Oct. 1902. Private Correspondence India, pt. II, vol. XXIII: Curzon to Hamilton 1 Oct. 1902.

8 FO 17 1535, Sir E. Satow Tel. No. 266 of 8 Sept. 1902. Papers Relating to Tibet 1904, p. 146: Lansdowne to Hardinge 22 Oct. 1902.

9 Private Correspondence India, pt. I, vol. VII: Hamilton to Curzon 27 Aug. 1902.

10 FO 17 1745, Note on Tibet by Sir W. Lee-Warner in IO to FO 17 Sept. 1902.

11 Letters from India, vol. 149, No. 1456a: Hamilton to Curzon 17 Sept. 1902.

12 FO 17 1745, Minute by Lansdowne in IO to FO 17 Sept. 1902.

13 Letters from India, vol. 150, No. 1590a: Minutes of the Political Committee of 6 Jan. 1903 discussing Curzon to Hamilton 13 Nov. 1902.

14 FO 17 1745, Mob. and Int. Dept. WO to FO 1 Oct. 1902.

15 Private Correspondence India, pt. II, vol. XXIV: Curzon to Hamilton 1 Jan. 1903.

16 FO 17 1745, Indian Foreign Letter of 8 Jan. 1903. This is printed in Papers Relating to Tibet 1904, but about one-half of the enclosures have been omitted.

17 Private Correspondence India, pt. II, vol. XXIV: Curzon to Hamilton 13 Nov. 1902.

18 Parliamentary Debates, series IV, vol. 130, p. 1141: Speech in the House of Lords 26 Feb. 1904.

19 Letters from India, vol. 152, No. 517: Minute by Sir D. Fitzpatrick 20 April 1903 on Tel. Viceroy to Sec. of State 16 April 1903.

20 FO 17 1745, Note on Tibet by Sir S. Bayley 11 Feb. 1903.

21 Private Correspondence India, pt. I, vol. VII: Hamilton to Curzon 13 Feb. 1903.

22 Private Correspondence India, pt. I, vol. VIII: Hamilton to Curzon 28 Jan. 1903.

23 Private Correspondence India, Pt. I, vol. VIII: Hamilton to Curzon 13 Feb. 1903.

24 Letters from India, vol. 154, No. 861: Memo on meeting of Political Committee 20 Feb. 1903.

25 Private Correspondence India, pt. I, vol. VIII: Hamilton to Curzon 20 Feb. 1903.

26 FO 17 1745, Minute by Sir T. Saunderson 11 Oct. 1902.

27 Papers Relating to Tibet 1904, p. 150: Lansdowne to Sir C. Scott 31 Dec. 1902.

28 Ibid., p. 178: Enclosure in FO to IO 3 Feb. 1903.

29 Papers Relating to Tibet 1904, p. 187: Lansdowne to Scott

8 April 1903. Ibid., p. 180: Lansdowne to Scott 11 Feb. 1903. Ibid., p. 181: Lansdowne to Scott 8 Feb. 1903.

30 Ibid., p. 186: Lansdowne to Scott 24 March 1903.

31 FO 17 1746, Lansdowne to Scott 1 April 1903.

32 Private Correspondence India, pt. I, vol. VIII: Hamilton to Curzon 8 April 1903.

33 Private Correspondence India, pt. I, vol. VIII: Hamilton to Curzon 15 April 1903.

34 Private Correspondence India, pt. II, vol. XXV: Curzon to Hamilton 3 April 1903.

35 Private Correspondence India, pt. I, vol. VIII: Hamilton to Curzon 28 May 1903.

36 Letters from India, vol. 153, No. 602: Minute by Sir D. Fitzpatrick on Tel. Viceroy to Sec. of State 7 May 1903.

37 Papers Relating to Tibet 1904, p. 196: Amban to Viceroy 6 April 1903.

38 Ibid., p. 177: Townley to FO 13 Feb 1903.

39 Papers Relating to Tibet, 1904, p. 196: Amban to Viceroy 6 April 1903.

40 Ibid., p. 189: Tel. Viceroy to Sec. of State 16 April 1903.

41 *The Heart of a Continent*, by F. E. Younghusband (London 1896).

42 Private Correspondence India, pt. II, vol. XXVI: Curzon to Hamilton 7 May 1903.

43 Papers Relating to Tibet 1904, p. 192: Tel. Viceroy to Sec. of State 7 May 1903.

44 Ibid., p. 193: Tel. Sec. of State to Viceroy 28 May 1903.

45 Private Correspondence India, pt. I, vol. VIII: Hamilton to Curzon 28 May 1903.

46 FO 17 1746, Minute by Lansdowne on Tel. Viceroy to Sec. of State 21 May 1903.

47 Private Correspondence India, pt. II, vol. XXVI: Curzon to Hamilton 4 June 1903.

48 Papers Relating to Tibet 1904, p. 192: Tel. Viceroy to Sec. of State 21 May 1903.

49 Ibid., p. 203: Tel. Viceroy to Sec. of State 16 July 1903; and p. 205: Tel. Townley to FO 15 Aug. 1903.

50 Ibid., p. 205: Tel. Townley to FO 15 Aug. 1903.

51 Papers Relating to Tibet 1904, pp. 219-21: Curzon to Brodrick 5 Nov. 1903.

52 Ibid., p. 292: Asst. Resident in Nepal to India 1 Nov. 1903.

53 Ibid., p. 293: C. Bell to Dist. Comm. Darjeeling 2 Nov. 1903.

54 Ibid., p. 284: Younghusband to India 8 Oct. 1903.

55 Ibid., p. 294: Tel. Sec. of State to Viceroy 6 Nov. 1903.

56 Ibid., p. 294: Lansdowne to Spring Rice 7 Nov. 1903.

57 Private Correspondence India, pt. II, vol. XXVI: Curzon to Hamilton 5 Aug. 1903.

58 FO 17 1746, W. F. O'Conor's Diary 10 Aug. 1903 in IO to FO 17 Sept. 1903.

59 FO 17 1746, Younghusband, Memo on Tibet, p. 41.

60 Ibid., p. 30.
61 Curzon, *Russian in Central Asia*, op. cit., p. 251.
62 For the history of the Khambajong negotiations and of the subsequent advance to Lhasa, see: *India and Tibet*, by Sir F. Younghusband (London 1910); *Lhasa*, by P. Landon, 2 vols (London 1905); *The Unveiling of Lhasa*, by E. Candler (London 1905); *Bayonets to Lhasa*, by Peter Fleming (London 1961); *The Younghusband Expedition. An Interpretation*, by P. Mehra (London 1968); *Trespassers on the Roof of the World*, by P. Hopkirk (London 1982); *Tibet on the Imperial Chessboard*, by P. Addy (Calcutta and New Delhi 1984).
63 FO 17 1750, Younghusband to India 27 May 1904 in IO to FO 5 July 1904.
64 *Military Report on Western Tibet*, by Capt. C. G. Rawling (Q.M.G. Dept., Simla 1905), p. 33. A copy of this report is to be found in the Library of the Royal Geographical Society, London.
65 Ampthill Papers (MSS Eur. E233/34/1 in the India Office Library, London): Ampthill to Younghusband 11 July 1904.
66 Ampthill Papers (E233/34/1): Kitchener to Ampthill 30 May 1904.
67 Ampthill Papers (E233/37): Ampthill to Brodrick 5 Oct. 1904.
68 Ampthill Papers (E233/37): Brodrick to Ampthill 6 and 13 Oct. 1904.
69 FO 17 1746, Younghusband, Memo on Tibet.
70 FO 17 1746, Minute by Lansdowne 29 Sept. 1903.
71 FO 17 1746, Memo on Tibet by St. J. Brodrick 4 Nov. 1903.
72 FO 17 1748, Darjeeling Frontier Report 7 March 1904 in IO to FO 7 April 1904.
73 FO 17 1749, Younghusband to India 10 May 1904 in IO to FO 6 June 1904.
74 FO 17 1746, Younghusband to India 17 Aug. 1903 in IO to FO 17 Sept. 1903.
75 FO 17 1746, Bengal to India 24 Sept. 1903 in IO to FO 27 Oct. 1903. FO 17 1748, Tel. Viceroy to Sec. of State 23 Feb. 1904 in IO to FO 24 Feb. 1904.
76 FO 17 1750, Younghusband to India 27 May 1904 in IO to FO 5 July 1904.
77 Ampthill Papers (E233/37): Curzon to Ampthill 19 July 1904.
78 Ampthill Papers (E233/37): Curzon to Ampthill 4 Aug. 1904.
79 FO 17 1746, Younghusband, Memo on Tibet, p. 8.
80 Ampthill Papers (E233/37): Brodrick to Ampthill 26 Aug. 1904. FO 17 1751, IO to FO 31 Aug. 1904.
81 FO 17 1752, Younghusband to India 14 and 15 Aug. 1904 in IO to FO 4 Oct. 1904.
82 FO 17 1751, Tel. Viceroy to Sec. of State 25 Aug. 1904 in IO to FO 31 Aug. 1904.
83 *British Documents on the Origins of the War: 1898-1914*, ed. G. P. Gooch and H. Temperley, vol. IV *The Anglo-Russian Rapprochement 1903-7* (London 1929), pp. 314-16.
84 Further Papers Relating to Tibet 1905 (Cd. 2370), pp. 265-6: Younghusband to India 9 Sept. 1904.

85 Ampthill Papers (E233/37): Brodrick to Ampthill 4 Nov. 1904.
86 Ampthill Papers (E233/37): Ampthill to Brodrick 14 Sept. 1904.
87 FO 17 1751, Brodrick to India No. 35 Secret of 5 Aug. 1904.
88 Further Papers Relating to Tibet 1905, p. 80: Younghusband to India 18 Oct. 1904.
89 Ampthill Papers (E233/11): Brodrick to Ampthill 8 Dec. 1904.
90 Ampthill Papers (E233/11): Brodrick to Ampthill 3 Feb. 1905.
91 Younghusband, *India and Tibet*, op. cit., pp. 298-300. FO 17 1752, Younghusband to India 9 Sept. 1904 in IO to FO 24 Oct. 1904.
92 Ampthill Papers (E233/37): Brodrick to Ampthill 1 July 1904.
93 Ibid., Curzon to Ampthill 26 May 1904.
94 Ampthill Papers (E233/37): Curzon to Ampthill 17 June 1904. FO 17 1749, Lansdowne to Spring Rice 4 May 1904.
95 FO 17 1752, Tel. Viceroy to Sec. of State 30 Sept. 1904 in IO to FO 1 Oct. 1904. For the Niti Pass question, see, for example: *The Northern Frontier of India, Central and Western Sector*, by S.C. Bajpai (Calcutta 1970), pp. 28-31.
96 Ampthill Papers (E233/37): Ampthill to Brodrick 14 Sept. 1904.
97 Ampthill Papers (E233/37): Ampthill to Curzon 16 June 1904.
98 Ampthill Papers (E233/34/1): Younghusband to Ampthill 11 May 1904.
99 FO 17 1749, Hardinge No. 274 of 30 May 1904.
100 Ampthill Papers (E233/37): Ampthill to Brodrick 16 June 1904.
101 FO 17 1753, Tel. Sec. of State to Viceroy 7 Nov. 1904 in IO to FO 11 Nov. 1904.
102 FO 17 1752, Tel. Sec. of State to Viceroy 3 Oct. 1904 in IO to FO 3 Oct. 1904.
103 Gooch and Temperley, *British Documents*, op. cit., vol. IV, p. 316.
104 FO 17 1752, Satow Tel. No. 205 of 22 Sept. 1904.
105 FO 17 1752, Memo by Sir F. Bertie 21 Sept. 1904 and Lansdowne to Hardinge 27 Sept. 1904.
106 FO 17 1752, FO Memo on the Agreement with Tibet 25 Sept. 1904.
107 FO 17 1755, Lansdowne to Hardinge 9 Aug. 1905.
108 FO 17 1752, Satow Tel. No. 230 of 22 Oct. 1904.
109 FO 17 1752, Sir F. Lascelles Tel. No. 23 of 22 Oct. 1904.
110 FO 17 1752, Satow Tel. No. 215 of 5 Oct. 1904.
111 *Out of My Past; the Memoirs of Count Kokovtsov*, ed. H. H. Fisher (Hoover War Library Publications No. 6, Stanford, California 1935, p. 590 n. 3). *Memoirs of Count Witte*, trans. and ed. A. Yarmolinsky (London 1921), p. 86. *The Decline of Imperial Russia*, by H. Seton-Watson (London 1952), p. 201. *The Rise of Russia in Asia*, by D. J. Dallin (London 1950), pp. 35-6.
112 FO 65 1621, Sir C. Scott No. 194 of 10 July 1901. Dallin, *Russia in Asia*, op. cit., p. 43. Seton-Watson, *Imperial Russia*, op. cit., p. 327n.
113 It now seems unlikely, as was suggested in BCCA p. 314, that Dorjieff was in fact ever a member of Prjevalski's last Tibetan expedition.
114 *Three Years in Tibet*, by E. Kawaguchi (Benares and London 1909),

pp. 493–508.

115 *Dawn in Siberia: the Mongols of Lake Baikal*, by G. D. R. Phillips (London 1942), p. 108.

116 *Sturm über Asien*, by W. Filchner (Berlin 1924). See also 'A Story of Struggle and Intrigue in Central Asia' (*JCAS* 1927 and 1928); 'Tibet and Russian Intrigue', by P. L. Mehra (*JRCAS* 1958).

117 Dallin, *Russia in Asia*, op. cit., p. 42. Li, *Tibet*, op. cit., p. 120.

118 *Pre-War Diplomacy*, by J. J. Korostovetz (London 1920), p. 48.

119 Fritters, *Mongolia*, op. cit., p. 35.

120 *Russia and Asia*, by A. Lobanov-Rostovsky (New York 1933), pp. 207–8.

121 FO 17 1752, Younghusband to India 17 Aug. 1904 in IO to FO 4 Oct. 1904.

122 Candler, op. cit. p. 277.

123 Kawaguchi, op. cit., p. 506.

124 FO 17 1753, Satow No. 404 Confidential of 29 Nov. 1904.

125 FO 17 1551, IO to FO 3 July 1902 enclosing a long and detailed analysis of the alleged missions between Russia and Tibet. For details of the career of Prince E. E. Ukhtomsky, see: *A History of Russia*, by Sir Bernard Pares (London 1962), pp. 458, 474, 484.

126 Ukhtomsky, Witte and the Russo-Chinese Bank were not, however, directly involved in the Yalu timber concession. This venture was the concern of a rival clique with which Witte's great rival, Plehve, was connected. Witte fell from power in August 1903. Whether the departure of Witte, which left Russian Far Eastern policy in the hands of men both more aggressive and less sophisticated in approach, increased or reduced the dangerous implications of the Tibetan situation is a matter for argument. The Government of India tended to take a monolithic view of Russian foreign policy which, in fact, was all too often the product of conflict between rival cliques. On the Yalu timber concession and the attitude of its supporters, such as Bezobrazov, towards both Witte and the Russo-Chinese Bank, see: *Russia: a History and an Interpretation*, by M. T. Florinsky (New York 1968), 2 vols, vol. 2 pp. 1268–9.

See, in the Bibliography to this book under Cybikov, Deniker, Narzounof and Oukhtomsky, for some references to the Russian side of the Tibetan ventures of the Dorjieff era.

127 See, for an exposition of the Tibetan question in the context of other aspects of Curzon's policy both internal and external: *Curzon in India*, by D. Dilks (London 1970), 2 vols.

For the Afghan question, see: *Afghanistan*, by W. K. Fraser-Tytler (London 1967); *Afghanistan 1900-1923. A Diplomatic History*, by L. W. Adamec (Berkeley and Los Angeles 1967).

XI The Aftermath: 1905 – 1910

1 *Tibet on the Imperial Chessboard*, by Premen Addy (Calcutta 1984).

2 Vol. IV, *The Anglo-Russian Rapprochement 1903-7* (London 1929).
3 *ML* 1, p. 20.
4 FO 535/5, No. 52, Satow to Lansdowne, 1 November 1904.
5 *ML* 1, pp. 16-31.
6 FO 535/7, No. 10, O'Connor to White, 23 November 1905.
7 *ML* 1, pp. 61-3.
8 Morley Papers (D 573/1 in India Office Library), Morley to Minto, 7 June 1906.
9 Quoted in *ML* 1, p. 47. Ch. III of *ML* 1 discusses the Calcutta negotiations in considerable detail.
10 For the text of the 1906 Convention, see: *The North-Eastern Frontier. A Documentary Study of the Internecine Rivalry between India, Tibet and China*, by P. Mehra, Vol. 1 (Delhi 1979), pp. 1-4.
11 *ML* 1, pp. 53-4.
12 *ML* 1, Ch. X.
13 It has been claimed that the Dalai Lama (then still in exile) repudiated this action by Tsarong Shape; and it is a fact that, shortly after his return to Tibet from the Calcutta negotiations, Tsarong Shape was assassinated. See: *Tibet. A Political History*, by Tsepon W.D. Shakabpa (New Haven 1967), p. 220.
14 For the history of the Dane Mission to Kabul, see, for example: *Afghanistan 1900-1923. A Diplomatic History*, by L. W. Adamec (Berkeley and Los Angeles 1967).
15 For an account of Anglo-Russian relations in Kashgaria at this period, see: *Macartney at Kashgar. New Light on British, Chinese and Russian Activities in Sinkiang 1890-1918*, by C.P. Skrine and P. Nightingale (London 1973).
16 *ML* 1, pp. 83-6.
17 The negotiation of the Anglo-Russian Convention of 1907 is the subject of Part Two of *ML* 1.
18 *ML* 1, p. 167.
19 *ML* 1, pp. 181-95.
20 Quoted in Mehra, op. cit., p. 15.
21 See: *ML* 2, Ch. XVII.
22 *ML* 1, p. 222.
23 For British policy towards Sinkiang up to 1895, see: *British India's Northern Frontier 1865-1895*, by G.J. Alder (London 1963).
24 These Mongolian agreements are reproduced in *ML* 2, pp. 615-17, 631-7.

BIBLIOGRAPHY

Abbreviations

FEQ: *Far Eastern Quarterly.*
IHQ: *Indian Historical Quarterley.*
JA: *Journal Asiatique.*
JASB: *Journal of the Asiatic Society of Bengal.*
JCAS: *Journal of the Central Asian Society.*
JNCBRAS: *Journal of the North China Branch of the Royal Asiatic Society.*
JRAS: *Journal of the Royal Asiatic Society.*
JRCAS: *Journal of the Royal Central Asian Society* (in continuation of JCAS).

UNPUBLISHED SOURCES

(1) *In the British Museum*

A certain amount of material relating to the earlier period of Anglo-Tibetan relations is to be found in the Additional MSS. The following have been consulted:

Add. MS. 19,283 f. 110	33,837 f. 60
29,204 ff. 340, 345	39,871 f. 51
29,210 ff. 1, 89	39,892 ff. 22, 26

(2) *In the India Office Library*

The following are among the many series of records of the British connection with India preserved in the India Office Library which have been consulted:

Home Miscellaneous
Board's Collections
India and Bengal Despatches
Bengal Despatches
Despatches to India (Political Dept.)
Secret Letters from India
Foreign Letters from India
Collections to Despatches
Enclosures to Secret Letters
Home Correspondence India
Secret and Political Letters from India
Elgin-Hamilton Correspondence
Curzon-Hamilton Correspondence
Bogle Papers
Hodgson MSS
Moorcroft MSS
Elgin Papers
Lansdowne Papers
Ampthill Papers
History of Sikkim (in typescript). Compiled by their Highnesses the
    Maharaja Sir Thutob Namgyal, K.C.I.E., and Maharani Yeshay
    Dolma of Sikkim, in 1908. (There is also a copy of this work in the
    Library of the Royal Central Asian Society, which was formerly the
    property of Sir C. Bell.)

(3)   In the Public Records Office

Copies of the greater part of the correspondence between the Indian
Government and the India Office relating to Tibet, which also concerned
the conduct of British relations with China, were sent by the India Office
to the Foreign Office. This correspondence can be found with ease in the
Foreign Office records, along with Foreign Office minutes, despatches
from the British Minister in Peking, Consular reports from Chungking,
and much other relevant material. The following series have been
consulted:

CO 77 29. This is an isolated volume containing letters on the Macartney
    Mission 1793-95.
FO 17 China. This series is divided into Various, in which correspondence
    from the India Office is to be found, Drafts, Despatches, Draft
    Telegrams, Telegrams. FO 17 1108, 1109, and 1745 to 1756 deal
    solely with Tibet and Sikkim.
FO 228. This series contains correspondence between the Peking
    Legation and its Consulates and the Indian Government.
FO 65 Russia.

(4)   In the Indian National Archives, New Delhi

Miscellaneous Bengal Political and General Consultations.

BIBLIOGRAPHY

PRINTED RECORDS, ETC.

Papers relating to the Nepaul War, printed in conformity to the resolution of the Court of Proprietors of East India Stock of 3rd March 1824.

East India, Sikkim Expedition, A. 9 P., 1862, XL.

Papers on the Hindustan-Tibet Road, A. & P., 1857, Session I, XI.

Papers Relating to Bhutan, A. & P. 1865, XXXIX.

Further Papers Relating to Bhutan, A. & P. 1866, LII.

China No. 2 1879, Report of Mr. Baber on his Journey to Tachienliu, A. & P. 1878-9, LXXII.

Report by Mr. Hosie on a journey through Central Ssu-Ch'uan, A & P. 1884-5, LXXX.

Papers Relating to Tibet 1904 (Cd. 1920).

Further Papers Relating to Tibet 1904 (Cd. 2054).

Further Papers Relating to Tibet 1905 (Cd. 2370).

Further Correspondence Relating to Tibet 1910 (Cd. 5240).

Report by Consul-General Hosie on the Province of Sauch'uan 1905 (Cd. 2247).

Report by Mr. A. Hosie H. M. Consul-General at Chengtu, on a journey to the Eastern Frontier of Tibet (Cd. 2586).

Punjab Government Records, vol. vi: Lahore Political Diaries 1847-9.

Selections from the Records of the Bengal Government, No. XVII: Report on Darjeeling, by W. B. Jackson, Calcutta 1854.

Political Missions to Bootan, Calcutta 1865.

Report on a Visit to Sikkim and the Thibetan Frontier in October, November, December 1873, by J. W. Edgar, Calcutta 1874.

Report on a Mission to Sikkim and the Tibetan Frontier, by Colman Macaulay, Calcutta 1885.

Summary of the Affairs of the Government of India in the Foreign Department for 1864 to 1868, by J. T. Wheeler, Calcutta 1868.

Frontier and Overseas Expeditions from India, compiled by the Intelligence Branch, Division of the Chief of Staff, Army Head Quarters, India, Simla 1907, Vol. IV, *North and North-Eastern Frontier Tribes.*

Notes on the Services of B. H. Hodgson, Esq., collected by a friend, for private circulation, no date.

British Documents on the Origins of the War 1898-1914, ed. by G. P. Gooch and H. Temperley, vol. IV, *The Anglo-Russian Rapprochement*, London 1953 (first published 1929).

Bengal Administration Reports.

Punjab Administration Reports.

Press List of Ancient Documents Preserved in the Imperial Record Room of the Government of India, Calcutta 1910.

Reports on the External Trade of Bengal with Nepal, Sikkim, and Bhutan, 1880-1905.

Report on the Internal Trade of Bengal for the year 1877-78, Calcutta 1878.

Reports on the Trade Statistics of the Punjab, 1870 to 1873.

Reports on the External Land Trade of the Punjab, 1881 to 1905.

Reports on the Trade between Assam and the Adjoining Foreign Countries, 1878 to 1905.

Imperial Gazetteer of India, Oxford 1908.
Punjab States Gazetteer, Vol. VII, Simla Hill States, Lahore 1911.
Punjab District Gazetteers, Vol. XXXa, Kangra District, Pts. II-IV.

SECONDARY SOURCES

Adamec, L. W., *Afghanistan 1900-1923. A Diplomatic History*, Berkeley and Los Angeles 1967.
Addy, P., *Tibet on the Imperial Chessboard*, Calcutta and New Delhi 1984.
Ahmad, Z., 'Tibet and Ladakh: a History', *St. Antony's Papers No. 14, Far Eastern Affairs Number Three*, London 1963.
Aitchison, C. U., *Collection of Treaties, Engagements and Sanads, etc.* 14 vols, Calcutta 1929-31.
Alder, G. J., *British India's Northern Frontier 1865-1895*, London 1963.
Alder, G. J., *Beyond Bokhara. The Life of William Moorcroft, Asian Explorer and Pioneer Veterinary Surgeon 1767-1825*, London 1985.
Aris, M., *Bhutan. The Early History of a Himalayan Kingdom*, Warminster 1979.
Aris, M., *Views of Medieval Bhutan, the Diary and Drawings of Samuel Davis 1783*, London and Washington, D.C. 1982.
Aspinall, A., *Cornwallis in Bengal*, Manchester 1931.
Auber, P., *China: An Outline of its Government, Laws and Policy; and of the British and Foreign Embassies to, and intercourse with, that Empire*, London 1834.
Baber, E. C., *Travel and Researches in Western China*, RGS Supp. Papers, vol. I, London 1886.
Bacot, J., *Le Tibet Revolté*, Paris 1912.
Bacot, J., *Introduction à l'Histoire du Tibet*, Paris 1962.
Bailey, F. M., 'Travels in Bhutan', *JCAS* 1930.
Bailey, F. M., *China, Tibet, Assam*, London 1945.
Bailey, F. M., *No Passport for Tibet*, London 1957.
Bajpai, S. C., *The Northern Frontier of India, Central and Western Sector*, Calcutta 1970.
Banerjee, A. C., *The Eastern Frontier of British India 1784-1826*, Calcutta 1946.
Barker, G. M., *A Tea Planter's Life in Assam*, London 1884.
Barooah, N. K., *David Scott in North-East India 1802-1831*, New Delhi 1970.
Barrow, J. A., *Some Account of the Public Life . . . of the Earl of Macartney*, 2 vols, London 1807.
Batten, J. H., *Official Reports on the Province of Kumaon*, Agra 1851.
Bayley, H. V., *Dorjé-ling*, Calcutta 1838.
Bell, Sir C., *Tibet, Past and Present*, Oxford 1924.
Bell, Sir C., 'The Dalai Lama; Lhasa 1921', *JCAS* 1924.
Bell Sir C., *The Religion of Tibet*, Oxford 1931.
Bell Sir C., *Portrait of the Dalai Lama*, London 1946.
Bhuyan, S. K., *Anglo-Assamese Relations, 1771-1826*, Gauhati 1949.

Bigham, C. A., *Year in China, 1899-1900*, London 1901.
Black, C. E. D., *Memoir of the Indian Survey 1878-90*, Calcutta 1891.
Black, C. E. D., *The Marquis of Dufferin and Ava*, London 1903.
Blakiston, T. W., *Five Months on the Yang-Tsze*, London 1862.
Bland, J. O. P. and Backhouse, E., *China under the Empress Dowager*, London and Peking 1939.
Blanford, W. T., 'Account of a visit to the Eastern and Northern frontiers of Independent Sikkim', *JASB* 1874, vol. XL, pt. II.
Bleichsteiner, R., *L'Eglise Jaune*, Paris 1937.
Blerzy, H., 'La Guerre du Bhutan', *Rev. de Deux Mondes*, Paris 1866.
Boulger, D. C., 'China via Tibet', *JRAS* 1878.
Boulger, D. C., *Lord William Bentinck*, Oxford 1892.
Boulger, D. C., *Life of Sir Halliday Macartney*, New York 1908.
Bower, H., *Diary of a Journey across Tibet*, London 1894.
Bredon, J., *Sir Robert Hart*, London 1909.
Bretschneider, E., *Medieval Researches from Eastern Asiatic Sources*, 2 vols, London.
Buchanan, F. (afterwards Hamilton), *An Account of the Kingdom of Napaul*, London 1819.
Buck, E. J., *Simla Past and Present*, Bombay 1925.
Buckland, C. E., *Bengal under the Lieutenant-Governors*, 2 vols, Calcutta 1901.
Buckland, C. E., *Dictionary of Indian Biography*, London 1906.
Burrard, S. G. and Hayden, H. H., *A Sketch of the . . . Himalaya Mountains and Tibet*, Delhi 1932.
Bysack, G. D., 'Notes on a Buddhist Monastery etc.', *JASB*, vol. LIX.
Cammann, S., 'The Panchen Lama's visit to China in 1780', *FEQ*, IX.
Cammann, S., *Trade through the Himalayas*, Princeton 1951.
Campbell, A., 'Journal of a trip to Sikkim in December 1848', *JASB*, vol. XVIII, pt. I, 1849.
Campbell, A., 'Notes on the Limboos etc.', *JASB*, vol. IX, pt. I, 1866.
Campbell, A., 'Note on the Lepchas etc.', *JASB*, vol. IX, pt. I, 1866.
Candler, E., *The Unveiling of Lhasa*, London 1905.
Caroe, Sir O., *Englishmen in Tibet*, Tibet Society Publication No. 4, London 1960.
Cavenagh, Sir O., *Rough Notes on the State of Nepal*, Calcutta 1851.
Chapman, C., 'Narrative of a Voyage to Cochin China', *Journal of the Indian Archipelago and Eastern Asia*, vol. VI. Singapore 1852.
Chapman, S., *Lhasa: the Holy City*, London 1938.
Chaudhuri, K. C., *Anglo-Nepalese Relations from the Earliest Times of the British Rule in India till the Gurkha War*, Calcutta 1960.
Christie, C. J., 'Sir Charles Bell: a Memoir', *Asian Affairs* (formerly JRCAS) VIII 1977.
Churchill, R. P., *The Anglo-Russian Convention of 1907*, Cedar Rapids 1939.
Clark, G., *Tibet, China and Great Britain*, Peking 1924.
Cooper, T. T., *Journal of an Overland Journey from China towards India*, Calcutta 1869.

Cooper, T. T., *Travels of a Pioneer of Commerce*, London 1871.

Cooper, T. T., *The Mishmee Hills*, London 1873.

Cordier, H., *L'Expulsion de MM. Huc et Gabet du Tibet*, Paris 1909.

Cordier, H., *Histoire des Relations de la Chine avec les Puissances*, vol. III. Paris 1902.

Cordier, H., *Histoire Generale de la Chine*, vol. IV. Paris 1921.

Cotton, H., *India and Home Memories*, London 1911.

Courant, M., *L'Asie Centrale aux XVIIe et XVIIIe siècles*, Paris 1912.

Cranmer-Byng, J. L. (ed.), *An Embassy to China: being the journal kept by Lord Macartney during his embassy to the Emperor Ch'ien-lung 1793-1794*, London 1962.

Cunningham, A., 'A trip through Kulu and Lahul to Ladak', *JASB*, vol. XVII, pt. I, 1848.

Cunningham, A., 'Memorandum of the Boundaries of Cashmir', *JASB*, vol. XVII, p.t I, 1848.

Cunningham, A., *Ladak, Physical, Statistical and Historical*, London 1854.

Cunningham, J. D., 'Notes on Moorcroft's Travels etc.', *JASB*, vol. XIII, pt. I. 1844.

Cunningham, J. D., *A History of the Sikhs etc.*, ed. E. L. O. Garrett, London 1918.

Curzon, G. N., *Russia in Central Asia*, London 1889.

Curzon, G. N., *Frontiers*, Romanes Lecture, Oxford 1907.

Cybikov, G. C., 'Journeys to Lhasa', *Geographical Journal*, 23, 1904.

Cybikov, G. C., 'Lhasa and Central Tibet', *Smithsonian Institution, Annual Report of the Board of Regents 1902-1903*, Washington 1904.

Cybikov, G. C., *Buddhist palomnik u svjatyn Tibeta. Po Dnevnikam, vedennym v 1899-1902gg*, Petrograd 1919.

Dainelli, G., *La Esplorazione della regione fra l'Himalaja occidentale e il Caracorum*, Bologna 1934.

Dallin, D. J., *The Rise of Russia in Asia*, London 1950.

D'Alviella, le Comte G., *Inde et Himalaya*, Paris 1877.

D'Anville, J. B. B., *Nouvel Atlas de la Chine, de la Tartarie Chinoise et du Thibet*, The Hague 1737.

Das, S. C., *Narrative of a Journey to Lhasa*, Calcutta 1885.

Das, S. C., *Indian Pandits in the Land of Snow*, ed. N. C. Das, Calcutta 1893.

Das, S. C., *Journey to Lhasa*, ed. W. W. Rockhill, London 1904.

Das, T., *British Expansion in Tibet*, Calcutta 1928.

Datta, C. L., *Ladakh and Western Himalayan Politics: 1819-1848*, New Delhi 1973.

Davies, A. M., *Warren Hastings*, London 1935.

Davies, H. R., *Yün-nan*, Cambridge 1909.

Davies, R. H., *Report on the Trade and Resources of the Countries on the North-Western Boundary of British India*, Lahore 1862.

Davies, Sir J., *China, during the War and since the Peace*, 2 vols, London 1852.

Davis, Sir J., *Chinese Miscellanies*, London 1865.

Deasy, H. H. P., *In Tibet and Chinese Turkestan*, London 1901.

Deb, A., *Bhutan and India. A Study in Frontier Political Relations (1772-1865)*, Calcutta 1976.

Deniker, J., 'Voyage de M. Tsybikov à Lhassa et au Tibet', *Géographie*, 9, 1904.

Deniker, J., see also: Narzounof, O.

Desgodins, C. H., *La Mission du Thibet*, Paris 1872.

Desgodins, C. H., *Le Thibet d'après la correspondence des Missionaires*. Paris 1885.

Desideri, I., *An account of Tibet*, ed. F. de Filippi, Intro. by C. Wessels, SJ, London 1932.

Dilks, D., *Curzon in India*, 2 vols, London 1969-70.

Diskalkar, D. B., 'The Tibeto-Nepalese War 1788-1793', *Journal of the Bihar and Orissa Research Society*, vol. XIX. Patna 1933.

Diskalkar, D. B., 'Bogle's Embassy to Tibet', *IHQ*, IX, 1933.

Dodwell, H. (ed.), *Warren Hastings' letters to Sir John Macpherson*, London 1927.

D'Orleans, Pere P. J., *Two Tartar Conquerors of China*, trans. the Earl of Ellesmere, intro. by R. H. Major, London 1854.

Dozey, E. C., *Darjeeling Past and Present*, Calcutta 1917.

Duka, T., *The Life of Alexander Csoma de Körös*, London 1885.

Eames, J. B., *The English in China*, London 1909.

Egerton, P. H., *Journal of a Tour through Spiti*, London 1864.

Ellis, H., *Journal of the Proceedings of the late Embassy to China*, London 1817.

Fazy, R., 'Le Cas Moorcroft: un Problème de l'Exploration Tibétaine', *T'oung Pao*, XXXV, 1940.

Field, A. R., 'A Note Concerning Early Anglo-Bhutanese Relations', *East and West*, NS Vol. 13, 1962.

Filchner, W., *Sturm über Asien*, Berlin 1924.

Filchner, W., 'A summary of Sturm über Asien, anon., entitled A Story of Struggle and Intrigue in Central Asia', *JCAS*, 1927 and 1928.

Fisher, M. W., Rose, L. E. and Huttenback, R. A., *Himalayan Battleground. Sino-Indian Rivalry in Ladakh*, London 1963.

Fleming, P., *Bayonets to Lhasa*, London 1961.

Florinsky, M. T., *Russia. A History and an Interpretation*, 2 vols, New York 1968.

Forrest, G. W., *Selections from the Letters, Despatches and other State Papers preserved in the Foreign Department of the Government of India 1772-1785*, 3 vols, Calcutta 1890.

Forrest, G. W., *The Administration of Warren Hastings*, Calcutta 1892.

Forrest, G. W., *The Administration of the Marquess of Lansdowne*, Calcutta 1894.

Forrest, G. W., *Selections from the State Papers of the Governors-General of India*, Warren Hastings, 3 vols, London 1910.

Fortune, R., *Three Years' Wanderings in the Northern Provinces of China*, London 1847.

Fortune, R., *A Journey to the Tea Countries of China*, London 1852.

Foster, Sir W., *The English Factories in India 1642-1645*, Oxford 1913.

Francke, A. H., *History of Western Tibet*, London 1907.

Fraser, D., *The Marches of Hindustan*, London 1907.

Fraser, J. B., *Journal of a Tour through part of the Himalaya Mountains*, London 1826.

Fraser, L., *India under Curzon and after*, London 1911.

Fraser-Tytler, Sir K., *Afghanistan*, Oxford 1953.

Freshfield, D., *Round Kanchenjunga*, London 1903.

Friters, G. M., *The International Position of Outer Mongolia*, Dijon 1939.

Fuchs, W., *Der Jesuiten-Atlas der Kanghsi-Zeit*, 1 vol, text plus 1 vol. maps, Peking 1943.

Furber, H., *Henry Dundas, First Viscount Melville 1742-1811*, Oxford 1931.

Furber, H., (ed.), *The Private Record of an Indian Governor-Generalship: the Correspondence of Sir John Shore etc. with H. Dundas etc.* Cambridge, Mass., 1933.

Furber, H., *John Company at Work*, Cambridge, Mass., 1951.

Gawler, J. G., *Sikkim etc.*, London 1873.

Gerard, A., *Account of Koonawur etc.*, ed. G. Lloyd. London 1841.

Gerard, A., 'Journey to Soobathoo and Shipke in Chinese Tartary', *JASB*, vol. XI, 1842.

Ghosh, S., *Tibet in Sino-Indian Relations 1899-1914*, New Delhi 1977.

Gill, W., *River of Golden Sand*, 2 vols, London 1880.

Gillard, D., *The Struggle for Asia 1828-1914. A study in British and Russian Imperialism*, London 1977.

Gleig, G. R., *Memoirs of the Rt. Hon Warren Hastings*, 3 vols, London 1841.

Gould, Sir B., *The Jewel in the Lotus*, London 1956.

Grenard, F., *Tibet*, London 1904.

Grey, Viscount of Fallodon, *Twenty-Five Years 1892-1916*, 2 vols, London 1928.

Griffith, W., 'Visit to Bootan', *JASB*, vol. VIII, 1839.

Griffith, W., *Journal of Travels in Assam, Burma, Bootan etc.*, Calcutta 1847.

Grousset, R., *Histoire de l'Extrême Orient*, 2 vols, Paris 1929.

Gundry, R. C., *China and her Neighbours*, London 1893.

Gupta, K., 'Distortions in the History of Sino-Indian Frontiers', *Economic and Political Weekly*, XV No. 30 1980.

Gupta, S., *British Relations with Bhutan*, Jaipur 1974.

Gutzlaff, C., *China Opened*, 2 vols, London 1838.

Hambly, G. (ed.), *Central Asia*, London 1969.

Hamilton, W., *The East India Gazetteer*, London 1815.

Hamilton, W., *A Geographical, Statistical, and Historical Description of Hindostan etc.*, 2 vols, London 1820.

Harcourt, A. F. P., *The Himalayan Districts of Kooloo, Lahoul and Spici*, London 1871.

Harrer, H., *Seven Years in Tibet*, London 1953.

Hastings, Marquess of, *Summary of the Administration of the Indian Government from October 1813 to January 1823 by the Marquess of Hastings*, London 1824.

Hastings, Marquess of, *The Administration of the Indian Government*, Edinburgh 1825.

Hastings, Marquess of, *Private Journals*, ed. the Marchioness of Bute, 2 vols, London 1858.

Hawthorn, J. G., *A Hand-book of Darjeeling*, Calcutta 1863.

Hedin, S., *Trans-Himalaya: discoveries and adventure in Tibet*, 2 vols, London 1910.

Herbert, J. D., 'Particulars of a visit to the Siccim Hills etc.', *Gleanings in Science*, Calcutta 1830.

Herbert, J. D., 'Journal of a visit to Kumaon', *JASB*, vol. XIII, 1844.

Hertslet, G. E. P., *Treaties between Great Britain and China*, 2 vols, London 1908.

Hodgson, B. H., *Essays on the Languages, Literature and Religion of Nepal and Tibet*, London 1874.

Hoffmeister, W., *Travels in Ceylon and Continental India*, London 1848.

Holdich, Sir T., *Tibet the Mysterious*, London 1908.

Hooker, J., *Hamalayan Journals*, 2 vols. London 1855.

Hopkirk, P., *Trespassers on the Roof of the World*, London 1982.

Hosie, A., *Three Years in Western China*, 2nd edn, London 1897.

Hügel, Baron C. von, *Travels in Kashmir and the Panjab*, London 1845.

Hummel, A. W., *Eminent Chinese of the Ch'ing Dynasty*, 2 vols, Washington 1943-44.

Hunter, Sir W. W. A., *Statistical Account of Bengal*, vol. X, London 1876.

Hunter, Sir W. W. A., *Life of B. H. Hodgson*, London 1896.

Husain, A., *British India's Relations with the Kingdom of Nepal 1857-1947*, London 1970.

Hutchison, J. and Vogel, J. P., *History of the Punjab Hill States*, 2 vols, Lahore 1933.

Hutton, T., 'Journal of a Trip through Kunawar etc.', *JASB*, vol. VIII, pt. II, 1839.

Iggulden, H. A., *The Second Battalion Derbyshire Regiment in the Sikkim Expedition of 1888*, London 1900.

Imbault-Huart, C., 'Histoire de la Conquête du Nepal par les Chinois', *JA*, Paris 1878.

Irwin, J., *The Kashmir Shawl*, London 1973.

Jacquemont, V., *Letters from India*, 2 vols, London 1834.

Karan, P. P. and Jenkins, W. M., *The Himalayan Kingdoms: Bhutan, Sikkim and Nepal*, Princeton 1963.

Kawaguchi, E., *Three Years in Tibet*, Benares and London 1909.

Khosla, G. D., *Himalayan Circuit*, London 1956.

Kiernan, E. V. G., *British Diplomacy in China 1880-85*, Cambridge 1939.

Kiernan, E. V. G., 'India, China and Tibet: 1885-86', *Journal of the Greater Indian Society*, vol. XIV, No. 2, 1955.

Kiernan, E. V. G., 'India, China and Sikkim: 1886-90', *IHQ*, vol. XXXI, No. 1, March 1955.

Kipling, R., *Kim*, London 1901.

Kirkpatrick, W., *An Account of the Kingdom of Nepaul*, London 1811.

Klein, I., 'The Anglo-Russian Convention and the Problem of Central Asia, 1907-1914', *Journal of British Studies*, XI 1971.

Kolmas, J., *Tibet and Imperial China. A Survey of Sino-Tibetan Relations up* to the End of the Manchu Dynasty in 1912, Canberra 1967.

Körös, A. Csoma de, 'Tibetan Studies', ed. E. D. Ross, extra no. JASB, vol. VII, 1911, Calcutta 1912.

Krausse, A., The Far East, its History and its Question, London 1900.

Krick, N. M., Relation d'un voyage au Thibet en 1852 et d'un voyage chez les Abors en 1853, Paris 1854.

Lahiri, R. M., The Annexation of Assam, Calcutta 1954.

Lamb, A., 'The Spiti Valley Today', JRCAS, July-Oct. 1956.

Lamb, A., 'Tibet in Anglo-Chinese Relations 1767-1842', JRAS, December 1957 and April 1958.

Lamb, A., 'Lord Macartney at Batavia, March 1793', Journal of the South Seas Society, Singapore 1958.

Lamb, A., 'Some Notes on Russian Intrigue in Tibet', JRCAS, 1959.

Lamb, A., The China-India Border. The Origins of the Disputed Boundaries, London 1964.

Lamb, A., The McMahon Line. A Study in the Relations between India, China and Tibet 1904-1914, 2 vols, London 1966.

Lamb, A., Asian Frontiers. Studies in a Continuing Problem, London 1968.

Lamb, A., The Mandarin Road to Old Hue. Narratives of Anglo-Vietnamese Diplomacy from the 17th Century to the Eve of the French Conquest, London 1970.

Lamb, A., The Sino-Indian Border in Ladakh, Canberra 1973.

Landon, P., Lhasa, 2 vols, London 1905.

Landon, P., Nepal, 2 vols, London 1928.

Landor, A. H., In the Forbidden Land: Tibet, 2 vols, London 1898.

Lansdell, H. H., Chinese Central Asia, 2 vols, London 1893.

Latourette, K. S., A History of the Expansion of Christianity, vol. VI, London 1945.

Lattimore, O., Inner Asian Frontiers of China, New York 1951.

Launay, A., Histoire de la Mission du Thibet, 2 vols, Paris and Lille 1904.

Lee, W.-K., Tibet in World Politics, New York 1931.

Lehault, P, La France et l'Angleterre en Asie, vol. I, Paris 1892.

Levi, S., Le Nepal, Paris 1905.

Li, T.-T., The Historical Status of Tibet, New York 1956.

Little, A. J., Through the Yang-tse Gorges, London 1898.

Little, A. J., Mount Omi and Beyond, London 1901.

Lloyd, G. (ed.), Narrative of a Journey from Caunpoor to the Boorendo Pass etc., 2 vols, London 1840.

Lobanov-Rostovsky, Prince A., Russia and Asia, New York 1933.

Louis, J. A. H., The Gates of Thibet, 2nd edn, Calcutta 1894.

Ludwig, E., The Visit of the Teshoo Lama to Peking, Peking 1904.

Lyall, Sir A., Life of the Marquess of Dufferin and Ava, 2 vols, London 1905.

Lyall, Sir A., The Rise and Expansion of the British Dominion in India, London 1920.

Macdonald, D., Land of the Lama, London 1929.

Macdonald, D., Twenty Years in Tibet, London 1932.

Macdonald, D., Tibet, Oxford 1946.

MacGregor, J., *Tibet. A Chronicle of Exploration*, London 1970.
Mackenzie, A., *History of the Relations of the Government of India with the Hill Tribes on the North-East Frontier of Bengal*, Calcutta 1884.
MacMurray, J. V. A. (ed.), *Treaties and Agreements with and concerning China 1894-1919*, Vol. 1, *Manchu Period (1894-1911)*, New York 1921.
Malcolm, Sir J., *Political History of India from 1784 to 1823*, 2 vols, London 1826.
Mariani, F., *Secret Tibet*, London 1952.
Markham, Sir C., *Narratives of the Mission of George Bogle to Tibet, and of the Journey of Thomas Manning to Lhasa*, London 1876.
Markham, Sir C., *Memoir of the Indian Survey*, 2nd edn, Calcutta 1878.
Markham, C. R., *Major James Rennell and the Rise of Modern English Geography*, London 1895.
Marshall, J. G., *Britain and Tibet 1765-1947: The Background to the India-China Border Dispute*, Bundoora, Australia 1977.
Marshman, J. C., *History of India*, 3 vols. London 1867.
Martin, R. M., *China; Political, Commercial, and Social; in an official report to Her Majesty's Government*, London 1847.
Mason, K., *Abode of Snow*, London 1955.
Mason, K., 'Great Figures of Nineteenth-Century Himalayan Exploration', *JRCAS*, 1956.
Maybon, C. B., *Histoire Moderne du Pays d'Annam*, Paris 1919.
Mayers, W. F., 'The Lamaist System in Tibet', *JRAS*, 1870.
Mayers, W. F., *The Chinese Government*, Shanghai 1878.
Mehra, P., 'Tibet and Russian Intrigue', *JRCAS*, Jan. 1958.
Mehra, P., 'Kazi U-gyen: "a paid Tibetan spy"?', *JRCAS* 1964.
Mehra, P., *The Younghusband Expedition. An Interpretation*, London 1968.
Mehra, P., *The McMahon Line and After*, New Delhi 1974.
Mehra, P., *Tibetan Polity, 1904-37*, Wiesbaden 1976.
Mehra, P., *The North-Eastern Frontier. A Documentary Study of the Internecine Rivalry between India, Tibet and China*, Vol. 1, New Delhi 1979.
Mersey, Viscount, *The Viceroys and Governors-General of India 1857-1947*, London 1949.
Michie, A., *The Englishman in China during the Victorian Era*, 2 vols, London 1900.
Midleton, Earl of, *Records and Reactions 1856-1939*, London 1939.
Millington, P., *Lhasa at Last*, London 1905.
Minto, Mary Countess of, *India, Minto and Morley, 1905-1910*, London 1932.
Mojumdar, K., *Political Relations Between India and Nepal*, New Delhi 1973.
Monger, G., *The End of Isolation: British Foreign Policy 1900-1907*, London 1963.
Moorcroft, W., 'A Journey to Lake Manasarovara etc.', *Asiatic Researches*, vol. XII. Calcutta 1816.
Moorcroft, W., and Trebeck, G., *Travels in the Himalayan Provinces of Hindustan etc.*, ed. H. H. Wilson, 2 vols, London 1841.

Morgan, G., *Ney Elias. Explorer and Envoy Extraordinary in High Asia*, London 1971.

Morgan, G., *Anglo-Russian Rivalry in Central Asia 1810-1895*, London 1981.

Morrison, G. E., *An Australian in China*, London 1895.

Morse, H. B., *International Relations of the Chinese Empire*, vol. II London 1918.

Morse, H. B., *The Trade and Administration of China*, London 1921.

Morse, H. B., *Chronicles of the East India Company Trading to China*, vols II, III. Oxford 1926.

Narzounof, O., 'Trois voyages à Lhasa (1898-1901). Présentés par J. Deniker', *Tour du Monde*, ns., 10, 1904.

Nicolson, H., *Lord Carnock*, London 1930.

Norman, H., *Peoples and Politics of the Far East*, London 1895.

Northey, W. B., *The Land of the Gurkhas*, Cambridge 1937.

O'Connor, Sir F., *On the Frontier and Beyond; A Record of Thirty Years Service*, London 1931.

O'Connor, Sir F., *Things Mortal*, London 1940.

Oldfield, H. A., *Sketches from Nipal*, 2 vols, London 1880.

O'Malley, L. S. S., *Bengal District Gazetteers: Darjeeling*, Calcutta 1907.

Oukhtomsky, E., 'The English in Tibet; a Russian view', *North American Review*, 179, 1904.

Panikkar, K. M., *Founding of the Kashmir State*, London 1953.

Panikkar, K. M., *Asia and Western Dominance*, London 1953.

Pares, Sir B., *A History of Russia*, London 1962.

Parker, E. H., 'Wei Yuan on the Mongols', *JNCBRAS* (NS), vol. XXII, 1887.

Parker, E. H., 'Letter from the Emperor of China to King George the Third'. *Nineteenth Century*, vol. XV, 1896.

Parker, E. H., 'Nepaul and China', *Imperial and Asiatic Quarterly Review*, VII, 1899.

Parker, E. H., *China Past and Present*, London 1903.

Parker, E. H., 'How the Tibetans Grew', *Imperial and Asiatic Quarterly Review*, vol. XVIII, 1904.

Parker, E. H., *China*, London 1917.

Pelliot, P. (ed.), *Travels in Tartary, Tibet and China, by Huc and Gabet*, 2 vols, London 1928.

Pemberton, R. B., *Report on the Eastern Frontier of British India*, Calcutta 1835.

Pemberton, R. B., *Report on Bootan*, Calcutta 1839.

Pemble, J., *The Invasion of Nepal. John Company at War*, Oxford 1971.

Perry-Ayscough, H. G. C. and Otter-Barry, R. B., *With the Russians in Mongolia*, London 1914.

Petech, L., *The Chronicles of Ladakh*, Calcutta 1939.

Petech, L., *China and Tibet in the early 18th Century*, Leiden 1950.

Petech, L., 'The Missions of Bogle and Turner according to Tibetan Texts', *T'oung Pao*, vol. XXXIX, 1949-50.

Petech, L., *The Kingdom of Ladakh c.950-1842 A.D.*, Rome 1977.

Phillips, C. H. (ed.), *The Correspondence of David Scott*, R. Hist: Soc., Camden 3rd Series, vols. LXXV and LXXVI, London 1951.

Phillips, G. D. R., *Dawn in Siberia: the Mongols of Lake Baikal*, London 1942.

Plaisted, B., 'An account of the countries . . . adjacent to Bengal', *Bengal Past and Present*, IV, Calcutta 1909.

Prasad, B., *The Foundations of India's Foreign Policy*, Calcutta 1955.

Pratt, Sir J., *The Expansion of Europe into the Far East*, London 1947.

Prinsep, H. T., *A Narrative of the Political and Military Transactions of British India, under the Administration of the Marquess of Hastings*, London 1820.

Prinsep, H. T., *History of the Political and Military Transactions in India during the Administration of the Marquess of Hastings*, 2 vols, London 1825.

Pritchard, E. H., *Anglo-Chinese Relations during the 17th and 18th Centuries*, University of Illinois Studies in the Social Sciences, Urbana, Illinois, 1929.

Pritchard, E. H., *The Crucial Years of Early Anglo-Chinese Relations 1750-1800*, Research Studies of the State College of Washington, vol. IV, 1936.

Pritchard, E. H., 'The Instructions of the East India Company to Lord Macartney on his Embassy to China and his Reports to the Company, 1792-94', *JRAS*, London 1938.

Rahul, R., *The Himalayan Borderland*, New Delhi 1970.

Rahul, R., *The Himalaya as a Frontier*, New Delhi 1978.

Ramsay, H. L., *Western Tibet*, Lahore 1890.

Rao, G. N., *The India-China Border: a Reappraisal*, Bombay 1968.

Rao, P. R., *India and Sikkim (1814-1970)*, New Delhi 1972.

Raper, F. V., 'Narrative etc.', *Asiatic Researches*, vol. XI, Calcutta 1810.

Rawling, C. G., *The Great Plateau*, London 1905.

Rawlinson, H. G., *The British Achievement in India*, London 1948.

Ray, P., *India's Foreign Trade since 1870*, London 1934.

Rayfield, D., *The Dream of Lhasa. The Life of Nikolay Przhevalsky, Explorer of Central Asia*, London 1976.

Regmi, D. R., *Modern Nepal: Rise and Growth in the Eighteenth Century*, Calcutta 1961.

Reid, Sir R., *History of the Frontier Areas Bordering on Assam from 1883-1941*, Shillong 1942.

Rennell, J., *Memoir of a Map of Hindoostan*, 3rd edn, London 1793.

Rennie, Dr., *Bhotan and the Douar War*, London 1866.

Richardson, H. E., 'The Karma-pa Sect. A Historical Note', *JRAS*, 1958.

Richardson, H. E., *Tibet and its History*, London 1962.

Riencourt, A. de, *Lost World: Tibet, Key to Asia*, London 1950.

Riseley, H. H. (ed.), *Gazetteer of Sikkim*, Calcutta 1894.

Robbins, H., *Our First Ambassador to China*, London 1908.

Roberts, P. E., *History of British India*, contd. by T. G. P. Spear, Oxford 1952.

Rockhill, W. W., 'Tibet: History of Tibet derived from Chinese sources', *JRAS*, vol. XXIII, 1891.

Rockhill, W. W., *Land of the Lamas*, New York 1891.

Rockhill, W. W., 'The Dalai Lamas of Lhasa', *T'oung Pao*, Series 3, vol. XI, 1910.

Ronaldshay, Earl of, *Lands of the Thunderbolt*, London 1923.

Ronaldshay, Earl of, *Life of Lord Curzon*, 3 vols, London 1928.

Ross, C. (ed.), *The Correspondence of Charles, First Marquis Cornwallis*, 3 vols, London 1859.

Ross-of-Bladensberg, Major, *The Marquess of Hastings*, Oxford 1893.

Rouire, A. M. F., *La Rivalité Anglo-Russe au XIXme Siècle en Asie*, Paris 1908.

Rupen, R. A., 'Mongolian Nationalism', *JRCAS*, 1958.

Saint-Martin, V. de and Rousselet, L., *Nouveau Dictionnaire de Geographie Universelle*, vol. VI. Paris 1894.

Sandberg, G., *Bhotan, the Unknown Indian State*, Calcutta 1897.

Sandberg, G., *The Exploration of Tibet*, Calcutta 1904.

Sandberg, G., *Tibet and the Tibetans*, London 1906.

Sanwal, B. D., *Nepal and the East India Company*, Bombay and London 1965.

Sargent, A. J., *Anglo-Chinese Diplomacy and Commerce*, Oxford 1907.

Sarkar, S. C., 'Some notes on the intercourse of Bengal with Northern Countries in the second half of the 18th Century', *Proc. Indian Hist. Records Comm.*, vol. XIII, 1930.

Scott, Sir J. G., *Burma*, London 1924.

Seaver, G., *Francis Younghusband*, London 1952.

Seton-Watson, H., *The Decline of Imperial Russia*, London 1952.

Shakabpa, Tsepon W. D., *Tibet. A Political History*, New Haven 1967.

Shakespear, C. W., *History of Upper Assam, Upper Burma, and North-East Frontier*, London 1914.

Shen, T.-L. and Liu, S.-C., *Tibet and the Tibetans*, Stanford, Cal., 1953.

Sherwill, J. L., 'Journal of a trip . . . in the Sikkim Himalaya', *JASB*, vol. V Calcutta 1862.

Sinha, J. C., *The Economic Annals of Bengal*, London 1927.

Sinha, N. K., *Fort William-India House Correspondence 1767-1769*, India Records Series, vol. V.

Skrine, C. P. and Nightingale, P., *Macartney at Kashgar. New Light on British, Chinese and Russian Activities in Sinkiang 1890-1918*, London 1973.

Smith, V. A., *The Oxford History of India*, 2nd edn revised by S. M. Edwardes, Oxford 1923.

Snelling, J., *The Sacred Mountain: travellers and pilgrims at Mount Kailas in Western Tibet*, London 1983.

Spate, O. H. K., *India and Pakistan*, London 1954.

Staunton, Sir G., Bart. *An Authentic Account of an Embassy from Great Britain to the Emperor of China etc.*, 2 vols, plus 1 vol. of plates, London 1797.

Staunton, Sir G. T., Bart. *Miscellaneous Notices relating to China*, London 1822.

Sumner, B. H., *Tsardom and Imperialism in the Far East and Middle East, 1880-1914*, Hamden Connecticut 1968.

Sykes, Sir P., *Sir Mortimer Durnad*, London 1926.

Sykes, Sir P., *A History of Exploration*, London 1934.

Sykes, Sir P., *The Quest for Cathay*, London 1936.

Sykes, Sir P., *History of Afghanistan*, 2 vols, London 1940.

Taboulet, G., *La Geste Française en Indochine*, 2 vols, Paris 1955.

Tavernier, J. B., *Travels in India*, ed. V. Ball, 2 vols, London 1889.

Teichman, Sir E., *Travels of a Consular Official in Eastern Tibet*, Cambridge 1922.

Teichman, Sir E., *Affairs of China*, London 1938.

Temple, Sir R., *Journals kept in Hyderabad, Cashmir, Sikkim and Nepal*, 2 vols, London 1887.

Thomas, L., *Out of this World; Across the Himalayas to Forbidden Tibet*, New York 1950.

Thompson, E. and Garratt, G. T., *Rise and Fulfilment of British Rule in India*, 2nd edn, London 1935.

Thomson, J. O., *History of Ancient Geography*, Cambridge 1948.

Thomson, T., *Western Himalaya and Tibet*, London 1852.

Tichy, H., *Tibetan Adventure*, London 1938.

Torrens, H. D., *Travels in Ladak, Tartary and Kashmir*, London 1862.

Traill, G. W., 'Statistical Sketch of Kumaon', *Asiatic Researches*, vol. XVI, 1828.

Tsybikoff, G., see: Cybikov, G. C.

Turner, S., *An Account of an Embassy to the Court of the Teshoo Lama in Tibet*, 2nd edn London 1806.

Ukhtomsky, Prince E. E., see: Oukhtomsky, E.

Varg, P. A., *Open Door Diplomat: the Life of W. W. Rockhill*, Urbana, Illinois, 1952.

Vigne, G. T., *Travels in Kashmir, Ladak, Iskardo etc.*, 2 vols, London 1842.

Waddell, L. A., *Among the Himalayas*, London 1899.

Waddell, L. A., *Lhasa and its Mysteries*, London 1905.

Walrond, T. (ed.), *Letters and Journals of James, Eighth Earl of Elgin*, London 1872.

Wang, S. T., *The Margary Affair and the Chefoo Convention*, Oxford 1940.

Watt, G., *Dictionary of the Economic Products of India*, vol. VI, pt. II, London and Calcutta 1893.

Welby, M. C., *Through Unknown Tibet*, London 1898.

Wessels, C., *Early Jesuit Travellers in Central Asia*, The Hague 1924.

West, A., *Sir Charles Wood's Administration of Indian Affairs from 1859 to 1866*, London 1867.

Wheeler, J. T., *A Short History of India*, London 1889.

Whistler, H., *In the High Himalayas*, London 1929.

White, J. C., *Sikkim and Bhutan*, London 1909.

Williams, E. T., *Tibet and her Neighbours*, Berkeley 1937.

Willoughby, W. W., *Foreign Rights and Interests in China*, Baltimore 1920.

Wilson, A., *The Abode of Snow*, London 1876.

Wilson, H. H., *History of British India from 1805 to 1835* (in continuation of Mill), 3 vols, London 1846.

Winnington, A., *Tibet, the Record of a Journey*, London 1957.

Witte, Count, *Memoirs*, translated and edited by A. Yarmolinsky, London 1921.

Woodcock, G., *Into Tibet. The Early British Explorers*, London 1971.

Woodman, D., *Himalayan Frontiers*, London 1969.

Wright, D., *History of Nepal*, Cambridge 1877.

Wright, S. F., *Hart and the Chinese Customs*, Belfast 1950.

Wyllie, J. W. S., *Essays on the External Policy of India*, ed. by W. W. Hunter, London 1875.

Yakhontoff, V. A., *Russia and the Soviet Union in the Far East*, London 1932.

Younghusband, F. E. (later Sir F.), *The Heart of a Continent*, London 1896.

Younghusband, Sir F., *India and Tibet*, London 1910.

Younghusband, Sir F., *Our Position in Tibet*, London 1910.

INDEX

Abdul Kadir Khan, 27, 28, 39, 40
Abdur Rahman, Amir of
  Afghanistan, 254
Aberdeen, 115
Adam J., 33
Aden, 233
Afghanistan, ix, 31, 53, 64, 117,
  128, 136, 164, 190, 194, 209,
  211, 226, 241, 245, 253, 254,
  255, 269, 270, 271, 272, 280,
  281, 283
Agnew Mr, 17
Agnew, Vans, 58, 60, 66, 91
Ahmad Ali, 39, 40
Alcock Sir R., 96, 99, 112
Alder, G. J., x
Alexander III, 250
Almora, 198
Alsatia, 166
Altan Khan, 2
Amban (Chinese Resident at
  Lhasa), 2, 8, 19, 34, 54, 62, 64,
  83, 92, 93, 99, 102, 108, 109,
  116, 117, 123, 130, 131, 132,
  133, 142, 143, 144, 146, 147,
  149, 150, 151, 152, 154, 155,
  156, 157, 158, 160, 161, 168,
  169, 170, 171, 175, 176, 182,
  183, 189, 190, 195, 196, 203,
  204, 214, 215, 216, 218, 227,
  231, 232, 233, 234, 235, 243,
  252, 258, 274, 275
America, 220
Amherst, Lady Sarah, 41
Amherst, Lord, 14, 36, 37, 38, 40,
  41
Ampthill, Lord, 240, 242, 243,
  244, 245, 246, 247, 248, 263,
  265, 267
Amritsar, 47, 52, 58, 65; Treaty of
  1846, 58
Anant Ram, 60, 61, 188
Anglo-Chinese Convention (1906),
  266, 272
Andkhui, 31
Anglo-French Agreement on
  Egypt, 246
Anglo-Russian Convention (1907),
  255, 266, 269, 271, 272, 273,
  275, 278, 279, 283, 284, 285
Annam, 117
Ardagh, Sir John, 191

Arghun, 45, 199
Argyle, Duke of, 101, 105, 106
Arsenals, 183, 230
Assam, xiii, 5, 22, 25, 61, 65, 82,
83, 84, 85, 86, 89, 95, 97, 100,
101, 173, 264, 277, 278; Tibetan
Trade with, 84, 85, 86
Assam Himalayas, Chinese interest
in, 277, 278
Auckland, Lord, 83
Australia, 264
Austria, 119

Baber, E. C., 118, 119, 120, 121,
159
Badengieff, 218
Badmaev, Dr, 205, 206, 218, 230,
250, 251, 253
Bahadur, Sir Jang, 95, 108, 109
Baikal, Lake, 184
Bailey, Lt. Col. F. M., 136
Balfour, A., 228, 241, 266, 269
Balkans, 269
Balkh, 31
Baluchistan, 194
Banks, Sir J., 16
Baranoff, 194
Bareilly, 47
Barker, Mr, 159
Basevi, Capt. J. P., 91
Bashahr, 43, 44, 47, 50, 54, 56, 59,
60, 61, 65
Batang, 148, 276
Begar, 46, 65
Bell, Sir C., 221
Benares, 12, 20, 26, 27, 28, 29
Benckendorff, Count, 229, 230,
236, 237
Bengal, xiii, 3, 5, 6, 7, 8, 9, 10, 14,
15, 21, 26, 31, 32, 44, 47, 67, 69,
70, 85, 89, 90, 100, 102, 103,
104, 109, 110, 121, 122, 124,
125, 126, 141, 149, 163, 167,
169, 170, 172, 173, 175, 176,
177, 180, 196, 197, 202, 203,
204, 208, 216, 246; Curzon
views on Bengal Government,
208; Government views on

Sikkim Tibet Frontier, 169, 170;
Lieutenant Governor of almost
captured at Gnatong, 149
Bentinck, Lord William, 69
Berlin, 250
Bertie, Sir F., 213
Bezobrazov, 321
Bhatgaon, 3
Bhim Sen Thapa, 29, 30
Bhutan, ix, 3, 5, 6, 7, 8, 10, 11, 15,
25, 26, 28, 29, 30, 33, 34, 36, 39,
41, 51, 61, 63, 68, 73, 76, 77, 78,
79, 81, 82, 83, 84, 86, 100, 101,
105, 108, 115, 123, 124, 141,
142, 143, 144, 145, 149, 152,
153, 158, 159, 168, 172, 173,
188, 196, 198, 202, 210, 216,
242, 275, 277; Anglo-Bhutanese
Treaty (1910), 275;
Anglo-Bhutanese War (1865),
82, 87, 100; Bhutan-British, 89;
see also Tongsa Penlop; Paro
Penlop
Bihar, xiii
Birmingham, 49, 127
Black Sect, 181
Blakiston, Capt., 92
Blandford, W. T., 106, 107
Blue Books (Tibet), 178, 219, 221,
227
Boer War, 211, 224
Bogle, G., xiv, 7, 8, 10, 11, 12, 13,
14, 16, 19, 23, 24, 33, 34, 39, 43,
64, 82, 83, 84, 100, 106, 111,
125, 184, 189, 190, 232
Bokhara, 205
Bombay, 186, 208
Bonga, 90
Bonin, M., 185
Bonvalot, M., 220, 237
Borax, 44, 81
Boulger, D. C., 115, 117
Boundary Commissions, *see*
Ladakh; Sikkim-Tibet
Boundary Pillars, Sikkim-Tibet
Border, 170, 171, 178, 179, 210,
212, 213; Chinese, 179, 180
Boury, Father, 90

Bower, H., 166, 174, 186, 187
Bowring, Sir J., 93
Boxer Rebellion, 190, 217, 218, 274
Bradford, 99, 115, 175
Brahmaputra, 5, 6, 44, 85, 86, 115, 240, 277
Brennan, B., 113
Bretherton, Major, 238
Bristol, 99
British Documents on the Origins of the War 1898-1914, 257
British Mission to Tibet, false rumours of (1878), 119
Brodrick, St J., 240, 241, 242, 244, 245, 246, 248
Browne, Col., 115
Browne, Col. (military attaché in Peking), 208
Bruce, Sir F., 91, 127
Buchanan, Dr, 32, 33
Buddhism, 1, 44, 46, 69, 89, 90, 106, 112, 127, 132, 147, 148, 162, 181, 184, 196, 205, 207, 215, 218, 240, 251, 254, 272, 273
Buriats, 184, 185, 205, 207, 218, 250, 251, 253, 262, 272
Burma, x, 3, 63, 89, 96, 97, 99, 101, 114, 117, 131, 132, 133, 135, 136, 137, 139, 140, 152, 154, 162, 197, 198
Burma-Tibet Convention (1886), 134, 135, 139, 141, 145, 157, 162, 165, 185, 186, 195
Burne, Sir O., 109

Cabinet, 227, 228, 231, 233, 241
Calcutta, 7, 11, 12, 26, 31, 32, 34, 36, 48, 97, 105, 121, 122, 125, 126, 159, 166, 169, 196, 197, 207, 208, 216, 264, 265, 267, 268
Calcutta Englishman, 196
Calcutta Review, 89
Campbell, Dr A., 72, 73, 74, 75, 76, 77, 78, 79, 80, 86, 88, 97, 105, 120, 141, 159
Campbell-Bannerman, Sir H., 261, 269

Canada, 264
Candler, E., 252
Canning, Stratford, 245
Canterbury, Archbishop of, 186
Canton, 9, 10, 13, 16, 17, 20, 21, 23, 24, 31, 36, 41, 54, 62, 92; English Trade at, 13, 16; Select Committee at, 31, 37, 38, 42
Capuchins, xiv
Carey, A. D., 186
Cathcart, Lt. Col., 16, 17, 21
Catholics, 90, 95, 96, 129, 131, 148, 150, 159, 184, 189, 218
Cartier, J., 5
Cavagnari, Sir L., 211
Cayley, Dr, 67
Central Asian Khanates, 44, 271
Central Asia, Russia, 270
Ceylon, 283
Chamberlain, Joseph, 240
Chambers of Commerce, 89, 97, 99, 127, 135, 145, 157, 159, 166, 175, 176, 185
Chandra Shamsher Jang, Maharaja of Nepal, 216
Chang Yin-T'ang, 264, 267, 268, 274, 275
Channer, Maj. Gen., 187
Chao Erh-Feng, 182, 255, 259, 275, 276
Chapba, 45, 46, 200, 201, 202
Chapman, Dr, 71
Cheauveau, Mgr, 98
Chebu Lama, 72, 73, 74, 76, 78, 79, 80
Chefoo Convention, 113, 116, 117, 119, 121, 265, 279, 281; Separate Article of, 116, 117, 118, 120, 126, 127, 130, 133, 134, 135, 165
Chenevix Trench, Capt., 198
Chengtu, 97, 149, 182
Cheshire, 99
Chi Chih-Wen, 148, 149
Ch'ien Lung, 2, 12, 20, 22, 93
China, *see under* Anglo-Chinese; Chinese Maritime Customs; Dalai Lama; Mongolia; Opium War; Panchen Lama; Peking;

Sinkiang; Szechuan; Tea; Tibet
China, British Communications
  with, 62
China Consular Service, 113, 118,
  132, 189
China, Emperors of, 112
China, Emperor of, Nepalese letter
  to, 32
China, military power in Tibet, x,
  xii, xiii, xiv
China Times, 217
China, Western trade with, 98,
  99
Chinese Communists, 239, 285
Chinese interest in Nepal
  (1814-16), 34, 35, 36
Chinese legation in London,
  129
Chinese Maritime Customs, 128,
  154, 167, 214, 236, 264
Chinese Revolution (1911), 94,
  278, 284
Chinese Turkestan, *see* Sinkiang
Ch'ing Dynasty, 1, 2, 10, 112, 129,
  147, 148, 218, 258, 274, 276
Ch'ing Prince, 216
Chini, 65
Chirang Palgez, 198, 199
Ch'i-shan, 62
Chita, 208
Chitral, 191
Chola Pass, 74, 81, 102
Chumbi Valley, 72, 74, 75, 81,
  102, 106, 110, 111, 121, 125,
  130, 140, 144, 145, 149, 152,
  158, 159, 161, 167, 168, 170,
  171, 174, 175, 178, 181, 203,
  210, 213, 229, 233, 236, 238,
  242, 244, 248, 249, 263, 264,
  268, 273, 275, 276, 278
Ch'ung-Hou, 148
Chungking, 98, 99, 118, 120, 182,
  185
Churchill, Lord Randolph, 127,
  136
Church of England, 89
Clerk, Sir G. R., 52, 53, 54, 55
Clive, Lord, 6

Cochin China, 10, 31; *see also*
  Annam
Columbo, 128
Conservative Government, 269
Constantinople, 279
Gooch Behar, 5, 6, 7, 10, 29, 100;
  War with Bhutan, 6, 7
Cooper, T. T., 85, 96, 97, 98, 99,
  100, 101, 102, 104, 105, 106,
  120, 129, 159
Cornwallis, Lord, 17, 18, 19, 20
Cossacks, 218, 236, 251
Cresswell and Co., 159
Cross, Lord, 154, 157
Csoma De Körös, 51
Cunningham, A., 48, 58, 61, 63,
  91
Cunningham, J. D., 48, 55, 57, 60,
  63, 65, 161
Currie, Sir P., 136
Curzon, Lord, x, 25, 169, 176,
  177, 185, 189, 190, 191, 192,
  193-221, 222, 223, 224, 226,
  227, 228, 229, 230, 231, 232,
  233, 234, 236, 238, 240, 241,
  242, 243, 244, 247, 253, 254,
  256, 257, 359, 260, 261, 263,
  264, 268, 270, 280, 281, 282, 285

Dalai Lama, x, 1, 8, 9, 12, 19, 27,
  28, 31, 45, 46, 64, 73, 83, 84, 86,
  89, 93, 108, 118, 122, 128, 130,
  146, 151, 152, 166, 172, 183,
  273, 275, 284; Eighth, 183;
  Ninth, 183; Tenth, 183;
  Eleventh, 183; Twelfth, 183;
  Thirteenth, 23, 148, 173, 182,
  183, 184, 185, 186, 190, 193,
  195, 196, 197, 199, 200, 201,
  202, 203, 204, 205, 206, 209,
  210, 211, 213, 215, 218, 221,
  223, 226, 234, 238, 239, 243,
  250, 251, 252, 254, 257, 258,
  260, 262, 272, 276, 277, 278, 283
Dalhousie, Lord, 62, 65
Dane, Sir L., 247, 248, 254, 268,
  270
D'Anville, xiv, 287

Dardanelles, 279
Darjeeling, 41, 51, 65, 69, 70, 71,
  73, 74, 76, 77, 78, 79, 81, 86, 88,
  89, 97, 101, 103, 105, 107, 110,
  111, 120, 121, 124, 127, 132,
  134, 140, 141, 145, 146, 149,
  152, 154, 159, 163, 177, 181,
  188, 194, 196, 207, 216, 223, 232
Darjeeling Frontier Reports, 208
Darjeeling Improvement Trust,
  177
Darrang District, 85
Das, Sarat Chandra, 122, 124, 125,
  128, 129, 132, 144, 188, 196,
  200, 205, 208
Davis, Sir J., 60, 62
Deasy, H.H.P., 186, 187
Deb Rajah of Bhutan, 8, 82, 142,
  143
Delhi, 32, 65
Desgodins, Father, 90, 150, 159
Desideri, I., xiv
Dewsbury, 127, 135
Dharla River, 6
Dharma Raja of Bhutan, 82
Dhurkey Sirdar, 177, 184, 203,
  213, 214
Dilke, Sir C., 117
Dogras, xiii, 48, 51, 52, 53, 54, 55,
  258; Treaty with Chinese and
  Tibet (1852), 55-7, 59, 61
Doko Pass, 171
Donchuk Pass, 171
Donkya Pass, 74
Dorjieff, 185, 205, 206, 207, 208,
  209, 210, 211, 215, 216, 219,
  242, 243, 251, 253, 254, 271,
  272, 273, 280, 282, 283
D'Orleans, H., 220
Drebung Monastery, 85, 126, 171,
  207
Duars, 5, 29, 101, 152
Dufferin, Lord, 126, 128, 132, 134,
  135, 136, 137, 139, 140, 141,
  145, 146, 147, 149, 153, 169
Du Halde, xiv
Duncan, J., 20, 26
Dundas, H., 17, 27

Dundee, 115
Durand, Sir M., 150, 151, 152,
  153, 154
Dutreuil Du Rhins, 220, 237
Dzungars, 191, 258

East India Company, ix, xiii, xiv,
  3, 4, 9, 14, 20, 23, 26, 27; Board
  of Control, 16, 17; Court of
  Directors, 4, 5, 6, 7, 11, 16, 17,
  31, 37, 47, 51, 59; Trade with
  China, 4, 24
Eden, Sir Ashley, 76, 80, 81, 86,
  92, 100, 122, 141, 179
Edgar, Sir J. W., 107, 110, 111,
  112, 121, 124, 125, 136, 141, 159
Edward VII, 213, 240
Egerton, P. H., 66
Egypt, 246
Elgin, Lord, VIII Earl, 86, 88, 91,
  171; IX Earl, 169, 173, 174, 175,
  176, 177, 179, 187, 189, 193,
  213, 215, 234, 252
Elias, Ney, 137, 150, 190
Elliott, Sir C., 170, 171, 174
Elwes, Capt., 132
Empress Dowager of China, 217

Fage, Father, 90
Filchner, W., 251
Firearms, 183, 242, 252
Fitzpatrick, Sir D., 228
Foochow, 217
Foreign Office, 104, 127, 133, 134,
  135, 138, 145, 147, 154, 155,
  156, 166, 174, 187, 195, 212,
  213, 216, 222, 224, 235, 244,
  269, 275, 279
Forsyth Mission, 67, 115
Fort William, 48
Foster, Mr, 16
France, 40, 50, 64, 90, 95, 96, 98,
  112, 118, 119, 131, 148, 150,
  159, 162, 184, 185, 189, 209,
  220, 237, 246, 250, 269
Francis, P., 11
Fraser, Mr (chargé at Peking), 119
Fraser, S. M., 264

Fu-K'ang-an, 21
Fukien, 250
Furber, H., 11

Gabet, Father, 31, 62, 93
Gaden Monastery, 126, 171
Galing, 143
Ganges, 3, 44, 115, 278
Gangtok, 121, 153, 171
Gardner, Resident at Katmandu, 35, 36
Garpons, 46, 47, 49, 50, 59, 60, 62, 66, 198, 199, 200, 201, 202
Gartok, 31, 44, 47, 49, 52, 55, 57, 59, 60, 61, 62, 65, 66, 84, 92, 198, 199, 200, 201, 202, 240, 243, 247, 248, 260
Garwhal, xii, 3, 25, 33, 35, 39, 40, 43, 51, 154, 247
Gates of Tibet, 179
Gaussen, Lt., 186
Gawler, Lt. Col., 80, 105
Gellong, 102
Gelupka (Yellow) Sect, 1, 2
George III, 23
Gerard, A., 49, 50
Gerard, Dr J. G., 48
Germany, 209, 220, 248, 250, 251
Giaogong, 168, 170, 173, 174, 175, 176, 177, 178, 179, 180, 184, 192, 204, 210, 211, 213, 214, 231, 232, 234
Gilgit, 61
Gillman, Mr, 47
Glasgow, 99, 115
Gloucester, 99
Gnatong, 111, 149, 154, 175
Godley, Sir A., 211
Gold, 3, 10, 28, 29, 44, 81, 120, 125, 127, 220, 221, 242, 253
Golden Urn, 19, 148
Goloss, 118
Goom Monastery, 207
Gorchakov, Prince, 80
Goschen, E., 147
Gosein, 11
Gracey, Mr, 198
Graevenitz, Baron, 229

Graham, Brig.-Gen., 149
Graham, Maj., 85
Grand Trunk Road, 65
Grant, G. W., 69
Granville, Lord, 101
'Great Game', 283
Greek Orthodox, 218
Groot, Von, 220
Gulab Singh, 3, 51, 52, 53, 54, 55, 56, 57, 58, 59, 61, 62, 64, 161, 185
Gurkha, xiv, 3, 4, 5, 7, 8, 9, 12, 21, 32, 33, 53, 57, 69, 70, 78, 94, 103, 107, 109, 123, 190, 223, 224, 225, 240, 258, 262; War with Tibet 1788, 17-25; see also Nepal
Gurkha War (1814-16), xii, 23, 24, 25, 29-33, 43, 47, 48, 51, 64, 68, 80, 90, 109
Guru, 238
Gützlaff, 89
Gwatkin, Capt., 132
Gyalpo of Ladakh, 45, 46, 48
Gyantse, 131, 136, 158, 232, 233, 234, 236, 238, 241, 242, 243, 244, 245, 246, 248, 260, 261, 263, 267, 268

Haas, M., 185
Habibullah, Amir of Afghanistan, 259, 270
Haji Wazir Shah, 199
Halifax, 99, 135
Hamilton, A., 8, 11, 12, 82, 83
Hamilton, Lord George, 174, 194, 202, 203, 206, 210, 211, 214, 222, 225, 226, 227, 228, 229, 231, 233, 236, 240, 241
Hankow, 92
Hanle, 62
Hardinge, Lord of Lahore, 59, 60, 61
Hardinge, Lord of Penshurst, 205, 218, 224, 230, 248
Hart, James, 154, 155, 156, 157, 158, 161
Hart, Sir R., 128, 137, 150, 154, 156, 265

Hastings, Marquis of, 30, 32, 34, 35, 36, 37, 39, 40, 41, 51, 64
Hastings, Warren, x, xiv, 5, 7, 8, 10, 11, 12, 13, 14, 15, 16, 17, 18, 23, 24, 25, 30, 34, 39, 41, 42, 48, 82, 84, 101, 105, 106, 118, 125, 189, 220, 257
Haughton, Col., 100, 101, 102, 103, 104, 107
Hearsey, H. Y., 31
Hedin, Sven, 220, 261, 262
Henderson, Dr, 48
Herat, 194
Herbert, Capt., 69
Hindu, 3, 4, 43, 44
Hindu Kush, 31
Hindustan-Tibet Road, 65, 66, 106
Ho Chang-jung, 161
Hodgson, B. H., 51, 53, 54, 57, 64, 70, 88, 105, 120, 159
Ho Huang-hsi, 214, 227, 231
Holdich, Sir T., 85, 221
Holland, 220
Hong Kong, 38, 42, 60, 61, 62, 93
Hong Kong and Shanghai Bank, 267
Hooker, Dr J., 73, 74, 75, 76, 77, 78, 105, 141, 179
Hopityant, M., 207
Hopkinson, Major, 83, 86
Hosie, A., 120, 159
Hsü Ying-k'uei, 217
Huc, Father, 31, 62, 90
Huddersfield, 99, 135
Hungary, 51
Hunza, 61, 152, 161

Iggulden, Major, 213
Ilam Singh, 72, 74
India, War with China, xi, xii
India and Tibet, 255, 278
India Office, 105, 109, 134, 135, 141, 145, 154, 155, 187, 206, 211, 212, 215, 220, 221, 222, 224, 225, 228, 231, 236, 241, 261, 271, 275
Indian Army, 225
Indian Mutiny, 108

Indian Tea Association, 160, 227
India, transfer of power (1947), 285
Indore, 232
Indus River, 44, 51, 58, 115
Irrawaddy River, 115
Isvolski, A., 272
Italy, 250

Jackson, Lt. D'Aguilar, 91
Jackson, W.B., 89
Jacquemont, V., 50
Jammu, ix, 3, 51, 54, 55, 57, 58, 64
Jampay, 177
Jang Bahadur, *see* Bahadur, Sir Jang
Japan, 166, 167, 174, 182, 188, 220, 248, 250, 251, 257; Sino-Japanese War (1894-5), 23, 166, 174, 182, 190
Jehol, 21
Jelep La Pass, 106, 111, 121, 140, 159, 168, 170, 175, 238
Jenkins, Major, 61, 83, 84, 85, 100
Jerdon, Major T., 91
Jesuits, xiii, xiv, 287
Jones, Captain, 7
Journal De St Petersburg, 205
Jung Lu, 217, 218, 219, 222

Kabul, 53, 190, 194, 211, 241, 254
Kailas, Mount, 44
Kalimpong, 181, 223, 164
Kalmuks, 64, 205
Kanawar, 48, 55
K'ang Hsi Emperor, xiv, 2
Kangra District, 66
Kangralama Pass, 74, 179
Kang-Yu-wei, 216, 218, 219
Kansu, 3, 116, 182, 272, 275, 285
Karakoram, 31, 43, 114, 161, 191, 271, 284
Karo La, 240
Kashak, 2, 163
Kashgar, 32, 67, 114, 116, 129, 130, 137, 161, 191, 194, 237, 271, 282, 283
Kashmir, ix, 25, 32, 39, 43, 44, 45, 46, 47, 48, 52, 57, 58, 59, 61, 63,

66, 67, 92, 103, 111, 114, 115, 152, 155, 161, 197, 198, 199, 200, 247, 255, 297

Katmandu, 3, 20, 26, 27, 29, 32, 53, 94, 95, 108, 190, 215, 223; British Resident at, 28, 29, 35, 36, 51, 57, 64, 88, 92, 95, 188, 197, 216, 222

Kawaguchi, E, 188, 220, 251, 252

Kennion, R. L., 198, 199, 200, 201, 202, 203

Kerman, 66

Khalon, 2

Khambajong, 124, 168, 229, 232, 233, 234, 235, 236, 238, 241

Khotan, 114, 191

Kiachta, 106, 250, 284

Kim, 188

Kimberley, Lord, 133

Kinloch, Captain, 4, 5, 286

Kipling, R., 188, 251

Kirkpatrick, Col., 20, 26

Kishen Kant Bose, 34, 36, 82, 83

Kitchener, Lord, 240

Knox, Capt., 28, 29, 32

Koko-Nor, 116

Korea, 209, 251, 253

Korostovetz, 215

Kotgarh, 47, 89

Kozlov, 219

Krick, Father, 90

Kuen Lun Mountains, 247, 284

Kulu, 54, 58

Kumaon, xii, 3, 25, 33, 35, 36, 37, 39, 40, 43, 44, 49, 51, 84, 89, 90, 91, 186, 247, 256

Kumbum, 272

Kunga, Leader of *Chapba*, 200, 201

Kuo Mission, 129

Kuropatkin, 251

Kwei Huan, Amban, 175, 182, 189

Lachen Valley, 125, 136, 168, 175, 179

Lachung, 235, 236

Ladakh, xiii, 3, 32, 43, 44, 45, 46, 47, 48, 49, 50, 51, 52, 53, 54, 55, 56, 58, 59, 61, 62, 67, 85, 90,

101, 104, 182, 186, 188, 198, 199, 216, 297; Boundary Commission (1846-7), 58-66, 84, 91; British agent in, 67; Dogras Invasion of, 51-5, 67; *see also* Kashmir; Gulab Singh; wool

Lahore, 48, 49, 51, 53, 55, 56, 59; Treaty of 1846, 58, 59

Lahul, 3, 25, 43, 44, 54, 58, 60, 64, 86, 90

Lama Serap Gyatso, *see* Serap Gyatso

Lamb, Charles, 31

Lamsdorff, Count, 206, 219, 262

Landon, P., x

Landor, A. H., 186, 187, 235

Lansdell, Dr, 186

Lansdowne, Lord, 154, 155, 156, 157, 162, 166, 169, 186, 191, 202, 222, 224, 225, 228, 229, 233, 236, 237, 241, 246

Lapchak, 45, 198, 199, 200

Latter, Capt., 34, 39

Lay of Lachen, 136

Lays of Ancient Rome, 136

Lazarists, 62, 90

Leakey, Dr, 132

Leeds, 99, 135, 157

Lee-Warner, Sir W., 212, 224, 225, 226, 228

Leh, 45, 46, 48, 49, 55, 56, 66, 198, 200

Lepchas, 68, 69, 70, 72, 76, 121

Lessar, M. de, 216, 217

Lhasa, x, xiv, 1, 2, 4, 8, 9, 11, 19, 26, 27, 28, 31, 32, 34, 35, 36, 43, 44, 45, 46, 50, 54, 60, 61, 62, 64, 66, 74, 78, 79, 81, 82, 83, 84, 85, 86, 87, 88, 90, 91, 92, 93, 94, 95, 98, 99, 100, 102, 103, 104, 106, 108, 110, 112, 117, 118, 119, 123, 124, 125, 126, 128, 129, 131, 136, 142, 143, 144, 146, 148, 158, 159, 160, 164, 166, 168, 171, 176, 183, 184, 188, 189, 190, 194, 196, 198, 201, 202, 203, 204, 208, 211, 212, 213, 214, 216, 219, 223, 224,

228, 229, 231, 232, 235, 239, 241, 244, 245, 246, 247, 248, 251, 252, 255, 256, 258, 260, 261, 263, 264, 265, 269, 271, 272, 273, 282, 275, 276; British resident at, 225, 226, 228, 233, 242, 244, 259, 278, 282; Chinese in, 32, 40, 276, 277, 278, 279; Regent at, 8, 12
Lhasa Convention (1904), 239, 240, 243, 244, 245, 247, 248, 249, 250, 257, 259, 260, 261, 262, 265, 266, 267, 268, 272, 274, 275, 276, 278; Chinese adhesion to, 239, 244, 248, 259, 260, 263; Indemnity, 244, 245, 248, 263, 264, 266, 267, 275, 276
Li, Prefect, 176
Liberal Government, 266, 269, 278
Licoloff, 218
Li Hung-chang, 116, 129, 130, 147, 148, 253
Likin, 129, 137, 160, 224
Lingtu, 140, 144, 145, 146, 147, 148, 149, 157, 165, 178, 180, 280
Lintin Island, 37
Lin Tse-hsu, 54
Little, A., 189
Littledale, Mr and Mrs, 191
Litton, Mr, 120, 185
Livadia, 205
Livadia, Treaty of (1879), 148
Liverpool, 99, 115
Lloyd, Capt., 69, 71
Lobanov-Rostovsky, 251
Logan, J., 4, 5
Lohit River, 264
London, 115, 129, 133, 135, 220, 269
Lords, House of, 227
Louis, J. A. H., 179
Ludhiana, 47, 52
Lumsden, Capt., P., 91
Lumsden, Mr, 26, 28
Lyall, Sir A., 136, 137, 211
Lyon, 185
Lytton, Lord, 117

Macaulay, Colman, 91, 107, 124-37, 139, 140, 141, 143, 153, 159, 173, 184, 190, 227, 256, 281
Macaulay, Lord, 136
Macao, 31
Macartney, Lord, 14, 16, 17, 20, 21, 22, 23, 29, 33
Macartney, Sir George, 129
Macartney, Sir Halliday, 129, 147, 150
MacDonald, Brig-Gen., 238, 240
MacDonald, Sir C., 195
MacGregor, J., xiv
Macpherson, Sir J., 10, 14, 15
Madras, 17
Malaya, 283
Malaysia, 10
Manasarowar, Lake, 44, 49, 52, 61, 187
Manchester, 99, 115, 127, 135
Manchu Dynasty, see Ch'ing Dynasty
Manchuria, 209, 233, 251, 253
Manning, Thomas, 31
Marathas, 41
Margary Affair, 105, 113, 115-16, 129, 132
Markham, Sir C., 125, 179
Marseilles, 207
Matho, 46
Maxim Gun, 216, 237
Mayers, W. F., 112, 147
McMahon Line, 256, 221
M'Cosh, J., 114
Mediterranean Sea, 279
Medlicott, J. S., 91
Menkujinov, 189
Merv, 137
Meshed, 194
Metcalf, Sir C., 70
Military Intelligence, 166, 186, 191, 225
Miller, Mr, 221
Minsar, Jagir of, 199, 200, 201, 202
Minto, Lord, 261, 262, 265, 267, 268
Mir Izzut Ullah, 32, 291
Mishmis, 90

Missionaries in Tibet, *see* Tibet, Christian misisons in

Moghuls, xiii

Moira, Lord, *see* Hastings, Marquis of

Molesworth, Mr, 85

Monasteries in Tibet, 134, 144, 160, 171, 183, 184

Mongolia, 2, 12, 97, 127, 147, 182, 206, 207, 208, 209, 218, 220, 250, 252, 257, 272, 284, 285

Mongolor, 220

Montgomerie, Major, 65

Moorcroft, William, 31, 32, 39, 40, 47, 48, 49, 50, 61, 64, 291

Moravians, 89

Morley, J., 261, 262, 267, 268

Morning Post, 276

Morrison, Lt., 6

Morung, 30, 34, 77

Moslems, 43, 44, 45, 46, 104, 105, 196, 199

Mönpas, 85

Möwis, P., 194, 195, 196, 207

Mumm, Baron, 250

Musk, 81, 97, 120

Nagar, 152, 161

Naini-Tal, 48

Namgyal, Sidkyong, Raja of Sikkim, 121, 141, 164

Namgyal, Tchoda, 164

Namgyal, Thutob, 121, 141, 164

Namgyal, Tokhang Donyer, 72, 75, 76, 77, 78, 79, 80, 86, 107, 111, 121, 141

Nanking, Treaty of 16, 42, 60

Napier, Sir C., 78

Napoleon III, 95

Nazir Deo, 6

Needham, Mr, 85

NEFA, xiii

Nepal, ix, xiv, 3, 4, 5, 6, 18, 20, 21, 25, 26–42, 52, 53, 54, 63, 68, 69, 70, 76, 78, 81, 85, 86, 90, 94, 99, 101, 105, 107, 121, 142, 144, 152, 164, 167, 172, 173, 188, 190, 197, 208, 210, 211, 216, 222, 223, 224, 225, 226, 227, 228, 230, 258, 275, 277, 280, 282; Anglo-Nepalese Treaty (1801), Chinese intervention in 1792, 108, 109, 166; Mission to Peking, 94, 95, 96, 108, 119, 166; Nepal-Tibet Treaty (1856), 94, 107, 123, 223, 225 *see also* Gurkhas; Gurkha War

Newars, 3, 4, 5, 28

New York Herald, 196

Nicholas II, 205, 215, 250, 251, 253, 272

Nicolson, Sir A., 272

Niti Pass, 247, 256

Nolan, Mr, 172, 173, 174, 181

Northbrook, Lord, 104

North China Herald, 218

North West Frontier, ix

Norzunoff, 207, 208, 252

Novoe Vremya, 205

Nurpur, 47

Nyechung Oracle, 144

Obishak, M., 207

O'Connor, Sir W. F., 260

O'Conor, Sir, N., 127, 128, 129, 130, 131, 132, 133, 134, 137, 138, 140, 160, 167, 174, 182, 189, 252

Odessa, 208

Oldham, Dr, 132

Opium, 127, 137

Opium War, 62

Orissa, xiii

Osservatore Romano, 218

Oxford, 169

Paisley, 115

Pamirs, 31, 137, 161, 191, 194, 279

Panchen Lama, 51, 122, 125, 151, 166, 232; sixth, x, 2, 5, 7, 8, 9, 10, 11, 12, 13, 14, 17, 18, 23, 87, 125, 126, 184, 286; seventh, 15; ninth, 243, 260, 261

Panikkar, K. M., 52
Panjdeh, 137, 161
Panthay Rebellion, 105
Paris, xiv
Paris Geographical Society, 207
Parkes, Sir Harry, 126, 186
Parliament, 145
Parliament, Commons, 271
Paro Penlop, 82, 124, 142
Parr, Capt., 214, 217, 236
Pashm, see Wool
Patan, 4
Patna, 4, 5, 31, 32
Paul, A. W., 132, 150, 155, 158, 159, 161
Pears Col., 216
Peking, 1, 10, 12, 13, 14, 16, 17, 18, 19, 20, 21, 22, 34, 36, 37, 38, 42, 49, 50, 54, 55, 60, 78, 88, 91, 92, 93, 94, 96, 99, 101, 102, 104, 105, 106, 107, 111, 116, 118, 126, 127, 128, 129, 132, 133, 136, 143, 145, 147, 148, 149, 155, 156, 171, 182, 183, 189, 195, 207, 215, 218, 250, 252, 257, 258, 259, 264, 265, 266, 274, 275, 276
Pemberton, J. B., 51, 64, 83, 84, 86
Penang, 10
Persia, 194, 269, 271, 272
Persian Gulf, 194, 271, 272
Phari, 81, 102, 103, 107, 110, 111, 124, 125, 142, 152, 158, 159, 167, 168, 172, 177, 181, 193, 194, 195, 197, 204, 210, 211, 214, 233, 238, 239
Pindaris, 41
Plassey, Battle of, 3, 5
Plehve, 321
Pön Sect, 181
Porcelain, 44
Potola, 223, 276
Prithvi Narayan, 3
Prjevalski, 126, 194, 219
Punjab, 43, 66, 67, 173, 246, 247
Purangir, 11, 15, 16

Railways, 121, 158, 207, 224, 248, 250, 254
Rajshahi Division, Bengal, 169
Rakas-Tal, Lake, 52
Rampur, 43, 47, 48, 52, 57, 58, 59
Ramsay, Col., 56, 92, 95, 96
Ranbahadur of Nepal, 28, 29
Rangoon, 99, 132
Rangpur, 6, 8, 16, 33
Ranjit River, 78
Ranjit Singh, 30, 48, 53
Ravenshaw, Lt. Col., 222, 223
Rawling, C. G., 239, 260, 261
Rennell, James, 6, 7, 287
Renou, Father, 90
Reuters, 216
Rhenok, 121
Rijnhardt, 220
Rima, 247, 264
Rinchingong, 168, 177, 204
Riseley, H. H., 143, 163, 179
Roberts, Lord, 225
Robertson, Lt. Col., 225
Rockhill, W. W., 220
Rosebery, Lord, 227
Rothschild's Bank, 220, 221
Rothschild, Walter, 196
Royal Asiatic Society, 115
Royal Geographical Society, 91, 95
Rudok, 46, 52, 57
Russell, Lord, 66
Russia, 40, 44, 48, 49, 61, 64, 67, 91, 98, 105, 118, 119, 123, 126, 137, 138, 139, 148, 150, 157, 162, 166, 177, 178, 182, 184, 185, 186, 189, 190, 191, 192, 193, 194, 195, 197, 203, 204, 205, 206, 208, 209, 210, 211, 214, 215, 216, 217, 218, 219, 220, 222, 223, 224, 225, 226, 227, 228, 229, 230, 232, 233, 234, 236, 237, 241, 242, 244, 246, 247, 248, 251, 252, 253, 254, 255, 257, 259, 261, 262, 265, 266, 269, 270, 271, 272, 273, 274, 278, 279, 280, 282
Russia in Central Asia, 238
Russo-Chinese Bank, 217, 219,

220, 221, 222, 253, 321
Russo-Mongol-Chinese Treaty
   1915, 284
Rutherford, Lt., 85

Sadya, 97
Salisbury, Lord, 154, 155, 174,
   187, 195
Salt, 44, 81, 183
Sandberg, Rev. G., 206
Sanyasis, 5, 6
Satow, Sir Ernest, 217, 218, 222,
   224, 250, 252, 259, 264
Saunders, Trelawney, 179
Saunderson, Sir T., 156
Schlagintweit, 220
Scott, D., 27, 33, 34
Scott, Sir J. G., 162
Sechung Shape, 267
Segauli, Treaty of (1816), 34, 36,
   41
Seistan, 66, 194
Serap Gyatso, 207, 208
Sera Monastery, 126, 171
Shanghai, 96, 99, 130
Shantung, 250
Shapes, 2, 163, 184, 196, 203, 267
Shata Shape, 163, 184
Sheng Tai, 157, 214, 252
Sher Ali, Amir of Afghanistan,
   211
Shigatse, 2, 19, 44, 81, 106, 122,
   124, 125, 131, 179, 189, 232,
   235, 236, 260, 261
Shore, Sir J., 22, 26, 27, 28
Siberia, 64
Sikang, 278
Sikhs, 30, 43, 47, 48, 51, 53, 55,
   56, 57, 58, 59, 240
Sikkim, ix, xiii, 3, 5, 25, 26, 30,
   33, 34, 35, 36, 38, 39, 40, 61, 63,
   64, 68-87, 88-113, 115, 121, 149;
   Nepalese incursions into, 39;
   Raja of, 141, 144; representative
   at Darjeeling, 73, 74, 76, 78, 80
Sikkim Expedition (1861), 79-82,
   87, 92, 184, 198; Anglo
   Sikkimese Treaty (1861), 80, 81,

88, 106, 140, 141; Expedition
   (1888), 149, 153, 157, 161, 167,
   168, 184, 190, 280, 281
Sikkim Gazeteer, 143, 163, 179
Sikkim-Tibet Boundary
   Commission, 168, 169, 170, 171,
   172, 174, 175, 176, 177
Sikkim-Tibet Convention (1890),
   157, 158, 159, 161, 164, 165,
   167, 168, 169, 173, 174, 175,
   178, 180, 183, 184, 185, 195,
   202, 230
Sikkim-Tibet Trade Regulations
   (1893), 158-64, 165, 167, 168,
   169, 172, 178, 181, 183, 202,
   230, 234, 266
Silhet, 38
Siliguri, 121
Silk, 44, 120
Simla, 40, 43, 48, 49, 65, 69, 169,
   262, 267
Simla Hill States, 43, 86
Simla News, 194
Sinkiang, xi, 44, 66, 67, 93, 105,
   106, 114, 116, 148, 182, 186,
   191, 209, 218, 255, 271, 272,
   274, 279, 282, 283
Sino-Indian Boundary Question,
   259, 279, 297
Sino-Indian War (1962), xi, xii
Sino-Nepalese Treaty (1792), 33;
   see also Tibet, Chinese
   Intervention In, 1792
Smyth, E., proposed mission to
   Tibet, 91, 92, 93
Sobraon, Battle of, 57
Society of Arts, 105; deputation
   from, 105, 106
Society for the Suppression of the
   Opium Trade, 127
Somaliland, 233, 241
Song-Tsan Gam-Po, 1
South Africa, 209
Spiti, xii, 3, 25, 43, 44, 54, 58, 60,
   63, 64, 66, 90
Spring Rice, Sir C., 220, 262
Staunton, Sir G., 21
Stewart Dr I. L., 91

Stok, 46
St Petersburg, 49, 64, 185, 206, 207, 208, 215, 218, 220, 229, 241, 266, 269, 270, 272, 273, 283
St Petersburg Geographical Society, 207, 253
Strachey, H., 61, 62, 63, 64, 83, 91
Suchow, 217
Sumatra, 17
Sung Kuei, 130
Survey of India, 65, 122, 188; native explorers of, 188; see also Rennell
Sutlej, 25, 30, 43, 44, 47, 48, 49, 54, 55, 58, 89, 106, 240, 260
Szechenyi, Count, 119
Szechuan, 36, 89, 90, 92, 95, 96, 97, 98, 101, 112, 115, 116, 117, 119, 120, 121, 133, 148, 149, 159, 182, 184, 189, 197, 258, 259, 268, 275, 276, 285

Tachienlu, 98, 119, 120, 121, 160, 172, 182
Taghdumbash Pamir, 191
Taiping Rebellion, 93, 129
Taklakot, 247
Talbot, Sir Adelbert, 198, 201
Tali, 104, 105
T'ang Dynasty, 1
T'ang Shao-yi, 252, 264, 266
Tanner, Col., 132
Tashi Lama, see Panchen Lama
Tashlhunpo, 2, 7, 8, 11, 12, 14, 15, 16, 18, 19, 46, 122, 124, 125, 126, 127, 129, 135, 243
Tawang, xiii, 84, 85, 277
Taw Sein Ko, 197
Taylor, Mr (Chinese Customs), 167
Tea, 10, 44, 46, 55, 56, 89, 93, 97, 98, 101, 102, 120, 121, 145, 159, 160, 161, 172, 182, 184, 200, 221, 227; Chinese, 10, 16; trade with Tibet in, 16
Teheran, 194
Tehri-Garwhal, 43
Teichman, Sir E., 165

Telegraph, 182, 248
Tenzing, Wangpu, 172, 173, 176, 184
Terai, 4, 5, 29, 30
Thomason, J., 52
Thompson, Sir Rivers, 126
Thomson, Dr, 61
Tibet: see Dalai Lama; Garpons; Gartok; Lhasa; Shigatse; Tashlumpo; Panchen Lama; Chinese Intervention in (1792), 19, 20, 21, 26, 30, 49, 94, 148, 183; 1910, 221; Christian missions in, xiii, xiv, 62, 89, 90, 95, 96, 98, 99, 112, 118, 119, 131, 148, 150, 159, 184, 189, 217, 218; Chinese Power in, x, xiv; Eastern, 95, 96, 97, 98, 118, 160, 182, 189, 221, 247, 268, 275, 276; Western, 31, 40, 41, 43–67, 84, 161, 185, 187, 198, 199, 200, 201, 202, 220, 247, 261, 6
Tibeto-Nepalese Relations, ix, 107, 108, 109; crises, (1883), 122, 123; (1891), 183
Tibet Trade Regulations (1908), 267, 268, 275, 276
Tientsin, 129
Tientsin, Treaty of, 91, 92
Times, 127, 128, 249, 250
Ti Rimpoche, 243
Tista River, 73, 81, 179
Titalia, Treaty of (1817), 39, 41, 68, 69, 71
Tongsa Penlop, 82, 87, 142, 143, 149
Tonkin, 162, 237
Topaz HMS, 37, 42
Trade Agent at Gyantse, see Gyantse
Trade Marts, see under Chumbi; Gartok; Gyantse; Rinchingong; Yatung; Zayul
Trans-Siberian Railway, 208, 220
Travels of a Pioneer of Commerce; 98
Trench, Capt. Chenevix, 198
Tromos, 167, 181

Tsangpo River, xiv, 61, 238, 240, 260, 287
Tsar of Russia see Alexander III; Nicholas II
Tsarong Shape, 267
Tseng Chi-tse, 129
Tseng Kuo-fan, 129
Tsongdu, 243
Tsong Ka-Pa, 1
Tso Tsang-t'ang, 274
Tsungli Yamen, see Yamen
Tsybikoff, 219
Tu, Major, 170
Tumlong, 73, 74
Tuna, 238
T'ung-chih Emperor, 112
Turkestan, Chinese, see Sinkiang
Turner, S., 14, 15, 16, 17, 19, 23, 34, 39, 43, 82, 83, 84, 100, 106, 125, 126, 189, 232
Turner, Storrs, 127

Udalguri, 85
Ugyen Gyatso, Lama, 122, 203
Ugyen Kazi, 188, 196, 197, 202, 203, 204, 208, 212, 221
Ugyen Wangchuk, 143, 149, 196; see also Tongsa Penlop
Ukhtomsky, Prince, 253, 321
Ulanov, 189, 251
United States of America, 98, 250
Urga, 257, 272, 284

Vanderheyden, Mr, 28
Van der Putte, xiv
Victoria, Queen, 124, 125
Volga River, 89

Waddell, L. A., 167
Wade, Sir, T., 96, 102, 104, 109, 112, 113, 115, 116, 117, 120, 190
Wai-wu-pu, 217, 227, 264, 266
Wales, Prince of (later George V), 260
Wallace, Mackenzie, 140
Walsham, Sir J., 145, 146, 147, 149, 155, 186
War Office, 225

Warry, Mr, 132, 135
Wazir Shah, Haji, 199
Webb, Capt., 40
Welby, M. C., 186, 187
Wellesley, Lord, 29
Wellington, Duke of, 136
Wen Hai, Amban, 175, 182
White, J. C., 167, 168, 169, 170, 171, 172, 175, 177, 179, 180, 181, 184, 193, 203, 212, 213, 214, 231, 232, 233, 234, 238, 260
Witte, Count, 250, 253, 321
Wool, Sale in Tibet, 27, 81, 125, 127, 135, 160, 172, 173; Shawl Wool, 40, 44, 46, 47, 48, 52, 55, 56, 58, 59, 61, 66
Worcestershire, 99
Wu Kuang-k'uai, 182
Wu T'ang, Viceroy of Szechuan, 112

Yachou, 182
Yakub Bey, 105
Yalu Timber Concession, 321
Yamdok Lake, 240
Yamen, Tsungli, 104, 111, 112, 117, 119, 120, 127, 130, 131, 132, 133, 134, 137, 140, 146, 147, 148, 150, 154, 156, 160, 167, 171, 186
Yangtze River, 92, 97, 118
Yarkand, 66, 67, 114
Yatung, 159, 161, 167-92, 193, 209, 213, 214, 217, 223, 226, 227, 232, 234, 235, 243, 247
Yellow Temple, 132, 143
Yorkshire, 160
Younghusband, F., x, xiii, 96, 186, 211, 219, 232, 233, 234, 236, 237, 245, 255, 260, 263; subsequent career after 1904, 255, 257, 259, 264, 265, 278, 280
Younghusband Mission, x, xi, xii, xiii, 76, 85, 137, 221, 232, 238-55, 256, 257, 258, 259, 268, 269, 271, 272, 274, 275, 278, 280, 281, 282, 283, 285
Younghusband, Mrs, 240

Yuan Dynasty, 1
Yuan Shih-k'ai, 218
Yunnan, 3, 38, 89, 93, 98, 99, 104, 105, 113, 114, 115, 116, 197, 250, 258, 275, 285
Yu T'ai, Amban, 215

Zayul, 85, 247
Zerempil, 251
Zorawar Singh, 51, 52, 53, 55
Zungars, *see* Dzungars
Zungtson, see Chapba

For Product Safety Concerns and Information please contact our EU
representative GPSR@taylorandfrancis.com
Taylor & Francis Verlag GmbH, Kaufingerstraße 24, 80331 München, Germany

www.ingramcontent.com/pod-product-compliance
Lightning Source LLC
Chambersburg PA
CBHW070546270326
41926CB00013B/2215